AMERICAN BADASS

AMERICAN BADASS

— The Future is Freedom —

Dan Castell

AMERICAN BADASS: THE FUTURE IS FREEDOM

Contact info: AmericanBadass.store

Front Cover Design: Russell Castell

Pulp Lit Press, West Columbia, SC

ISBN-13: 979-8865761778

<u>To the Iconoclasts</u>
And after you have rent to rusting dust,
Every last statue and vestige of the past,
Whom will the children admire?
To what dark idol will your babes aspire?

Table of Contents

PART II - SELF-RELIANT

PART III - UNCONQUERABLE

Chapter V - 10-foot Tall and Bulletproof Badass:
                Nation & Unconquerability

Prologue

Pure Americanism: all badass, all the time

"The secret of happiness is freedom.
The secret of freedom is courage."
— Thucydides, *The Peloponnesian War*, II.43 —

BADASS.

THE VERY TERM UNSETTLES our polite sensibilities, barging into the gilt-edged parlor of the mind with the roughcut indelicacy of an unshaven stevedore. It skates on the unapologetic razor's edge of danger. It asks no quarter, gives no ground, upending the tessellated tea sets of our to-do lists and AppleWatch inventories, leaving our cutout cubicle-squared day in heaps and shards.

Your first thought is to run. To hide. To have no acquaintance with such uncouth, roughhewn ruffianism.

And yet.

Underneath. Underneath that pock-marked exterior there may lie a straightness and softness that makes that seeming rudeness somehow good.

That rough with the smooth is, I contend, the truth of that special kind of badass we find in its American expression.

And it's not that America is the only country to ever have badass individuals, or even to be badass as a people. You can think of Genghis Khan, whose merciless bowman swept across Asia and much of Europe, stacking cairns of severed heads and widely spreading Mongol seed. Or the Spartans, who threw their own children out of the house at twelve so they would learn to scavenge and steal and fend for themselves, to mold them into warriors of pitiless, relentless resolve.

That is one type of badass. It is one side of badass, the obvious side, the foundational root of all badass: the tough guy side. It's the first stage—and an essential component—but only its initial, elementary expression.

Because badass can be refined.

Badass can build out beyond mere thuggery. Beyond physical toughness, there lies mental and spiritual refinement. Not just the conquest of things, but the inner conquest: *Masakatsu agatsu*—true conquest is self conquest. This conquest of the human heart, because of one's faith in a Higher Order, enables the outer conquest of evil in the world by evoking the fortitude to concretely manifest goodness through giving of self and living in love. That is the kind of fully-realized, two-sided human excellence Genghis Khan and the Spartans could never comprehend.

American Badass—at its fullest, best expression—is that unique flavor, a strong musk with a rosy afterglow, the double-edged sword of grit *with* good, tough *with* tender.

In its American expression, it has taken on a peculiar—and, I would submit, peculiarly beautiful—set of admixtures which has not only built one of the most long-lasting and exemplary republics of all time, but which may serve as the wellspring from which this nation can recall itself to its true vocation and serve once again as a light and beacon to the world.

The badass at the cultural heart of America—the spirit of a people who were to bring freedom to a new world, blossom into the great industrial boom of the 19th century and defense of democratic ideals in the 20th century—traces its ideological roots to the tiny, leaking, creaking *Mayflower* buffeting the wind and waves of the North Atlantic in 1620.

The Pilgrims on that storm-tossed craft carried with them a handful of Bibles and a burning desire for independence from authority over their minds so great, they would risk their lives and families to set out into a wild and hostile land, rather than submit to the dictates of overlords in the comforts of their homeland.

They carried with them, in inchoate form, the four great pillars of American Badass:

For their *freedom*, if necessary, they would forsake every comfort, rather than be enslaved.

For their independent *self-reliance*, if necessary, they would go it alone, into an unknown wilderness, rather than do so under subjugation.

From their undying *unconquerability*, because necessary, they would endure any trial, rather than fail in their attempt.

And by their faith that—through the divine—they can indeed do the *impossible*, if necessary, they would overcome any obstacle, rather than fail to build His kingdom on earth.

Without knowing it, these intrepid souls were—in a single act—laying the cornerstone for a nascent civilization, shaping a new way of life never before attempted upon the earth. If you will, they were striking the first coin on the glowing anvil of their yearning for freedom of an ethos which would become the birthright of all citizens of this imminent republic: American Badass.

Yet today, the forces of freedom unleashed by those Puritan ancestors seem perhaps more beleaguered than at any time since our founding revolution. Encroaching on liberty are the forces of despotism, crony capitalism, mandarinism (both through the natural rot of institutional ossification and the malign design of purposeful mismanagement), and our own widening cultural torpor, vapidity, and ignorance. Yes, we have met the enemy, and "he is us." This treatise is not an attempt at anodyne. It is a spark for a powder keg; it is a bullet aimed between the red-rimmed eyes of the monster of tyranny which has haunted the history of humankind from its infancy and which—as implacable as a ghost, as inescapable as nightmare—can only be fought back by the light of truth and reason, though never fully eliminated.

Our age will be a time of calling out, of pushing back, and, if necessary, fighting back this Beast. We will fight this fight whether we wish it or not, for the prosperity of our times brings out the worst kinds of men and parts of our ourselves; surfeit and surplus always and inevitably elicit sloth and self-indulgence so that—as Plato tells us in Bk VIII of the *Republic,* as Gibbon recounts in voluminous detail of imperial Rome—order is inverted, debauchery elevated, profligacy commonplace, deviancy celebrated, and probity scorned. Such a society soon finds itself on the edge of ruin...and, indeed, may topple inevitably into complete chaos.

Or...

Rediscover its badass. The Romans righted themselves for many decades under the "golden" emperors—like Trajan and Marcus Aurelius—who rediscovered their people's heroic natal ethos and rebuilt their empire. Our age can do the same by rediscovering and rebuilding the American Republic.

The American Badass to be rediscovered is, I submit, a particularly nuanced and powerful articulation of our national spirit, an orientation and engagement with life which not only reshaped this continent but can regain its stature as a watchword for all human possibility. It was—and will be again—a beacon of hope and herald of the call to greatness in every human heart: to reach out, to strive, to imagine, and to remake self and world into more than the merely given, more than the merely expected, more than the merely possible. It was—and is—a reminder to every person of their infinite power to reinvent and remake themselves at every moment with the infinite power of free choice.

This is not to say there aren't many types of badass, and even badasses elsewhere that fit the American model. But there does seem a certain rough-cut heroism which is the core of the American self-concept, the Yankee spirit of independence, self-reliance, Puritanical work ethic, underlaid with the foundations of the Western Christian ethos which molded a paradoxically powerful *imago* from which this continent was shaped and which still haunts the dreams and visions of this people. And, since we cannot shape the course of our lives without models and heroes, it may be well for us to reflect on and, indeed, celebrate the core character which forms that American spirit

Nor is American badass either the only—nor even necessarily the most expeditious—form of planetary badassery. It's just that the American flavor has historically worked to shape much, if not all, of those earmarks of American exceptionalism. This American exceptionalism arises, in my estimation, from the confluence of several of Western's civilizations core concepts. But it is only marked by such notions as individualism, independence, and the sanctity of individual life that lie within our civilizational value stack. At least as important are the ways in which such values are stacked, in other words, what values sit atop and become most prominently displayed and pursued.

American Badass may be seen as the American Bushido code of freedom and the means by which to manifest it. There is a combination of toughness, resolve, independence of spirit, and godly compassion which encompasses what has become the value stack, the American ideal of badass: you can Get-R-Dun, while helping thy neighbor; live with warlike vigor, yet with open-handed brotherhood; display individual pertinacity, but with social conscience—these seeming paradoxical traits, crafted and balanced in a character fitted to the amelioration of pragmatic necessities, characterize this kind of Americanism and, indeed, a kind of "badass" swagger which makes each person their own sovereign and node of power and potential, but also always with a potency which is most properly directed only toward a good serving not just the personal but the common weal.

Whence comes this paradoxical paradigm...this humanitarian warrior, this fierce philanthropist? In essence, American Badass can only come late in the development of civilization, for it is nothing short of the full flowering of the Western value system. That is, the ideals of the Colonists that founded this country wove the democratic aspirations born in ancient Athens—where they named their warships such things as *Liberty* and *Freedom of Speech*—around the admonitions to Christian selflessness and Stoic self-control. These multiple strains, plus a bit of good old-fashioned Yankee pragmatism, make a heady stew of potentiality and power. For, there is nothing more powerful than a free person with self-restraint, because such a person's energies are thereby most fully manifest without being dissipated in dissolution; their will and actions are unified around a moral singleness of purpose, their reason unclouded by greed—and such impulse control and focus gives every action its maximal impact, backed up by maximal follow-through and unyielding commitment.

The truth is that moral virtue builds integrity, and integrity—the integration of all of one's energies in each act because one has no internal contradictions of purpose—generates maximal potentiality. When body, mind, and soul are all of one accord—when one has complete harmony of one's values with one's action at every moment—the person realizes the most complete, continual, and potent manifestation of all their capacities. Or, as was once said long ago, *"When you eye is single, your whole body shall be filled with light."* In contrast, the wayward mind—the criminal, dissolute, vicious soul—is always somewhat at war with itself, for there is indeed a conscience within every human heart and thus always some degree of hesitation, some division of energy, some self-initiated incapacity in every dissolute character. Yes, the wastrel may know an act is wrong yet do it anyway...but part of them is still holding back; they are, at one and the same time, both repulsed and compelled by their own acts...and live in the continual chaos which is the divided, broken soul. Thus, it is only the fully virtuous...and free...person who will be most splendidly and spectacularly productive, for only they live in maximal inner harmony and unity.

For that reason, the truest expression of American badass is not mere brute force. True, in its crudest form, badass might be envisioned merely as a form of roughness, pertinacity, even as some kind of sneering relentlessness bordering on ruthlessness. Such toughness is sometimes a necessary good, but it's not the ideal of badassery, at least not in its American instantiation. American soldiers, fathers, and protectors are expected to abide by their moral compass, and when they fall down on this moral duty, they are called out and their reputations torn asunder in a virtual public pillory. Thus, we berate ourselves and our soldiers for Lieutenant Calley's platoon raping and massacring Vietnamese civilians or the brutalities of Abu Ghraib prison. And, the best of our soldiers will admit and decry the ugliness of war. Thus, General Sherman's famous speech proclaiming that *"war is hell"* and *"its glory all moonshine."* Thus did Robert E. Lee, in his short tenure as president of Washington College after the Civil War, purposefully march out of step during military cadet drills. Thus did two-time Medal of Honor recipient General Smedley Butler publish his military memoirs under the title *War is a Racket*.

Therefore, American Badass is neither a mere exercise in individual libertinism, nor a brutal dominion of the strong over the weak, but it is rather an attempt at producing a sound and sensible political expression of the Kantian "kingdom of ends" in both our domestic politics and international accords. The unspoken quest of America was making real the promise of freedom envisioned so long ago in Athenian democracy. These were civilizational aspirations which—long held and much nuanced—had fermented to the point of possibility and potency. In its full expression—grounded on that small, defiant resolve of the Puritan ancestors—these ideals became an ethos of those four primary personal qualities which gives American Badass such vibrancy, efficacy, and power: The American badass is:

FREE

SELF-RELIANT

UNCONQUERABLE

IMPOSSIBLIST

That is:

1. As the Pilgrims sought freedom, the American Badass hungers for *freedom* like a drowning man gasping for air, fighting for it like a wolf over the last bone.

2. As the Pilgrims prized independence, the American Badass seeks *self-reliance,* the ability to bootstrap one's way up

7

and stand on one's own two feet.

3. As the Pilgrims evinced endurance, the American Badass displays *unconquerability*, the granite fortitude to withstand and overcome every challenge on the way to one's goals.

4. As the Pilgrims were moved by boundless faith, the American Badass acts on *impossibilism*, the undying belief that nothing is impossible to God and the human spirit, that the end point of human flourishing is chasing and achieving the greatest challenges, choosing to pursue and manifest dreams so great that others will call them impossible.

And, as we shall see, these four qualities are not separate, but are mutually intertwined, building upon one another to form a coherent and—when fully-realized—well-nigh unassailable dynamism which explains the power of American Badass.

We shall trace here that peculiarly American form of badassery, from its roots, through its struggles and triumphs, to the present day...and towards that shining future which awaits us on the other side of today's looming gloom. We shall meet its embodiments in unlikely persons and obscure places, in unusual events and unbelievable challenges, and thereby come to see how—with slow, inevitable power—the American Badass has built today's cultural landscape, and will next shape the world to come.

This work will unpack and explore these ideals, weaving them within a (more or less) chronological story of the people who came to the American continent, shaped its landscape, and turned it from the dreamy utopia of Francis Bacon into the thrumming industrial colossus of Thomas Edison and Ayn Rand. We shall begin with the Pilgrims battered by the winds in their wave-tossed boat, and wind up with William Shatner "kirking" his 90-year-old self atop a rocket, to the very edge of the stars.

We shall tell you the story of a people hungry to suck the sweet marrow of the bones of life, diving into life's maelstrom with a joyful ferocity which can only be called badass. This is their story; this is your story.

Listen:

PART I
FREE

Chapter 1

The Birth of Badass:
Nation & Freedom

The birth pangs of American Freedom began with the liberty-loving Pilgrims aboard the ship Mayflower: The tiny craft—less than 100 feet from stem to stern—sat idle on the quay in Britain on September 16, 1620, taking on the last of the passengers from its ill-fated companion, the Speedwell.

These people were English Separatists, the most radically independent of the Puritans, whose religious views had made them pariahs in their homeland. Rather than recant their deeply-held beliefs, they would take their chances in the wilds of the New Land across the savage seas. They would rather die seeking freedom for their faith, than succumb, seeking security under another's creed.

In the early 1600s, they sojourned to the freer climes of Holland, but even there could not find sufficient ambit for their religious expression. They would need someplace else, some blank slate upon which to write their story. So, in 1620, they would set off across the wild Atlantic for the new world.

They had twice before set out into the great Atlantic swells in the Mayflower alongside her sister ship the Speedwell, but twice had been forced back as the Speedwell faltered. Despite the many setbacks, they refused to quit. Their desire to practice their religion without restraint from an overweening church and intervening state—and faith that their God would see and bless their loyalty— gave them clarity of vision and determination of purpose.

Few would notice and fewer care as the barely 100 souls abandoned the Speedwell and crammed all their dreams and belongings into just the one overworked barky, Mayflower, and embarked. They watched from the deck as their homeland dipped below the horizon with pensive wistfulness and then turned to face what was to come, with nothing but their own hands, hope, and grit to sustain them, leaving behind them their homeland for what they were sure was nothing but a fierce crossing and unforgiving wilderness.

Once again, they were blown and buffeted by storms and rough seas; for 66 days, the intrepid settlers cleaved southerly toward Virginia but were eventually forced far off their intended course, finally reaching land at Plymouth in the frigid Massachusetts Bay on Christmas Eve. These 102 colonists would establish the first permanent colony in New England.

From their Chronicles on their reasons for persevering (pp. 24 - 26):

"So after they had continued together about a year, and kept their meetings every Sabbath in one place or another, exercising the worship of God amongst themselves, notwithstanding all the diligence and malice of their adversaries, they seeing the could no longer continue in that condition, they resolved to get over into Holland, as they could, which was in the year 1607 and 1608...

{I]t was by many thought an adventure almost desperate, a case intolerable, and a misery worse than death...But these things did not dismay them, (although they did sometime trouble them,) for their desires were set on the ways of God, and to enjoy his ordinances. But they rested on his providence, and knew whom they had believed."

Free

IN THE BEGINNING—MUCH LIKE those Pilgrims eking out their meager survival in unknown soil during that first frozen winter of 1620—the infant nation knew itself not. The settlements that would grow around them were just a collection of scattered, disparate outposts: tiny, little hamlets with little mutual connection or overarching structure. They spoke English, came from England, and enjoyed a good cup of tea, but otherwise were isolated, ill-formed, undefined outcroppings of human hope.

They had what some might consider naive—even childish—dreams of freedom from restraint, notions that they could simply walk away from the troubles of the Old World and start anew. But, in the settlement at Plymouth, the Pilgrims added personal grit and practical perseverance to their hope. These early colonists came prepared not just to pray but to work, to dig and delve...to earn their dreams through gumption, guts, and grit. Over the next century, the infant nation learned to crawl, then walk, then run: the hamlets became villages, the villages became towns, and those towns gathered into proper colonies with roads and markets...and, eventually, governors were sent by the British Crown as overseers to take a cut of all the money changing hands from the ships plying lumber, tobacco, and iron ore from these busy settlements back to the mother country.

Still, for over a century, the colonists were largely left to their own devices, working out their nascent dreams of freedom. They built their houses of faith to their liking. They gathered in democratic assemblies according to their charters. They built schools and workshops, mines and harbors to trade and provide for their dreams of independence as more and more people began to follow them to this new land.

It would take the Crown's interference to knit these far-flung libertarian experiments into a single whole. It would take the crucible of tyranny to evince the unconquerable love of liberty which energizes this unique people—those who would leave all behind and come, often with nothing, seeking freedom above all else. It would take overweening governmental intrusion to bring to the fore the badass leaders who would becomes Founders and Framers of a new nation.

It would take the oppression of the British Crown testing the Colonists, taxing their monies, and trammelling their rights, to give them the gut check which would cause AmRev 1.0, the first American Revolution.

And here is how it happened:

1750 - The Iron Act is passed by Parliament. The British government decides to extend to America the predatory mercantilism they have used in so many other lands on so many others peoples: extract the raw materials from a colony, ship them back to England and produce finished goods in British factories, and then sell those raw materials as retail wares back to their place of origin for a tidy two-way profit. To accomplish this government-mandated grift, the Iron Act instituted an excise tax which essentially forced the Colonists to export the pig iron dug from American mines exclusively to London. At the same time—as in India and Ireland and Australia, etc.—the Crown declared it illegal for the Colonists to manufacture any finished goods from iron. Instead, the Colonists were to first export their raw iron ore duty-free to Britain, where the British would manufacture all the finished goods, and then turn around and force the Colonists to buy all the finished products of the iron (pins, belt buckles, axes) from Britain which they had previously produced themselves—not to mention far more cheaply and easily, while also employing and enriching the people who actually lived and worked with all the foundries and blacksmiths aplenty living right there where the ore was produced.

Fortunately for everyone involved, this enactment was largely ignored, honored more in the breech than the observance. Still, after nearly 150 years largely characterized by benign neglect, this act was an opening shot across the bow for any sensible citizen in the Americas, and a precedent for taxation which would soon balloon beyond tolerability. As with most government programs, once fed, the beast grows. The natural course of lawmaking is that, once enacted, a proposal transmutes into a program, and that program metastasizes into a department, and finally eventuates into a permanent grant for government theft and abuse. Soon enough, finding new ways to tax the Colonies would become one of Parliament's most engaging pastimes.

1764 - The Sugar Act is passed, much along the same lines as the Iron Act, it creates a virtual monopoly on molasses for the British West Indies sugarcane plantations while also increasing the search and seizure powers of customs officers enforcing the regulations imposed on colonial merchantmen. As maritime trade suffers, seafaring colonists and producers are outraged, and protests begin. Adding to the colonial burden, the Currency Act follows, which restricts the Colonies from issuing legal tender for public and private debts. It was this act which began Benjamin Franklin's lobbying efforts for greater colonial self-determination and which, he later reported, was also one of the primary causes of the revolutionary movement.

1765 - The Stamp Act, the first direct tax on the Colonists, is passed, which ups the ante on taxation, imposing taxes on a wide range of paper goods, from newspapers and playing cards to legal documents which meant it soon affects nearly every adult...and even forces them to pay in British currency, not Colonial scrip. It meets with stiff resistance and outright defiance: vehement broadsides and editorials, protests, British ministers hanged in effigy, intimidation of stamp commissioners who resign under the public opprobrium, and finally an outright embargo on the importation of British goods as Colonial merchants boycott British trade. The Colonies simply refuse to pay. In mere months, the pushback will force its repeal, along with the equally unpopular Sugar Act.

1767 - In response to the turmoil in the Colonies, Parliament pivots in the Townshend Acts. Miffed at having to repeal their earlier tax efforts—rather than reverting to the long-standing excise taxes of earlier times—Parliament oafishly asserts its authority by enacting an entire raft of seemingly random taxes on everything from glass to lead, paint pigment to tea.

1768 - The Colonists are naturally restive under all the new taxes. Sam Adams publishes a Circular Letter arguing the unlawful and impractical nature of taxation by a far-off Parliament. The Massachusetts Assembly endorses the Letter; the King's ministers order the Assembly to recant their endorsement; the Assembly refuses. In a classic case of continuing the beatings until morale improves, the Crown dissolves the Assembly and deploys British troops—and even a 50-gun warship—to occupy Boston. In return, the Colonists return to boycotting British goods, and the protesting, rioting, and smuggling to avoid the taxes all continue apace. Customs officers target John Hancock and his sloop *Liberty*, charging the man and the craft separately on suspicion of smuggling. Hot shot local lawyer John Adams appears as attorney to defend Hancock, and the charges against Hancock are dropped. The *Liberty* itself, however, is impounded, tried, convicted, and turned into a British customs cruiser. Boston's patriots will have none of that absurdity of putting a bunch of lumber on trial. Enraged, Sam Adams' Sons of Liberty swarm to the harbor, seize a British customs boat, hoist it out of the water, drag it overland across town, set it under the Liberty Tree at Boston Commons, and put the customs boat on trial for treason. Duly finding the boat guilty, they promptly burn it. Pure, unadulterated badass. Those are your ancestors; those are the people you come from, showing you what happens when tyrants mess with American patriots.

The sorts of street protests, oratory, and theatre which Sam Adams and the Sons of Liberty undertook beneath their Liberty Tree so inspire other patriots, no less a light than Thomas Paine later writes this celebratory paean to it:

"Liberty Tree"

In a chariot of light from the regions of day,
The Goddess of Liberty came;
Ten thousand celestials directed the way,
And hither conducted the dame.

A fair budding branch from the gardens above,
Where millions with millions agree,
She brought in her hand as a pledge of her love,
And the plant she named Liberty Tree.

The celestial exotic struck deep in the ground,
Like a native it flourished and bore;
The fame of its fruit drew the nations around,
To seek out this peaceable shore.

Unmindful of names or distinctions they came,
For freemen like brothers agree;
With one spirit endued, they one friendship pursued,
And their temple was Liberty Tree.

Beneath this fair tree, like the patriarchs of old,
Their bread in contentment they ate
Unvexed with the troubles of silver and gold,
The cares of the grand and the great.

With timber and tar they Old England supplied,
And supported her power on the sea;
Her battles they fought, without getting a groat,
For the honor of Liberty Tree.

But hear, O ye swains, 'tis a tale most profane,
How all the tyrannical powers,
Kings, Commons and Lords, are uniting amain,
To cut down this guardian of ours;

From the east to the west blow the trumpet to arms,
Through the land let the sound of it flee,
Let the far and the near, all unite with a cheer,
In defence of our Liberty Tree.

As the riot and rebellion in defense of liberty continues in Boston, the colonial Governor thrashes about for a way to quell his intractable subjects. Yet, when he tries to find someone to testify against John Hancock, Sam Adams, and the mob leaders so he can charge these men with sedition and then extradite them to London for trial, not a single Colonial will rat out his fellow countryman. He can find no way to stage a show trial for treason. At the same time, in response to the oppression, a growing number of Colonies are joining in Committees of Correspondence to set up lines of constant communication and mutual support. Naturally, the first such committee was instituted in Boston, and it was Sam Adams who assembled his Committee...and under the Liberty Tree.

Soon, Liberty Trees are springing up around the Colonies. The Colonists assemble around these as places of communal gathering to agitate for their freedoms. In Rhode Island, Silas Downer and the Sons of Liberty dedicate their favorite elm as a Tree of Liberty thusly:

> *"We do therefore, in the name and behalf*
> *of all the true SONS of LIBERTY in America,*
> *Great Britain, Corsica, Ireland or wheresoever*
> *they are dispersed throughout the world,*
>
> *dedicate and solemnly devote this tree to be a*
> *TREE of LIBERTY.*
>
> *May all our councils and deliberations*
>
> *under its venerable branches be*
> *guided by wisdom, and directed to the support*
> *and maintenance of that liberty, which our*
> *forefathers sought out and found*
>
> *under trees and in the wilderness.*
>
> *—May it long flourish, and may*
> *the SONS of LIBERTY often repair hither,*
>
> *to confirm and strengthen each other.*
>
> *–When they look towards the sacred ELM,*
>
> *—may they be penetrated with a sense of duty*
>
> *to themselves, their country, and their posterity:*

— And may they, like the house of David,

grow stronger and stronger,
while their enemies, like the house of Saul,
grow weaker and weaker. AMEN"

1770 - The Boston Massacre takes the struggle to a new level: citizens are shot, five killed, for the dread crime of pelting redcoat soldiers with snow balls. Unfortunately for the King's security forces, you can kill a few protestors, but you can't kill an idea. The protests and boycotts for liberty only intensify. John Hancock leads a delegation to London which demands, and gets, the removal of the British troops occupying Boston. Parliament, seeing that its actions are backfiring, largely abandon the massive public relations failure of the Townshend Acts.

1772 - Sam Adams et al. turn up the heat against their British overlords via increasingly incendiary editorials. At the same time the Committees of Correspondence begin organizing a parallel governing structure and political agenda; these will eventually form the basis for the new revolutionary government. The other colonies will follow Adams' model in quick succession.

1773 - Ironically, Parliament, in looking to mollify their boisterous Colonists, now drop all of the taxes, but codify into law the single most onerous part of the Townshend Acts in the Tea Act. This attempt by Parliament to retain a cosmetic vestige of its authority will prove to be precisely what pushes the Colonists to overt action. On December 16th, a crowd of patriots—roused by one of Sam Adams' fiery orations—swarm Boston harbor to enjoy a "Tea Party" wherein thousands of pounds of tea are dumped overboard. The Crown's authority is snubbed, the British East India Company takes a loss worth millions, and John Adams records in his diary that, *"the People should never rise, without doing something to be remembered—something notable And striking. This Destruction of the Tea is so bold, so daring, so firm, intrepid and inflexible, and it must have so important Consequences, and so lasting, that I cant but consider it as an Epocha in History."*

1774 - Their feathers ruffled, Parliament responds to the Colonial imbroglio with its harshest measures ever in what the Colonists term the Intolerable Acts: Boston harbor is closed; the Massachusetts elected assemblymen are replaced with Crown appointees; the Assembly itself—a 150 year old democratic tradition—is forbidden to meet without official approval; British officials will now have their crimes tried in friendly Britain (not Boston); and, the redcoats soldiers can freely requisition unoccupied buildings for their own use. Rather than kowtow, Boston's patriots continue to refuse the tea, and the other Colonies band together with their Boston brethren by convening in Philadelphia for the first, though brief, Continental Congress. Massachusetts forms a breakaway patriot government—the Massachusetts Provincial Congress—and calls for the citizen militias to begin training...just in case.

1775 - Parliament declares Boston in rebellion. British troops begin undertaking random, warrantless, search-and-seizure raids. Patriots begin stockpiling arms and ammunition—including cannonade—in anticipation of matters going kinetic. British troops continue breaking into houses, especially keen to seize people's firearms. One poetic patriot, in response to this warrantless British pilfering, declared:

> That whosoe'er keeps gun or pistol,
> I'll spoil the motion of his systole.

Alarmed at the Colonial intransigence, the Crown orders General Gage and his redcoats to sortie from Boston and seize a reported cache of contraband weaponry at Concord. The patriots learn of the British plan and prepare themselves. At the break of dawn on the 19th of April, a thin line of some 70 American militiamen stand on the dewy sward of Lexington Green to block the advance of over 700 British regulars, creating a tense stand off...until an unknown someone fires their musket, in "the shot heard around the world." Instantly, gunfire erupts from both sides, and the militiamen begin to beat a fighting retreat toward Concord; the British follow close behind but are only able to find and disable three cannons, since the rebels had already moved most of their munitions. Yet, throughout that same night and dawn, Paul Revere and others have been riding hard, alerting the minutemen...and now the patriot militia begins arriving in numbers. From the surrounding regions of New England—from every corner and hamlet—armed patriots are rushing to the sound of the guns. The British, cut off by a rising tide of riflemen, begin their own retreat, back towards Boston. A hail of militia gunfire and sniping from the woods now accompany the redcoats on their daylong withdrawal. Throughout the afternoon, the British are harried, harassed, ambushed, and assaulted as increasingly large and well-organized militia groups arrive. At the end of the gruelling engagement, the rebels' cache of weapons remains secure, the vaunted British army has been outgunned and badly bloodied by Yankee farmers with muskets, and, from all over New England, over 15,000 militiamen— a *de facto* Colonial army—ring General Gage's embattled British garrison of 3,000 troops now trapped in Boston. More importantly, this day has turned the political tide: no more a mere riot, the Colonial resistance has undoubtedly become an open rebellion to be decided by force of arms. Hearing news of Lexington, George Washington remarks, *"the once-happy and peaceful plains of America are either to be drenched in blood or inhabited by slaves."* The minutemen militia's unflinching stand was the spark that lit the fire of the first American Revolution.

As was ever the case, liberty is never given; it must be taken. The patriots of the land thereby served their God with guns and guts. From that very first determination to stand their ground at Lexington, the American people stopped being mere Colonists and became separatist rebels. Those patriots had used a church spire to signal the news of the British advance, grabbed their weapons, and jumped without hesitation into the fight—their fury, their glory, came from a successive reliance on God, guns, and guts. This luminous action demonstrated the spirit of American resistance encapsulated in Benjamin Franklin's oft-quoted catch phrase, *"Resistance to tyranny is service to God."*

The two sides will settle into an armed siege of Boston, an open but undeclared war. The Colonists call a second Continental Congress in Philadelphia, and it sets about the long work of wrangling over make-or-break relations with Britain.

1776 - On January 10th, Thomas Paine publishes *Common Sense*, a plain, clear treatise on the case for independence. It instantly becomes—and remains—the best-selling book per capita in American history; it is read aloud with great approbation in meetings and taverns, kindling the love of liberty and the embers of revolution.

On March 17th, George Washington outmaneuvers the British by having nearly 60 cannons, including heavy 20-pounders—guns extracted from British Fort Ticonderoga captured by Ethan Allen and dragged 300 miles through the snow by bookseller-turned-warrior Henry Knox—all wrangled to the top of the commanding Dorchester Heights in a single night so that, at dawn, British replacement General Howe finds his troops staring down their massive barrels. Upon arising, the British commander instantly knows he has been checkmated and exclaims, *"My God, these fellows have done more in one night than I could make my army do in three months!"* He immediately orders his "lobsterbacks"—plus many timid loyalists—to begin slinking away to Canada in over 100 ships. This first great success liberates Boston from its 11-month siege, invigorates the revolutionary cause, and forever after marks the bloodless triumph of March 17th as "Evacuation Day," the day the British occupiers evacuated their fort before Washington's guns.

On July 4th, the Continental Congress at last produces, signs, and publishes a Declaration of Independence, which marks the seemingly inevitable result of all that has come before. Colonies no more, these now united American States resolve to take on the challenge of life independently...and thereby also, by implication, declare open war against the Crown.

Now, as the legislature of a proper nation, Congress formally elevates one of their own to the position of commander-in-chief of the military, tasked with molding the patchwork militia bands into a proper army. In shouldering that task (for free, taking no salary), George Washington—veteran of the Indian wars with decades of battlefield experience—will prove to be the paradigmatic American badass who will lead the American armies to victory in war and later, as President, lead the entire American citizenry to triumph as a nation.

George Washington: Epitome of American Badass

"[T]here is no truth more thoroughly established, than that there exists...an indissoluble union between virtue and happiness."

— George Washington —

First President of the Republic, and first in American Badassery, there is a reason George Washington's name and stolid face are plastered across all those one "dollar" Federal Reserve notes and elementary schools. It starts with him lighting what he called "the sacred fire of liberty" in the siege of Boston and ends with the Order of Cincinnatus.

Washington would first lead the army of the fledgling Republic against the world-straddling British Empire, whose scarlet-clad troops, renowned for their discipline and marksmanship, had built history's largest and wealthiest empire. It was his to take the untrained, ill-supplied American militia, stay in the field, and show the world (most especially the French, with all their treasure and naval might) that the Colonists could muster the will and might to stand against such an army.

It was his to relieve the redcoat siege of Boston by chasing off the British with the siege cannons purloined from Fort Ticonderoga in March of 1776; to manage the skilful fighting retreats from Manhattan that summer; cross the Delaware that Christmas night to surprise the slumbering Hessian mercenaries, capturing nearly 1,000 prisoners; devise a combination of Fabian withdrawal, Hannibalian encirclement, and Pattonesque boldness to win the battles of Trenton and Princeton in January, 1777; endure having his forces' flank turned by General Howe at Brandywine Creek and see the capital of Philadelphia invested by the enemy; face the rising criticism after further Continental losses at Germantown; dispatch his best forces to enable General Gates' critical victory in the battle of Saratoga—for which Gates received the acclaim, while he took the blame for the loss of the Delaware river area and a gruelling winter of deep cold and scant provisioning in the encampment at Valley Forge; stave off assaults of the Continental army's main base at Morristown at the battles of Connecticut Farms and Springfield; but finally, in the summer of 1781, to slip away, concealed from the enemy, combine his two largest French and Continental armies, and trap Cornwallis at Yorktown, effectively breaking the back of British resistance...all while skilfully fending off political backstabbers and naysayers calling for his ouster, building from scratch an intelligence network far superior to his adversary's, and overcoming continual logistical and recruitment shortages.

And it was his to do so not only with tactical boldness and personal courage, but an unwavering piety which was an inspiration for his troops and nation alike. Thus we find our inaugural President seek divine intercession:

Before the war, his diary of June 1, 1774 records, *"Went to church and fasted all day."*

Prior to battle in 1776, he reminded the Continental Army that, *"[T]o be well prepared for an engagement is, under God, (whose divine Aid it behooves us to supplicate) more than one half the battle."*

At the critical juncture when France joined the Continental cause, he promoted an attitude of pious gratitude by declaring a day of thanksgiving: *"It having pleased the Almighty ruler of the Universe propitiously to defend the Cause of the United American-States and finally by raising us up a powerful Friend among the Princes of the Earth to establish our liberty and Independence upon lasting foundations, it becomes us to set apart a day for gratefully acknowledging the divine Goodness & celebrating the important Event which we owe to his benign Interposition."*

Reflecting on colonial military victories at the climax of the struggle, he wrote to Reverend Samuel Cooper that, *"[I]t is our Duty...to exert our utmost powers to bring to a happy Conclusion...a Contest in which we have so long been engaged, and in which we have so often, and conspicuously experienced, the Smiles of Heaven."*

As the war wound down, his General Orders to the troops, of February 15, 1783 commanded his officers to promote, *"that public Homage and adoration which are due to the supreme being, who has through his infinite goodness brought our public Calamities and dangers (in all humane probability) very near to a happy conclusion."*

His resignation from command of the army in 1783 concluded with what is now called Washington's Prayer: *"I now make it my earnest prayer, that God would have you, and the State over which you preside, in his holy protection, that he would incline the hearts of the Citizens to cultivate a spirit of subordination and obedience to Government, to entertain a brotherly affection and love for one another, for their fellow Citizens of the United States at large, and particularly for their brethren who have served in the Field, and finally, that he would most graciously be pleased to dispose us all, to do Justice, to love mercy, and to demean ourselves with that Charity, humility and pacific temper of mind, which were the Characteristicks of the Divine Author of our blessed Religion, and without an humble imitation of whose example in these things, we can never hope to be a happy Nation."*

Such appeals to the godhead were hardly just rhetorical flourish or theological nicety on Washington's part, for the belief that our moral foundation flows from divine authority is found throughout world cultures. From Zeus of the ancient Greeks to Olodumare of the Yoruba, people hold that the moral law is propounded by godly wisdom and thence justly obeyed by the prudent soul. Such moral law upholds two modalities of virtue, first, towards virile strength, fortitude, and self-reliance, and second—most especially in the Christian tradition—toward selflessness, sacrifice, and compassion. As noted above, these twin modes of goodness—i.e. the tough with the tender, the rough with the righteous—this balance of characteristics, are mutually maximized in the American Bushido code of freedom which Washington embodied, that prayerful warrior who was our first figurehead of Americanism.

While he showed great humility and deference when serving the Republic, Washington proved most jealous in matters of his personal honor. His desire to be perfect in duty and sacrifice was perhaps best shown in April, 1781, when he learned his cousin, Lund Washington—who was tasked with managing Washington's Mount Vernon estate while the general was off fighting the war—had preserved Washington's house by finagling away a unit of British troops who had been burning down estates on the Potomac River. Lund was proud at having talked the British out of immolating Washington's lands. Washington, however, a man of immense self-control, was as short, sharp, and blunt as he ever allowed himself to be in telling Lund how disappointed he was: *"It would have been a less painful circumstance to me, to have heard...they have burnt my House, & laid the Plantation in Ruins."* Lund's connivance—though well-intentioned—came from the calculus of a smaller man, as it could give the appearance that Washington valued his property above his honor, or was somehow not willing to sacrifice everything for the cause of liberty. Most importantly Lund's actions would set a bad example and, *"certainly Have a Bad effect, and Contrasts with Spirited Answers from Some Neighbours that Had their Houses Burnt Accordingly."* It was possible that this act, even at this one remove, would disgrace the nation, cast a pall on its army's commander in chief, and even undermine the spirit and determination of others. No matter how taken, Lund's actions were a stain upon Washington, a man who spent his life fortifying his character. That's how finely-honed and exacting was Washington's standard of probity. Washington's magnanimity demanded the sacrifice which meant honor, which is the emblem of a life well-lived. His personal commitment was to, *"never suffer private convenience to interfere with what I conceive to be my official duties."*

After winning the brutal war while maintaining his Christian sensibility, Washington went on to provide exemplary leadership in the political realm. His august presence and steady resolve helmed the 1787 convention in Philadelphia which produced the Constitution. He then served two terms as the first President of these fledgling united States of America, declining to run for a third term, thereby setting a precedent in political humility that stood for nearly 150 years.

Washington's greatest political contribution, however, may have been in something else he did *not* do. He did not make himself a king, but instead followed in the footsteps of noble Cincinnatus.

Cincinnatus was a legendary figure from early Roman history, the iconic model of civic virtue. According to the story, in 438 BC, the fierce Aequi tribe descended upon the Roman people, and the Senate knew there was only one man for the job of fending off the invaders: Cincinnatus, a patrician and former consul whose once noble circumstances had been reduced to a mere four acres along the Tiber river. When they petitioned him, they found the now elderly patrician personally tilling the fields of his small family farm. Hearing of the trouble, he immediately threw down the plow, donned the ceremonial purple robes of his senatorial class, and took to the head of the legions. As part of the public emergency, he was granted dictatorial powers for six months, one man with complete public trust, plenary power over anything in the nation. With bold dispatch, he kitted out the troops, marched upon the invaders, and decisively crushed their forces, all in less than a fortnight. Having completed this difficult and distasteful civic duty, now sitting at the apex of power, rather than—as so many of history's small-minded, acquisitive sociopaths have—use it to glorify himself and enrich his friends from the public coffers, he quietly resigned the office, slipped back into his simple farmer's robes, and once again took up his plow. (And, according to legend, would apparently repeat the exercise of saving the republic without reward a second time years later, proving once again his mettle, indomitability, and selflessness.)

It was selfless devotion to duty—leadership undaunted,

unwavering, and unsurpassed. In March, 1783, Washington—as a second Cincinnatus—faced his own moment of truth. His officers were preparing to mutiny, to march on Congress and seize the government; Washington showed up unexpectedly at the tavern where they were hatching their treasonous plans and gave two speeches which quelled their rebellious aims. He then, that December—despite being the recipient of universal acclaim and expected to ascend to power as potentate of the nation—quietly resigned his post as commander-in-chief, retiring to private life; he renounced all talk of a crown for him. Because of Washington, there would be no royalty ruling Americans. His was the quintessential model of badass: the courage and fortitude to withstand years of military service; the prudence and cunning to ply the rapids of political intrigue; and then the piety to do what is right, and only what is right...all those with a constant reliance on the will of God. That is what shaped him as the epitome of American badass: toughness beyond measure, tempered by morals without stint. Washington set a standard for American Badass which stands to this day.

Washington's contributions were, however, not the only ones that shaped the Revolution. And, as our story unfolds, we shall meet seven more of the great spirits who shaped this Republic in its fledgling days: Sam Adams, James Madison, Benjamin Franklin, Thomas Paine, Patrick Henry, John Adams, and Thomas Jefferson. Each of these will serve as both a type and token of American badass demonstrated by the founding generation.

Revolutionary Ladies

"If we do not lay out ourselves in the service of mankind, whom should we serve?"

— Abigail Adams —

And, of course, there were any number of badass colonial women doing the work of birthing the Republic. For instance, Abigail Adams not only gave her husband John immense moral, intellectual and emotional stability as wife and confidante in their constant correspondence during the trying days of the Continental Congress and Presidency, but provided the very practical aid of organizing a local Ladies Auxiliary to manufacture essential salt peter to assuage the nascent Continental army's gunpowder shortage. Likewise, we have all heard of Betsy Ross stitching up the first flag as emblem of the nation.

And then there are the Molly Pitchers of the war, who threw their shoulder to the wheel in the bravest and most selfless ways. During the war, Molly Pitcher became an archetype: the woman loading the cannon and blasting away with the boys on the battlefield. It is possible that the name itself conveys not so much an historical person as a type: first, the timely, anonymous maiden (good, ole "Molly") bringing a *pitcher* full of much-needed water to the boys in the field. But it is also applied to any of several actual ladies who stood in the breech during the height of battle. At least two such heroic women are recorded by name. First is Mary Hays, who was a "camp follower" accompanying her artilleryman husband in the field; when he was killed in battle, she jumped into his place at the cannon—swabbing the barrel, loading the cannon balls, and giving the redcoats a good drubbing. The second is Margaret Corbin, who similarly took her artilleryman husband's place when he fell in action, only retiring from battle herself after being badly wounded; she would eventually be awarded a life pension from the state of Pennsylvania for her brave service.

The Dream of Freedom
"Our unalterable resolution should be to be free."
— Samuel Adams —

Want to sell something to the American people? Tell them about freedom. Want to boost your political campaign in the polls? Promise the voters more freedom. At least, historically, that was the battle cry and self-concept which sat atop the American totem pole, the value stack of our ideals. From the days of the Revolution, America was born in freedom, stood for freedom, was regarded as the world's bastion of freedom. This is why immigrants have teamed to these shores for centuries, with the promise of liberty, with that statue in New York harbor boldly harkening as a beacon to do, be, and become yourself without undue hindrance from government functionaries and the nattering fault-finding of petty minds. It was foundational that Americans believed in finding your own way, pulling oneself up by one's own bootstraps, and then reaping the rewards (and, yes, facing the challenges and burdens) which come from standing on one's own before the world. The continual influx of liberty-loving blood—the self-transfusion, if you will, of people drawn to this land by the clarion call of freedom—is part of what keeps enkindling that ethos of freedom first. American citizenship is thus largely self-selective: you become truly American by your love of American ideals, most especially if you are amongst those people who burn with a love of freedom. In one sense, Americans are distinguished by their heart, their core values, and cannot be distinguished by race, religion, or homeland. America is less a place, than an idea, and being American is less about where you were born than what you believe.

And it is real. Native born Americans may not realize the difference between this nation and so many other places and time; native-born Americans imbibe with the air they breathe the assumption of personal liberty and opportunity, the indisputability of personal worth and the expectation of self-development; they accept it without thought and act upon it, largely without reflecting upon or ever expressing it. But such liberty is a rarity. So rare, people will risk everything for it; they will die for it. For example, I have met many families that fled Iran at the fall of the Shah, but one especially. Their son's best friend came from an impoverished family who could not afford to get out. A young lad of ten, this friend hungered so much to likewise flee to America, that he stuffed himself inside a suitcase, thinking he could stow himself aboard an airplane and safely fly to the States. He was indeed packed aboard the airplane, but, as he was simply bunged in the cargo hold with the luggage, he sadly asphyxiated from the thin atmosphere en route.

He is not alone in risking everything for a taste of liberty, not alone in literally dying for freedom. The people yearning for freedom who come here—especially as they pass through citizenship training and come to recognize the long, deep constitutional roots of American freedom—revitalize this Republic, renew its youthful vigor and explain much of its continual optimistic energy.

American Badass, then, starts and ends with freedom, a kind of ongoing field test of the possibility of political freedom which has simply not been tried with such unstinting abandon anywhere else. And that kind of freedom is what elicits most completely one's character. For good or ill, given full freedom to express and act, your true self will reveal itself. The human person can only fully develop to their glory and dignity by having the capacity to try, to strive, to fail, and to find their true worth and way in the world. Thus, they must have the room to spread their wings, to rise or to fall, to pass or fail the test. Only the fullest freedom elicits the fullest expression of the individual.

Individual human autonomy implies a dignity for that person, which implies a kind of sanctity in personhood. This valuation of the individual arises because the course of Western civilization rests on the Christian supposition of the incommensurate worth of each and every human individual—the infinite, irreplaceable value of each unique, unrepeatable human life—and thus that the full efflorescence of that life's potential and purpose is of infinite, incalculable value. Hence, a proper political system must undergird our individual freedoms to enable that exploration and development of self, so that each of us individually and all of us universally will thereby prosper. As a result, then, the protection of liberty which seems at first a mere political nicety with beneficent ends becomes a grave moral imperative.

To induce people's best, you must furnish liberty most.

It further follows that even the most selfish, violent, and self-aggrandizing impulses of the American populace should be circumscribed by the recognition of the need to protect and defend the rights and worth of the other. If every life has worth, then an implicit bound is set by which one can be morally leveraged to discard the practice of slavery, to quell imperialist impulses, to become the most generous charitable givers on the planet, to temper xenophobic distrust with compassion, to mete out mercy with justice, to end our most spectacular triumphs in war with unparalleled largesse and forgiveness in peace. A people and republic founded on such values is no normal historical circumstance. The American republic was not your everyday empire. This was an experiment, yes, in freedom, but also one lit by the lights of the larger Western moral tradition and its Christian underpinnings. It was not an exercise in mere individual libertinism, nor of oligarchic dominion of the few over the many, but to actualize the autonomy of each priceless person in the public realm within the bounds of moral excellence.

The American experiment represents, then, the furthest reach of that experiment in personal self-development begun in Athens, reborn in the Renaissance, and codified in the American Constitution. It's not just an American heritage, nor even just a civilizational tradition; it's a human aspiration to find the code to maximize personal freedom within the nurturing weave of the social network; it's the vision of a tapestry of life whose every strand glows with undulating individuate color and potency, yet binds with effortless grace into a harmonious whole, thrumming with vibrant life and limitless possibility. Such magnitude of purpose and perfection of outcome can only come through care in design of governance and the recognition of the duty of each person to lawful responsibility.

Thus, the twin acts—Revolution and Constitution—are the fullest expression of the "American genius," that spirit which conjoins the love of liberty with the practical grit and moral purpose to maximally manifest it despite life's manifold practical challenges. It is pure idealism conjoined with that pragmatic Yankee wisdom which John Adams recounts of his father's saw that, *"To get atop an oak tree you either climb it...or sit on an acorn and wait."* Plainly, the American people had no interest in sitting and waiting on anything. And so they climbed atop the task of nation-building with the same zeal with which they had opposed the Crown and won their independency.

Having won the war for freedom, the real work began: manifesting and maintaining it in a republic. No people had ever before undertaken such a bold political endeavor: declare themselves a nation and wrench that land from the grips of the world's largest empire. Now, these freedom-loving Founders would follow that precedent with another: framing their new republic under a Constitution codifying liberty and justice for their posterity. And it is perhaps impossible to surpass the beauty, brilliance, and eloquence of the resultant documents crafted by the Founders and Framers in the matter of liberty. It is perhaps best to simply record in wonder and gratitude the legacy of their words.

Lex Rex: A Nation of Laws, Not Men
"A republic, if you can keep it."
— Benjamin Franklin —

Now more than ever, today's citizens need to rediscover, reclaim, and restore the protections embodied in that Constitution. Not since the first American Revolution have the people of this nation been so controlled and coerced, their rights so infringed and ignored by a distant, bloated government bureaucracy. Never has freedom been more needed, yet less appreciated. The history of the world is a history of despotism and tyranny, slavery and sacrifice by millions of faceless minions to the powerful, the ruthless, the privileged 1% of the 1%. The neglected undercurrent of history is that nameless mass of humankind born into bondage who—their days burdened by the dictates of distant masters and rapacity of local overlords—become a desperate peasantry grinding their teeth as they and their children are borne down by misery, brutality, and helplessness. "If only..." has been the cry for hundreds of nations; "If only..." has been the unfulfilled hope of a thousand generations.

The American charter set about rectifying this legacy. One of the banners often carried by the patriots of the Revolution read simply, *Lex Rex*, Latin shorthand for the Law (*lex*) is King (*rex*), i.e. true justice is a nation runs by laws, not by men. Thus, in creating the government of our new nation, there was little debate that it would be a republic, for a republic—going back to its early use by the Romans for the time after they threw off their monarchy—is precisely such a commonwealth: a nation not of kings, but of laws.

The four-page Constitution hatched in Philadelphia in 1787 aimed at establishing that American *Lex Rex* through the codification and protection of your individual freedom. And the resultant charter—this unprecedented, unparalleled repository of opportunity for everyman—should be loudly celebrated and fiercely defended. That a couple hundred years ago, a few thousand ragtag dreamers on this continent rose up, stirred their fellow citizens to shake off the torpor of bondage, and break their shackles; that the wild call of courage could enable the common folk to free themselves from their common bondage; and that, finally—someplace, somewhere in the drear passage of unending tyranny—one People had wedded the idealist's temerity with a visionary's tenacity; that they had rallied to the cause of universal justice, that they had unflinchingly challenged the mightiest empire on the planet, and through dauntless courage and unstinting sacrifice won their way to freedom...and that you are the recipient of that victory...and its precious, irreplaceable inheritance is your gift...if you can keep it...that is why the skies blaze with fireworks every July 4th.

We shall unpack the provisions and repercussions of the Constitution in the ensuing chapters. Note, for now, however, that the Constitution itself is, in reality, a mere "auxiliary precaution." In other words, the written law is merely a backstop. The spirit of the People is always and everywhere the *primary* protection of freedom. You, the citizen, are the surest, ultimate safeguard of your own liberty. Your determination to be free—your willingness to act and speak out, your refusal to be bullied or silenced—these are the true determinates of a nation's political direction.

In this regard, we have only to think of what the Founders did when they considered their taxes too high: they flouted the tax and destroyed the tea. When they considered the Stamp Act too onerous and intrusive, they boycotted British goods, then tarred and feathered the government agents and ran them out of town. When the government told them to turn over the weapons they were amassing at Concord, the Americans, in effect, said, "Come and take it!" When the customs officers stole John Hancock's sloop *Liberty*, the Sons of Liberty promptly grabbed, convicted, and burned their boat.

The Founders didn't play.

The government, of course, warned against this protesting and stockpiling weapons (and these were not just muskets those Colonists were caching at Concord but artillery: gunpowder, cannons, and cannon balls). The British overseers had, in their infinite wisdom, declared it illegal for ordinary people to keep such weapons of war and decided to seize them, to which the Americans answered, "Fool around and find out!"

The next steps wrote the history books.

The American colonists were unflinching, uncompromising, and by most standards even unreasonable in their demands for their sovereignty. But that seems to be what is necessary to declare, defend, and live in freedom. They fought a war which killed almost 1 in 100 in the land, surpassed only by the Civil War in its cost in blood. Seeing the bedraggled, dishevelled wraiths in mismatched uniforms who marched alongside Washington at the victory celebrations in New York in 1783, one witness noted the victorious troops were, "*ill-clad and weatherbeaten and made a forlorn appearance. But then they were our troops, and as I looked at them and thought upon all they had done and suffered for us, my heart and eyes were full and I admired and gloried in them the more, because they were weatherbeaten and forlorn.*"

It ain't easy being free...only glorious.

And the question becomes whether such a commitment to liberty can be maintained, whether (and how fast) it might be neglected by its inheritors, eroded by its detractors, and finally destroyed by its enemies.

The answer—for every generation—is up to you.

"Proclaim liberty throughout the land unto all the inhabitants ."

— Leviticus 25:10 —

Chapter 2

You and your Constitution:

Citizen & Sovereign

As the Pilgrims sought freedom, the American Badass hungers for <u>*freedom*</u> *like a drowning man hungers for air. But their courage and determination to make the daunting trip across the Atlantic was the merest beginning of their adventure in manifesting freedom. The Pilgrims' real work began when they landed. They had to actually build a community—house and road and farm— laboring to produce a polity from whence a nation could grow. Thus, before they even left the ship, they enacted a founding concord, a declaration of essential laws to shape their time together living in freedom via a written Compact—a model of government codified and circumscribed by the Rule of Law which would reach its culmination in the Constitution of the United States 150 years hence.*

— *The Mayflower Chronicles, p. 121:*

Mayflower Compact

In the name of God, Amen. We, whose names are underwritten...Do by these Presents, solemnly and mutually, in the Presence of God and one another, covenant and combine ourselves together into a civil Body Politick, for our better Ordering and Preservation, and Furtherance of the Ends aforesaid: And by Virtue hereof do enact, constitute, and frame, such just and equal Laws, Ordinances, Acts, Constitutions, and Offices, from time to time, as shall be thought most meet and convenient for the general Good of the Colony; unto which we promise all due Submission and Obedience. In witness whereof we have hereunto subscribed our names at Cape-Cod the eleventh of November, in the Reign of our Sovereign Lord King James, of England...anno Domini 1620.

Righteous Rebellion

ONCE A REVOLUTION IS WON, the question becomes, how will its victory be utilized? For the fledgling American nation—as a great testing lab of liberty—that question became, how free will we be, how free can a whole country be? And can we bequeath that freedom to our posterity? The challenge was to find just how far and how long a people can keep the flame of freedom going...and pass along that burning torch of American Badass.

The first step in the adventure of America embodying political freedom was becoming not just a hodge-podge amalgam of renegade colonies, but a nation. Fortunately for the Colonists, the British Parliament—in all its venality and hubris—had provided the annealing fire to forge the disparate, obstinate sensibilities of independent-minded settlers into one single coalition with one shared purpose: get up off my back, redcoat!

Samuel Adams: Captain "No!" of the Colonial Cause

"The truth is, all might be free if they valued freedom, and defended it as they ought."

— Samuel Adams, in the *Boston Gazette* (1771) —

There was a reason the British so badly wanted to hang Sam Adams. One of the most outspoken standard bearers for independence, Sam Adams always riled up the British oppressors with his calls for outright revolution—though he who would himself later helm the post-revolutionary state government. Adams always stood in the forefront for Colonial rights. Firebrand of the first American Revolution, maker of malt and trouble, from the1740s, his voice was one of the earliest—and perhaps loudest—publicly crying for American liberty and "independency." His was that stalwart, uncompromising battle cry of freedom, the tireless, unwavering spirit who worked feverishly to turn words into deeds, to make real the ideal...to the highest degree. Agitator-in-chief, propagandist *par excellence*, he declaimed in *"The Rights of the Colonists"* (1772): *"If men, through fear, fraud, or mistake, should in terms renounce or give up any natural right, the eternal law of reason and the grand end of society would absolutely vacate such renunciation. The right to freedom being a gift of Almighty God, it is not in the power of man to alienate this gift and voluntarily become a slave."*

His endless broadsheets, letters, and speeches stirred the patriots while his practical political machinations got the right men elected to the right posts in Boston to move policy and practice toward independence. As a leader of the Sons of Liberty, Adams and his cohorts fomented non-cooperation and direct street action against his British oppressors, from embargoes of British imports to the famed Tea Party in Boston harbor. His endless energies created the Committees of Correspondence to organize resistance alongside the other colonies; this network of leaders was the backbone upon which the American independence political movement grew from talk to successful rebellion...and then became the cadre which formed the eventual independent American government. It was he—and John Hancock—that the British authorities most sought to arrest that fateful day in April, 1775 when the Battles of Lexington and Concord sparked the actual Revolution.

Adams offered no compromise to anyone who inveighed against our declaration of full American independence: *"If you love wealth greater than liberty, the tranquility of servitude greater than the animating contest of freedom, go home from us in peace. We seek not your counsel, nor your arms. Crouch down and lick the hand that feeds you; and may posterity forget that ye were our countrymen."*

And, when the young nation set to governing itself, he turned from rabble-rouser to statesman, shouldering the duty of public service by serving as both state senator and Governor of Massachusetts. For, as he had reminded his readers in an essay in the *Public Advertiser* in 1749, a nation's happiness arises precisely from service in virtue and adherence to duty: *"Neither the wisest constitution nor the wisest laws will secure the liberty and happiness of a people whose manners are universally corrupt."*

A Constitution of Freedom
"Let us raise a standard to which the wise and honest can repair. The rest is in the hand of God."
— George Washington,
opening the Constitutional Convention —

As great as Sam Adams' political infighting was to move the people and Congress towards independence, as important as Washington's military action was to oust the redcoats from our land, the ultimate test for the young nation was forging a set of laws which could turn America's bold independence into viable self-government. What would be the political character of this rebellious People?

The Revolution being won but the Articles of Confederation proving ungainly, a Constitutional Convention was called in the summer of 1787 to form a government. It brought together three of our exemplar Founders—Washington, Madison, and Franklin—along with 36 other delegates to the capital in Philadelphia for a parlay which shaped the continent's future. The Articles of Confederation which had heretofore stitched the 13 disparate Colonies together had proven so amorphous and ineffectual that they could neither reliably fund the Colonial confederation nor provision Washington's army. The Framers were therefore looking to forge fundamental laws which might both hold together a vibrant, independent nation, while preserving the liberty and autonomy of each sovereign citizen and state.

The task of putting freedom first was one rarely set by a political council. Remember, the history of humankind is primarily of warlords and autocrats, of gangs of ruffians riding into town, knocking heads together and announcing they are now the new "government" and that every word from their mouths is now "law," whether fair or not. Historically, revolutionaries like our Founders— once having grabbed the reins of power—do not then turn around and hand that power over to the masses. Rather, most changes of government—especially if brought about through war—simply seat a new ruling class, enthrone yet another aristocracy which gathers power and wealth to the few at the top. Authoritarianism— i.e. sheer brutality and tyranny—is the norm in human governance, and constructing a system which provides for both stability and freedom is a rare and challenging undertaking.

Thus the physical battle to oust the redcoats from our land was the merest precursor; the greater task was the mental and spiritual challenge of shaping this bold, unprecedented experiment in self-government. Fortunately, the people who undertook that challenge in Philadelphia had a rare set of qualities uniquely suited to the task. First, many had been classically educated from both the Bible and histories of the Greco-Roman era, giving them a broad knowledge of history, political types and outcomes, and the limits and vagaries of human nature. Second, their ancestral history from Magna Carta wherein the King conceded the rights of his subjects at Runnymede, to the challenges to that rule of law under Cromwell's dictatorship and the English Civil War, plus the cultural legacy of such works such as Hobbes' *Leviathan* and Locke's *Second Treatise on Government*—all of these gave them a sense of the dangers of authoritarianism as well as the intellectual framework to seek justice via a more libertarian modality. Third, they had their own immediate experience of the tyranny wrought by Parliament and Kind George counterpoised by the weaknesses revealed in the 1781 Articles of Confederation which had stitched the Colonies together through the Revolution, but too loosely to function as a single, cohesive body. It would be a fine balancing act indeed, requiring the finest political craftsmanship, to render a nation at once founded in its laws but free in its People.

Would patriots such as these—so passionate and self-sacrificing in defense of essential liberties—have crafted a form of government which circumscribed their personal liberties? Or would they not rather have limited government power first and forever? Indeed, mission one was limiting government, for they knew history's one great political lesson: evil men will always try to turn the power of government to evil purpose. As John Adams said, *"Power in every form...when directed only by human Wisdom and Benevolence is dangerous."* In other words, to keep the people free, keep the government shackled. They knew that while self-restrained men like Washington or Jefferson may rise and serve—helping the public first and themselves last—that evil people are also born in every land and in every generation. Sooner or later, wicked men would skulk to the political forefront, men rapacious for power, unfettered by duty, heedless of morality. There is no way to stop the wicked from seeking—and probably no way to keep some from acquiring—access to power. The only solution is to keep government sufficiently small, poor, and weak that it cannot become a useful cudgel for state-sponsored robbery and villainy. Thus, in framing a government of personal liberty, the Framers understood—as Jefferson formulated it in the Kentucky Resolutions in 1798—that, *"in questions of power then, let no more be heard of confidence in man, but bind him down from mischief by the chains of the constitution."*

It was this understanding of the need to keep governance good by keeping it restrained—and the sort of civil society and citizenry that could uphold it—which informed the minds of those who gathered at the Constitutional Convention. The resultant Constitution of these united American States is thus intended as a codification of *limitation* on government, not an unlimited grant of power. In fact, the Constitution acts and speaks primarily as a continual reminder of limitation; it restrains our politicos by—in the space of just four pages—using the word *"no"* 34 times and *"not"* 31 times; it is a continual remonstrance to our bureaucrats that they are manacled, restricted, and hidebound to the proper limits of just governance. Its primary purpose is to grant only the minimal size and scope of authority to the state—just the necessary allotment of power to keep things running—while allowing maximal scope for citizen action. But even then, the Anti-Federalists—having the ancestral memory of Cromwell and his Roundheads and Locke's admonitions ringing in their ears—had the good sense to demand we append to that document a Bills of Rights, ten explicit, black-letter statements of those <u>lines which SHALL **NOT** BE CROSSED</u>.

The founding documents of this nation, then, form a philosophical whole, a rationalist anthropology underscoring a libertarian public policy. As John Quincy Adams said at the Constitution's 50th anniversary celebration, our Constitution is, "*the complement of the Declaration of Independence, founded upon the same principles...[They] are part of one consistent whole.*" These twin documents arise from an understanding of a natural law which underwrites a form of governance directed toward individual self-development. The Constitution's structure flows from that vision of government so admirably and succinctly outlined in Jefferson's immortal words—cribbed from George Mason's brilliant, earlier declaration for Virginia—in the American Declaration of Independence:

We hold these truths to be self-evident, that all men are created equal, that they are endowed by their Creator with certain unalienable Rights, that among these are Life, Liberty and the pursuit of Happiness. — That to secure these rights, Governments are instituted among Men, deriving their just powers from the consent of the governed.

There, in a single passage, is the Founders vision of the godly design for human government. It is, if you will, the mission statement for the American People. The Constitution turns that vision into an action plan, a blueprint for a working truth. And, for generations, the American People's moral compass and love of freedom has been strong enough to make that blueprint into concrete reality.

Though few citizens realize it, the core principle of the American Constitution is a guarantee, by law, of all possible rights, liberty, and powers to the People. Then, from that infinite field of individual liberty, we, the citizenry, grant to government a *short, specified* list of powers for the limited purpose of protecting those freedoms. Depending on how you parse the relevant sections, we have allowed the federal Congress the power to act on only 21 matters (twenty in Article I, Section 8 and one in Article IV, section 3), <u>and that's all</u>!!! The federal government has, in short, less than two dozen matters upon which it may legally act.

Put another way, the Constitution is a contract wherein the People agree to create and support a restricted administration to manage a handful of large, complex tasks (like provisioning a navy), but to otherwise leave the citizens alone. In other words, we have decided to let some bureaucrats handle those challenges which are cumbersome but essential to keeping us all safe, while we apply our energies to the twin tasks most fundamental to building a nation's economy and culture: productive work and responsible citizenship. Towards that end, the Constitution enshrines one golden principle at the heart of our law: that the powers of governmental power must be kept small, so the People's freedom may be great. As Madison put it in Federalist 45: *"The powers delegated...to the Federal government are few and defined. Those which are to remain in the State governments are numerous and indefinite."*

This codification of your range of freedom may be called the principle of *presumptive liberty*, wherein you, the citizen, live in an endless vista of infinite possibilities for expressing your creative faculties; you are assumed the freedom to act in any way not circumscribed by law, while the federal government via Congress may licitly act *only and solely* to restrict a citizen on matters *explicitly enumerated* in Article I, Section 8. In other words, Congress must be *minimally busy* and *sparingly funded*, so that you, the Citizen-sovereign, are guaranteed to be *maximally free* and *fully empowered*. In plain speech, then, the Constitution is itself, one long "No!" to government overstepping its bounds, and any unconstitutional federal undertaking is not only an empty pretence but a crime. Anyone—including and especially Congress, federal functionaries, or judges—who tells you otherwise is either ignorant or lying. Anyone who knows American law, knows the Founders' vision: God created us free, and good government has first and last one mission: to guarantee and guard that freedom...in writing...and by law.

If you doubt any of this, read the Constitution for yourself and decide. After all, the document clearly states that "we the People"—not a king, not a Congress, nor any other political priesthood—are the ones who promulgated it, and so we are the ultimate arbiters in adjudicating its meaning and enactment. In case there is any doubt about the Constitution's overall design, we need only glance at the Bill of Rights' final two Amendments, IX and X (more thoroughly covered in Chapter 7). These twin enactments make clear—as do voluminous quotes from the Founders and Framers (provided in Appendix 1)—that any act attempted by any branch or agent of the federal government outside the Constitution's explicit, written limits is not only dangerous in principle, but legally null, void, and of no effect. (To easily check this, see the quick-read version of that Constitution—keeping the core parts related to rights and modestly updated to contemporary English usage—which is attached at the end of this chapter.)

To accomplish this end of maximal liberty, the Constitution creates a carefully-crafted balance and division of power, splitting political power two ways. First, "horizontally", it creates three side-by-side separate branches of governance—legislative, executive, and judicial—designed to make them as much competitors amongst themselves as allies subjugating the citizenry. Second, top-to-bottom, our government is allotted into three levels—federal, state, and local—where each serves their own ends and interests and thus should as much struggle betwixt themselves as with their subjects. As Madison explains this purposeful intergovernmental competition in *The Federalist Papers,* No. 51, it serves as a bulwark against despotism, especially against the legislative branch, for "*{I}t is not possible to give to each department an equal power of self-defense. In republican* *government, the legislative authority necessarily predominates. The remedy for this inconveniency is to divide the legislature into different branches; and to render them, by different modes of election and different principles of action, as little connected with each other as the nature of their common functions and their common dependence on the society will admit. It may even be necessary to guard against dangerous encroachments by still further precautions."*

The American Constitution, therefore, is purposefully constructed to produce a slow, divided, and "inefficient" government, and that design has withstood the test of time: nearing 250 years strong, the American Constitution now stands as the longest-extant written national charter on the planet. That alone is living testament to the sagacity of its design, for it has proven its mettle as a guiding light in shielding the American people through rebellion, invasion, and innumerable assaults from demagogues and traitors, plutocrats and quislings, and the endless parade of grafters, grifters, and gangsters who always accrete to the centers of power. Indeed, this Constitution—read as a blueprint for political justice—is an invitation to everyone, not just American-born but anywhere in the world, to examine and demand that every person, in every land, lay claim to the dignity of freedom, the indispensability of justice, and the sanctity of each and every incommensurate human life.

In short sum, then, the Constitution's carefully-crafted lawyer-speak means you are free. It means a collection of brilliant men—bent on a protecting the rights of the people and believing in Divine justice—gifted to you an unmatched heritage: a framework for freedom. Your Framers produced a form of governance which devolved freedom down towards the states, the localities, and the People. None of them seized power as dictator or king. As noted above, when Washington's officers begged him to declare himself king, he followed the example of Cincinnatus and retired to private life on his farm. He and his soldiers fought, foraged, and froze at Valley Forge for freedom. Too many other patriots—from ordinary militiamen to the signers of the Declaration of Independence—likewise suffered the burning of their homes and lands, scattering of their families, or outright death in that cause. Such sacrifice was not to be so readily discarded. The sovereign power of decision had not been wrested from the British Crown at such cost to immediately be stolen again by its very rescuers. Such an undertaking would make the whole revolution a mere exercise of giving a new, American face to the old, British tyranny. The American People would put freedom first.

Liberty and Anthropology

"Rightful liberty is unobstructed action according to our will within limits drawn around us by the equal rights of others. I do not add 'within the limits of the law' because law is often but the tyrant's will, and always so when it violates the rights of the individual."

— Thomas Jefferson —

To truly bind a nation's bureaucrats and apparatchiks to justice, one needs a sure foundation. For the Framers of our political system, that foundation was ultimately spiritual. The Constitution grew not just from political *desiderata*, but from the Framers' understanding of human nature, that your rights come from your inherent human nature; they come first from God, from your created nature in God's own image. Specifically, your nature, your anthropology, is a creature whose essential personhood arises from two elements, mind and will; you are a being born both rational and free, evincing: (1) *reason* -the ability to move and act on the basis of reflection, of mind, your ability to think, to understand, to plan and to create, and (2) *free will*- the capacity to choose, to act upon decisions which either improve or degrade your condition. These twin human capabilities are those which empower you—a frail, forked creature—to survive in both the natural and social wilderness. This understanding of your need to exercise your nature and capabilities in order to flourish was therefore codified in the protections guaranteed to you in the Bill of Rights, those first ten amendments explicitly protecting these essential freedoms.

First Freedoms: The Spirit

"Without freedom of thought, there can be no such thing as wisdom; and no such thing as public liberty, without freedom of speech."

— Benjamin Franklin —

The political protections instantiated in the Bill of Rights serve to guarantee the freedom necessary for you to manifest your reason and volition. First, let us understand the character of that freedom. Political freedom for such a creature must allow you the ability to think and act without restraint; to maximally instantiate your capacities without constraint; to act with least limit; to exercise, in physical form, your capacity for thought, and your potentiality to intend and will. Thus, actualizing freedom is giving body and mind the latitude to move, produce, and explore under the agency of thought and will...and freedom in both reflection and volition becomes, therefore, the test of all real political freedom. For, short of when clapped in iron bonds, the body is continually and automatically under the operation of your own thought and will.

A well-ordered republic, then, prizes first and foremost the freedom of the mind, giving it full compass to explore, to reflect and express its reflections. Therefore, the very First Amendment protects your ability to acquire and disseminate information, i.e. the right to think, to speak, and to meet with others to share your thoughts and theirs. Thence, to protect your freedom of thought and mind, government shall never interfere with your ability to:

• Say what you wish to say

• Hear what your fellows wish to say

• Think and believe and worship as you wish

• Publish your thoughts and beliefs so that your fellows might share them

• Gather with others to mutually express all such thoughts and beliefs

• And that includes thoughts for, about, and even against the government and its agents

These prohibitions barring government from censorship are simply the logical conclusion of leaving the citizen's mind to do its work. In this way, the First Amendment enshrines freedom of the mind. And despite being a member of the Continental Congress who voted to ratify the initial Constitution which had failed to explicitly provide this protection, Sam Adams—that tireless voice and mover of men's minds in speech and print and assembly—quickly sided with the Anti-Federalists in demanding the Bill of Rights, with its First Amendment protection of such freedom of thought and expression. A rabble-rouser like Adams immediately recognized the necessity of protecting the right to think, speak, and publish unpopular opinions, as he had done so vigorously for decades in laying the groundwork for the liberation of his countrymen from the oppressive hand of British colonial rule over American minds.

Freedom Next: Your Body

"Always remember that an armed and trained militia is the firmest bulwark of republics—that without standing armies their liberty can never be in danger, nor with large ones, safe."

— James Madison —

After protecting our freedom of thought, the Bill of Rights moves on to protecting one's voluntary action, the ability to manifest one's thought and will in physical form. Preeminent in preserving physical freedom is preserving one's physical form, the body itself. To be able to act, one must remain alive, and one must therefore have means of self defense. The Second Amendment— second only to your freedom of mind—therefore enshrines the right to defend one's body, family, property, and polity. For, after the work of freeing the mind, the most important work is protecting life and limb. And, since the most powerful, effective means of such protection is weaponry, *"the right of the people to keep and bear arms shall not be infringed."*

There is a reason that final, independent clause in the Second Amendment is one of the most blunt and unambiguous in the whole document. Plainly, the patriots who had just fought a bloody war to throw off the chains of tyranny—begun by a gunfight when the British sought to seize the cache of weapons at Concord—wanted their citizen militiamen well-armed and sufficiently dangerous to keep the government fearful of assaulting anyone's life or liberties. Hence, the right of the people to own and carry weapons shall not even be so much as touched at the *fringe*, the edges...not even along its hairline border. As Mao notoriously noted, "political power flows from the barrel of a gun," and the Framers wanted that power, first, foremost, and always in the hands of the People.

Fully Free: Your Property

"Now, one of the most essential branches of English liberty is the freedom of one's house. A man's house is his castle; and whilst he is quiet, he is as well-guarded as a prince in his castle."
— James Otis —

The ensuing amendments likewise protect the physical means of survival. Since human beings survive only through their tools—the artifacts by which they plow their fields or run their workshops—a citizen without the means of employment is at best a slave, at worst a starveling. When John Locke penned the *Second Treatise on Government*, he declared the essential political rights to be threefold: "life, liberty, and *property*." He was pointing—as would such later libertarian writers as von Mises—that, to physically enact freedom, we must engage, modify, and produce in the material world; we therefore have both a need for and right to retain our productive output and the means to produce, i.e. our property. Hence, protection of property is as much a part of true political freedom as the right to speak, seek redress of grievance, or defend ourselves. Without maximal access and protection of the material means of his own maintenance and flourishing in the material world, the citizen is not free, but hampered, bound to a serfdom wherein he cannot reap the bounty of his own labor, nor pass along whatever abundance he produces to his progeny. A failure to protect personal property is thereby not only the formula for servitude, but for a perpetual enslavement, generation after generation of people who can never acquire the wealth to fully enjoy freedom. As Madison said in his essay "Property", *"Government is instituted to protect property of every sort...This being the end of government, that alone is a just government, which impartially secures to every man, whatever is his own."* The Third through Eighth Amendments therefore serve to protect oneself *and* one's property; they safeguard the material means to enact one's freely-chosen decisions and the wealth acquired thereby.

The Third Amendment protects the sanctity of one's household from having soldiers domicile themselves in your house, that no one may make free use of your property by government decree, an actual practice at the time of the Revolution. (Indeed, the Colonists were expected not only to house but also *feed* the occupying troops!)

The Fourth Amendment protects all of one's chattel property—basically all the stuff inside the house—from bureaucrats snooping, grabbing, or messing with things that are none of their business, without reasonable, specific court order arising from witness testimony.

The Vth, VIth, VIIth, and VIII amendment protect our persons and property in cases of law and dispute overseen by that third branch of government, the court system.

The final two Amendments serve, perhaps most importantly, as a final reaffirmation of limitation: the IXth Amendment reminds the government that the People retain innumerable rights...and, just because a right has not yet been written down or codified, does not mean it does not exist. Likewise, the Xth Amendment reminds the government that all power—

unless specifically granted to the government in writing—is retained either by the People, or their state.

...and that's it!

That's all there is to it. That is all the federal government can lawfully do. The Constitution is, properly, a short, sharp reminder on the limited scope of federal action, and a protection of the rights of American citizens to realize their full capacities. The bulk of the Constitution (Articles I - VI) are the operational framework for the federal government, its forms, functions, and limitations. Those articles are, in essence, of no real importance to the citizen in their everyday undertakings, since those provisions, properly enacted, establish a republic which keeps the citizen safe to go about living a free, flourishing life. As long as the government is doing its job properly, an American citizen should rarely see or hear from the government or its agents. A citizen in a free republic will be too busy producing and enjoying an abundance of freedom to have much concern with the government, which is itself too busy attending to its few, limited duties—like defending the borders and collecting import duties—to wheedle, cajole, or harass a private citizen in her everyday business.

These documents, at their core, then, reflect a philosophical anthropology, an understanding of your human nature whose capacities, limitations, and rights are inherent and therefore antecedent to any government. Put another way, as a child of God, your rights can never be taken away; no matter how ferociously your rights are attacked, abused, ignored or trampled by bad government, they remain inherently and inalienably yours, part of what makes you human. But the self-conscious awareness and agency inherent in your humanity can only be fully expressed and explored under liberty, under a governmental system wherein the possible evils of tyranny are proscribed by law, and where the rewards of freedom can most fully flow to those who prove most upright, self-disciplined, and self-reliant.

The question becomes, then, can today's citizenry—with all the doubts and assaults upon belief in this nation and faith in the

Creator—restore the sense of civic virtue and personal honor to serve others and defend this Republic? For, no manifesto, no mere piece of paper—no matter how finely crafted—will stay the course of wickedness all by itself. Rather, it is the spirit of the People which most determines the course of government. Indeed, even the worst form of government, if enacted by a people with a heart for liberty and soul for justice, would doubtless protect the common people. Likewise, one could parade a hermetically-sealed Constitution under all the red-white-and-blue bunting in the world and have a nation of citizens behaving like thugs and petty despots. Only a people with a strong moral compass and burning will for freedom can maintain a constitutional republic.

As Madison famously put it, elsewhere in *Federalist* No. 51: *"If men were angels, no government would be necessary. If angels were to govern men, neither external nor internal controls on government would be necessary. In framing a government which is to be administered by men over men, the great difficulty lies in this: you must first enable the government to control the governed; and in the next place oblige it to control itself. A dependence on the people is, no doubt, the primary control on the government; but experience has taught mankind the necessity of auxiliary precautions."*

Survival of the Finest: Liberty and Probity

"Today it would be progress if everyone would stop talking about values. Instead, let us talk, as the Founders did, about virtues."

— George Will —

Thus, the through line which cannot be forgotten—the thread which cannot be unwound in the tapestry of American Badass—is the patina of virtue which informs truly mature badass. If the personal power of liberty is released—that infinite creative capacity and agency of the fully-realized human—it must be properly channelled toward beneficent ends, or it will bring disaster upon both self and others. Without the tempering walls of self-discipline, liberty quickly devolves into libertinism, anarchy both personal and social. A system of most complete freedom depends for its survival on a people of most complete virtue. Freedom demands virtue: temperance, honesty, industry, conscientiousness, frugality, courage, and a dozen other qualities of everyday self-restraint. Otherwise liberty becomes license to licentious indolence and a self-indulgence which wreaks ruin on citizen and republic alike, and the once free person soon becomes a wretched wastrel, slave to their own vices. Thus, after cleaving off the bonds of British tyranny and gathering in Philadelphia to write the Constitution of liberty, the Framers always interlaced their dreams of liberty with a monitory call for virtue...and even divine help...in their endeavors.

Near the opening of the Constitutional Convention, Franklin encouraged the presiding officer, George Washington, and the assembly to prayerfully seek divine assistance: *"In the beginning of the contest with Britain, when we were sensible of danger, we had daily prayers in this room for Divine protection. Our prayers, Sir, were heard, and they were graciously answered. All of us who were engaged in the struggle must have observed frequent instances of a superintending Providence in our favor....and have we not forgotten this powerful Friend? Or do we imagine we no longer need His assistance? I have lived, Sir, a long time, and the longer I live, the more convincing proofs I see of this truth: 'that God governs in the affairs of man.' And if a sparrow cannot fall to the ground without His notice, is it probable that an empire can rise without His aid?"*

Such appeals to the Divine, and the virtue which was expected to follow from such piety, were commonplace in that generation. Again and again—virtually to a man—the Founders and Framers admonished us that, *to be a great nation, we must be a good people.*

Here is just a smattering of the statements of the Founders on the essentiality of virtue in a republic:

"[I]t is religion and morality alone which can establish the principles upon which freedom can securely stand. The only foundation of a free constitution is pure virtue."

— John Adams —

"If virtue & knowledge are diffused among the people, they will never be enslav'd. This will be their great security."

— Samuel Adams —

"Only a virtuous people are capable of freedom. As nations become more corrupt and vicious, they have more need of masters."

— Benjamin Franklin —

"Bad men cannot make good citizens. It is when a people forget God that tyrants forge their chains. A vitiated state of morals, a corrupted public conscience, is incompatible with freedom. No free government, or the blessings of liberty, can be preserved to any people but by a firm adherence to justice, moderation, temperance, frugality, and virtue; and by a frequent recurrence to fundamental principles."

— Patrick Henry —

"Without virtue, happiness cannot be."

— Thomas Jefferson —

"It is certainly true that a popular government cannot flourish without virtue in the people."

— Richard Henry Lee —

"The aim of every political Constitution, is or ought to be first to obtain for rulers men who possess most wisdom to discern, and most virtue to pursue, the common good of society; and in the next place, to take the most effectual precautions for keeping them virtuous whilst they continue to hold their public trust."

— James Madison —

"No free government, or the blessings of liberty, can be preserved to any people, but by a firm adherence to justice, moderation, temperance, frugality and virtue, and by frequent recurrence to fundamental principles."

— George Mason —

"Whenever we are planning for posterity, we ought to remember that virtue is not hereditary."

— Thomas Paine —

"If men be good, government cannot be bad."

— William Penn —

"Without virtue, there can be no liberty."

— Benjamin Rush —

"[T]he manners of the people in general are of the utmost moment to the stability of any civil society. When the body of a people are altogether corrupt in their manners, the government is ripe for dissolution."

— John Witherspoon —

"Can it be that Providence has not connected the permanent felicity of a nation with its virtue?"

— George Washington —

"[V]irtue or morality is a necessary spring of popular government."
— George Washington —

As we shall see in the ensuing chapters, the result of such freedom is precisely the development of autonomy, the learned responsibility—or, more simply, self-reliance—which is the second element of American Badass. (And for scores of similar admonitions by the Founders and their ilk on the essentiality of virtue for the maintenance of liberty, see Appendix 2)

The inverse of the development of virtue is the outcome if the vicious person accedes to power...or the citizens themselves succumb to self-indulgent vice. And the challenges brought on by malignancy and monetary malfeasance will indeed eventually prove problematic for the Republic. At the end of the Constitutional Convention, Franklin spoke with almost oracular prescience when declaring, *"I believe...that this [new government under the Constitution] is likely to be well administered for a course of years, and can only end in Despotism, as other forms have done before it, when the people shall become so corrupted as to need despotic Government, being incapable of any other."*

The Bankers War, Round 1: Jefferson vs. Hamilton

"And I sincerely believe...that banking establishments are more dangerous than standing armies; & that the principle of spending money to be paid by posterity, under the name of funding, is but swindling futurity on a large scale."
— Thomas Jefferson (*Papers*, 10:89) —

At the same time freedom was being codified in law, its enemies were laying the groundwork for undermining it, eating at its foundations with the tirelessness of termites. Big money always has a way of turning the heads of greedy minds, and a pair of men in whom Washington placed great trust were thusly turned. Their names were Benedict Arnold and Alexander Hamilton.

Benedict Arnold is well enough known for his treachery in betraying Washington and the revolutionary cause. Despite having failed in the Montreal campaign of 1775 to liberate the Canadian people from the British—thereby keeping them from becoming part of the American Republic, as they properly had the right to be, instead of remaining subjects of the Crown (for the solution, see Appendix 4)—he was given command of the fort at West Point by Washington. Oft accused of embezzlement to support his profligate lifestyle, the embittered Arnold conspired to surrender that critical fortification overseeing the Hudson River to the British for £ 20,000. When, however, his accomplice was captured and hanged for espionage, Arnold fled, exacerbating his treachery by taking a post as general in the British armies, going on to burn colonial cities and slaughter American prisoners. After the war, he lived a long, justifiably miserable retirement, shunned not only by Americans but also by both the British military alongside whom he had fought and the Canadians whom he had failed.

Because no one likes a betrayer.

Of the Founders, Hamilton is one of the most ambiguous figures, who still today has some bedazzled by his brilliance. A dashing figure of notable wit and charm, Hamilton was an ambitious illegitimate son of nobility with an eager eye for opportunity. A complex figure who loved liberty, money, and the ladies, Alexander Hamilton, as America's first Treasury Secretary, was instrumental in cajoling President Washington into setting up the first National Bank of the United States. This occurred, despite then Vice President Thomas Jefferson's strenuous objections to the idea. While it is certainly true that Hamilton's efforts as Treasury Secretary laid the groundwork for the robust commercial dynamism which would characterize the coming century in America, many of those same enactments undermined the foundations for sound political economy and finance codified in the Constitution. At the time of its opening, the young New York Stock Exchange on Wall Street was trading only four instruments, all of which Hamilton had initiated. Was there self-interest in his policy making? Was Hamilton simply doing well by doing good, or was there perhaps a little more self-interest in his schemes than needful?

This issue of central banking caused a tremendous rift between Washington's two top advisors, Treasury Secretary Hamilton and Vice President Thomas Jefferson. Jefferson's stance on central banking had, amongst other elements, a clear constitutional foundation, warning of the illegitimacy of a national bank in 1791: *"I consider the foundation of the Constitution as laid on this ground: That 'all powers not delegated to the United States, by the Constitution, nor prohibited by it to the States, are reserved to the States or to the people.' [Xth Amendment] To take a single step beyond the boundaries thus specially drawn around the powers of Congress, is to take possession of a boundless field of power, no longer susceptible of any definition...The incorporation of a bank, and the powers assumed by this bill, have not, in my opinion, been delegated to the United States, by the Constitution."*

Despite such republican objections, in 1791, Hamilton and the Federalists finally persuaded Washington to back the first central bank of the united American States with a 20 year charter, initially capitalized for a whopping $10 million, with significant backing from European moneyed interests (80% of this "national" bank was privately owned), whose pockets would be lined with the interest on the initial loan and would further profit from the central banking system thenceforth. This enactment, then, was both (a) a centralization of monetary power—in itself an invitation to both financial chicanery and a weakening of national economic strength by centralizing rather than diversifying banking and monetary exchange—and (b) a step toward the debasement of the monetary system through the hidden tax of inflation.

Thieving Scraps and the Scrip Scam

"Bank-paper must be suppressed, and the circulating medium must be restored to the nation to whom it belongs."
— Thomas Jefferson —

Little did the American People realize that, with their victory over the British army, the real war was just beginning, the Bankers War. The moneyed interest would come again and again to insinuate themselves and their financialization into the thriving American economic free market, an ongoing war between the bankers and the People which has continued, off and on, over the history of the Republic. The struggle for control over money, its form and issuance, would be an oft-misunderstood and continually overlooked challenge to the full liberty and prosperity inherent in the Constitution's promise. The forces of the international moneyed class have worked with tireless, fervent effort to institute their schemes within the Republic's marrow and thereby vitiated much of its vital energy through vampiric financial subterfuge. Through obscurantist language, euphemism, and political legerdemain, they have managed to undermine the simple, direct, and effective intentions of our founding document to protect the People's wealth through sound money, and have instead continually fought to wrest the control of the currency—and thereby much of the economy—by manipulation of the type, issuance, and amount of currency.

The Framers had foreseen and attempted to forestall such financialized manipulation. Specifically, Article I, Section 10 of the Constitution prohibits any State from emitting bills (paper money), but instead mandates the use of hard currency, specifically the precious metals silver and gold. The Framers had already tried the experiment with paper money under the Articles of Confederation, whereby the Colonies issued millions of "Continental" notes in the form of scrip. These debt notes had been quickly inflated by the penurious revolutionary government, and, by the end of the war, one was lucky to get 1% of its face value for a Continental note. Those debt notes were so debased that their very name became a watchword for lack of value, with any worthless thing being called "not worth a Continental."

Hence, when the first Congress turned to the issue of money in the Coinage Act of 1792, they mandated hard currency, not scrip. Specifically, Congress authorized two metal coins, one of silver, one of gold. The actual and true American *Dollar* was instituted as a silver coin, consisting of 371.25 grains of fine silver. A real dollar in the United States is, therefore, 371.25 grains (or 0.7734375 of a troy ounce) of fine silver...or at least a bearer note of scrip redeemable for such. The second coin, the gold *Eagle*, was declared *"to be of the value of ten dollars or units, and to contain two hundred and forty-seven grains, and four eighths of a grain of pure ... gold."*

Properly, then a "dollar" is a weight of silver, and any scrip "dollar bill" is a promissory note redeemable for actual money in the form of 371.25 grains (0.7734375 troy oz.) of fine silver. Calling a Federal Reserve debt note (that everyday greenback in your back pocket) a "dollar" is, therefore, a lie. Such a note is a promise of nothing; it is redeemable for nothing real; it is a smokescreen of debt, a bankers' buck, a flim-flam forced into the economy by government threats and bankers' lies. It conveys no value, transfers no wealth, effects no barter when moved from citizen to citizen; its issuance neither stabilizes trade nor maintains the free flow of actual productive value through actual peer-to-peer mercantile exchange. What it actually does do, however, is allow for the continual, arbitrary, inflationary release of money units which thereby bloats easy government spending and enriches bankers who issue this currency as a debt owed by the American People to them in the form of US bonds.

There is a reason that scrip—paper money...or, these days, mere digits on a computer screen—is called "fiat" money. *Fiat* means by declaration, by mere say-so; it means the government declares or says this piece of paper (or cowrie shell or tobacco leaf, etc.) is hereby money, and the citizens must accept it...or else. When we all play this make-believe game that a mere piece of paper is something of substantial value that we can freely exchange for someone else's real property or real time in labor, we put the controller and issuer of that make-believe money in a position of incredible power. By the simple act of counterfeiting real money on a printing machine, they get a virtual cut of every transaction throughout the economy, a continual "override" of everything that happens in the real *economy* through the mechanism of *financing* make-believe money units. Through that make-believe mechanism, greater and greater power and wealth is accumulated by the counterfeiting *financial* operators while the citizens doing the actual labor in the real *economy* see the value of their work and property evaporate. It is a subtle, insidious process, just slow enough and abstract enough to remain hidden from the ordinary citizen's gaze, especially when purposefully obscured by such obfuscatory verbiage as calling their wanton money-printing "quantitative easing" or "contingent liquidity arrangements"...or trying to soften the gut-wrenching impact of a straight-up, orphan-starving economic *depression* with such temporizing semantic elides as "recession" or "slow down."

In contrast, actual money in the form of precious metals (or notes redeemable for such), conveys actual convertible commercial value when exchanged. Using real money turns every transaction into a ready, civilized form of fungible barter. Using real money, you are, in actuality, conducting a simple, direct trade, i.e. moving a real asset (e.g. a coin having real world value) for someone's property or labor. Using real money, there is no phony financialization of the transaction, simply a straight-up economic event, a meeting of the minds which produces an agreeable transfer of assets. When such exchanges use a portable, fungible, imperishable, universally-recognized commodity like precious metals the economy operates on a solid foundation—at once fluid and unassailable—from whence to construct and maintain a healthy economy. The valuation of assets thereby becomes more stable, as they are all tied to other measurable, tangible assets. Commodity money is self-regulated by market forces, neither controlled nor issued in back rooms by insiders. Likewise, hard money minimizes extremes of market dislocation due to misallocation of assets, bubble price expansion or contraction. What ensues is productive, stable, continual growth.

Such an economy's largest challenges are in producing sufficient liquidity (i.e. hard currency monetary units) as the markets grow. Since, however, a free economy quickly finds someone seizing the opportunity to produce what is needed, such challenges are readily met by the market. This ongoing challenge of the healthy market outgrowing its monetary base also implies that sound money economies are naturally deflationary; in other words, as the economy grows somewhat faster than the monetary units, that makes each monetary unit more valuable. Thus, the value of one's savings tends to increase as the economy grows. All hard assets are therefore—although nominally lower in numeric price—more valuable, since the money units are incrementally harder to acquire. In other words, in a hard-money economy, the wealth of the citizenry is best preserved while the stability of the nation's productive activity maintained.

Again, calling today's circulating Federal Reserve Notes "dollars" is a lie, and that lie is the primary weapon used in the Bankers War against the Republic. Real American dollars are hard currency (silver) which tend toward deflationary economic stability; Federal Reserve debt notes are fiat currency (paper) which tend toward inflationary financialized instability. An economy built of the financier's lies of fiat currency will—since a scaffold of merest paper nothings—eventually topple into the spectacular morass of nothing which it actually represents. In contrast, an economy built of the actual blood, sweat, and sinew of real trade in actual money—while occasionally struggling through the up-and-down challenges as do all vibrant systems—can slow down, can stumble, but has the sure base of real property to which it can always revert and from whence it can readily re-emerge.

The greatest—and seemingly inescapable—danger of fiat currency is the continual temptation to inflation it gives the government and banks. Because there is no inherent limit to the amount of fiat currency which can be emitted (for, unlike metals, one does not have to physically produce it via protracted effort), the merry Keynesian can pretend he can print his way to happiness. And so he does...for a while. Initially, inflating the currency in circulation like a gigantic balloon does agitate activity in the economy, much like the jittery, febrile agitation of the addict's first, sweet taste of a toxic narcotic. But—after that first dizzying rush of fiat money frenzy is gone—the government, the speculators, and the public will ask for more. And then more. And, soon enough, everyone is addicted to the joy juice of ever-expanding stock markets, credit booms, and speculative bubbles of every sort. And the masses cry out: "Aren't we all winning? Isn't this financialized money scam amazing?" But the underlying economy—the actually production, distribution, and utilization of physical artifacts—is much the same. The crazy numbers on the stock market board—and most especially those on the "derivative" markets, which are simply speculation on the speculations by the speculators—are all just a doped-up pipe dream of arbitrary numbers "derived" from the mass psychosis of their consensual hallucination that anything of actual real-world value is happening on their flickering computer screens. They have taken the unreality of transmitting no-promise, no-value fiat money and turned second-order products bundled from that phony casino into a virtual video game version of a real economy. And that, my friends, is "financialization," when real economics is supplanted by the speculation of the speculators on the financing of the financiers obscuring the real economics of the real economy.

That upside-down pyramid of debt on top of debt on top of the real work of real people moving real products is the upside-down outcome of fake, say-so money, and it always ends badly, especially for the little guy who just stays at the bottom of the upside down pyramid, carrying the burden of doing actual grunt work fixing pipes and growing potatoes, while the speculators drink champagne and jitterbug on top. Indeed, because the phony money is king, it actually causes misallocation of resources, moving activity away from really productive building and planting and saving, and into speculative derivatives and NFTs and bubbly SPACs. It is the financialized equivalent of an absinthe-fueled debauch in the Moulin Rouge, and the next day's aftermath is just as ugly.

Thus, in matters of money and economy—rather than follow the claptrap agitprop proffered by the financial agents—watch the movement of actual lumber and labor, trucks and ships, food and factories. Pay no attention to the magician's trick of distracting you with their fine double-speak about their controlled "markets" and contrived "GDP" and massaged "reports" and manipulated "chairmen." Demand real payment in hard assets. Watch what the moneyed elites actually do: convert their phony money into land and gold and rental property and yachts. Watch how they freely spend during the easy-money, expansion, inflationary part of the boom-bust cycle, and then revert to cash during the tight-money, contraction, deflation part so they can buy up all the real things for pennies on the dollar.

The issuance of paper currency by such manipulators is, then, a destructive inflationary undertaking, a long-play grift. While it may increase tax revenues by incrementally increasing the nominal value of property (e.g. over time doubling the value of one's house, for instance), it likewise slowly steals the value of one's earnings by debasing the value of the paper money earned. Inflationary practices such as these are, in effect, an insidious, continual theft of one's earning power and wealth by debasement of the currency. It is theft by stealth by moneyed elites and— because obscure and little understood by those citizens—it is readily instituted and rarely confronted.

The net result of this ongoing inflationary Bankers War is seen in most ghastly form today, wherein the amount of money units (Federal Reserve "dollars") flooding the nation are measured in *trillions*, as opposed to the *millions* which served to fund the entire federal government of the early Republic. A trillion is an immense number. A trillion is one million *times* one million! Like this:

1,000,000 x 1,000,000 = 1,000,000,000,000 !!!

While the capitalization of Hamilton's first National Bank was measured in tens of millions (and the federal debt for the entire Revolutionary War $18 million), today's U.S. national debt is measured in tens of trillions. Yet, our nation is certainly not a million *times* larger. While the early Republic numbered a few million persons, our nation currently numbers a few hundred million; so, we have grown, roughly, 150 to 200 times bigger in population. But the money masters have multiplied the number of money units by *1 million times* over. In other words, since the Revolution, while our population has grown less than 200 times larger, our supply of money units (falsely called "dollars") has ballooned over *1 million times*. That is precisely the mechanism of manipulation expected when you have "fiat" currency which Jefferson (and so many others) warned about. In other words, our money's value has been evaporated by the bankers who were putatively tasked with protecting its value and defending our economy.

With so many money units sloshing around, is it any wonder your money buys so much less, that you pay so much more for a loaf of bread, a gallon of gas? The money masters are stealing the value of your labor, the wealth of your savings, by making the money units (their phony paper "dollars") increasingly worthless...and at an increasing rate. In contrast to their financialized mumbo-jumbo, the acid test of real-world *economics* is simple: where did the real stuff go? Who owned the houses and steel mills and ships yesterday, and what bank or corporation owns them today? Are you buying more bread and milk with your money units ("dollars") these days or not? Pay no attention to the pedantic rodomontade purveyed by bankers and politicians; put your eyes on the real movement of the medium-sized dry goods of the world. If you aren't getting more real goods and services for your money units, someone is ripping you off. And maybe, just maybe, it's the guy running the money mill. Maybe, because he's standing there at the money tap, he's sloshing out a little extra to his friends in big government and big business—because, let's be real, what's not owned by Black Rock, State Street, and Vanguard these days?—while he gives you a pitiful "stimulus" or "benefit" check, you poor peasant you. Maybe, just maybe, it was a bad idea to create a mechanism whereby bankers can produce as much make-believe "money" as they want, not limited by the need to ground its issuance on something of real value, like silver and gold, as the Framers had planned. Maybe the People—through their Treasury Department—should issue their own currency, as Lincoln did, and not let that be done by a private entity owned by European interests which remains unaccountable, unaudited, and unknown. Maybe, allowing nameless foreign bankers to inflate our currency a million times over was not such a good idea. Maybe it is time for the People to take their money back. (For more quotes and reflections of these money matters, see Appendix 3)

President Jefferson Fights Back
"Money is gold, nothing else."
— Banker J.P. Morgan testifying to Congress (1912) —

Aside from direct, foreign invasion of our shores, the false promises and fincialized theft arising from fiat currency represent perhaps the greatest threats to this Republic. Having experienced the ugly outcome of inflationary fiat scrip during the war years, Thomas Jefferson fought against the institution of a central bank, and, as president, worked assiduously to make possible its closure by reducing the federal debt. In a 1799 letter, he wrote: *"I am for a government rigorously frugal and simple, applying all the possible saving of the public revenues to the discharge of the national debt and not for a multiplication of officers and salaries... [nor] for increasing, by every device, the public debt, on the principle of it's being a public blessing."*

When Jefferson and his Democratic-Republican party came roaring into office in 1801, he got the chance to practice such government frugality: he took on the national debt and the National Bank which Hamilton had championed and immediately set about rectifying the government's spendthrift ways. In his first message to Congress, he wrote, *"Sound principles will not justify our taxing the industry of our fellow citizens to accumulate treasure for wars to happen we know not when and which might not perhaps happen but from the temptations offered by that treasure."*

He cut spending, by fighting to keep the federal budget over his two terms below $10 million, even as low as $7 million. He cut the size of the bureaucracy to a total workforce of just 130 employees...for the entire federal government...for a nation of millions! The foreign embassies were likewise reduced to only three essentials, viz. Britain, France, and Spain. He cut the size of the standing army to 3,000 soldiers and 172 officers. The navy was reduced to six frigates, even while he dispatched that navy and its marines to defeat the Barbary pirate enclaves at the famous shores of Tripoli, thereby ending their maritime "white slave" trade.

With the debt paid down and budget restrained, Jefferson was then able to reduce taxes on the citizens, including the very unpopular whiskey tax. As he would explain later in a letter to Lafayette (1823): *"A rigid economy of the public contributions and absolute interdiction of all useless expenses will go far towards keeping the government honest and unoppressive."*

What was the result of cutting the size of government and reducing taxes? By the third year, the federal revenue actually grew...because when a free people are unburdened by taxes and left to work and strive and innovate, they produce mightily and the economy booms. Freedom actually works! As Jefferson reduced federal spending, the resultant soaring economy produced $17 million in federal revenue. Jefferson used that surplus revenue to pay down the national debt; from $83 million in 1801, he would pare it back to $57 million by 1809. By the time he left office, Jefferson had put the country on the pathway to solvency and shedding itself of the bondage of central banking. In 1811, the Congress, led by the Democratic-Republicans, would follow through on the opportunity Jefferson had created to cut the ties with Hamilton's Bank, by voting to terminate its charter and close it down.

Over his tenure, Jefferson—by trimming the federal budget and bureaucracy—would reduce the national debt by $26 million...even while also spending an additional $13 million for the Louisiana Purchase, which added New Orleans, the entire Mississippi Valley, and immense swaths of western land for a whopping 3¢ an acre...simply the greatest real estate deal in the history of history. Broadly put, during his presidency, Jefferson opened the frontier, cleared the sea of pirates, and cut the nation's debt by a third while doubling its size.

Simply badass.

With the Bank laid out flat and the economy booming, Round One of the Bankers War went to Jefferson and the Republic.

Yet, winning one battle is not winning the war.

It is rumored by some that it was Congress' 1811 disavowal of national banks and debt slavery which would lead European banking interests to coerce the British Parliament into open hostility with the United States a year later in the War of 1812. Perhaps suggestive of the covert machinations underlying that war was the assassination in May of British Prime Minister Spencer Perceval, a devout Christian and opponent of bellicosity. A mere month after Perceval's murder, despite some attempts at conciliation, war had been declared. Regardless of whether the War of 1812 was itself an engineered counterattack by the moneyed interests, the Bankers War against the Republic was far from over.

"Those who lend money without charging interest, and who cannot be bribed to lie about the innocent, such people will stand firm forever."

— Psalm 15:5 —

The Ten-Minute Constitution
a.k.a.
The One-Page Constitution

*"I want a government small enough
to fit inside the Constitution."*
— Harry Browne —

The "Ten Minute Constitution" gives every citizen a quick and easy understanding of our most important public document. This version does two things: first, it keeps only those sections related to grants of action given to government and the rights guaranteed and retained by the people (omitting procedural details). Second, it seeks to make these passages maximally understandable by rendering them in a contemporary idiom. While keeping as close as possible to the clean, concise language of the original, this version reworks and updates some words for modern readers. The hope is the result shines with some of the Framers' reflected brilliance.

A couple notes:

On spelling: since the original document capitalized such substantive nouns as "Senate" and "State", we have kept the practice for "State" and likewise capitalized "Citizen" to underscore the position of authority retained within this charter by the states and citizens of this union, respectively.

On copyright and format: permission and encouragement is given to freely distribute this "One Page Constitution" in any form which will best help people understand their rights and freedoms, provided it be free of charge and with attribution. A "One-Page" version of this Constitution (formatted to print on one double-sided page) is also available free of charge on our website.

The Constitution of the United States of America

WE, THE PEOPLE of the United States of America, in order to form a more perfect union, establish justice, insure domestic tranquility, provide for the common defense, promote the general good, and secure God's blessings of freedom to ourselves and our posterity, do ordain and establish this Constitution for the United States of America.

Article I
(Powers of Congress & the States)

Section 1. All national law-making powers are granted solely to a Congress of the United States, which shall consist of a Senate and House of Representatives.

Section 2. The number of Representatives and amount of direct taxes shall be divided among the States according to their population.

Section 7. All laws for raising money shall come only from the House of Representatives;

Section 8. In order to pay the debts, support the armed forces, and provide for the universal good of the United States, Congress shall have the following delegated powers:

• to impose taxes by duty, tariff, and excise; all such indirect taxes shall be uniform throughout the United States.

• to borrow money on the credit of the United States

• to regulate trade with foreign nations, among the States, and with the Indian tribes

• to establish a uniform process for naturalization as a Citizen

• to provide uniform bankruptcy laws throughout the United States

• to mint coins for money, regulating the value of these and foreign coins, and fixing a standard for weights and measures

• to provide for punishment for counterfeiting United States coins and securities

• to establish post offices and post roads

• to promote arts and science by establishing patent and copyright laws, providing exclusive rights for limited times to authors' writings and inventors' discoveries

• to constitute courts inferior to the Supreme Court

• to define and punish piracy, felonies at sea, and offenses against international law

• to declare war

• to grant Letters of Marque and Reprisal, establishing rules concerning captures on land and sea

• to raise and fund armies, provided no such appropriation be for more than two years

• to provide and maintain a navy

• to provide rules and regulations for the army and navy

• to call up the citizen militia to execute the laws, suppress rebellion, and repel invasion

• to provide for organizing, arming, and regulating such parts of the citizen militia when actually in the service of the United States; but the States shall appoint their own officers and train their own militias according to the discipline prescribed by Congress

• to exercise exclusive legislative power over whatever district (not exceeding ten square miles) is appointed the seat of government for the United States; and to exercise like authority over all places purchased by consent of any State legislature for forts, dock yards, etc.

- to make all laws which shall be necessary and proper for executing the foregoing powers

Section 9. The writ of habeas corpus cannot be suspended, unless public safety requires it during actual rebellion or invasion.

No laws may be passed which are retroactive or single out a person or group for punishment without a trial.

No direct tax can be laid, unless it is divided among the States according to their population (as determined by census or enumeration)

No tax or duty can be laid on exports from any State, nor can there be customs or tariffs between States, nor shall any State's trade be given preferential treatment.

No money may be drawn from the Treasury unless appropriated by law

Section 10. No State is allowed to engage in any of the following actions:

- enter into foreign treaty or alliance

- grant Letters of Marque and Reprisal

- coin money

- print paper money

- use anything but gold and silver coin as payment

- pass any laws which are retroactive, single out a person or group for punishment without a trial, or limit the obligation of contracts

- grant any titles of nobility

Article II

(Powers Granted the Executive)

Section 1. The power to administer the law shall be placed in a President of the United States of America.

Section 2. The President shall be commander in chief of the army and navy, and of the State militias during actual service to the United States; he shall have power to grant reprieves and pardons for offenses against the United States.

First getting the advice and consent of the Senate, he shall have power to make treaties and to appoint ambassadors, Supreme Court judges, and other officials of the United States.

Article III

(Powers Granted the Judiciary)

Section 1. The judicial power of the United States shall be vested in one Supreme Court, and in such lower courts as Congress provides.

Section 2. The judicial power of the United States extends to all cases of law and justice concerning the following:

• the Constitution

• federal law and public officials

• foreign treaties and ambassadors

• naval and maritime jurisdiction

• controversies involving the United States or between two of more States

• disputes between a State and Citizen of another State; between Citizens of different States; between Citizens of the same State with claims arising from different States; and between a State or Citizen(s) and a foreign entity.

The Supreme Court shall act as a court of appeals, both as the laws and fact. It shall have original jurisdiction, however, in all cases affecting ambassadors, public officials, and matters in which a State is a party.

Except impeachment, all criminal trials shall be by jury and in the State where the crime is purported.

Section 3. Treason against these United States shall only be defined as waging war against them or giving aid and comfort to their enemies. No one shall be convicted of treason except by confession in open court or the testimony of two witnesses to the same, overt act.

Article IV
(Duties and Privileges of the States)

Section 1. Each State shall honor and accept every other State's laws, records, and court decisions.

Section 2. The Citizens of each State shall have the rights, privileges, and protections guaranteed to the Citizens of the United States.

A person charged with a crime who flees to another States, shall be delivered to the State having jurisdiction of the crime upon demand of that State government.

Section 3. The Congress shall have power to enact rules and regulations for any territory or property within a State which belongs to the whole United States.

Section 4. The United States shall guarantee to every State in this union a republican form of government, and shall protect each from invasion or rebellion.

Article V
(Amending the Constitution)

The Congress may propose Amendments to this Constitution by either a two thirds vote of both Houses or by calling a convention for proposing Amendments if two thirds of the State legislatures have applied for it. Such Amendments shall only become valid when ratified by three fourths of the States' legislatures or conventions.

Article VI
(Constitutional Supremacy & Loyalty)

This Constitution, the laws enacted pursuant to it, and treaties made under its authority, shall be the supreme law of the land.

All senators, representatives, legislators, executive officials and judicial officers—both Federal and State—shall swear by oath (or affirm) to support this Constitution. No religious test shall ever by required to qualify for any United States office.

The Bill of Rights
(its first ten Amendments)

Article I Congress shall make no law establishing a national religion, or preventing free religious exercise; or limiting freedom of speech, or of the press; or of the right of the people to peacefully assemble, or to request the government to correct injustice.

Article II Since a well-equipped militia is necessary for the safety of a free nation, the right of the people to own and carry weapons shall not be limited.

Article III No soldier shall, in time of peace, be quartered in any house without the consent of the owner; nor in time of war, except in a manner to be prescribed by law.

Article IV The right of the people to be safe in their bodies, homes, files, and belongings, against unreasonable searches and seizures, shall not be violated; and no warrants shall be issued, unless having both probable cause and support by oath (or affirmation); and all warrants must describe the particular place to be searched and the persons or things to be seized.

Article V No person shall be held to answer for a capital or other major crime, unless requested or indicted by a grand jury (except in cases arising in the army, navy, or militia during actual service in time of war or public danger); nor shall any person be tried for the same offense twice; nor forced in any criminal case to be a witness against himself; nor lose life, liberty, or property, without due process of law; nor shall private property be taken for public use, without fair payment.

Article VI In all criminal prosecutions, the accused shall enjoy the right to be tried quickly and publicly, by an impartial jury in the State and district where the crime was committed (such district having been previously determined by law); to be informed of the nature and cause of the accusation; to be confronted with the witnesses against him; to have compulsory process for obtaining witnesses in his favor, and to have legal assistance for his defense.

Article VII Trial by jury shall also be preserved in common law suits, where the value exceeds twenty dollars; and any fact tried by a jury shall be re-examined by a court of the United States under the rules of the common law.

Article VIII Excessive bail shall not be required, nor excessive fines imposed, nor cruel and unusual punishments inflicted.

Article IX The Constitution's listing and enumeration of some rights, does not deny or belittle all the other rights retained by the people.

Article X All powers are retained by the people and the States, except for those powers specifically delegated to the United States and prohibited to the States by this Constitution.

(other Amendments affecting rights)

Article XIII There shall be no slavery or involuntary servitude within the United States, except as a punishment for crime.

Article XIV Every person born or naturalized in the United States is a Citizen of the United States and of the State where they reside. No State shall make or enforce any law which limits the rights or privileges of Citizens of the United States; nor shall any State deprive any person of life, liberty, or property, without due process of law; nor deny to any person the equal protection of the laws.

Article XV No United States Citizen's right to vote shall be denied on account of race, color, or previous condition of servitude.

Article XVI The Congress shall have power to tax income derived from sources, but not by apportionment among the States according to census or enumeration.

Article XIX No United States Citizen's right to vote shall be denied on account of sex.

Article XXVI No United States Citizen's right to vote shall be denied on account of age once eighteen years old.

PART II
SELF-RELIANT

Chapter 3

Built like a Brickhouse Badass: National Independence & Self-Reliance

The Pilgrims knew that, to live a life in freedom, one must earn it through self-reliance. As soon as they landed in Plymouth, they set to work, building out their settlement. From the Mayflower Chronicles, pp. 173 - 179:

"Tuesday, the 9th of January, was a reasonable fair day; and we went to labor that day in the building of our town, in two rows of houses, for more safety. We divided by lot the plot of ground whereon to build our town...We agreed that every man should build his own house, thinking by that course men would make more haste than working in common. The common house, in which for the first we made our rendezvous, being near finished, wanted only covering, it being about twenty foot square. Some should make mortar, and some gather thatch; so that in four days half it was thatched. Frost and foul weather hindered us much. This time of the year seldom could we work half the week...

Friday the 12th we went to work; but about noon it began to rain, that it force us to give over work...

Tuesday, Wednesday, Thursday, were very fair, sunshiny days, as if it had been in April; and our people, so many as were in health, wrought cheerfully...

Saturday, 20th, we made up our shed for our common goods.

Sunday, the 21st, we kept our meeting on land.

Monday, the 22d, was a fair day. We wrought on our houses; and in the afternoon carried up our hogs-heads of meal to our common storehouse. The rest of the week we followed our business likewise."

Self-Reliant

WITH THE DAWNING OF THE 19th century, the work of nation-building began. Moving from the dreams of revolutionaries, America entered the gritty but rewarding work of turning the ideal of freedom into the reality of a nation. No longer the time of Founders and Framers, this epoch would be the age of the Builders and Inventors.

Now must the young nation learn self-reliance. Now must its citizens learn to stand on their own two feet, or fail forever. Much as the Pilgrims prized independence—and were unashamed to dig and delve in the dirt to carve out their homestead—the American Badass honors *self-reliance*, bootstrapping your way up, willingly shouldering life's necessary burdens which turn wistful dreams into sparkling reality. For, without the wherewithal to earn your freedom, to produce the physical means of supporting, defending, and improving yourself, there can be no independence. To be really and actually free, you must be self-reliant.

The president who would help shape America's youthful energy and vigor towards its full strength and sovereignty was James Madison. His scholarly efforts, endless industry, pragmatic calculus, and expansionist vision would help America achieve a self-conscious persona of liberty everywhere.

JAMES MADISON

"All men having power ought to be mistrusted."

— James Madison —

James Madison shares the distinction of being one of only two men who served the early Republic in all three pivotal roles as Founder, Framer, and President. The first was Washington, that most preeminent hero of the Revolution, chairman of the Constitutional Convention, and then that inaugural figurehead of leadership, our first President. Yet, so beloved was Madison at his retirement from public life, that—in honor of his service—he has had more American counties, towns, and memorials named after him than Washington. For, while Washington won the Revolution, Madison both shaped our national Constitution and then helmed the nation through its first war. He stepped into the Presidency in the early 19th century, precisely when our young country began the serious work of building out its nascent dreams of freedom into a concrete, dynamic reality. There seemed no one better suited to lead the federal government at the dawning of a golden age of American constitutional governance, than this small, tireless man generally accredited as the "father of the Constitution," who was one of those rare souls able to be at once dreamer and doer, man of both vision and action.

As Founder and young politician, he scoured the ancient histories and European writers seeking an answer to the "sighs of humanity" (*Federalist* 10) sent up by all of history's downtrodden peasants seeking a just form of governance. Believing he had found the formula in a democratic republic with just and clear limitation of powers granted, he continually agitated for such a republican confederation, first while serving in the Virginia House of Delegates and later the Continental Congress. He envisioned the vast American landscape as the ideal setting for enacting a government of such grand scope and noble purpose. Though the youngest member of Congress, he was often the finest in intellect and foremost is speaking and soon won many over to his way of thinking.

As Framer, Madison's tireless energies made him the prime

mover, and, indeed, the primary intellectual and practical "father" of the written Constitution. In intellectual terms, its republican design—with a tripartite division of powers via an elected executive, bicameral legislature, and judicial review—was simply a rewrite of the luminous constitution he had drafted in partnership with George Mason for the state of Virginia in 1776. In practical terms, Madison's efforts were essential: coaxing Washington to lend his august presence by presiding over the Constitutional Convention; arriving early to draw up the agenda; drafting the Virginia Plan which steered the convention's debates; recording its every speech for posterity in shorthand notes; speaking more than anyone else during those debates; and then, to ensure the Constitution's adoption, penning two of America's most important political documents—*The Federalist Papers* to motivate its public acceptance and the Bill of Rights to ensure its legislative passage.

As Builder, Madison was thus a man who knew what he was about when he stepped into the presidency to institute the Constitution's promise. Having personally laid out its foundations, he was well placed to build out its black-letter legal promise into the actuality of a nation, making real in wood and iron across a continent an American republic made sure and strong in the promise of liberty.

As much as he was the scholar and pedant of the revolutionary generation—once, hoping to change trade policy with Britain, he researched and wrote a 200-page treatise on trade law in a fortnight, distributing it to recalcitrant congressmen—he was also a decisive, pragmatic President. When France and Spain dithered on acknowledging American land rights in Florida, Madison simply ordered the army to march in and seize the territory—closely followed by eager homesteaders—which settled the matter once and for all.

Along with his wife Dolley, Madison made Washington, D.C. during its nascent years—then half construction site, half mud pit—a model of republican camaraderie. For decades, Dolley made herself the de facto doyen of national politics; she opened their home in receptions, called "squeezes", to anyone across the political spectrum, a place where one could drop in for easy conversation, fine food and—rather outré for the time—whiskey punch. A statuesque beauty in exotic satin turban topped with a feather, Dolley would deftly work the room, coddling the shyest guest, sitting down to a pinch of snuff or game of cards, or even grabbing the smaller Madison by the hands, hoisting him up behind her, and then capering along with the diminutive president clinging to her back. Their inviting charm and engaging partnership made them, and their houses at Washington and Montpelier, the center of political society.

Madison—and Dolley—would also shepherd the young nation through its rematch against Britain in the War of 1812. Before the Revolution, the British had enjoyed a finely-honed neo-mercantilist system whose genteel enslavement kept the colonies as agrarian, preindustrial sources of raw materials, mere fonts for the extraction of raw materials and labor—and they wanted their de facto slaves back. Since then, Britain's navy had continually "impressed" (i.e. kidnapped) sailors from American ships, despite continual Yankee protest and remonstrance. Madison, a spunky fellow with no back-down in him, at last went to Congress seeking a declaration of war. He recognized that although Americans had won their freedom—wresting this land from the cloying hand of the British aristocracy (and, by extension, the European banking kleptocracy which itself held Britain in thrall)—the infant nation would have to fight again...and then again if necessary...to keep it.

A bloody affray fought on a shoestring by both sides, the War of 1812 proved a close-run contest. The British were initially too deeply entangled with fighting Napoleon in Europe to bring their full might to bear, while the American forces were initially poorly trained and led. The low point came in 1814 when the British, having at last dispatched Napoleon, debauched 4,500 men—know as "Wellington's Invincibles" for their success in conquering the French emperor—at Chesapeake Bay in Maryland to march on America's half-built capital. They were met by a gaggle of hastily-gathered militia near the town of Bladensburg. In an ignominious defeat—wryly characterized by one newspaper as the "Bladensburg Races"—the American militia took one look at the daunting array of British imperial might and scampered away, disappearing deep into the woodlands. Despite the danger, being a mere half dozen miles away at the White House, President Madison—all 5′ 4″ of him—decided to personally ride to the front lines, had to be practically dragged away from the firing line, and would spend the next 60 hours almost continuously in the saddle overseeing the safe evacuation of the government before the inexorable British march to sack the capital.

No one who signed the Declaration of Independence ever backed away from a fight.

For her part, Dolley proved to be no mere socialite. With the British now moving from Bladensburg towards the White House, she acted quickly to protect national treasures. Despite being defenseless (her bodyguards having already fled), she tarried long enough to have Gilbert Stuart's iconic life-sized portrait of George Washington—an item the British would have dearly loved to desecrate—broken loose from the frame fixing it to the wall, carefully rolled up and carried to safety. She thereby preserved the painting for posterity, for it now once more proudly adorns those same White House walls.

Although the British troops would soon enjoy a night's plunder, burning government buildings and leaving behind a pall of smoke and destruction, Madison and company had managed to safeguard the government and would marshal the remaining American forces in the field. In the end, the US Navy soon pulled off a pair of brilliant victories which halted the British assaults in the west. These would be capped by Andrew Jackson's spectacular—albeit after-the-buzzer—triumph at the Battle of New Orleans in 1815. These victories left Madison and the Americans in possession of the field and turned the entire affair, ultimately, into a protracted draw, if not straight-out American triumph. The British Empire had twice tried to corral their wayward American serfs back into bondage, and twice had wound up scurrying back, bloodied and beaten, to their island.

Constitutional Coda

"The very definition of tyranny is when all powers are gathered under one place."
— James Madison, *The Federalist Papers*, No. 47 —

One of Madison's last acts as President showed his constitutional resolve, when he vetoed a bill which he not only wanted but had publicly supported. It was a federal program to build roads and canals which would have meant much for the young nation, but, when Congress precipitously enacted it, Madison balked. The lawmakers had simply voted to undertake the plan, completely ignoring the fundamental principle that the power to enact such a measure was not granted by Article I, Section 8 and was therefore not constitutional. Madison therefore, in effect, vetoed his own plan. He urged Congress to instead do the right thing and send a preliminary proposal to the states to first pass an amendment granting Congress the power to build such roads and canals. Rebuking the legislators, he explained that attempting an enactment outside constitutional bounds would, in effect, grant to Congress *"a general power of legislation"* far beyond their brief. Defender of constitutionality to the end, it would be a remarkable thing to see today's presidents, let alone representatives, halted by such clear, obvious, and necessary constitutional limits.

Even in his retirement, Madison would continue to oversee the health of the Republic he had helped found and shape. In an 1819 letter (to Spencer Roane, Sep. 2), he decried the latitude the Supreme Court had granted the Congress, by ruling a national bank is legal as a secondary power necessary in order to undertake such explicitly constitutional acts as levying and collecting taxes, funding a navy, etc. Madison noted that this decision created an area of legislative *"discretion...having for its general object the national welfare,"* for, in truth, *"everything is related immediately or remotely to very other thing; and consequently, a Power over any one thing...may amount to a Power over every other."* He noted, in short, that the precedent being set here would hand to Congress the broad latitude to pass whatever legislation it wanted, in effect, licensing a wanton legislative grant of power whose consequences we still face today.

Like the best of his revolutionary brethren, Madison's time in office had been an act of duty, of sacrifice for his people and nation. For him, the presidency was a means to public service, not personal advancement, and therefore—like Washington and Jefferson—he actually came out poorer for the experience (unlike many later presidents, who used the office as a springboard to wealth), so much so, that, after his death, Dolley struggled for years with debts and poverty. In the eyes of his fellows, Madison's commitment to dutiful service made him ever mindful of what was due from him to everyone, while likewise cautious to never wound the feelings of anyone. Reflecting on Madison's legacy, no less a light than John Adams said of his colleague's presidency that Madison had, *"acquired more glory and established more union than all his three predecessors, Washington, Adams, and Jefferson, put together."* Madison had been intent on making real, as national poet laureate Robert Frost later framed it, *"a dream of a new land to fulfill with people in self-control. That is all through his thinking....To fulfill this land—a new land—with people in self-control."* Together, he and Dolley gave a badass example of the republican ideal of generous service to that land and its People: bringing forth its fundamental laws, shepherding it through its first war under those laws to face down the British Empire, and forever establishing these united American States as a nation of strength and independence by a self-disciplined People.

Frontier of Freedom

"The establishment of civil and religious liberty was the motive which induced me to the field—The object is obtained—And it now remains my earnest wish and prayer, that the citizens of the United States could make a wise and virtuous use of the blessing placed before them."

— George Washington —

Despite the struggles of war and challenges of cultivating a raw frontier, the continuous constitutional stewardship of three consecutive Democratic-Republican presidents (Jefferson, Madison, Monroe) enabled the country to flourish. The 1800s may, indeed, be accredited as the time of the purest instantiation of the constitutional Republic, demonstrating the sagacity of its provisions in the nation's massive geographic, industrial, economic, and demographic growth. Not yet fifty years old, the nation had already demonstrated a burgeoning military might which shrugged off the British Empire in the War of 1812. Likewise, it flourished economically.

Much economic wisdom born of hard, practical experience was baked into the final formulation of the Constitution, and Jefferson once remarked how amazed he was at how quickly commerce grew: within only a few years of the new Constitution's instantiation, the economy boomed. For the other genius inherent in the document is there are no handouts from the government; there is no attempt to shape private action through public policy. It does not try to tip the scales for anyone's particular hobbyhorse. The main work of the central government is to protect the borders and shoreline (hence a permanent navy) and help settle disputes (hence a court system). Beyond that, the People—with the world at their feet and no limits to their choices—are free to work out, on their own, how best to live. Thus, in the early Republic, there were few taxes, and those were imposed as excise, which meant, as long as one did not engage in that particular taxable activity (e.g. import or export goods overseas, buy or sell whiskey), a citizen could live and work tax-free. For most of the century, the states were obliged to use sound money—gold or silver—and thus would avoid sinking into extremes of debt by emitting paper scrip. With an open field of endeavor, unhindered by arbitrary taxation from far-off bureaucrats, and a sound currency, the People could fully employ their ingenuity and industry in any art, science, or business. They could—and, indeed, had to—explore and invent in order to survive and thrive.

And thrive they did. The cities grew. The waterways and roads bustled. One could easily move out to the land, lay out a farm, raise family and livestock, and live out one's life without ever having seen, thought, or sent a penny to the federal government. As documented in the next chapter, the individual citizen could thereby flourish, expanding across the continent, with little thought of government...as well it should be.

Two great political questions, however, would plague the new Republic. One was the rather slow-burning somewhat esoteric controversy of central banking. But the most morally exigent, public, and ultimately explosive was slavery.

Freeing Ourselves from Slavery

"[I]t being among my first wishes to see some plan adopted, by the legislature by which slavery in this country may be abolished by slow, sure, and imperceptible degrees."
— George Washington —

Slavery—for the Christian sensibility—remained an obvious contradiction at the heart of a republic of freedom. Many of the Founders attempted to address this ugliness during (or even before) the Revolution. A running political fight in the early 1800s, it was only decided by arms when the People—as was inevitable— finally faced this great unaddressed stain upon the Constitution, and eradicated that blemish on the country's claims to love freedom above all.

Early on, that same Christian sentiment which motivated the Quakers and Wilberforce to fight for the abolition of slavery in Britain, stirred in the Colonies. The First and Second Great Awakenings in America would not only create a groundswell of religious revival, but also generate an evangelical spirit of universal fellowship and amity which would elicit advocacy for a post-racist equality through the Christian faith. That Christian faith impels reform and repentance not just of self, but also outwardly within society at large. But, such reforms typically arise not from the top down, but from the citizens up. Thus, as early as 1652, a Christian upwelling had persuaded the Rhode Island legislature to outlaw slavery (which, sadly, lapsed by 1700). Likewise, it was a collection of Quakers in Pennsylvania, who in 1688 promulgated the "Germantown Petition Against Slavery," which declaimed: *"There is a saying that we shall doe to all men licke as we will be done ourselves; macking no difference of what generation, descent or Colour they are. and those who steal or robb men, and those who buy or purchase them, are they not all alicke? Here is liberty of conscience wch. is right and reasonable; here ought to be likewise liberty of ye body, except of evildoers, wch is an other case. But to bring men hither, or to robb and sell them against their will, we stand against."*

In the south, Governor Oglethorpe founded Georgia in 1733 as a slave-free colony, modelling the ideal of liberation and emancipation which the northern states would make permanent less than a century later. Such early stirrings of Christian conscience would continually force this issue to the political table at the national level.

By the time of the revolutionary generation, many of the Founders and Framers would move and inveigh against the institution. Before the Revolution, Jefferson introduced a modest form of emancipative legislation in the Virginia assembly wherein slave owners would be allowed to voluntarily free their slaves; it did not pass. He wrote an early draft of the Declaration of Independence excoriating King George for the slave trade; Congress, at the behest of representatives from southern states, removed it. Similarly, George Washington's final will *commanded* that his slaves be emancipated upon his death; they, at least, were freed. But the long-standing practice—with its perverse economic incentives and social prejudices—was not to be eradicated in a moment by a few idealistic visionaries. As Franklin realized, the practice was so foul and deeply ingrained, that even its removal may, in the near term, prove immensely painful: *"Slavery is such an atrocious debasement of human nature, that its very extirpation, if not performed with solicitous care, may sometimes open a source of serious evils."*

In the *real politik* of the 1776 Congress, the only path to a unanimous break with England included accommodating the southern states—which would brook no emancipation of slaves. That meant leaving the sordid practice alone. Slavery was, in fact, the single hardest-fought issue of the Continental Congress, much as it would prove, later, to be the bone stuck in the craw of the Republic. The ugly compromise which allowed the adoption of the Constitution was agreeing not to touch the practice for 20 years; this was done. The Founders and Framers side-stepped the dark question in order to manifest AmRev 1.0. Only later, as the nation prospered and grew, was there more time—and, frankly greater moral necessity—to honestly address the issue: can we really call ourselves a free people, while enslaving others?

The Abolitionists recognized early the need to eradicate the practice, and such sentiment burgeoned throughout the late 18th and early 19th century. Many rode the spirit of the Revolution to push forward emancipatory legislation. In 1778, Jefferson was finally able to lead Virginia to become one of the first jurisdictions anywhere in the world to ban the importation of slaves. In 1780, Pennsylvania became the first state to outlaw the practice of slavery outright. In 1801, Jefferson sent the navy (and marines) to the famed shores Tripoli to rout the enslaving pirates. By 1804, every single northern state had outlawed slavery. The tide was turning. On January 1st, 1808—the very first day permitted after the 20 year hiatus written into the constitutional compromise—Congress permanently banned the importation of slaves to the United States of America.

An importation ban, however, only barred the growth of slavery; it still left many in bondage. Slavery therefore remained for the better part of another century, and its ugly resolution was only finally settled by war. The handwriting was on the wall, but it would take several decades and over a half million lives to alleviate the stain of slavery. When the final paroxysm came in the Civil War, the practice was so deeply entrenched—and of such social and economic import—amongst the Southern gentry that only America's bloodiest war could wrest if from their hands.

Similarly, the cultural vestiges and aftereffects redounded

for generations. A century later, a preacher from Alabama named Martin Luther King, Jr., would force us to repent and clean out the last vestiges of legislative discrimination. And, to the final credit of the nation, those battles were fought, the deep moral wound addressed, the work of emancipation was undertaken, and restorative legislation enacted.

In the struggle over resolving slavery, we see again the continual movement of badass from rough and tough to smooth and tender as needed to enact the moral outcome, from warrior to monk, from pirate to poet, and back again. The aspiration of the 17th century pacifist Quakers matched the libertarian goals of the militant revolutionary Minutemen; these, conjoined with the abolitionist demands for emancipation for the entire nation enforced by northern armies, to the street marches and protests of the 1960s were necessary to finally eradicate the last legal vestiges of institutionalized slavery. The struggle for freedom is neither single-step nor obvious, neither simple nor easy. The path is often varied, disjoint, wayward, and treacherous. For that reason, one must be prepared to move with gentleness and tact when possible, but suddenness and force when needful. The fully developed badass uses the means least confrontational but most optimal for the circumstances.

At the time of initial emancipation, the adolescent nation was finding its strength and axiological orientation; as one of the first nations to forgo slavery, it was demonstrating the value of—and its adherence to—a moral compass. Coming out of the paroxysms of civil war, the nation would discover not just its moral vision, but renewed strength in the economic freedoms and opportunities of the age of invention. With the completion of the transcontinental railroad in 1869, the rails would enable fast, free movement of people and goods from coast to coast. Where before, the crossing of the nation was a matter of extreme danger and hardship taking weeks—even months in a Conestoga wagon—now in, a matter of a few days, one could take a train from New York to San Francisco while sleeping comfortably and dining lavishly. The other central struggle of the century would be economic, and would revolve around the issue, once more, of a national bank.

The Bankers War, Round 2:
Jackson Ushers in an Age of Gold

"I wish it were possible to obtain a single amendment to our Constitution...I mean an additional article, taking from the federal government the power of borrowing."
— Thomas Jefferson —

In the 19th century, the lessons of the dangers of economic monopolies possible in a free economy were visited upon this nation in several ways, perhaps primarily through the ongoing Bankers War. Early on, when Hamilton's first national bank's charter lapsed, the European banking interest had sprung into action, launching a war of reclamation and retribution. The British military had been dispatched to the Americas to corral the wayward Yankees bank into the fold, for you may undertake almost any action as an independent nation, as long as you do not interfere with the international money monopoly's central bank grift.

To his eternal shame, although he won the war, Madison eventually succumbed to the blandishments of those who sought to reinstitute the central bank. Perhaps we must forgive him, for the nation was facing the exigencies of funding the War of 1812 and the dangers of central banking are not as obvious as piles of war debt and the tempting ease of monetary inflation.

Nonetheless, as Jefferson said, one of the core responsibilities of government is thrift and husbandry of the public purse...and the larger the class of government, the more essential it is to act with frugality in protection of the public good. Though he had by then retired from public life, Jefferson continued to remonstrate against central banks and fiat currency. In an 1813 letter he wrote, *"Bank-paper must be suppressed, and the circulating medium must be restored to the nation to whom it belongs."* (*Papers*, 6:494)

National banks, in the opinion of our third President, were not simply illegal but straight out dangerous. And, he therefore not only fought them politically but worked to end them practically.

Still, under the pressures of the debt from the second war against Britain and bankers' agents in Congress, in 1817 Jefferson's successor signed the bill instituting another central Bank of the United States with another twenty year charter. It typically has been the greatest of Presidents who fought with greatest urgency against the money interests. Still, although winning the war in the field, it was Madison who laid the groundwork for a great economic war with the moneyed elites. The fight would wait another twenty years—until that second national bank's charter neared its end—when Andrew Jackson's adamantine spirit would take up the task of fending off the banks for the sake of the People.

Old Hickory and Economic Liberty
"One man with courage makes a majority."
— Andrew Jackson —

There is a reason that Andrew Jackson's image was put on the 20 "dollar" Federal Reserve Note in 1928: he practically single-handedly ushered in a Golden Age of American prosperity by his heroic struggle with the banks. Celebrated conqueror of the vaunted British invaders at the Battle of New Orleans, renegade statesman, and roughhewn man of action—Jackson's bluff, no-nonsense style won him few friends in Congress and fewer in the press. But, as an unapologetic populist widely celebrated by the People, he had little regard for such niceties. He was a man on a mission to free the America's citizens from a malign force which few seemed to recognize, and fewer had the temerity to oppose.

A valiant solider, he had risen from the ranks in the endless fracas along the Frontier. By the time he marched his Tennessee volunteers down to New Orleans at the close of the War of 1812, he was a sharp-eyed major general with years of field experience. Once there, his sleepless leadership and exacting tactical dispositions in the weeks before the fight would allow an ill-trained, outnumbered, hodge-podge militia to overawe thousands of veteran British invaders, forever cementing his reputation in the public imagination. He took that same tireless energy and ferocity of purpose with him to Washington after winning the presidential election of 1828, and his prime mission was a determination to retire the central bank, believing it a creature of predatory and foreign moneyed interests at odds with the good of the American People.

Jackson Beats the Banksters

"I am one of those who does not believe the national debt is a national blessing...[I]t is calculated to raise around the administration a moneyed aristocracy dangerous to the liberties of the country."
— Andrew Jackson, Letter to L. H. Coleman (1824) —

When Jackson entered the White House in 1829, he pared back the federal behemoth by firing 2,000 of the government's 11,000 workers and began investigations of the second national Bank of the United States. He argued against a federal bank being owned by private, foreign stockholders, noting the absurdity of a *United States* bank being owned by *European* kleptocrats: *"More than $8,000,000 of the stock of the bank is held by foreigners who are more dangerous than the military power of an enemy."* He also began inquiries into reinstituting gold and silver money, rather than the national Banks' scrip...and, indeed, whether the people might not be better off in general issuing their own constitutionally-sound currency, rather than allowing a privately-held, for-profit Bank to control the issuance of currency.

His primary opponent in this fight would be Nicholas Biddle. President of the second Bank of the United States since 1822, Biddle was as brilliant he was arrogant in defending the interests of the Bank. Seconded by newspaper hirelings from coast to coast, Biddle immediately delivered a tocsin of broadsides against Jackson's impertinence at questioning the Bank's machinations. As the political contretemps grew, Biddle was called before the Senate finance committee, where—rather than taking a conciliatory, let alone remorseful, tone—Biddle brashly lashed out, bragging that his Bank of the United States could crush the many independent state banks which Jackson advocated. Thus began a long-running political fight between Jackson, defending state banks, and Biddle with his minions, championing the European moneyed interests and their central Bank.

By 1832, the political Banking War roiled towards its climax. A coterie of industry operatives came as emissaries to the President, pleading with him to accede to a renewal of the Bank's charter. After years of their attacks in public and private, their unending hectoring and importuning, Jackson at last exploded, pounding the desk and declaiming: *"Gentlemen, I too have been a close observer of the doings of the Bank of the United States! I have had men watching you for a long time, and am convinced that you have used the funds of the bank to speculate in the breadstuffs of the country. When you won, you divided the profits amongst you, and when you lost, you charged it to the bank. You tell me that if I take the deposits from the bank and annul its charter, I shall ruin ten thousand families. That may be true, gentlemen, but that is your sin! Should I let you go on, you will ruin fifty thousand families, and that would be my sin! You are a den of vipers and thieves. I have determined to rout you out, and by the Eternal, I will rout you out!"*

In the face of Jackson's intransigence, the bankster wing of Congress—especially senators Henry Clay and Daniel Webster—pushed through a bill to renew its charter. One week later, Jackson returned his veto of the bill with a carefully crafted explanation wherein he argued that the country should pursue the good of the majority, not the funding of the wealthy. He provided an extensive explanation of the rationale for his demur: that a national bank concentrated the nation's financial strength into a single institution; exposed the government to control by foreign interests which served mainly to make the rich richer; exercised too much control over Congress; favored the northeastern over the southern and western states; and placed the entire banking industry in control of a handful of families.

Jackson's detailed disavowal exposed the inordinate power vested in the Bank and stopped the charter—its renewal was dead—but he had also exposed himself to their ire. He was up for re-election that year, and the Bank threw its considerable support behind Jackson's opponent, who just happened to be that most public Bank mouthpiece, Senator Henry Clay. In a wholly illegal and unprecedented maneuver, Biddle poured an unheard of $3,000,000 into Clay's presidential campaign. Nonetheless, running under the slogan "Jackson and No Bank!" Old Hickory roused the Jeffersonian spirit of the country; the American People rallied 'round, saw through Biddle's smoke and agitprop, and elected Jackson over Clay, with the Jackson-Van Buren ticket demolishing Clay 239 to 49 in the electoral count for a resounding landslide victory.

Entering office for his second term, Jackson—first dutifully verifying through whistleblower testimony by its own officers that the Bank had used public money in its own self-interest as a means of attempting to control the election—undertook to stop feeding the Bank, which he called "that hydra of corruption": he ordered his cabinet to cease depositing federal funds with the Bank; instead the federal government was to begin employing a combination of 89 state banks for federal procurement and disbursement. To his astonishment, the Secretary of Treasury refused to enact his presidential Executive Order to that effect. Jackson therefore fired him and appointed a successor. Yet, so deeply entrenched was the money interest in the bureaucracy, that the fellow appointed as replacement Secretary by Jackson also refused to comply. So Jackson fired him too. Finally, Jackson appointed a third man, and he finally had the guts to follow through. At last, the government stopped funding its enemy by ceasing to move funds through the Bank.

Undaunted, Biddle responded by political and economic warfare against Jackson and the People. And he was brutally frank in explicating the ruthlessness of his methods, saying: *"Nothing but widespread suffering will produce any effect on Congress...Our only safety is in pursuing a steady course of firm restriction, and I have no doubt such a course will ultimately lead to restoration of the currency and the recharter of the Bank."*

Biddle's Bank therefore contracted credit and called in loans, which did indeed cause a credit crisis, economic slowdown, and financial hardship. At the same time, the Bank's irrepressible claque in the Senate—Clay, Webster, and John C. Calhoun—led that body to vote for a symbolic censure of Jackson for removing the money from the Bank. But—as that act was not passed over to the Jackson-friendly House for scrutiny as a formal impeachment, nor had given the President an opportunity to speak in defense of his actions—it was essentially an unconstitutional political temper tantrum.

At the same time, America's economy and citizenry proved too resilient to be much incommoded by Biddle's financialized machinations. Contemporary reports by the Treasury Department show that—with the exception of those entities directly undermined by the Bank's action—the nation as a whole prospered. The economy quickly recovered, and the People properly placed the blame for the whole affair at the Bank's feet.

For his part, President Jackson doggedly continued withholding any deposits from the Federal Government to the second Bank of the United States. In fact, by early January 1835, Jackson's actions and frugality with the budget had so blessed the public coffers that he paid the national debt down to essentially zero. For the first and only time in our nation's history, America would not carry the burden of a national debt. Flourishing economically, growing by leaps and bounds in the West, and at peace with the world, Jackson's vision of a populist government of and for the People was proving its worth.

As he neared the end of his second term and seemed to have finally overcome the banksters, Jackson would soon receive the same dark recompense delivered to so many other populist advocates of the people's money: Lincoln, McKinley, McFadden, Huey Long, John and Robert Kennedy. For it is a dangerous thing to stand between powerful people and their pot of gold. Potential opponents to moneyed interests typically face bribery, intimidation, public vilification, and assassination, in that order. On January 30, 1835, a would-be assassin by the name of Richard Lawrence tried to shoot President Jackson outside the Capital but failed when both his pistols misfired (and was subsequently tackled by a strapping frontiersman-turned-Representative from Tennessee named Davy Crockett). One can draw their own conclusions on the matter, but Jackson's account of the event to his vice president, Van Buren, was characteristically frank and laconic: *"The bank, Mr. Van Buren, is trying to kill me."*

At the end of his two terms, Jackson had balanced the federal budget through a combination of frugality, tariff revenues, and the sale of public lands. At the same time, he was, like Jefferson, able to underwrite large federal expenditures, like internal improvements on roads and canals. Again, lowering tax rates paradoxically produces more federal tax revenue because constitutional restraint on taxation allows the economy to grow larger, and this larger economy produces more tax revenue even with such lower rates; in effect, the government gets a skinnier slice but of a much larger pie, in the end getting more sweets for its pie hole. The original constitutional plan ordained no direct taxation of the populace internally; as a result, the marketplace within the borders of these united American states became the world's most dynamic free market. In their daily lives, the People were free to trade and work internally, with no government interference. Taxation—as provided by the Framers—derived from some excise taxes, but primarily from import and export duties from those who wished to participate in the economic dynamo which was Jackson's America. In other words, foreign producers could import (or citizens export) for a slight fee to create transnational participation in the nation's fruitful economy, but, otherwise, internally, the People were given a boundless, unfettered economic opportunity. As a result, business burgeons and the economy expands. Jackson's stewardship thereby produced a land where the government was debt-free, the Bank defunded, the economy booming, the borders secure, and the People prospering. In sum, his administration had proven that freedom works, both politically and economically.

Determined to follow the established two-term precedent of Washington and Jefferson, a triumphant Jackson retired in 1837 to his homestead, the Hermitage. When asked what his greatest accomplishment had been, he replied, *"I killed the Bank."* And Jackson kept on winning, even in retirement. When the new Senate was sworn in, Thomas Hart Benton led his colleagues to permanently expunge from the Senate journal by formal vote Clay's perfidious, foundationless censure of Jackson for his actions against the Bank. Soon after, Jackson's vice president, Van Buren, would win the next presidential election and would, in his turn, complete the work of giving the second National Bank its quietus; by July, its coffers were completely emptied of all federal deposits and—its charter having failed renewal and its business now completed—within a year it would be forever closed. The election of Van Buren—and the later electrion of President Polk, hailed as "Young Hickory" for being Jackson's protégé—are testaments to the lasting admiration for Jackson's populist programs which wrested the control of finance from the banks and put hard money and real power back in the People's hands.

Cycles, Economic Autophagy, and Success
"One of the greatest delusions...is the hope that the evils in this world are to be cured by legislation."
— Thomas B. Reed (1886) —

Economies—the full, free, multitudinous money exchange by millions of people—are immensely complex. Their rise and fall, growth and decline, their moments of strength and periods of weakness—all these arise from the myriad microdecisions of innumerable participants. A free market is a maximally productive market, and a free people will create an economy which runs hot and hard. But success also brings its own challenges. Thus, an efficient economy can overshoot, overproduce, as it tempts overly hopeful but unprepared entrepreneurs to open businesses which are destined for ruin.

In the post-Jacksonian economy, the citizens experimented with free silver, state banks, an entire "wild west" of economic activity. There would be many examples of financial overextension leading to personal ruin, such as the oversold, undercapitalized banking scrip issued by the "wildcat" banks. Likewise, there would be overbuilding of rail lines during the railroad boom of the1870s. Such times of unrestrained exuberance, however, bring their own correction, as the foolish and feckless fail in ill-conceived attempts at easy riches. Thus, markets heat up and gull the incompetent into the ill-conceived, leading to the inconvenient.

But here is the question: in the long run, are these slowdowns and their results truly harmful? Failure is the price of success, for you must often first test all the things that don't work to winnow out those that do. Furthermore, closer inspection of many of these "downturns" will show that they are often localized (to particular industries or regions) and therefore of interest only to a few, not the many. And what the economists and financiers are primarily decrying is not the change of economic pace, but price deflation.

So, let us consider price deflation. How are you hurt by price deflation? Do you want to pay more for a loaf of bread and gallon of milk...or less? If producers are increasingly competing for your (real, silver) dollar so effectively that they give you more food for less money...is that okay with you? When it is time to spend some money from your savings account, do you want it to buy more or less? Doesn't price deflation actually help your bottom line?

Hence, the way in which such shifts in economic activity are characterized by the financiers as some kind of "emergency" seems questionable, arbitrary, if not downright tendentious and self-serving. Why is a normal process of balancing out overbuilding by a time of slowdown so terrifying? Why would we seek to normalize continual price *inflation*, rather than the more enriching action of price *deflation*? Sure, the banks get to spend extra money when they issue bags of inflationary "dollars," but does that make inflation itself better for the public? Is it not more "normal" for prices to both rise and fall and to, in fact, do so continually, and to varying degrees, depending on the myriad conditions extant and emergent around the world? The more insane outlook is to expect perpetual, flat-lined price stability or, likewise, to attempt to create a continual arbitrary 2 % inflation rate, year after year. This 2% target seems to be the Federal Reserve's presumptive "sweet spot," perhaps because that is where they can continually debase the value of the fiat currency without riling the ire of the populace it is fleecing. As its Chairman Jerome Powell testified before Congress (June 21, 2023), the Fed seeks that place where *"inflation is low enough that people don't think about it."* In other words, they see their mission as keeping you asleep while they produce a steady, subliminal inflationary destruction of your money, which they perversely call "price stability." In reality, however, wouldn't an increasingly efficient, competitive economy drive the cost of everything *down*? For, in such a marketplace, there would be more and more companies, competing with larger scale industrial factories, using more advanced and efficient processes seeking to produce more with less, and then pass along those efficiencies by competing with lower prices in order to win more consumers. Deflation, then, would seem to be the natural price tendency of a truly free advanced economy. And a beneficent price deflation was indeed often the case for the real (silver) American dollar during the 1800s. If was more common for your great-great-great-grandparents to buy more and more year after year with their (real) dollar than not.

Likewise, at the same time, a vibrant economy will challenge both individual companies and whole industries to upgrade, transform, and, if necessary, even quit. Poorly funded or mismanaged businesses will simply close, as well they should. In turn, rival startups with better ideas and teamwork will rise, grow into a comfortable complacency, and perhaps eventually falter of their own success in their turn. Entire industries—whale oil, corset-makers, telegraphy offices, Pony Express mail riders—will disappear as better options arise. A free economy engenders innovation, encourages development, and thus necessitates change and transition.

The willingness and ability to adopt and adapt are part of a free market. So too are the continual ups and downs of its varied participants and industries. They will come and go, decline or grow, with the vagaries of markets, technology, customers, and history. This means that attempting to characterize the market action of tens of millions of participants via a single total number—some meaningless cumulative "GDP" or stock index enumeration—is to fail to understand the nature of this forest, whose many trees come and go but itself thrives because of it. What is most needful is to preserve the *freedom* of the market, not some combinatory, manipulated number.

The primary selling point proffered by national banks has been that they will somehow "manage" the economy as a single entity through a kind of financial wizardry; they purport to make a kind of science of emitting "just enough" inflation via currency manipulation to keep economic activity continually running smoothly. Yet, a close comparison of the 1800s (largely operating without central banks thanks to Jefferson and Jackson) with the 1900s (largely helmed by the Federal Reserve thanks to Wilson, FDR and an unending string of ensuing sycophants), shows strong parallels. In both the 19th century—with free silver and "wildcat" banking—and the 20th century—with its single, centralized Fed—shows that during both periods, broadly speaking, approximately half the time the economy was growing, and half the time shrinking. In both cases, recessions occurred about half the time, while rallies occur during the other half. In other words, the economy is trending up approximately half the time, and down approximately half the time. Now, if one were to step back and calmly reflect on the matter, isn't that what you would expect? Like a healthy organism breathing in and breathing out, an economy will have times of growth in production, which nurtures both the weak and the strong, followed by times of slowing into parsimony, shaking off the weak while toughening the strong. At the end of such shakeouts, an economy will have grown overall and be ready to begin another growth cycle, though now from a base both larger and healthier for the next run. This is simply any natural developmental cycle. (At the same time, it is instructive to compare the strength of the currency, and one will note the relative stability (or even increasing value via deflation) of the (true, silver) dollar in the 1800s, compared to the diminishing value of the Fed's paper notes, which have lost well over 90% of their value within the last century which via the Fed's supposedly carefully-titrated inflationary drip. Which approach seems to be doing a better job of defending the value of the currency and thereby the People's wealth?)

In contrast with such organic unfolding economic processes, an interventionist central bank seeks to intrude itself. It will use its large slush fund of make-believe money notes to arbitrarily determine winners from losers. Some companies or industries will be considered "too big" or too "systemically important" to fail. These will be given "loan packages" or other forms of unearned payouts in order to maintain themselves, even when their own mismanagement and malinvestment has put them into virtual bankruptcy. In effect, money taken by government from healthy businesses directly via taxation (or indirectly via phony-paper bond issuance) is given to unhealthy businesses. Stealing from productive businesses and giving it to failing enterprises, however, merely creates "zombie" corporations which will then simply continue to stumble along, sucking public monies out of the healthy economy and paying their people to continue acting stupidly. It is an obvious formula for eventual failure but it obtains, solely because of the coercive power of government to extract tribute in the form of taxes by the implicit threat of force and then hand the proceeds over to the central banks who dole it out to their buddies.

Perhaps we are better off *not* letting governments declare a "crisis"...and insinuate their fumbling, bumbling bureaucratic fingers into arenas they can neither understand nor control. After all, these are bureaucrats, many or most of whom—having gone straight from school to government—have never held a job demanding actual productivity in the real economy and who thereby have little sense of what is necessary for actual street-level effectiveness. For whatever degree of kind-heartedness they may personally possess, they likely have never had to understand wages, prices, output, payroll, resourcefulness, innovation, gumption, guts, or grit. They receive hefty checks which appear with magical regularity for the simple feat of showing up every day. Their degree of accountability to their "customers"—i.e. the ordinary taxpayer—is minimal; their pay and perks for a 40-hour week (often occasioned by simply answering a few phones calls or enduring a couple committee meetings) is extraordinary...especially by comparison to the boot-strapping entrepreneur's scant return for trying to keep herself afloat whilst juggling the challenges of deadlines, payroll, callbacks, quarterly tax filings, RFQs, and everyday customer complaints.

Rather than attempt Soviet-style rule-by-committee (for the word *soviet* simply means committee), here's how you fix an economy: leave it to the millions of practically-minded, hard-working, grounded individuals who daily grind it out on the actual playing field of doing the real work. Someone—or, most likely, a combination of many individual "someones"—will figure it out. In seeking solutions to a nationwide economic challenge, a committee of cloistered, coddled drones with little real-world experience have essentially no chance of out-thinking or out-planning the collective efforts of millions of innovative entrepreneurs.

When in doubt, try freedom first.

In economics, then, start with this prime directive: leave the economy alone. Like any other growing, organic, vibrant system, it must cycle. It will expand and contract; parts of it will be dynamic and growing, while parts or it will be moribund and dying...all at the same time. But, left alone, it will tend to right itself. The dynamic, vibrant parts will flourish and grow, while the moribund shrink and disappear, all on their own, without any external meddling needed. Interfered with—especially by those who have more power than sense, hubris than experience—the economy will tend to falter more than flourish, to stumble more than progress.

In forestry, we have discovered that we must allow the

detritus in our forests to burn for them to thrive. Likewise, the economy must clear out the zombie corporations and weak hands to maximize its strength. In the near term, it will be tough on those players who are shaken out, but it optimizes the health of the overall economy in the long run...and those who fail in today's venture will have the opportunity to step back, regroup, and come back stronger and better tomorrow. Allowing old, decrepit businesses to fail is analogous to the body's self-eating (*autophagy*) of its old senescent cells. Hence, slowdowns are, if you will, a kind of necessary *economic autophagy*. It is the nature of life's adventure to fail and fail and fail again until you get clear and strong on the means to your chosen goal...and the bigger and harder—the more "impossibler"—the goal, the more fail needed until you get there. But getting through the fail, and removing the deadwood, is essential to reach one's full vibrancy—in economics and in life.

In sum, economies are large, multivariant, organic engines...systems of inordinate size and complexity which move by the actions of innumerable individuals. If the individual agents are given the maximum latitude of action, they will naturally work, test, experiment, and churn their way to the best possible solution for their tiny corner of the economy...and so too will millions of others. As the amorphous but active outcome of millions of intelligent, intentional actors, an economy will tend towards self-correction. Large, ham-fisted intervention by a handful of elite manipulators in finance or government committees will only tend toward overcorrection, misdirection, misallocation, and retardation of the corrective process. The necessity of allowing for "economic autophagy," the death of unproductive zombie corporations, the final collapse of flailing companies, is a necessary part of the ongoing process of growth, maturation, and winnowing which produces true health in commerce and trade. To think and act otherwise is to imagine a handful of technocrats with fancy titles somehow have more wisdom in their handful of tiny heads than in the hundreds of millions of equally intelligent, successful, mature, and responsible adults actually running the myriad specialized trades in the real world.

For the proof, look at the economic strength of the country under presidents with a *laissez-faire*, small-government approach to federalism. Jefferson doubled the size of the country while reducing the war debt of the Revolution and slashing the size of the bureaucracy; Polk doubled the size of the country again, while actually reducing the federal budget; and, later, Coolidge would cut income taxes until only the top 2% of wage earners paid anything, thereby unleashing the "roaring" growth of the 20s. For the people to grow, the government must remain small, giving them the room to do so. A people left to rely on their own resources and trained to cultivate their personal virtues will find more strength than they know, more innovation than the central planners can ever imagine. Hence, economic "management" is far simpler than the bankers like to pretend.

To the technocrats: sit down, shut up, and let the professionals solve the problems in their field. You may go back to studying your pretty, little charts and graphs and let the pros solve the issues about which they, not you, have expertise.

To the People: keep on truckin'!

"And Jesus entered the temple of God and drove out all who sold and bought in the temple, and he overturned the tables of the money-changers and the seats of those who sold pigeons. He said to them, 'It is written, My house shall be called a house of prayer, but you make it a den of robbers.' "

— Matthew 21:12-13 —

Chapter 4

Badass Bootstrapping Your Better You: Citizen & Self-Reliance

As the settlers struggled to bring nourishment from the soil and make their stand in this new land, they encouraged each other. From the Mayflower Chronicles, pp. 263 - 265:

"Now, brethren, I pray you, remember yourselves, and know that you are not in a retired, monastical course, but have given your names and promises one to another, and covenanted here to cleave together in the service of God and the King. What then must your do? May you live as retired hermits, and look after nobody? Nay, you must seek still the wealth of one another, and inquire, as David, How liveth such a man? How is he clad? How is he fed? He is my brother, my associate; we ventured out lives together here, and had a hard brunt of it; and we are in league together. Is his labor harder than mine? Surely I will ease him. Hath he no bed to lie on? Why, I have two; I'll lend him one. Hath he no apparel? Why, I have two suits; I'll give him one of them. Eats he coarse fare, bread and water, and I have better? Why, surely we will part stakes. He is as good a man as I, and we are bound each to other; so that his wants must be my wants, his sorrows my sorrows, his sickness my sickness, and his welfare my welfare; for I am as he is. And such a sweet sympathy were excellent, comfortable, yea, heavenly, and is the only maker and conserver of churches and commonwealths; and where this is wanting, ruin comes on quickly.

"I wonderfully encourageth men in their duties, when they see the burthen equally borne; but when some withdraw themselves, and retirn to their own particular ease, pleasure, or profit, what heart can men have to go on in their business? When men are come together to lift some weighty piece of timber, or vessel, if one stand still and do not lift, shall not the rest be weakened and disheartened? Will not a few idle drones spoil the whole stock of laborious bees? So one idle belly, one murmurer, one complainer, one self-lover, will weaken and dishearten and dishearten a whole colony. Great matters have been brought to pass, where men have cheerfully, as with one heart, hand and shoulder, gone about it, both in wars, buildings and plantations; but where every man seeks himself, all cometh to nothing."

WHEN THE UNITED STATES FOUGHT off the second British assault on American independence in the War of 1812, it had firmly and finally established itself as an independent nation and rival of the European powers. It was now the largest ship-building nation on earth, had more than doubled its size with Jefferson's Louisiana Purchase and, through the Lewis and Clark expedition, had opened a road through the West clear to the Pacific Ocean which would soon generate even more explosive growth and expansion.

At the same time, this was the golden age of maximum constitutionality for the American Republic. With the exception of a couple tussles with the central bankers, there would be negligible taxation—indeed, there was little federal involvement inside the borders at all, besides rarities like scattered canal and road building. The citizens were largely left alone, to seek, to strive, to prosper and ponder as they will. What followed was the natural and expected result of such purposeful, far-reaching liberty: long stretches of exemplary growth, development, and innovation. The older cities burgeoned, newer settlements grew, and the country transitioned from its revolutionary agrarianism to an industrial might on par with any nation on the planet, and an innovative, technological dynamism unrivalled anywhere. From Jefferson's presidency until Teddy Roosevelt's gilded progressive interventionism, America maximized its constitutional freedoms, personal responsibility, and the autonomous, educated, moral citizenry of the free republic prospered. By every measure, leaving the people unhindered to personal liberty and self-reliance under the constitution's guarantee of 100% freedom proved its worth.

Again, the core genius of the American Constitution and cultural spirit is not any legal particularity such as the disposition of voting privileges, bicameral legislative processes, or even enumeration of guarantees to the citizenry; it is the central principle of *laissez faire*. The conclusion, therefore, for lawmakers now and forevermore:

Hey, politicos, just leave the folks alone!

And the historic icon who perhaps showed most clearly what a free citizen could do, starting from nothing and disciplining himself to pursuing excellence throughout one's life, was Benjamin Franklin.

BENJAMIN FRANKLIN
"Man will ultimately be ruled by God or by tyrants."
— Benjamin Franklin —

Benjamin Franklin may be the most complete model of American self-reliance, whereby a free republic allows one the pursuit of anything possible while demanding self-discipline, thereby eliciting the most and best from each individual citizen. Franklin's story is a exemplary rags-to-riches tale of a lad who, with just two years of formal schooling, rose to eminence in not just one but several fields, whilst donating of himself lavishly through philanthropy and public service in shaping a new nation. Founder of a successful printing business which he leveraged to prominence by both writing and printing his best-selling annual *Poor Richard's Almanack* series, world-renowned inventor and scientist, diplomat, Founder, and Framer, Benjamin Franklin perfectly exemplifies the self-reliant, self-made, self-starting ideal: an American who bootstraps himself from poverty to riches. Tireless, innovative, and productive across many fields, Franklin gloriously demonstrates the timeless worth of his signature maxim that "Early to bed and early to rise makes a man healthy, wealthy, and wise"...and, furthermore, thereby shows that once one achieves a basal subsistence level of self-reliance, one can pursue the full efflorescence of inventiveness and creativity with unconquerable purpose...as a person or a nation. Again, a libertarian republic will elicit from every citizen first initiative, closely followed by the core elements of self-reliance: determination, industry, and inventiveness. Because you cannot wait to feed yourself, but must go and do and make things happen, you will naturally continue forward to develop, build, and grow ever more magnificently in your life.

Here is how this happened for this inspiring exemplar:

Ben Franklin: Aspiring Moralist
"Wish not so much to live long as to live well."
—Benjamin Franklin —

Coming from Puritan roots, Franklin was reared with a wont to do the good, to instantiate a moral legacy. As a youth, he wrote an essay, "Bonifacius: Essays to Do Good," recapitulating these moral ideals. Having struck out on his own from the family home, he set himself on a path towards self improvement, so much so that his *Autobiography* details him systematically cultivating what he considered the 13 core virtues, cycling through the list on a weekly basis—focusing on improving one virtue at a time—in an attempt to thereby move to ever-improving perfection of his character. He thereby looked to make himself a better man by forcing himself to spend a full week, 4 times a year, scrutinizing how well he exhibited each of these essential qualities:

Temperance - Eat not to dullness; drink not to elevation.

Silence - Speak not but what may benefit others or yourself; avoid trifling conversation.

Order - Let all your things have their places; let each part of your business have its time.

Resolution - Resolve to perform what you ought; perform without fail what you resolve.

Frugality - Make no expense but to do good to others or yourself; i.e., waste nothing.

Industry - Lose no time; be always employed in something useful; cut off all unnecessary actions.

Sincerity - Use no hurtful deceit; think innocently and justly, and, if you speak, speak accordingly.

Justice - Wrong none by doing injuries, or omitting the benefits that are your duty.

Moderation - Avoid extremes; forbear resenting injuries so much as you think they deserve.

Cleanliness - Tolerate no uncleanliness in body, clothes, or habitation.

Tranquility - Be not disturbed at trifles, or at accidents common or unavoidable.

Chastity - Rarely use venery but for health or offspring, never to dullness, weakness, or the injury of your own or another's peace or reputation.

Humility - Imitate Jesus and Socrates.

By the practice of keeping a personal ledger, noting every time he "missed the mark" (which is the literally meaning of the Hebrew word *sin*), he curated his moral worth. As he built his *resolution, frugality, industry,* etc., his effectiveness grew, his business grew, and his ability to help others grew. When not printing others' material, he produced his own material in his *Poor Richard's Almanac*, an ongoing collection of homey sayings and aphorisms, from "A penny saved is a penny earned" to "A child and a fool imagine twenty shillings and twenty years can never be spent." Displaying immense energy and pragmatic agency, Franklin lived his life striving to become great by practicing being good. In this way, he became a model of both the Renaissance man who may be molded by a society of freedom, and the pragmatic, self-reliance Yankee, that American *imago* who weds thought with action, vision to backbone, i.e., a Jefferson, a Madison, a Franklin.

Ben Franklin: Philanthropist
"When you're good to others, you're best to yourself."
—Benjamin Franklin —

As much as one can make the case for the spiritual or ideological foundation of American Badass, there is the continual duality of its nature. Though the American Badass likes a good idea as much as the next person, that innate, uncompromising Yankee pragmatism wants to ask, "Great, but does it work in practice?"

The voluntarist Franklin demonstrates in resplendent fullness how doing things well can indeed reap practical rewards which allow one to turn about and bless others by creating numerous organizations and enterprises for the public good. From the time he landed in Philadelphia and opened his print shop, he was a whirlwind of practical community action. Looking for a way to improve his book club, he opened the first subscription library in1731. This was to be followed by initiating or helming numerous public works projects, many or most of which were firsts for the Colonies, including:

• Philadelphia Fire Department, the "Union Fire Company" bucket brigade, 1736

- University of Pennsylvania, 1751

- Pennsylvania Hospital, 1752

- Philadelphia Contributorship, first homeowners insurance company, 1752

- Postmaster General of the Colonies, 1753; of the American Confederation, 1775

Ben Franklin: Natural Philosopher
"Hide not your Talents, they for Use were made. What's a Sun-Dial in the shade!"

—Benjamin Franklin —

As Franklin prospered, he acquired the leisure to pursue his interests as a natural philosopher, scientist, and inventor. Even as a child, he was a clever inventor. An avid swimmer, he devised a set of oval flippers to attach to his hands and improve his speed through the water. Wanting to both read up close and see afar off, he invented bifocal glasses. His Franklin Stove used the fire's heat to create convection to better circulate and warm the room while minimizing smoke. Franklin purposefully never patented the design, believing it best to offer such designs to "freely and generously" serve others.

Although such inventions had pragmatic value, Franklin made a more lasting mark in the basic sciences. He founded the American Philosophical Society in 1743 to encourage systematic work on science and invention. He improved his time whilst sailing back and forth betwixt Britain and America by undertaking the study of hydrology, especially by charting the course of the Gulf Stream. But his most lasting contributions to the practical arts were in the investigation of electromagnetism. One of the earliest investigators in the fundamentals of electricity, he advanced the conception of its action as analogous to a fluid, an "electric fluid." He initiated the terminology of calling this "electric fluid's" two pathways of action "positive" and "negative." And of course, his famous kite flight would prove that lightning was a kind of "electric fire." In 1752 he launched this kite into a lightning storm hoping to ground a lightning strike—a hazardous undertaking best not tried at home! He did manage to draw "electric fire" down the string through an iron key, collecting it in a Leyden jar (a crude capacitor), thus proving the aerial phenomenon was indeed a kind of electrical discharge. On the basis of this understanding, he would develop the lightning rod to protect persons and property from sudden atmospheric discharges. He would also be received into the Royal Society and awarded its highest honor, the Copley Medal, in recognition of his contributions to the basic sciences.

Ben Franklin: Slow-Burn Patriot

"Where liberty dwells, there is my country."
—Benjamin Franklin —

And then, of course, there is the arena of politics. Franklin was *exemplum primum* of American proto-voluntarism. He would, in the autumn of his life, spend much time in public service at the highest political levels: governor of Pennsylvania, diplomat to Britain and France, Founder and Framer. Over that time he would move from staunch British patriot to colonial rebel, from slave owner to abolitionist. But much of this celebrated patriotic effort would stem from a detestation of political brutality that began with a single incident.

The turning point came on January 29, 1774 while Franklin was in London lobbying the Crown on behalf of the Colonies, shortly after the Boston Tea Party:

Now called to Whitehall Palace by the King's Privy Council, Franklin—in his finest bottle-blue coat—stands at the center of a confined octagonal chamber; this small arena, with close-in surrounding stadium seating is called the Cockpit for its use as a cockfighting arena by King Henry VIII. Royal officialdom has just received word of the Sons of Liberty and their little escapade with a Tea Party in Boston harbor the preceding month, and, furious beyond measure, they mean to vent their ire on the nearest Colonial.

Thus, Franklin—despite being an eminent 68 year old man of letters, fellow of the Royal Society, founder of the American Philosophical Society, and overseas emissary—is viciously pilloried and excoriated for well over an hour by a political nabob half his age while a crowd of London's potentates and high society, many of whom Franklin had considered friends, jeer and cackle. Alone, isolated, abandoned, the enraged Franklin stands stock still, holding his piece, maintaining a stoic inscrutability...but by the time he walks out, he is a changed man. In short order, he will resign his royal posts and, after delivering final petitions from the Continental Congress to the Crown, set sail back to America, having resolved to turn his considerable talents to the cause of revolution.

Franklin had become an American patriot and would dedicate the rest of his life to that cause.

His was the kind of backbone exhibited by the rest of the Colonials, the sense of self-worth and contempt for tyranny which undergirded the entire revolutionary enterprise. No self-respecting American would abide being treated to such indignities, much as they would never acquiesce to swinging taxes, commandeering of their houses by British soldiery, seizure of their papers, nor confiscation of their guns.

That's the difference between a badass and a slave.

That's also why Franklin proposed that his personal motto adorn the Great Seal of the United States: *"Rebellion to Tyrants is Obedience to God."*

Self-Reliance: a Master Virtue

"Government never furthered any enterprise but by the alacrity with which it got out of its way."

— Henry David Thoreau —

One of the things most evident from Ben Franklin's story is the complexity of building self-reliance. Yes, building a successful business all by itself would have made him financially self-reliant, but the qualities and characteristics which made him able to build such a business (initiative, industry, confidence, focus, doggedness, etc.) were those which—when continually and widely applied, as Franklin did—can be leveraged into a kind of superpower producing well-nigh superhuman results. Thus, he went from entrepreneur to author to philanthropist to inventor to scientist to diplomat to statesman, seemingly without missing a beat...all from the same characteristics, the same moral core and dispositions to determined, disciplined action.

Because America's limited, libertarian approach to governance produces a *tabula rosa*—an open field for action—it puts the burden of decision and agency back on the individual; it necessarily evokes the maximal thought, decision, and action by the citizen. And a nation of free citizens—acting both singly and in manifold cascading associations—will quickly and always produce far more options, outcomes, and pure productivity than any central planning committee ever will. Despite what may appear like a chaos of energies, and even seeming outright lawlessness at the edges, this Brownian movement of millions of individual agents exploring and experimenting in innumerable ways with possible commercial, scientific, artistic, social, and political approaches to self-improvement is quite simply—and most obviously—the quickest way to discover the most (and least) pragmatic solutions.

And to participate in this hurly-burly of activity, each citizen must develop that master virtue so tellingly and masterfully demonstrated by the Pilgrims: self-reliance. Both the Plymouth and Virginia colonies prospered only when each member of the colony was given his own plot of land to hoe and—as much as they pitched together to build the stockade and common house—only when each thrived primarily through their own efforts to feed and equip themselves individually; even when living as an isolated settlement in a hostile wilderness, it was the task of each individual householder to build, maintain, and grow their own plot through their own daily toil; it was theirs alone to do, or to die. The first, and most successful, colonies were those which stressed the necessity to put *your* hand to *your* plow and *your* back to *your* work. Self-reliance was therefore baked into the very marrow of this nation from its inception and realized in fullest efflorescence in the 19th century—and only thereby does one becomes personally responsible and empowered, can one evince that hardest, but most gloriously rewarding stage: the full self-development of all one's faculties and goals which is Ben Franklin's story.

But self-reliance is, however, not a single trait, but rather the outcome from a *combination* of many virtues. Self-reliance relies on a broad moral foundation for its instantiation; it is the *result* of a raft of virtues properly inculcated in every young child, including, but not limited to, such fundamental virtues as temperance, empathy, fortitude, and patience. Before you can be free, you must be self-reliant, and to realize self-reliance, you must first manifest the most basic virtues. The development of self-reliance is thus a long, late, adult outcome, only fully realized by earlier mastery of many antecedent traits.

Because it is a kind of multi-textured characteristic, one cannot discern self-reliance via a single quality—you cannot glance over and exclaim, "Oh, look at Eddie being so self-reliant!" Rather, self-reliance arises only as a result of the cumulative work of an entire set of smaller, ongoing virtuous acts, arising only as an outcome of mastering many lesser, more rudimentary virtues. Therefore, self-reliance may be called a second-order, master, or *mother virtue*, which sits at the apex of a set of antecedent or prerequisite virtues from which it emerges only when such precursor virtues are mastered and combined. These lesser, primal, or *daughter virtues* would encompass, for instance, many of those which we expect children to learn before age ten which engender self-mastery of their present impulses and immediate everyday environment, such as politeness and punctuality, kindness and cleanliness. Requisite for self-reliance would also be those virtues we expect from folks before they reach age twenty, which would make them capable of beginning to master the larger challenges of social and financial independence: focus, determination, self-control, honesty, frugality, industry, etc. Of course, the virtues necessary to realize self-reliance are not readily enumerable in an exact list—and, indeed, will vary by particular circumstance—but essentially entail the qualities necessary to face the responsibilities and challenges of maintaining a household in one's particular social and cultural setting.

In general, then, self-reliance is a master virtue revealed by a range of activities; that is, self-reliance is not a single mode of action or achievement, but rather the emergent outcome of developing a range of underlying, basal virtues. For, to be able to properly stand on one's own through the myriad challenges of wind, weather, flood, illness, heartache, and life's thousand twists of fate, requires a raft of personal strengths. One must have honesty to earn the trust of your fellows; industriousness to produce a surplus needful for times of winter and want; conscientiousness to continually meet commitments to produce that surplus for self, family, and customers; thrift to store up for tomorrow's famine; temperance to quell urges to indulge in such distracting temptations as laziness, lust, or liquor; courage to stand against rascals and raiders who would grab all one has gained; wisdom to know the rascal from the righteous; etc., etc. Thus, you cannot achieve self-reliance until you have formed the character to consistently tend and care for yourself and others in a sound, sensible manner. Only someone sufficiently well-reared and empowered to control their impulses and rigorously attend to their duties will continually evince a self-reliant life.

Thus, when French scholar de Tocqueville visited these united States in the 19th century to learn the secret of America's stunning success in having—over the space of just a couple generations since twice fighting off the British, established great fishing, whaling, and trading fleets for their wares, built cities and factories from coast to coast, and invented all manner of productivity-enhancing mechanical agricultural and industrial gizmos from threshers to steamboats, he reported: *"I sought for the greatness and genius of America in her commodious harbors and her ample rivers, and it was not there; in her fertile fields and boundless prairies; and it was not there; in her rich mines and her vast commerce, and it was not there. Not until I visited the churches of America and heard her pulpits aflame with righteousness did I understand the secret of her genius and power. America is great because she is good, and if America ever ceases to be good, America will cease to be great."*

As ever, it is the spirit and not the substance that tells the tale.

There is a kind of "forcing function" inherent in a libertarian republic which necessarily engenders the morality to become self-reliant, and that maximizes one's individual capacity to render such immense commercial and economical productivity. Why? Because the single most productive thing on the planet is the human mind: its limitless potentiality will continually, iteratively produce unknown, unforeseen wonders. Therefore, that system of governance, education, and familial upbringing will almost always win which elicits the courage, confidence, and curiosity of the child, which encourages that child to try and to try and to try again until they find the innovative solution. This was the cultural mindset, the familial setting, which plainly was underlying so much of the early Republic. And those inventive souls had a historical mentor to follow in the person of Benjamin Franklin, that Founder and Framer whose polymath proclivities had him turning his considerable talents not just to the political arts of statesmanship and diplomacy, but also to literature, and—most importantly for the growing industrialism of the 19th century—scientific investigation and practical invention.

Into the Want

The road to Badass is long and hard. The mere hankering for liberty is no guarantee. Having the spirit of autonomy and a love for freedom is far from an assurance of gaining so dear a prize. The mere wish, no matter how hungry the hankering, is no delivery. Franklin's road to his successes came only after many long, lonely hours of work, the many years of "early to bed, early to rise," which make success possible.

To, like Franklin, manifest the real thing out of the wishful dream, one must master the fine art of self-deprivation. All of the distractions of little pleasures and dainty pursuits must be stripped away, sacrificed on the altar of purposeful action. Thus, the Pilgrims broke with the homeland, friends, and family, plunged across the unforgiving seas, and toiled in the frigid, rocky soil; Ben Franklin would leave family to work day and night, ink to his elbow, printing the works of others, then toil into the night, scribbling his own verse to build a business, to amass the wealth which enabled him to undertake the charitable work of building schools and hospitals, fire departments, libraries, and even a new nation; and, likewise, as we shall see, much as frontiersmen like Daniel Boone and Kit Carson would plunge headlong through miles of unhewn wilderness to carve out an encampment, fending off predators and ruffians to scratch out a life of independence.

All of these exemplars dove deep *into the want*: they voluntarily faced the dry, the empty wasteland of self-deprivation, self-discipline, self-denial for hours, days, and years for the purpose of making possible through action in the real, that freedom which was their ideal. The badass must be prepared to go into and spend as long as it takes going *into the wanting time*. It may take years. It may take all the gumption, guts, and grit you can muster. But, as is most often the case: the hardest road usually proves to be the easy way.

You can't avoid sacrifice.

You can't fake results.

And to undertake the sacrifice that produces the results, you have to first go *into the want*. The badass, then, must first go through the wanting. To fully reach badass, you have to be willing to run headlong straight *into the long wanting*.

There is nothing more to it than to just go through it.

To earn your badass, you have to go *into the want*.

Daniel Boone: Self-Reliant Man

"I firmly believe that it takes but a little philosophy to make a man happy in whatever state fortune many place him."
— Daniel Boone —

One man who knew how to go *into the want* was Daniel Boone. Pathfinder, pioneer, frontiersman, Boone would open the way into the West. While most Colonials were still fretting over the great political battles in the East, Boone was out exploring the highlands of what would become Tennessee. Boone may at first seem just another semi-literate hunter roaming the backwoods of the Carolinas and Kentucky, bringing back deerskins for $1 each (which is the reason a one-dollar note is called a "buck"), plus more than his share of bears—there is more than one tree still standing carved with such declarations as: *"D. Boon Cilled a Bar on the tree in year 1760."*

But Boone would prove to be much more than a skilled hunter. He may be the Americana folk hero of the West who best exemplifies the tough and tender, manly and moral, the rough with righteous. Before the Revolution, seeking better hunting grounds to feed his family, Boone moved to the western frontier of the Kentucky territory. During an initial attempt to settle the area, an ambush—by the native Cherokee, Shawnee, amongst others—overran part of Boone's expedition, including his oldest son, who was tortured and killed. This event, with other skirmishes in the area, opened Dunmore's War in 1774, an affray which would be settled the next year, but which also began the long struggle between the natives and settlers in the "Dark and Bloody Ground" of the Ohio River Valley which continued, off and on, for decades.

Boone would join the militia and earn great acclaim and a captaincy, but he also wound up deeply indebted at the end of the campaign. A wealthy investor offered him a challenging means to pay off his debts: open the Indian lands of the lush Cumberland Gap. Boone accepted and—although he had lost his son to these people through torture and taken arms against them just the year before—he elected to use a diplomatic approach with the Cherokee before moving into their territory. Avoiding militarism, in March of 1775, he invited the Cherokee leaders to negotiate what became a mediated sale of the Cherokee claim on the lands of Kentucky. With that done, Boone lead a group of 30 intrepid pioneers, hacking a path over 250 miles deep into the unsettled region. This path Boone blazed—initially known as "Boone's Trace"—would be followed by first hundreds, then thousands, and finally over 200,000 settlers as it became the "Wilderness Road" which opened the frontier for American westward expansion.

Having found a suitable site, Boone built his own permanent, fortified compound, aptly named Boonesborough. That September, he ventured back to North Carolina to fetch his long-suffering family to their new home. But there was to be little time for respite and reunion, as the Revolution of July, 1776 brought unending challenges to the Boone clan. Many Indians saw the war as the opportunity to push the settlers out by making common cause with the British, who, in their turn, eagerly armed and provisioned the natives as supplementary combatants alongside their regulars. As this alliance reignited the troubles along the frontier, Boone would again be called to militia leadership.

Within a month, this resurgence of war came to Boone in a most immediate and harrowing way, when his eldest daughter, Jemima, and two of her friends went for a canoe excursion only to be kidnapped by a Shawnee raiding party. Fortunately, the accomplished woodsman Boone was able to lead a rescue team, track the hostages down in two days—thanks in large part to Jemima's resourcefulness in leaving snapped twigs along the way—fight off the kidnappers, and rescue the lasses.

As the war unfolded, the fighting in the West raged from the British headquarters at Detroit in the north clear down to the Gulf, providing Boone many more challenges of his gumption, grit, and guts. In January, 1778, leading an expedition to far off salt flats which could reprovision Boonesborough's dwindling supply of that ingredient essential for preserving meat, Boone and his party would be captured by Chief Blackfish of the Shawnee. The Chief led Boone and his party far to the north, way up to Chillicothe, Ohio. There, however, Boone's toughness and courage saved the team from possible massacre. Challenged to run the gauntlet, Boone fought with such courage and toughness, that he earned the admiration of Chief Blackfish, nicknaming Boone *Sheltowee* ("Big Turtle") and "adopting" (or perhaps more accurately, enslaving) him by baptism into the chief's own household. Biding his time, Boone learned that Blackfish was outfitting a large war party to return for an attack on Boonesborough. Finding his opportunity during a turkey hunt, Boone escaped and travelled nonstop—covering 150 miles in just five days, first by horse and then, when the horse faltered, on foot—to warn his family and settlement. There was little time to bolster the defenses before Chief Blackfish appeared outside the stockade, leading a troop of native warriors supported by a dozen European mercenaries numbering over 400 men altogether. Although outnumbered 10 to 1, the sharp-shooting settlers beat back the initial assaults by Blackfish and his allies. A ten day siege followed during which Blackfish tried first frontal assaults, then throwing burning flambeaux at the garrison's roof, and even tunnelling beneath the walls. The defenders maintained their posts and marksmanship, and even employed a makeshift wooden cannon. At last, the frustrated chief undertook a final attack, a massed assault with bullet, flame, and arrow, but that was drown out in a hail of gunfire and providential heavy rain. Boone, although only a captain and by rank the subordinate officer during the siege, proved the savviest tactician and natural leader by keeping the settlers steady and disciplined throughout the ordeal.

Ironically, Boone would be court-martialled just months later because of suspicions arising from his ordeal with Chief

Blackfish's Shawnee. Not only had he spent several months away while captured by the natives—and thus near the British northern settlements—but many in Boonesborough sought vengeance on the natives by sending out war parties to exact reprisal. Boone—despite having his daughter kidnapped, his son hideously murdered, and been personally kidnapped by natives—counselled peace. Ever true to the Christian upbringing of his Quaker roots, he recognized the Indians were, like himself, children of the living God and thus properly due the same consideration as any other human being. He refused to spill blood for blood's sake. In the end, his clear, sound principles won over the military court so thoroughly that he was not only acquitted but given a promotion to the rank of major. Boone found, however, that the townspeople were still determined to undertake hostilities. He knew it was better to leave rather than surrender his principles, so in 1779 he moved on, founding an entire second settlement, soon known as Boone's Station. From there he began a long and varied life over the next several decades, from shopkeeper to surveyor's assistant, but most often either in the militia, as state representative, or other public service. He had no cause or grievance with any person. He had run his race and run it well, with as much grace and dignity as a poor boy with so little learning could muster, slave to no man and enemy of none, master of his own fate on the land he carved from the unforgiving wilderness and held onto through his indomitable fortitude.

Davy Crockett: Not Yours to Give

"Be sure you are right—then go ahead."

— Davy Crockett —

Famed frontiersman from the same Tennessee region as Boone, Davy Crockett also initially made his mark in the hills as a skilled hunter, most especially by his accounts of fearlessly taking on bears, once claiming over 100 kills in a single year. This "King of the Wild Frontier" also served as militiaman. In the War of 1812, he fought against both the British at Jackson's famed victory at New Orleans and also against the "Red Stick" Creek tribe in the wild border struggles, but he would ultimately leave that service after his unit participated in the massacre at Tallushatchee of over 200 people, warriors, women and children alike. As he later wrote remorsefully of the slaughter, "We shot 'em down like dogs."

He would spend much of the next decade pursuing assorted occupations attempting to cobble together a living. He would work concurrently as entrepreneur while a militia officer or representative in first the Tennessee General Assembly and then US Congress, where he served three terms. In 1831, Crockett's fame skyrocketed on the success of a popular farcical play, *The Lion of the West*, which people took to be modelled on his life. Overnight, the homey backwoodsman went from country legislator to national legend.

It is as a legislator, however, that Crockett showed he was more than a mere sharpshooting bumpkin. One day, while out on the hustings stumping for re-election, he had the opportunity to acquire perhaps his greatest political lesson from one of his constituents...and, more importantly, he had the humility to take it to heart. This fellow, named Bunce, would give Crockett a powerful reminder of the importance of maintaining the boundaries of constitutional self-restraint, that legislatures should deliver not handouts, only opportunities. Years later, this principle was tested when the House of Representatives looked to appropriate $10,000 for the benefit of a widow of a distinguished naval officer. Several splendid speeches had been made in its support. The Speaker was just about to put the question to the vote when Davy Crockett rose to speak against this well-meaning but unconstitutional gift. In a speech that startled many in the Congress, Crockett said: *"We have the right, as individuals, to give away as much of our own money as we please in charity; but as members of Congress we have no right so to appropriate a dollar of the public money...I am the poorest man on this floor. I cannot vote for this bill, but I will give one week's pay to the object, and if every member of Congress will do the same, it will amount to more than the bill asks."*

Crockett sat down. The hall was silent, and many moved by the gesture. When a reporter asked later why he had voted against such a kindly humanitarian effort, Crockett recounted the lesson he had learned from that man named Bunce:

It was early in Crockett's congressional career when he encountered Mr. Bunce while canvassing for votes. When he asked for Bunce's vote, the fellow frankly answered that, while he had previously voted for Crockett, but planned to never vote for him again. Bunce said it was because of Crockett's previous vote of $20,000 of relief money for businesses after a great fire in the Georgetown district of Washington. Shocked, Crockett asked why anyone would object to gifting such a relatively small amount from the federal treasury for the good of the people in need at the Capital. Bunce replied that nothing could be more injurious and dangerous than such a vote, which was a clear violation of constitutional bounds. Bunce said that, for the Constitution to be worth anything, it must be *"held sacred, and rigidly observed in **all** its provisions."* It was not the amount that mattered, but the principle of the thing. The public treasury was held by Congress as a sacred trust to be used for the *greater* good of the *general* public, not the *private* good of any *particular* group. The money power was the most dangerous, far-reaching of any power given to government, for it reaches into every man's back pocket. Bunce said that, once legislators decide to give freely to whomever they wished, they have set the precedent that the government can take any amount from anyone to give to anyone else, for whatever reason they decide. The principle must be: Congress follows the Constitution, or else Congress is, in essence, a house of thieves. Congress may give freely from their own wallets whatever amount they wanted, but they must jealously guard the people's purse, spending only what is lawful.

No, Bunce concluded, government money did not belong to Congress; it was, *"not yours to give."*

To his credit, Crockett listened closely to Bunce and made the old man's words his own. He retold the story a hundred times and made it a principle of his congressional action from then on.

The wisdom of Bunce was the wisdom of the Framers: disbursements are, as codified in the written law, for the general good under the enumerated, specific powers; everything else is mischief and malfeasance. And, to his credit, Crockett was wise enough to listen...besides wily enough to use the anecdote as a crowd-pleasing stump speech.

Let this stand as a notice to all legislators: the monies conveyed to you in trust are solely for the general weal, and not for the personal or private furtherance of any single person; they confer a fiduciary responsibility on the lawmaker to be used, not with plenary discretion, but under the anxious privilege of acting in the public's behalf and for their benefit. Anything else is conversion, misappropriation, usurpation, embezzlement, if not outright theft and treason.

Get it right, Congress.

That money is not yours to give.

After his third and final term in the US Congress, Crockett once again stood for re-election, but, as had happened twice before, lost. This time, Crockett would foreswear politics once and for all, famously saying, *"I told the people of my district that I would serve them as faithfully as I had done; but if not, they might go to hell, and I would go to Texas."*

In Texas, a small converted mission called the Alamo awaited Crockett, General Santa Anna, and destiny. There Crockett would make the ultimate sacrifice of self for the service of his people, as—fighting under the famous cannon-emblazoned "Come Take It" flag—he and the rest of the fort's defenders were killed in the service to the cause of Texas independence. Though the tyrannical and double-dealing Santa Anna did indeed come and take all the arms and lives of the men at the Alamo that day, he himself would be overawed a month later at the battle of San Jacinto by Texas' independence fighters, setting the Lone Star republic forever free.

Crockett had all the bluster and bravado to take down bears, face down Congress, and fight against tyrants, but he also knew his limits. In his willingness to face and decry the moral horror of the slaughter of innocent natives, in opening his ears to the advice from Bunce on the proper limits of federal spending, Crockett demonstrated that a true badass needs not just courage and determination, but also moral self-reflection and humility...yes, even when a U.S. Congressman.

Cowboy Critters

"The cowboy has been called America's folk hero."
— Charles W. Harris —

As the frontier of America moved west, the moccasin-shod frontiersmen hunting with flintlocks were supplanted by the cowboys, those who would roam in what remained of the buffalo herds and the vast spaces largely unclaimed between the great urban sprawls on the two coasts. Theirs was to tame not the woodland wilds overrun with bobcats and bears, but the ranging veldt of big skies and unforgiving desert.

The cowboy was largely an everyday work hand and so is a mostly anonymous *imago*, rarely an actual name or person...and, when named, is as often as a notorious outlaw as upright citizen. The average cowpoke was often enough a rather ordinary hireling, a man who could do some riding and roping and the hard, thankless work of working a ranch. These men seem hardly the stuff of legend, and so it is usually just the most notorious and unscrupulous whose names come down to us. We know of the gumption, grit, and guts which go into making such back-breaking labor a calling, but know few of these iconic representatives by name.

But there are a few of those prairie-riding cowfolks we can present as the best of the Wild West:

Kit Carson (1809 - 1868) Kit Carson was raised on land once owned by Daniel Boone's clan and would grow to become a legendary pathfinder and frontiersman in his own right, becoming the Western counterpart of Boone as he opened that great Pacific mountain range, the Rockies. Although a rough riding mountain man, fur trapper, and wilderness guide, he was also said to keep his word "as sure as the sun comes' up" and live his life as "clean as a hound's tooth." As was typical of the time, he lived both close to the land and to the native people, his first two wives being American Indians; he lost his first love, Singing Grass, to childbirth, and the second to an Indian style divorce. While scraping together a meager living by hunting for $1 a day in the hills around Bent's Fort, Colorado, his big break came in the person of John Fremont. Fremont had been dispatched from Washington by the War Department to map the West, and hired Carson as guide to the Rockies, later spreading Carson's fame in chronicles of their adventures.

On the last of their three expeditions in the hills, things took an oddly political turn. The scientific exploration had become a matter of settlement and conquest. President Polk wanted the entire West in the Union; he would soon add Texas, and he wanted California too. Thus—apparently at the behest of orders from Washington—Fremont began riling up the local Anglo settlers against the Spaniards, initiating what became the Bear Flag Revolt of 1848 which brought the California territories into the United States. Carson stayed on, essentially as mercenary, scout, and, as the need arose, dispatch rider. For, as Fremont's insurrection made headway, he asked Carson if his frontiersman's skills could enable him to carry critical dispatches clear across the 2,400 miles through the Badlands, forests, and hostiles back to Washington. Carson, whose unassuming manner matched his courage, said he believed he could.

Carson set out into the Badlands carrying his satchel and was well into the trek, when a military expedition—sent to reinforce the burgeoning Bear Revolt—intercepted Carson and ordered him to act as their guide. Thus returning to California once again as a scout and belligerent, Carson would become the hero of the Battle of San Pascual. His unit having been cut off by superior Spanish forces, Carson and two others slipped away in the night;

Carson slid off his boots to keep his movements silent, and made his way barefoot through the hard-scrabble desert, covering the 28 miles by morning. At dawn, a beaten and bedraggled Carson delivered his report, and a force of over 200 reinforcements was immediately dispatched whose arrival drove the Spanish from the field.

From such adventures, Carson's notoriety grew, and he became acclaimed as the "prince of backwoodsmen." His name and likeness became a constant motif of Western pulp fiction hawkers of his era; in such tales, he was the larger-than-life scourge of outlaws and "injuns" alike. In actuality, Carson was a slight, unpretentious man with little affinity for the limelight. Upon making Carson's acquaintance after the Battle of San Pascual and the publication of Fremont's accounts, young lieutenant William Tecumseh Sherman recalled, *"I was very anxious to see a man who had achieved such feats of daring among the wild animals of the Rocky Mountains and still wilder Indians of the Plains. I cannot express my surprise at beholding a small, stoop-shouldered man with reddish hair, freckled face, soft blue eyes, and nothing to indicate extraordinary courage and daring."*

Truly, the inner man is rarely revealed by the outer. And Carson would continue to live a life both bold and self-reliant. He would primarily provide for his third and final family by ranching, while leaving his mark in the military by tussling with rebellious Confederates and native tribes, eventually earning the rank of brevet general. Finally, he served as fair-minded Indian Agent for the Cheyenne and Arapaho, the people he once contested. He would likewise travel with a commission of Ute chiefs to plead their cause at the White House. Finally, in 1868, his lovely, beloved third wife Josela would die from the birth of their eighth child. Bereft, Carson's already diminishing health would fail as he perished in lovelorn sorrow a month later, as tender in death as he had been tough in life.

Stagecoach Mary (c. 1832-1914) Born into slavery but dying a free woman, Mary Fields was a hard-drinking, cigar-smoking, gun-toting mail rider for the US Postal Service. Known for her quick temper, fiesty language, and the no-nonsense comportment of "a grizzly bear," Fields was the first black woman to run a mail route for the Postal Service, riding her buckboard coach solo through the rural mountain roads adjoining Cascade, Montana. Over 6-foot tall and 200 pounds, she cut an imposing figure who was at once determined, even reckless, in dispatching her duties, keeping thieves and critters at bay with the rifle and handgun she always kept by her side. Fearless in the face of wind, weather, or snow, Fields stopped for nothing. Once, when heavy winter snows made the roads impassable for her coach, she strapped on show shoes and trudged 30 miles through the mountain passes to deliver her mail. On another occasion, when her coach overturned en route, she stayed at her station throughout the night, fighting off a pack of wolves with her trusty rifle. Simply badass, all day long.

Bass Reeves (1838-1910) Also born into slavery, Reeves grew to be a famous cowboy lawman. After possible military service in the Civil War, Reeves became a trail guide in the West before becoming the first black deputy in the Deep South. As a US Marshall in Arkansas and police officer in Oklahoma, he would tally 14 clean kills (all accounted as self-defense) and over 3,000 arrests—including his own son on the charge of killing his wife! A master of ambush and disguise, Reeves used his wits as much as his gun, managing to serve over 30 years unscathed by even a single bullet wound, all while maintaining a reputation for impeccable honor. Tough as nails, right as rain, he is believed by many to be the original model for the famed *Lone Ranger* radio and TV serials.

Annie Oakley (1860-1926) Perhaps the most famous cowgirl of them all, Annie Oakley was the stage name of Phoebe Ann Mosey who grew up in Ohio with a rifle in her hands, hunting to help her family survive, so skilful with her weapon she even paid off the mortgage on the family farm. Facing off against famed marksman Frank E. Butler in a shooting contest, she would win not only the contest but Butler's heart. The two would go on to marry and become the headline act of Buffalo Bill's Wild West Show, touring Europe and America, performing for presidents, princes, and potentates. As part of their act, "Little Sure Shot" Annie would shoot a cigar from her husband's hand, or cut a playing card in half...held sideways...at 30 paces.

Forced to retire after a railroad accident badly injured her back, Oakley continued performing in a stage play written to highlight her skills. She also took on the cause of self-defense for women, teaching over 15,000 women the shooting arts. Her goal was to *"see that every woman know how to handle guns, as naturally as they know how to handle babies."* By 1898, she could offer President McKinley a company of 50 "lady sharpshooters," armed, provisioned, and ready for action in the war with Spain. She shows us how to take care of yourself and others through the tenderness of toughness.

Bootstrapping: Cowboy Cool

"We have a sense that we should be like the mythical cowboy... able to take on and conquer anything and live in the world without the need for other people."
— Morrie Schwartz —

Such were the people who inhabited the Plains, the West, and other regions beyond the original Colonies. So when you ask, "Why the obsession with cowboys?" the answer may begin to clarify. Sure, one may wonder: why would anyone want to spend their days in all that scorching sun and swirling dust, wrangling stinking cattle across empty wilderness? It's a tough life, for tough folk. It's nothing but dirt, danger, indignity, desolation...and independence.

In that sense, the cowboy *imago* becomes the purest instantiation of Americanism. It's one person, alone, facing a vast horizon of potentialities, astride a horse which can speed one like the wind, while bearing a sidearm with the power of thunder, with no one to answer to but oneself and God. It is the purity of power wrought from the rawest of potential, continually on that edge where danger meets daring-do.

It is to be totally alive, continually challenged, and eternally triumphant in one's person and power. It is, in a sense, the potential and promise of Americanism realized. It is liberty and self-reliance in a single snapshot, and it is the instantiation of gumptions, guts, and grit...that won the West, and which won America itself.

That is why the cowboy.

All that "boot-strapping" spirit of do-it-your-own and grind your way through is just part of what made the flourishing growth of America possible in the 1800s. So that bootstrap, it's not just part of your footwear. It's how you face adversity; it's a way of life; it's how you win.

The bootstrapping stage is where the child becomes the adult, and it was at the age where America reached its mature potentiality so that, by 1898, no nation could overawe what it could produce in industry, invention, art, science, or war. That's the year the great Spanish Empire would discover its time had long past. It would declare war on the United States. In that brief, unequal Spanish-American War, the US forces would thoroughly trounce the failing vestiges of Spanish imperial ambitions in just five months, forcing Spain to relinquish Puerto Rico, Guam, the Philippines, and Cuba.

The baton was being passed from the old world to the new, and in 1907 Teddy Roosevelt would underscore the point by sending out the Great White Fleet in proof. Giving the world a little flex of American naval power, he sent 16 battleships painted peacetime white, with red-white-and-blue banners at their bows, circumnavigating the glove, showing off the nation's "good will"...and also maritime punch, for anyone thinking of messing with the U.S. It's was Teddy's boldest demonstration of how to *"speak softly, and carry a big stick."*

And, of course, the doughboys would pay off all that bluster in quick succession when, a decade later, they would come in to help close out the first Great War.

As the nation would sit down at the world table by

showing it had grown from its adolescent uncertainty into a self-starting adult to be reckoned with, so does the cowboy exhibit that initiative, that belief in the individual capacity to grow, to discover, to create, to develop internally and produce externally. The cowboy is a realization of full autonomy, a physical demonstration of power's devolution to the atomic level, i.e. that the individual human soul is the seat of power and potential. A cowboy is pure individualism, the personal pursuit of happiness, self-expression, directness, a meritocracy of one. A cowboy eschews the finery, frippery, and heraldry of Old World nobility. A cowboy's nobility is realized by work and muck and going into the suck. And that cowboy emerges triumphantly from the muck, covered in mud but just as good as anyone, and just as ready to do it again. It is the *Shane* of book and film, the Lone Ranger of TV and radio, who—though he can shoot with the deadly skill of any outlaw—would rather build a log cabin to keep the prairie safe and the settlers secure. Thereby does the cowboy become that most emblematic icon and epitome of independence, practicality, and industry...beneath whose rugged exterior lies a heart of gold.

And where your cowboy self rides best and breathes deepest is on a wide-open frontier 'neath endless skies, with nothing but your own bootstraps to pull yourself up. And there, self-reliance is wrangling and settling an unforgiving land, homesteading that fundamental human community of father-mother-children—and to do so with a combination of the kindness of spirit in defense of others of a blushing maiden, alongside the pragmatism of purpose of a shootin' iron. The cowboy arises only in that perfect cynosure of constitutional freedom, endless landscape, and ethos of merciful mettle which was most perfectly manifest in that one place, that one time.

So, when you're talking bootstrappin', it's most likely Western style:

Just a cowboy, the stars, and a Colt .45.

We Don't Need No Stinkin' Governing

"Destiny is not a matter of chance; it is a matter of choice. It is not a thing to be waited for; it is a thing to be achieved."
— William Jennings Bryan —

A People that can pour forth across the land and conquer a continent, bring endless light to the darkness, and enable humankind to fly are self-evidently competent and capable. Such a People need ask nothing more than to be given the room to run...and they will grow and prosper. They don't need top-down muzzling by ninnying busybody bureaucrats.

Americans have no need for "representatives" who mostly seem to represent their own self-interest with lifelong perks. We need no more legislative legerdemain, like one-line legalese exemptions for friends, family, and financiers hidden in 1,000-page pseudo-legal monstrosities of perk, pork, and payola shoved through committee without proper review or debate; no more technocratic Senior Executive Service overlords, who sit atop their vast bureaucratic empires, decade after decade, sneering and demeaning the people's demands and entreaties; no more internal federal armies—literal pistol-packing hordes, down to park rangers and IRS accountants—swarming over the landscape like jackals, seeing whose liberty and livelihood they can devour. If such a government—which has robbed, muzzled, browbeaten, defamed, impoverished, imprisoned, poisoned, and, yes, gunned down its own people—is not at war with the citizens, it is the best imitation of one possible.

We don't need no "leaders" like that. What we need are "leave-aloners." What we need is minimal interference with our already complex, fascinating, and productive lives. A self-reliant, self-starting, productive people have no need for interference and intervention. And if the self-appointed leaders can't learn some leave-alone, those self-starting people will darn sure start building their own alternate structures, alternative political communities, which shall supplant today's self-serving, self-satisfied overlords.

We can lead ourselves, thank you very much. We have led

ourselves for years. As husbands and wives, fathers and mothers, business owners and teachers, we know quite well how to manage our lives. We know how to balance our checkbooks and build our customer base, how to retool into a new trade while juggling multiple responsibilities...how to renovate a house or repair a relationship; we know how to raise our children, love our country, honor our commitments, and worship our Creator. We don't need to be led; we don't need to be numbered, cajoled, scolded, or herded like cattle at the whims of bureaucrats for the dreams of technocrats.

What we need are un-leaders, who know when to sit down, shut up, and listen how best to leave the folks well enough alone who know best how to manage their own affairs, thank you very much.

We need *listeners*, not lecturers; we need *representatives*, not pied pipers. We need *learners*, who have studied the precepts of the Constitution and stand by the principles of personal liberty and citizen sovereignty.

We need those who speak with *our* voice...those who come *from*, stand *with*, and speak *for* the people. We need servant citizens who take office as a duty, undertake their duties selflessly while speaking honestly, and leave. We need people who—in humility, and expecting no more gain than serving the public good—arise from the people, spend a couple years balancing the books at the Post Office, overseeing the readiness of the Navy...and then go home, needing no more payback than a pat on the back and the satisfaction of a job well done.

Let's face it—day in, day out, in every time and in all places:

We don't need no stinkin' governing.

We just need some leave-alone.

Yankee Inventiveness

"You have to be burning with an idea, or a problem, or a wrong that you want to right. If you're not passionate enough from the start, you'll never stick it out."

— Steve Jobs —

At the same time the American people were reshaping the West, they were remaking the shape of the world itself with their inventiveness. Franklin was not alone in adding to that ever-escalating asymptotic increase of technical competency and industrial capacity which went exponential at the end of AmRev 1.0. America was the world's best shipbuilder, with a knowledge garnered from British seafaring and built on timbers felled from our huge tracts of old-growth forests. The early American industrialists brought machining and automation to the largely agrarian nation which would, within a century, become the world's leading steel producer and auto maker. American ingenuity would produce a second Industrial Revolution wrought by mechanical and metallic industrialization of every type, from typewriters, adding machines, and cash registers, to reaping machines and canal dredgers.

While we can assume some part of this was the outcome of the general burgeoning industrial age founded on the fundamental scientific discoveries of the 17th and 18th centuries, the constitutional institution of patent protections for inventors, and the cultural ethos encouraging freedom of thought and self-reliance of action were almost certainly part of the disproportionate explosion of innovations which have flowed from the American people over the ensuing two hundred years. It seems doubtful Americans are somehow disproportionally smarter than any other group of folks. Rather, this creative cornucopia is most likely a cultural phenomenon, just another badass outcome which comes from a culture of freedom.

In sum, in less than a century—perhaps boosted by the establishment of the Patent Office in 1802—the nation transformed from an agricultural to an industrial base, in large measure via introduction of a raft of technical innovations. At the start of the century, Jefferson was president; he wrote his letters by candlelight, sent messages by express rider, and the only means of importing beaver pelts from the fur trappers around San Francisco was by sailing all the way down past Cape Horn and back up again.

Then came the inventors:

• Oliver Evans produced high-pressure versions of Fitch and Rumsey's steam engines as dredgers, grinders, and automatic grain mills (even installing a presidential model at Washington's Mount Vernon plantation)

• Fulton mounted a steam engine on a boat, enabling people to take advantage of the nation's increasing network of canals

• Steam engines were turned into train engines riding iron rails which soon crossed the eastern seaboard...and later the entire continent

• On May 10, 1869, a golden rail spike was driven into the ground at Promontory Point, Utah, demarcating the completion of a transcontinental railroad. Travelling coast to coast—which was impossible for Jefferson, a tiresome journey of long weeks at sea or harrowing danger by covered wagon for Polk—was now but a few days of urbane comfort and catered dining for anyone

• Eli Whitney's cotton gin was introduced, maximizing output of cotton fiber for the clothing industry

• McCormick's Virginia Reaper machine slashed the labor involved in harvesting grains

• Morse's telegraph began relaying messages down poles strung with "lightnin' wire," replacing hand-written hand-carried missives carted by Pony Express

• Alexander Graham Bell in 1876 enabled one to immediately telephone that story which before you would have had to post or telegraph

• Eastman empowered folks to capture the image of your loved ones by camera

• Not to be outdone, Edison let you put such pictures in motion with his kinetoscope (as he did for Annie Oakley), and then preserve the sound of their voice with his phonograph, and finally to see them day or night with his light bulb

• And, soon enough, the Wright Brothers in December, 1903, enabled you to fly to see your loved ones in person

• To be followed, in the following century, by the magnification of the speed and power of all this communication, investigation, and transformation by the introduction of radio, TV, radar, sonar, laser, X-rays, computers, internet, smartphone, etc., etc.

The unleashing of the inquisitive, determined creativity of the curious human mind would magnify the powers of the civilization, producing opportunity, adventure, and prosperity. The latent potential for limitless abundance locked in the material realm was finally being released through the power of disciplined imagination and focused effort. That abundance would have the knock-on benefits of increasing the lifespan and bounty for everyone, but it would also create a tremendous challenge: how to properly forestall the ambitions of the greedy.

Liberty, Plenty, Monopoly
"Liberty may be endangered by the abuses of liberty as well as the abuses of power."
— James Madison —

We've all played the board game *Monopoly*. You scoot your pieces around, happily grabbing properties and piling up cash...until the point where someone has amassed so many properties and so much cash that they can't lose; no matter where you land, and not matter what they buy, they have so much—and you have so little—that they will certainly win. That's the monopoly part of *Monopoly*, and a very important economic lesson.

What, in fact, *Monopoly* most starkly demonstrates is the

Pareto distribution. More broadly thought of as the 80/20 rule, the Pareto distribution seems to be a general phenomenon: a few individuals in any setting produce most of the results. This unequal production appears in nature as certain plants or animals most flourish and reproduce; in the arts and sciences, wherein a handful of writers and composers emit by far the greatest work, both by number and public consumption; and, in the immediate context, a small number of entrepreneurs and corporations will garner the greatest wealth by widely outselling everyone else. Because productivity is unevenly distributed, that means that whoever has some (even slight) advantage of talent and/or resources and/or training and/or luck will soon amass the disproportionate win, i.e. even small advantages, iterated over sufficient time and number of instances, will produce huge differences in final results.

In the first part of the board game, all of the players freely move across the board, choosing properties and gathering wealth. In the first century of the Constitution, physical open space was created by the land acquisition of Jefferson's Louisiana Purchase, plus Polk's additions of Texas and California. The people moved freely, enjoying an immense compass of land into which the adventurers and settlers poured and thrived. They also moved freely and thrived in the economic sphere because there was little or no taxation. Indeed, there was no federal income tax, meaning as long as you did not engage in activities subject to the few excise taxes, you could avoid taxes altogether.

Practically free from taxes and with a broad, bountiful land to develop, the People's inherent creativity and dynamism was given full compass; they planned and tested and invented and dreamed. Left to their own devices, the People then built and worked, multiplied and flourished. Productivity boomed in agriculture, industry, housing, transportation, and every form of innovation.

But, as in the board game, it is precisely the great freedom and opportunity afforded in that beginning of the game that allows monopoly to loom as a possibility. This is the exciting, fast-paced middle part of *Monopoly*, where anything is possible.

Because any player can make any play, some will prosper and some will falter. And, as some prosper, they can use the ensuing gained advantage in more or less scrupulous ways, with more or less craftiness and selfishness. In the 3D *Monopoly* game of life, it is often the more selfish—and less moral—player who more quickly and fully develops their monopoly. In fact, looking to bootstrap yourself on the back of everyone else, the truly unscrupulous can hire the whip hand of the government to do the dirty work for them. In that way, an open playing field afforded by constitutional freedom can be twisted into guide rails which turn freedom on its head. That is the way of the Robber Baron.

Barons of Robbery

"Within the highest circles of power and wealth, a lack of pity and remorse is practically a prerequisite to success, and only the psychopathic mentality can thrive."

— Stefan H. Verstappe —

In the big-boy *Monopoly* game of the 19th century, the Robber Barons amassed unimaginable wealth. On one level, you can say they were merely commercial cowboys, wild opportunist without compunction. They were given a vast wilderness of commerce to conquer, and they rode forth with gusto and bravado, conquering all before them, counting not the cost for anyone else. Pure freedom allows for the fullest expression of both the good and bad, and in a maximally open society, one naturally witnesses the most complete expression of greed.

The simple fact is that, to produce the maximal freedom and range of output, one must maximize opportunity, which opens the annulus for the full expression of both kinds of action, benevolent and malevolent. It is the maximization of freedom which allows for the greatest output by those with the best talent, intent, and effort. Unfortunately, such maximal autonomy also maximizes the range of possibilities of action and outcome for those of ill will and malign intent.

Thus, the rise of the Robber Barons was partly an outcome of their own greed, but it was also a predictable outcome of the *laissez-faire* economic circumstances. The burgeoning of national wealth arose from a fully free market alongside a rising population working through the increasing output afforded by industrialized production. The result was an unprecedented surplus output which generated a class of super-wealthy tycoons unlike any that had come before:

• *John Jacob Astor,* who is believed to have created the first monopoly, by cornering the fur trade early in the 19th century

• *Cornelius "the Commodore" Vanderbilt,* who built the world's largest shipping monopoly, then sold it off to leverage himself into becoming the richest man in the country by jumping early aboard railroad transportation

• *Andrew Carnegie,* who took the country from iron to steel when he threw the first steel bridge clear across the mighty Mississippi River in 1874 and would go on to smelt the structural steel which would become the backbone for the skyscrapers of the age to come

• *J.P. Morgan,* who, while also a steel magnate, was primarily active in the banking industry...and, perhaps not coincidentally, was also a mustachioed, top hat-adorned, moon-faced fellow like the *Monopoly* game's fat cat mascot. He seems to have been not only an inside player in New York high finance, but an emissary and bag man for European banking interests, backing business-friendly President McKinley's election in 1896, and also being especially closely connected to the creation in 1913 of the Third (the final, fatal) National Bank, called the Federal Reserve

• But the monopolist among monopolists, whom even Morgan couldn't beat, was *John D. Rockefeller* and his Rockefeller clan, whose first foray in monopolistic capitalism garnered well over 90% of the burgeoning oil industry across the continental United States, thereby piling up a fortune which, in today's reckoning, would approach 400 billions of money. From "Devil Bill" to John D. and on down the family line, it appears that the rapacious inclinations of the Rockefeller clan gave them the dark agency to—if we are to believe the muckraking chroniclers of their depredations like Ida Tarbell—by hook, crook, or outright murder, gain the advantage over their commercial rivals. Not content with perhaps the greatest commodity monopoly of all time in oil—certainly rivalled only by the British East India Company's tea holdings—the acquisitive clan rolled their empire forward perhaps most perniciously into medicine, turning the healing arts into a monopolistic for-profit industry. By a combination of funding specious research and publishing the self-serving, tendentious, and spurious *Flexnor Report* assailing any other long-standing or even more effective healing modalities, Rockefeller's minions were able to turn the American Medical Association into, essentially, a subsidiary branch of the petroleum industry. By the time the paid-for Rockefeller medical schools were done with them, the medicos in lab coats were converted into pill-pushing agents of the petroleum-derived pharmaceuticals...as if such nostrums were the *sine qua non* of medical practice. The question of an AMA-trained doctor became not, "How can we heal that?" but "Which pill for that?"

This model of monopolist destruction of the competition would be used again and again by the Rockefellers, as when they ginned up the "Reefer Madness" scare of the 30s to drive the both medically and industrially useful hemp plant from the field, a plant which not only produced rope and cloth but diesel oil to fuel the farmers' tractors. Such competition and independence was simply not to be allowed, and the Rockefellers let no trifling concerns about fairness, truth, or honor stand in the way of a measurable business advantage.

• At the same time, there were some who, at least at times, attempted to do good while doing well. *Henry Ford* profited massively from his assembly line automobile production, but also believed that well-paid workers were more productive and happier. He paid double the salary of other manufacturers, and, while most businesses scheduled a 60-hour work week, he instituted 40 hours for his people. Being wealthy does not necessarily make one a completely selfish pig—it just makes it easier.

The historical importance of the monopolistic Robber Barons is not so much to demonstrate human greed; that is a given. Rather, it highlights the need to recognize the limitations of an unfettered free market, the need for oversight and lawful bounds on commercial activity. They reveal a weakness—perhaps naivety—in the constitutional arrangement of purest economic freedom, for greed will never cease. Hence, American law must place clear and competent restraints on its exercise.

Corporation vs. Citizen: Asymmetric Economic Warfare

"The lesson is clear: if you are a thief, steal by the billions or trillions, and then no one can do anything about it...[I]f you want to indulge your criminal fantasies, lie and steal, profit from death and drugs, dominate and demand, be king and command, become the highly-functioning socially-acceptable sociopath you always knew you could be...Think big. Think bank. Serial killers, bank robbers and drug dealers go to jail; bankers get bailouts and get an unlimited insurance policy called 'too big to fail.'"

— Jurriaan Maessen, Global Research —

One area wherein the law is especially vulnerable to predatory abuse is in the matter of corporations. General incorporation law lays the groundwork for potential growth of monopolies and inequitable action in business and commercial practice. An artificially-created "corporation" (from the Latin *corpus*, meaning "body") is a single "body" treated with many of the legal protects afforded to a single human being. But a business corporation is not a human being; it is an entity which can employ thousands of human beings and bodies working ceaselessly...and which may never die. While a single human may well build a business through commercial acumen and concerted effort, a corporation competes with potentially limitless resources of human intellect, money, and time; it pits the many against the one; it has no need of sleep, rest, or refreshment; and it has no natural death.

A corporation is an inexorable, implacable foe, and to have the agency of the law on its side by granting it any of the privileges and immunities of a natural person is only to superadd the protection of the law to the natural inequities of the contest.

All "partnerships", "trusts", "corporations", etc. are social constructs, legal fictions. They were instituted for defined purposes in the realm of personal and business finance, and they have an obvious utility in that arena. But, like any entity, it has strengths and weaknesses, potential benefits and costs. On the level of particular moral harm to the overall economy, such socially-constructed—and thereby "artificial"—entities potentially create an uneven playing field. Artificial entities which can combine the abilities of many individuals with large material resources are inherently powerful economic forces. They therefore constitute an immense potential danger to the economic health of the nation which can prove disruptive, disordering, and eventually destructive to a freely-functioning marketplace within their particular competitive sector. As they scale up in size, they can theoretically deploy any amount of resources, making them capable of manipulating the market, competitors, and—especially if they are in any degree unscrupulous—create unfair competitive advantages for themselves which lock out the competition, garner insuperable market share, and then develop into monopolistic monoliths. In fact, such corruption is a virtual inevitability, for, when power meets crooked in pursuit of money, thievery and corruption surely follow. Regulators will be bribed; politicians will be bought; the entire system will be turned to suit the needs of one—or a few— on the inside; the free market will disappear in a crony capital big-boy game of *Monopoly* wherein the greedy pigs gorge at the money trough.

Hence, the open vistas of commerce afforded by maximized economic freedom also afford the largest purview for purest greed, if not outright malfeasance. So it was that the notorious Robber Barons arose during the heyday of the early republic, when the Constitution had been least overridden by federal enactments and bureaucrats. And the creation of corporations exacerbated the differential economic power in that

3D *Monopoly* game. To give equal protection to unequal entities is by default to create differential outcomes. There is no metric by which one can expect the legal fiction of a "corporation"—which has no physical embodiment outside law, and thence can take on any size or form, "live" for potentially any length of time, and bring to bear the talents and energies of any number of individual actual persons—to be outworked by one single, hairless bipedal human.

In contrast, the protections afforded to real, human persons under the law exist because human beings need such protections. Indeed, the whole purpose of law is to protect human persons in their inherent nature as free, rational beings who are likewise vulnerable to assault, theft, fraud, and other forms of malign intentional harm. Corporations, in contrast, are entities most in need of restriction, oversight, and regulation. Human beings need freedom, access, and privilege—not so paper fiction corporations made for financial convenience. The creation of corporations and the affordance of privilege to such entities is an affront to the basic fabric of the Republic. Their way must be made harder, for their advantages are legion. Corporations, unless closely controlled and judicially corralled, are an injustice. They are a dangerous legalized fiction which starts the individual citizen two lengths behind in the race of life.

Again, in the boardgame version of *Monopoly*, you scoot around the board collecting properties, charging others rent, and it's all free and fun...until someone builds a back-breaker, a lot so built-up that, when you land on it, it breaks you...your cash, your property, all disappear into their hoard as they grin at you with hungry, gleaming eye. That tipping point, wherein the leader has so much they can buy anything they land on and no one can catch them, spells the practical end of the game. At that point, the game is—in my grandfather's immortal phrase—*"all over but the shouting."* Today, we might call the boardroom version of that game *Corporation*, for that is the form in which the big money game is played today. The moneyed interests are today deep in that final acquisition phase of the swindle, wherein the largest corporations (Blackrock, State Street, Vanguard) roll immense piles of cash from project to project, setting up shell companies and pass-through entities to acquire virtually anything not nailed down, hoovering up entire neighborhoods of houses while middle class Americans shelter their whole family in a minivan...or tent. Fewer and fewer media corporations create the totality of "mainstream" media content, its fare a combination of mind-numbing fast-cut sports, gossipy distraction, and authoritarian psychobabble packaged as "news" to keep the sheep just sufficiently disturbed to stay fearful, but too titillated or confused to take effective action. A handful of monoliths—Amazon, Target, WalMart, and their ilk— siphon off the bulk of the retail trade, funnelling millions towards whatever cause *de jour* most demeans the history and heritage of this nation. We have reached the acquisition-and-consolidation phase of *n*-stage predatory capitalism...the stage right before the cure kills the patient. It is the stage where the People either badass up, or stoop to endless slavery.

Progressivism, Proto-Fascism, and the Age to Come

"Reader, suppose you were an idiot. And suppose you were a member of Congress. But I repeat myself."
— Mark Twain —

Rockefeller, Morgan, Carnegie, Vanderbilt, their partners in grift like the Tammany Hall or Oregon Land Scandal crews, and other suchlike malefactors originating in the Gilded Age made great hay whilst the sun still shone, racking up billions on the back of the penurious day laborers. And when Teddy Roosevelt and the Sherman Anti-Trust Act sought to rein in their depredations, the big boys called in Senator Aldrich and other well-paid politicos to use the newly-codified central power of Washington to their own advantage under the Wilson Administration (of which more, anon).

In the children's story, ole Br'er Rabbit cries out, "Don't throw me in the briar patch!" And, sure enough, poor, dullard Br'er Fox throws that wily rabbit back into his snuggly warren from whence he can never be routed out. In a similar manner, the wily money masters would beg not to be taken before Congress, before rows of well-bribed politicos pitching pre-scripted questions written for them by the financiers' spin teams in order to emit 1,000 page prewritten "blue ribbon" reports which just happen to justify the forthcoming legislation which...Well, Shazam!—while purporting to assuage public doubts and fears by delimiting corruption—will actually both enrich the very plutocrats it purports to punish while likewise empowering the very bureaucrats who mishandled the punishment. It's a homey little farce, played out in legislative halls across the land, but most especially under the resounding rotunda of the U.S. Capital, where the big boys play under big lights for big stakes. That's where sharks wearing four-figure suits practice smiling and smiling and smiling...until they can find where to stick the knife deep in the backs of the guileless public.

In the continual effort to separate fact from fiction at this highest level—Is the President robbing my family? Is the IRS going to starve my kids with these new taxes?—it can be difficult to pick up and follow the petty details of which of your Congresscritters have their snouts most deeply buried in the pork trough. But a continual attention will show that it's far more likely than not that your local politico is knee-deep in the porking...and you ain't in the club.

So, when they come along with whatever brand new, never-before-conceived amazing plan to greenify your planet while slimming your waist and hips...run.

Such a time was the administration of "rough-ridin'" Theodore Roosevelt.

"That we are to stand by the president, right or wrong is not only unpatriotic and servile, but is morally treasonable to the American public."

— Theodore Roosevelt —

A cousin of FDR (about whom, more anon), scion of New York blue bloods, "Teddy" was the first of the Progressivist presidents and, for that reason, probably the least interventionist.

As remarkable, even admirable, a man as Teddy seemed in so many ways, and as ennobling were his remarks in his "Citizenship in a Republic" speech, his legislation seemed largely undertaken with little thought to constitutional or economic aftereffects. He seemed to be all action, no reflection. Again, it is that ability to meld the two traits which enabled Jefferson, Madison, and Jackson to make such headway in the 19th century. The presidents which followed seem rather more challenged to accomplish that fine balance of sound reflection with effective action.

Although his "trust-busting", conservationism, food and drugs legislation were precedent-setting, they were also, by today's standards, relatively mild transgressions of constitutional bounds. And, indeed, at that time, the Republic having been so successful for so long, it seemed easy to think, what is a little tinkering with the Constitution amongst friends? So they did. After all, as Mark Twain quipped: *"There is no distinctly native American criminal class, save Congress."*

As a result, however, of that camel's nose in the tent, ever more constitutional encroachments would follow, so that today, it is not only the banks, but that other arm of predatory capitalist usurpation, the corporation, which the citizen must fight off. The growth of this twin-headed hydra of government-corporate overreach—euphemistically called "public-private partnership" by our mealy-mouthed politicos, but which Mussolini aptly denominated "fascism"—has now become part of the everyday legacy which has shaped the Republic for the last century.

As fine as completely unfettered economic freedom might sound in the abstract, its enactment in reality is a fool's errand, for it simply releases the unchecked passions of some very unseemly misers and actors. Much as we need restrictions on big government within the Constitution, we need bounds on the operations of financial predators. Largely, in both cases, the needful qualities are to be found in the moral precepts set down long ago. Properly inculcated and embodied, there is little need for anything else. Since, however, there will always be those too ambitious in politics and too greedy in finance, we must set clear and definitive bounds, enact and enforce laws of limitation.

Not every tyrant sits on a throne; sometimes they lounge athwart a pot of gold. In either case, they are twisted creatures in need of pushback from the People. Therefore, in the end, some curtailment of economic action must be undertaken in the public sphere. Hence, TR's instincts and the Sherman-Anti-Trust Act are probably closer to the needful approach than either a free-trading globe-roaming unchecked flow of financialization, or a heavily centralized and controlled Soviet system. TR's administration, thus, ushers in the twin dangers which would frame the fight for the next century: fascism's government-corporate duopoly vs. American constitutionalism. In short, the coming struggle would be between the global plutocracy and the American Republic.

Rose Wilder Lane: Little House of Freedom

"And how does a man on this earth get butter? Doesn't the government give butter? But government does not produce food from the earth; Government is guns. It is one common distinction of all civilized peoples, that they give their guns to the Government. Men in Government monopolize the necessary use of force; they are not using their energies productively; they are not milking cows. To get butter, they must use guns; they have nothing else to use."

— Rose Wilder Lane —

One citizen who saw both sides of the American Republic—and so personally presaged the fight to come—was Rose Wilder Lane. Most famous for being young Rose in her mother's *Little House on the Prairie* book series documenting their family's many trials homesteading in and about the Great Plains, she would seek greater adventures at the turn of the century and move to New York City. There, her intellectual bent took her through not only bohemian culture but into the extremes of leftist politics, becoming an avowed Communist during the Red Scare days. Like many of the most diehard of her fellow travellers, the rise of a true Communist state in Russia brightened her young heart, and she eagerly travelled there to experience firsthand the wonders of sovietism writ large.

It was, however, precisely getting to experience Communism firsthand that enabled her to see its limitations and dangers. By the rise of FDR's regime, she had reverted back to her ancestral roots and was looking to build a constitutional restoration as a bulwark against the rising tide of communistic socialism under FDR. She penned many an article and book in defense of libertarian Americanism, warning her fellow citizens of how Roosevelt's administration was at war with the Constitution. As Lane had discovered in speaking with the villagers in the Ukrainian prairie, a nation is too vast a space to run from some urban office. *"It's too big,"* the headman of one multigenerational farm commune told her. Those people had lived simply and successfully as a tight, communal village for centuries, but he saw with acute clarity that a nation cannot be run from a desk at the capital and pretend it is a communal village. For the microdecisions necessarily to maintain economic vibrancy are too manifold and the adverse outcomes of bad decisions too severe to leave such direction to a handful of time servers in a government office. It's too big. Protect the borders, pave the roads, and leave the people alone. Just leave us to do the work, and it will get done.

Even now, a hundred years on, it is not too late to follow Lane's sage advice, awaken from our socialist slumbers, and take back the constitutional cornucopia bequeathed to us.

"But seek first the kingdom of God and His righteousness, and all these things will be added to you."

— Matthew 6:33 —

PART III
UNCONQUERABLE

Chapter 5

10-foot Tall and Bulletproof Badass:

Nation & Unconquerability

As the Pilgrims gained a foothold, they became the subject of attacks from many sides. At long last, it was time to take their stand, for they refused to surrender; they resolved to be unconquerable. Mayflower Chronicles, pp. 331 -332

"{W]e came to this conclusion, that Captain Standish should take so many men, as he thought sufficient to make his party good against all the Indians in the Massachuset bay; and because, (as all men know that have to do with them in that kind,) it is impossible to deal with them upon open defiance, but to take them in such traps as they lay for others...and more fitly take opportunity to revenge the same; but should forbear, if it were possible, till such time as he could make sure [of] Wituwamat, that bloody and bold villain before spoken of; whose head he had order to bring with him, that he might be a warning and terror to all of that disposition."

Unconquerable

MUCH AS THE PILGRIMS HAD to demonstrate unstoppable resolve and defiance to overcome both the wilderness and their enemies, the American Badass develops *unconquerability*, the fortitude to face down any difficulty. This quality is the inevitable outcome of the constant application of the prior two badass qualities. That is, if you are first so thoroughly committed to protecting your freedom that you commit to developing self-reliance, then you must build a master skill set to face down life's many challenges. Your determination to remain free through self-reliant action enables you to overcome first one obstacle, and then another, over and over again. Repeated enough, this ability to engage and overcome manifold difficulties of multiple types becomes an emergent characteristic—*unconquerability*—which enables you to continually face and then overcome numerous challenges.

Unconquerability, then, is mental and emotional gumption, the grit to stay the course through the greatest hardships in order to win the victory. At the start of any project, you may not be sure how, but you know you will find a path. You simply *will* find a way—going under, over, around, or through. Somehow, you will find the way to reach your goal. Practicing this skill of relentless resourcefulness, you eventually reach a state wherein seemingly nothing can stop you from reaching your goal, nothing prevent you from achieving your mission. You attain, in short, badass unconquerablity.

The emergence of that unconquerable strength is what obtained in America as the 20th century opened: a nation bursting with inventive capitalist enterprise, a military strength which could topple even the greatest of enemies with a few years of effort. In short, the nation had emerged as an exemplar colossus of personal freedom and public magnificence. It seemed that the United States could do no wrong.

And that is also exactly where its enemies would lay their greatest trap.

THOMAS PAINE

"It is the duty of the patriot to protect his country from its government."

— Thomas Paine —

Perhaps the most unrelenting and uncompromising of the badass Founders, Thomas Paine embodied an adamantine unconquerability in his burning desire for absolute freedom. Lifelong revolutionary and eternal rebel, Paine continually challenged and reimagined himself in an ever-widening quest for ever more vigorous ways to express and manifest political autonomy. Born in England, Paine's youth was spent scraping together a living first as a tailor, then as a tax collector. A seemingly aimless fellow who happened to have an interest in politics but no real direction, Paine drifted through two marriages and several indifferent careers and business ventures. This seemingly feckless ne'er-do-well's life would change dramatically in 1774, however, when he was introduced to the post-Cockpit revolutionary Benjamin Franklin, a meeting which proved momentous for everyone. In London as unofficial ambassador for the Colonies, Franklin saw potential in this zealous Mr. Paine, and generously gave him passage to America, letters of introduction, and a position as magazine editor—and, by extension, writer—for Franklin's publication, *The Pennsylvania Magazine*.

Once ensconced as editor in Philadelphia, Paine would open his tenure with a bang, immediately turning the magazine's content to his favored political causes: the abolition of slavery, worker's rights, and, most importantly, colonial independence. He would interlard the work of others in the magazine alongside his own lambent pieces, displaying a previously undiscovered talent for polemical broadsides. As a result, the magazine prospered, and Paine seemed to have finally found his calling.

The magazine's success that first year was, however, mere prelude, for Paine's pen was busy at nights on a far bigger project. With the Revolution already alit in Boston by the tumultuous events of 1775, Paine wanted to give energy and impetus to the cause. In January, 1776, he anonymously released the manuscript he had been feverishly scribbling, a revolutionary manifesto which gave force and urgency to the rebellion, called simply *Common Sense*. The 47-page pamphlet proved an immediate sensation, becoming—in today's terms—so viral, that, by head count, 1 of every 4 Americans bought a copy. It was read, talked about, and lionized everywhere. And, a true believer in the cause, Paine donated the proceeds from its sale to the soldiers for the war effort,

Paine's tract gave the *de facto* revolution a plain, clear statement of its purpose, a spur to recruitment, and an argument for its acceptance by indecisive patriots standing on the sidelines. No one can undertake a great task without a great reason: for every great *what*, there must be an even greater *why*. Paine's treatise was, in essence, the work that gave the Colonists their *why*, expressing in clear terms the inchoate feelings roiling in the hearts of so many Americans.

Common Sense begins by describing the natural amity of human society which is corrupted under tyranny: *"Society in every state is a blessing, but government even in its best state is but a necessary evil; in its worst state an intolerable one; for when we suffer, or are exposed to the same miseries by a government, which we might expect in a country without government, our calamity is heightened by reflecting that we furnish the means by which we suffer! Government, like dress, is the badge of lost innocence; the palaces of kings are built on the ruins of the bowers of paradise."*

...and then, outlines the difficulties caused by monarchy: *"There is something exceedingly ridiculous in the composition of monarchy; it first excludes a man from the means of information, yet empowers him to act in cases where the highest judgment is required. The state of a king shuts him from the world, yet the business of a king requires him to know it thoroughly; wherefore the different parts, unnaturally opposing and destroying each other, prove the whole character to be absurd and useless...In the early ages of the world, according to the scripture chronology, there were no kings; the consequence of which was there were no wars; it is the pride of kings which throws mankind into confusion."*

...speaks against the idea of inheritance of power through royal families: *"For all men being originally equals, no one by birth could have the right to set up his own family in perpetual preference to all others forever, and tho' himself might deserve some decent degree of honours of his contemporaries, yet his descendants might be far too unworthy to inherit them...Men who look upon themselves born to reign, and others to obey, soon grow insolent; selected from the rest of mankind their minds are early poisoned by importance; and the world they act in differs so materially from the world at large, that they have but little opportunity of knowing its true interests, and when they succeed to the government are frequently the most ignorant and unfit of any throughout the dominions."*

...notes that, there being an implicit social contract, citizens have no obligation to a government acting contrary to the performance of its primary duty: *"Common sense will tell us, that the power which hath endeavoured to subdue us, is of all others, the most improper to defend us."*

...adds that a people's virtue—moral fiber—is the stuff of which a just and mighty nation is built: *"When we are planning for posterity, we ought to remember that virtue is not hereditary...When I was teaching children I began every day writing this on the blackboard: 'Do to others what you would like them to do to you,' telling them how much better the world would be if everybody lived by this rule."*

...and concludes that a unified American citizenry of such moral stuff is well-nigh insuperable and would create a model and palladium of liberty for the world: *"The cause of America is, in a great measure, the cause of all mankind. Many circumstances have, and will arise, which are not local, but universal, and through which the principles of all lovers of mankind are affected, and in the event of which, their affections are interested. The laying a country desolate with fire and sword, declaring war against the natural*

---

rights of all mankind, and extirpating the defenders thereof from the face of the earth, is the concern of every man to whom nature hath given the power of feeling...It is not in numbers, but in unity, that our great strength lies; yet our present numbers are sufficient to repel the force of all the world...In short, independence is the only bond that can tie and keep us together...Wherefore, instead of gazing at each other with suspicious or doubtful curiosity, let each of us, hold out to his neighbor the hearty hand of friendship, and unite in drawing a line, which, like an act of oblivion, shall bury in forgetfulness every former dissention. Let the names of Whig and Tory be extinct; and let none other be heard among us, than those of a good citizen, an open and resolute friend, and a virtuous supporter of the RIGHTS of MANKIND and of the FREE AND INDEPENDENT STATES OF AMERICA."

Paine's "common sense" appeal to the down-to-earth sensibilities of everyday folk, by codifying much of the general sentiment of colonial America, gave that sentiment an expression whereby it could be explicitly repeated and disseminated—and, indeed, itself became a model for much of the pragmatic, folksy homespun discourse which forevermore characterized effective American political rhetoric. It would become a through line underpinning the populist musings of Mark Twain, William Jennings Bryan, Huey Long, Will Rogers, Ronald Reagan, etc., who exhibited that implicit distrust of the coddled elite while lionizing the consensus wisdom of the general populace. It was a reflection of the democratic impulse which had initiated the Revolution and revivified its inheritors in their expectation of governmental accession to their aims while also underscoring the need for mutual association by the general populace in a kind of reciprocal protection for their common ends.

Throughout the war years, Paine would capitalize upon and amplify the success of *Common Sense* with an ongoing series of pamphlets, *The American Crisis*, which provided political commentary on the revolutionary struggle. The first edition was published during that drear, difficult first year of the war, and

Washington had its rousing encouragements read aloud to the troops: *"These are the times that try men's souls: The summer soldier and the sunshine patriot will, in this crisis, shrink from the service of their country; but he that stands it now, deserves the love and thanks of man and woman. Tyranny, like Hell, is not easily conquered; yet we have this consolation with us, that the harder the conflict, the more glorious the triumph. What we obtain too cheap, we esteem too lightly: it is dearness only that gives every thing its value. Heaven knows how to put a proper price upon its goods; and it would be strange indeed if so celestial an article as freedom should not be highly rated."*

Paine was feted everywhere, and soon found himself a member of the new Continental Congress. Ever the idealist, however, Paine was unafraid to denounce duplicity and self-interest, even amongst his august revolutionary comrades. In the Deane affair, he decried the corrupt profiteering off donations from France by such well-placed members of Congress as John Jay and congressional finance minister Robert Morris. Later, Paine discovered that other members of Congress—including such Virginia luminaries as Washington, Jefferson, Madison, and Lee—expected to retain, after the Revolution, huge tracts of land granted to them by the Crown. In response, he wrote a pamphlet, *The Public Good*, exposing the plan and argued that such lands should be used for the general benefit of all the people, not select individuals. In both these cases, he was initially vilified, even physically attacked, yet eventually vindicated—but as a result of such relentless pursuit of democratic justice, he wound up unpopular, isolated, and often penurious.

In part to escape the political and personal fallout from such controversies, Paine cajoled Congress into sending him on a mission to France in 1781, at the height of the revolutionary war. Just a few months later, he returned triumphant with over 2 million *livres* in silver coin, and a promise of another 8 million from the French king. The members of Congress, always short of funding for the Revolution, were elated. When General Washington generously moved that Congress remunerate Paine for his efforts, the cash-strapped idealist balked. Despite his circumstances, he objected to setting a precedent of taking payment for service to the Revolution.

Ever the restless revolutionary and absolutist in defense of individual rights, Paine would later join with the Anti-Federalists in 1787 during the fight to ensure the original bare-bones Constitution added the Bill of Rights. Then, in 1790, hearing news of the burgeoning citizen disquiet in France, he promptly emigrated, seeking always to be in the place of the greatest revolutionary foment. As was his wont, there he penned another landmark polemic, *The Rights of Man,* both as apologia for the French revolutionist cause and also as a universal broadside against extant political conventions like monarchies. This work, like *Common Sense,* proved immensely popular; his words galvanized the Frankish revolutionaries much as they had in America, and won him such acclaim that he was bestowed with honorary French citizenship. Naturally, the pamphlet also got him convicted in absentia in Britain of libel and sedition.

To avoid British censure, Paine made common cause with the French. He broadened his writing, releasing *The Age of Reason* in 1794, a foray into theology, espousing his Deist notions of free thought, including some rather sharp critiques of Christianity. He would follow that with the equally impolitic move of publishing an open letter attacking George Washington for military and political incompetence and personally as a man of questionable character. Eventually, his uncompromising public critiques also got him arrested and imprisoned even by the French revolutionary government, where he escaped beheading by only the merest luck, the chalk mark on his cell which should have marked him for beheading being obscured. Finally, in the early 1800s, Paine would escape the turmoil of French politics, returning once more to America, but—having alienated much of the populace with his more radical publications over the preceding decade—he found himself increasingly isolated and eventually died with little fanfare, largely ignored and forgotten, a mere handful of people attending his funeral.

Unrelenting and unrepentant to the end, Paine's

unwavering quest for unalloyed freedom for humankind never slackened. Opinion-shaper in two of history's watershed revolutions, he won the personal acquaintance of perhaps the two most famous political leaders of his age—George Washington and Napoleon Bonaparte—and had the temerity and honesty to publicly disparage both. Without the politesse or avidity to make himself a worldly success, Paine nevertheless seeded the world with ideas which shape political thought to this day. As the people of these united States of America entered the 20th century, they would face a set of challenges which would call for much the kind of unconquerable mettle Paine embodied.

Heroic or Hedonic
"A nation of sheep will beget a government of wolves."
— Edward R. Murrow —

As one reaches the stage of emergent unconquerability, one would seem predestined to ultimate victory. After all, you have moved past having mere love of liberty and practical self-reliance, to now have the ability to so thoroughly apply your capacities that it seems you almost cannot be stopped. And that is nearly true: an unconquerable spirit leaves you basically insuperable...except by one person: yourself. The challenge of the unconquerable stage is whether one continues in the discipline of selfless magnanimity, or succumbs to the temptation to self-indulgence on the fruits of one's conquests. The twentieth century is when the American people were led from their Puritanical Pilgrim's roots shaped around heroic ideals, to the sybaritic siren's song of sensuality; it was a century of ever-accelerating devolution from disciplined liberty towards those ever-entwined vices: barbarism and authoritarianism. For, an immoral and feckless people—lawless in their own lives—will soon surrender themselves to a lawless government which seeks power first and foremost. Material largesse and indulgence often lead to moral debasement and debauchery, wherein people give themselves over to a kind of

165

materialism which makes mere passing sensual pleasures their highest goal. Thus in the 20th century, as America amassed a material magnificence of towering cities and economic abundance—just as it seemed to be master of its own destiny and fitted to be a light and mercy to the nations—it would face its greatest challenge. For those malign forces who seek to overturn freedom and independence for their own purposes recognized that, while this Republic was truly too mighty to be conquered from without, it may well be destroyed...from within...by itself.

A nation and its people are oriented in one of two directions, either towards the heroic or the hedonic. The heroic mindset is stoic and sacrificial, the hedonic sensual and selfish. Societies will tend to lionize in art and word, act and song, one or the other of these life orientations and, indeed, over the life cycle of a people, may well shift back and forth between the two. In the classic formulation delivered in Plato's *Republic* (Book VIII) cultures often pass through a four part supercycle, devolving from the heroic to the hedonic. Such a society is initially shaped around heroic ideals, a vision of the self-disciplined traits exemplified by a noble, aristocratic class; then, in the succeeding generations, we may find that its people, while still seeking public honor and acclaim, become more enamored of money than honor, evincing a mere superficial pretense of nobility while actually pursuing opulence; their descendents, in turn, may then devolve into an ethos of using that wealth to seek pleasure in an era of self-indulgence and profligacy under pure democracy; in its fourth and final phase, such a people will finally succumb to an age of tyranny which inevitably follows as—having lost the moral foundations of restraint and self-control—the lawless, shiftless multitudes seek the external control of a political strongman to herd their wayward instincts.

Plato is not alone is seeing such archetypal transitions in cultural history. In contemporary literature, Strauss and Howe posit a loosely analogous four-stage cycle which they contend has been revealed over the course of the last 300 years in the history of this nation. While their characterization of this supercycle differs in several points from the Platonic model, it nonetheless follows a similar quadratic stepwise descent from a cultural "high" which may be envisioned as a heroic ideal which reverses and is supplanted by a moribund, unmoored, and self-critical culture, eventually initiating the need to found another cycle around a new set of core heroic principles. We may, then, take this schema as a kind of generalized cultural archetype from initiation of "heroic" ideals, followed by devolution to introspection, indirection, anomie, and eventual recrudescence. Broadly, this crude framework has been codified by the catch phrase: "Strong men make good times; good times make weak men; weak men make bad times; bad times make strong men...strong men make good times, etc."

Applied to the American experience in broad historical terms, then, the revolutionary generation who froze at Valley Forge would make possible the expansion of the nation through the West and its debt-free resurgence under Jackson, much as the internecine horrors wrought by the heroes of the Civil War in pursuit of the ideal of Emancipation would make possible decades of unparalleled prosperity in the Gilded Age. The simple psychological truth that early badass generations produce a plenitude which enables their descendents to wantonly indulge seems well-nigh unassailable, and should lead us to reflect on the underlying causes of the social changes seen over the last 100 years of the American Republic. For, having clawed by long effort to the upper echelons of abundance, it would be all-too-common and all-too-deplorable for America to devolve into indulgent materialism, sloth, and indebtedness.

But, beyond Puritanical finger-wagging at the human predilection to cultural degeneration and profligacy, lies a larger, more insidious possibility. What if malignant persons or organizations looked to exacerbate the phenomenon, mayhap giving an encouraging push "off the cliff" to the wastrel inheritor generations? What if this pattern of social devolution has, in fact, been studied, codified, and weaponized by super-political (i.e. global moneyed) persons who seek the maximum control over the greatest number of people? Such malign forces would look for means and opportunities to warp the inheritor generations into

167

their least virtuous and therefore most malleable form. In seeking to shape an authoritarian America, the conspirators-for-corruption would foment and exacerbate the people's worst tendencies towards anomie and helplessness—even going so far as to artificially generate self-indulgent and self-destructive habits if these were not happening naturally. Such a plan would see the initial American heroism of the 20th century first spectacularly triumphant...and then turned disastrously destructive. When misdirected like that, maximum badass devolves into mere bad acts. And when your enemy is a skilful manipulator of information and perception, you may find yourself working exactly to your own detriment, using you finest skills and capacities to undermine those persons and polities most precious to you. As the American people were called to heroism in battlefields again and again...and always answered the call, they would also be seductively wooed by the siren's enticement to both hedonism and authoritarianism, which sung louder and longer as the century wore on. But the groundwork of this struggle was, once again, laid in the halls of high finance, where the war over money would shape people's actions and expectations. Thus, as we trace the history of the surface, heroic movements of social and political forces over the last century, note how they are interwoven with the coils of the strangling moneyed python wrapping ever tighter around the citizenry's neck.

And this is how it happened:

The Bankers War, Round 3: Mr. Wilson's Opening Betrayal

"The government, which was designed for the people, has got into the hands of the bosses and their employers, the special interests. An invisible empire has been set up above the forms of democracy."

— Woodrow Wilson —

While previous presidents had their moments of constitutional indiscretion, Woodrow Wilson would prove to be the president who perhaps most decisively took a hatchet to the Constitution. Everyone should have seen Wilson coming, but they seemed to have thought him just an effete intellectual rube from the halls of academia. In fact, however, he was an immensely ambitious authoritarian with boundless political aspirations. Wilson's earlier work presaged the autocratic timbre with would mark his administration of the Republic as standard-bearer for the Progressive movement. His PhD thesis, "Congressional Governments: A Study in American Politics," advocated modifying the American presidency, adopting instead a more powerful executive model, akin to the British Prime Minister. Later, as reformist president of Princeton University, his ubiquitous radical rearrangements across the institution, from curricula and dormitories, to eating arrangements and observances of faith—while admittedly raising academic standards—also raised the ire of students, alumni, and faculty alike. Then, when he ran for governor of New Jersey in 1910, he pledged he would prove an *"unconstitutional governor,"* and, true to his word, he continued with his signature single-mindedly Progressive and autocratic approach which had made him so unpopular at Princeton. Thus, when the Republicans fumbled the election of 1912 by splitting their base's vote between Taft and Teddy Roosevelt's "Bull Moose" third party, Wilson's election by a thin plurality would usher in an unprecedented age of executive activism by his White House.

In foreign affairs, Wilson undertook continual raids, incursions, and invasions in Mexico, Haiti, and the Dominican Republic, culminating in the watershed entry of the US into the First World War in 1917. He justified America's greatest overseas undertaking to date as embarking on a *"war to end all wars"* which would make the world *"safe for democracy,"* even when our first president had warned against such *"foreign entanglements,"* and when this nation itself is, in fact, explicitly and purposefully not a democracy, but a constitutional republic.

As the emergency of war is always the most ready cloak for tyranny, Wilson paired his international adventuring with domestic oppression. He rammed through the most far-ranging and extensive set of anti-constitutional enactments yet attempted by a president. First, to assure that all American citizens maintained a proper degree of enthusiasm for his overseas crusade, Wilson's administration bloated the interior security forces of the United States to both suppress speech and disseminate propaganda. The Committee for Public Information was created as a federal propaganda ministry dedicated to ginning up war fever to override the initially reticent, isolationist instincts of the American public. With guidance and direction from Britain's "Wellington House" propaganda unit—directed by "change agents" Edward Bernays and Walter Lippmann, both of whom advocated for the "manufacture of consent" of the masses under direction of a technocratic elite—the American people's consent for war was manufactured by the use of bald-faced lies and childish imagery. The electorate were subjected to garish renderings of rabid, blood-drenched baboons in Germanic *Pickelhaube* helmets assailing helpless maidens; these were emblazoned with such captions as "Destroy the Mad Brute" and warnings of the murderous intentions of the Kaiser, that "Butcher of Berlin;" such images were paired with lurid stories about infants' arms being cut off and Belgian maidens being raped by endless lines of "Huns;" all such depictions were offered as if they somehow encapsulated the character of the people who gave the world Mozart, Einstein, Goethe, and Albert Schweitzer. Dubious about these reports, famed defense attorney Clarence Darrow personally travelled throughout France and Belgium in 1915, offering a cash reward to anyone who could substantiate any of the dramatic tales of German atrocities. Not one person came forward to provide evidence of the purported amputations, rapes, and bayoneted babies which were used to emotionally rile Americans (and Brits) against the German people. And, somehow, the files of alleged eyewitness testimony on the atrocities (the *Bryce Report*) which fueled the Administration's war fury were all "lost" after the war, preventing any historian from going back to settle the matter. Ain't that some amazing bad luck?

Not content with febrile propaganda, Wilson's administration nationalized control of the railroad, telephone, shipping, and food production industries. Then, they instituted a broad suspension of civil liberties, most especially the 1st and 4th Amendments. Newspapers were censored, or forcibly closed down. Mail was intercepted and censored. Protests and speeches in criticism of the government became criminalized; over a thousand people were jailed for exercising their right to proclaim their views. Famed union organizer Eugene Debs, for instance, was jailed for 10 years for daring to publicly voice his opposition to the war. Both the Army and Justice Departments set up internal investigation units, spying on thousands of Americans whose sympathies were deemed untrustworthy. And to underscore the point, the so-called Justice Department created a cadre of 250,000 roughneck vigilantes—the American Protective League—to patrol the streets making citizen's arrests of anyone not carrying a draft card...or simply giving a beat down to anyone speaking out against the war.

Thus, Wilson's first step in making the world "safe for democracy" was to turn America into a police state. After all, doesn't the end justify the means? But here's the catch: democracy is never safe. The Founders specifically sought to prevent pure democracy in these united American States. We are guaranteed a *republican* form of government, under the rule of law (like those 1st and 4th Amendments which Wilson abrogated). We are not to be ruled by a mob "democratically" voting for whatever they happen to want that day. Perhaps this was the source of the apocryphal tale which holds that, when Wilson was asked why he kept a herd of sheep on the White House lawn, he answered, *"Because they remind me of the American people."*

But it was not only on these issues that Wilson's policies undermined the Republic. His most destructive and long-lasting assault on American liberty was not herding the American sheep, but shepherding in the creation of the Federal Reserve. Amazingly, the man who let down the drawbridge to the American castle, would also, in this book *The New Freedom* (1913), pull back the curtain on the hushed halls of power: *"Since I entered politics, I have chiefly had men's views confided to me privately. Some of the biggest men in the United States, in the field of commerce and manufacture are afraid of somebody, are afraid of something. They know that there is a power somewhere so organized, so subtle, so watchful, so interlocked, so complete, so pervasive, that they better not speak above their breath when they speak in condemnation of it."*

On the matter of monetary policy and taxes, Wilson was the president who completely revolutionized and inverted America's long-standing, proven monetary and fiscal system. His innovations—which turned the economy into a controlled banker's plaything, in dark partnership with government—were instituted along two lines. First, on the pretext of the great risk to the public caused by the market "panic" back in 1907, his administration worked with Senator Aldrich and—according to the written confessions of participants like Paul Warburg and other representatives of political and banking concerns who participated—advanced a plan for creating a third national bank, to be called the Federal Reserve. Commonly referred to as the Federal Reserve Bank, this institution is neither a *federal* agency, nor holds *reserves* of any true money, nor is a *bank* in any proper sense. Rather, this financial monstrosity is owned and beholden to undisclosed foreign investors who serve the interests of the plutocracy, i.e. it allows the people with all the money to control all the People's money. The second, complementary piece of financialized theft of this Fed plan was upending the tax system. Rather than the proven constitutional and freedom-preserving paradigm of using import, export, and excise taxes to fund a small federal work force while leaving the People alone in their economic activity, Wilson destroyed the long-standing protective tariffs which enabled the American middle class to work, invest, and save freely, unfettered by internal taxation; instead, Wilson instituted a direct tax on the income of every American. For the first time in our nation's history, the entire populace would pass into direct indentured servitude to the Fedgov, i.e. some portion of the People's daily labor would be skimmed off by taxation. Such taxation served primarily to recycle back out of circulation the excess money printed by the Fed creature, thereby allowing the Fed "Bank" and FedGov to emit phony money far more freely, for they would get first use of all that new money but also be able to mute the ensuing inflation caused thereby by siphoning off the excess scrip on the back end—in essence, stealing it back via taxation to use it again! Plus, the plan added two extra bonuses: first, it gave the banksters an override of everyone's earnings every time the citizens used their ever-inflating, ever-more-worthless currency; second, it gave Fedgov an excuse to send out tax forms demanding details of the personal financial affairs of millions of private citizens. And they did all this while promising to never levy a federal income tax exceeding 10%...Scout's honor...Fedgov super-safe ultra-promise...income tax never above 10%...right?

Under the weight of Wilson's multidimensional assault, the American ship of state, that stately republic of freedom, would be deeply wounded—its magnificent lineaments blasted and blown asunder by a vainglorious autocrat—and beginning to sink. There would be a short respite during the next decade under the Coolidge administration, before the era of depression and war under FDR irrevocably cracked the hull.

The Quietest American

"There is no substitute for a militant freedom. The only alternative is submission and slavery."

— Calvin Coolidge —

Calvin Coolidge took a habitual reticence and caution which he learned growing up the in the tiny hamlet of Plymouth Notch, Vermont, and molded them into a kind of *laissez faire* libertarian statesmanship which is, in its way, a parallel of the Chinese Taoist sage, i.e. that fellow who wins through *wu wei*, a kind of action which succeeds through inaction, a "way" of doing by least doing. This hands-off approach, rather than limiting his efficacy, seems to have made him the single most successful president of the first half of the 20th century. Called "Silent Cal" for his laconic parsimony with words, one story has a Washington dowager—seated beside him at a Washington fete—confess she has a bet on that she can get him to speak more than two words at dinner, to which he replied, *"You lose."* Though no man to waste words, Coolidge was, ironically, both an accomplished and effective public speaker...and an equally adept essayist whose reflections on current events were eagerly sought for newspaper columns after his retirement.

Coolidge began his career as a young lawyer with political ambitions in Massachusetts, moving successively from city councilman, to state legislature, to governor of the state. His policies were, by today's standards, a progressive republicanism. He would support and enact increasing teachers' salaries, building rail lines, and limiting the work week for women and children. But he would also veto bills to increase legislators' salaries and continually trim budgets and protect individual liberties. He felt, *"it is much more important to kill bad bills than to pass good ones."*

Tapped to run for vice president under Warren G. Harding in 1920, he reached the presidency when a fatal apoplexy in 1923 took the life of the feckless and amoral Harding. Roused at 2 a.m. whilst vacationing at his father's home, Coolidge was immediately sworn in under kerosene lamp by his father, a notary public, and immediately inherited the chaos of a mismanaged and corrupt administration. Once installed, Coolidge acted quickly to send out investigators who unearthed and prosecuted the numerous tendrils of graft, bribery, kickbacks, embezzlement, and other forms of white collar malfeasance woven by the members of Harding's ill-chosen cabinet. Due to Coolidge's swift, concerted response, several members of Harding's team would be arrested, tried, and jailed. That handled, Coolidge set about the serious task of turning the federal government back onto a more constitutional course after the Wilson years, which meant trimming its size, scope, and functions. On general matters of policy, Coolidge would seek to restore a government that would do far less *for*—and thus take less far *from*—the American people. As he said, *"I am for economy in government—not to save money, but to save people."*

In the 1800s, it had been several Democrat presidents—Jefferson, Madison, Monroe, Jackson, Polk—who tamed the federal beast and gave more money back to the people. In the 1900s, it would be the Republicans who took up the cause of limiting the spendthrift and interventionist ways of profligate Democrats. When

Coolidge entered the presidency, the Fedgov budget was $3.1 billion; when he left seven years later, it was $2.9 billion. Calvin Coolidge was not only a president who cut the size of government; he was, now a full century on, the *last* American president to cut the size of government. As he cautioned, *"Government extravagance is not only contrary to the whole teaching of our Constitution, but violates the fundamental conceptions and the very genius of American institutions."*

Emblematic of his economic approach, when Coolidge was sent the gift of twin lion cubs from South Africa by the mayor of Johannesburg, he named one "Tax Reduction" and the other "Budget Bureau." It was government thrift and forbearance, both on the getting of money (tax) side *and* on the spending of money (budget) side which enabled him to corral the federal leviathan and leave the people free to save, invest, and grow their wealth. Over his tenure, Coolidge either shrunk or kept the annual budget flat while, at the same time, slashing the tax rate. When he took office, the tax rate in the top bracket was already at a whopping 58%; he slashed that rate in half, introducing what he called "scientific taxation." His plan was merely implementing the universal economic principle discussed earlier—known by the cognoscenti as the Laffer Curve—that lowering taxes actually raises tax revenue. This simple truth seems difficult for most politicians to accept, yet the mechanics are easy to understand: the more money people have in hand to invest means the more the economy grows; thus less government taxation produces a far bigger money pie from which people (and government) can take a slice.

At the same time Coolidge was reducing income taxes, he was also restoring tariffs, since those were the taxes initially envisioned as the backbone for Fedgov payroll. Because he was simultaneously shrinking the budget while his tax reductions increased revenues, he also continually produced a federal surplus. He used that surplus to pay down over 25% of the debt from Mr. Wilson's war. He held weekly early morning budget meetings to go over the Fedgov books, doing the heavy lifting of doing line-by-line economizing on matters large and small: reducing the size of the Navy's fleet, saving $50,000 a year simply by having the Postal

Service carry mail in plain grey canvas bags (rather than the previous bleached-white ones bearing a snazzy blue stripe), and even asking his White House cook to cut back on her menus, and, when she indeed reduced her annual budget—by federal standards, a rather modest $2,000—also taking the time to send her a note of thanks and encouragement. In other words, Coolidge succeeded by personally attending to all the dreary details and the simple principle of restoring proper constitutional governance, which thereby returned the country to its original economic model: freedom at home, taxation at the border, and proper husbandry of the national budget.

As a result, the country as a whole averaged a continual, steady economic growth of 3.5% year after year throughout his term. This was the basis upon which the bustling prosperity got Coolidge's era denominated as the "Roaring 20s." Again, nothing in life is static. An economy—and thus its money supply—is either inflating or deflating. Inflation rewards (and so induces) speculation, profligacy, short-term spending, short-term thinking, and risk. Deflation rewards (and so induces) savings, thrift, long-term investment planning, and safety. You either grow the Fed's money supply, or you grow the economy; you don't grow both. For Coolidge, money and its proper management was a matter of personal responsibility: you are either avoiding responsibility, or taking it on. In this regard, he said, *"Inflation is repudiation; deflation is assumption"* of fiscal responsibility. He sought to at least avoid inflation by minimizing expenditures from the national checkbook. As he put it, *"It is our theory that the people own the government, not that the government should own the people."*

Coolidge was, however, no mere miser. During the awkward interregnum after Harding's death, before the White House was ready for Coolidge to move in for his presidency, he and First Lady Grace were staying at the Willard Hotel. Early one morning, Coolidge awakened to find a young fellow standing in the room, rifling through his clothing, holding the president's wallet, a gold watch chain, and a small charm. *"I wish you wouldn't take that,"* Coolidge said mildly to the startled thief, indicating the personalized charm. The young man looked down and read the inscription—a gift to Coolidge from the "Massachusetts General Court"—and, palling in terror, stammered that he was a guest, short of cash to pay his tab and trying to return home. Coolidge, without missing a beat, offered to "loan" the thief the $32 in the wallet, and even told the fellow which route to take out of the room to avoid being arrested by the secret service guards outside. That was the calm, sense of proportion, humility, and grace which gave Coolidge his unassuming style of badass.

On broader matters of foreign and public policy, Coolidge was equally reticent to interfere and intervene. He avoided "foreign entanglements" by pulling the United States out of Wilson's pet project, the internationalist-run League of Nations. He sought no new wars, interventions, or invasions anywhere. He withdrew the troops from the Dominican Republic and made an abortive attempt to withdraw them from Nicaragua, but relented when the resultant power vacuum only produced chaos, making matters worse.

He was, thus, libertarian in principle but not thereby against all forms of government action. He strenuously advocated for cases he deemed justified and necessary. Thus, he readily signed a law giving full citizenship to Native Americans. He likewise lobbied for equal legal protections for African Americans, whose rights were, he said, *"just as sacred as those of any other citizen."* He therefore repeatedly proposed nationwide anti-lynching laws, which, however, Congress resisted. In sum, he advocated no wars, no interventions, while balancing budgets and reducing the size and scope of the federal government.

His administration was, in fact, simply the application of constitutional restraint, and, per usual, it worked. The country was peaceful, prosperous, and well-managed. In many ways, the self-discipline which Coolidge imposed upon the government (and people) was simply the gentle art of saying "No." And, as president, he seems to have developed his own, elegant kind of Taoist "non-doing" to deliver his denials to his petitioners. In 1929, as he was ushering incoming president Herbert Hoover to the White House, he explained his approach: *"As president, you have to stand every day for three to four hours to meet all sorts of visitors. Nine-tenths of them want something they ought not to have. If you keep dead-still they will run down in three minutes or less. If you even cough or smile they will start all over again."*

That was how our country's best do-nothing president explained his method of saying "No" by way of quiet, respectful *wu-wei* which saved everyone's dignity and the national treasury at the same time. Calvin Coolidge: America's semi-Taoist badass.

This short hiatus of constitutionalism amidst the galloping Progressivism of the age allowed the economy to flourish. At the same time, the very freedom afforded the people became extremely fertile ground upon which the scrip scam of Federal Reserve Notes could frolic. As Coolidge kept Washington under control, the Fed continued to float its worthless scrip throughout the land, which eventually made its every policy whim epochal for the American economy, as would become evident when economic depression took hold of the nation.

The Great Destruction

"The Great Depression was not accidental; it was a carefully contrived occurrence. The international Bankers sought to bring about a condition of despair here so that they might emerge as rulers of us all."
— Louis McFadden, Chairman,
    House Committee on Banking and Currency —

In the autumn of 1929, during the ensuing Hoover administration, the stock market fell in a "crash" that took off nearly half its value in just two months. Incoming President Hoover initially followed in the footsteps of his predecessors, and could have done a fine job of nothing—as had been done with great success in the downturn of 1920-1921 which then led to a quick recovery...a story which would recur in 1987, when Reagan did a whole lotta nothing as the market first crashed, then slowed, and finally reversed upward, fixing the crash and unemployment all by itself.

But Hoover, a long time Fedgov functionary, decided instead to dither and diddle. For long months, while Hoover dawdled, the pundits in the newspapers squawked that someone needed to "do something!" Naturally, the economy was beginning to recover on its own. But, with the 1931 election season looming and an uptick in bank runs, Hoover was finally goaded into beginning to goose the nation with fancy Washington programs. His fumbling undertakings would actually undermine confidence and stability, but it would take a full-bore government assault to turn a market dip and a couple banks runs into a full-on Great Depression, and, for that, you needed someone like FDR. But before we get to FDR, let's take a moment to look at bank runs.

Full Reserve Banking

"Those that think banks and governments are making them poor haven't seen the whole picture. Poverty is the act of trusting their system."
— Robin Sacredfire —

It's that famous scene from Frank Capra's classic *It's a Wonderful Life*: there's that swell fella, Jimmy Stewart, explaining to the crowd gathered around him at the good, ole Saving-and-Loan that your money's in Joe's house, and you can't be wanting your money back from poor, downtrodden Joe, now could you? After Wilson's Federal Reserve got hold of the money printing press, and FDR got hold of the government ledger book, there would be many "runs" on banks just like that, such runs being one of the immediate outcomes of economic hard times.

But here's the thing: if times are hard, heck yes, you want your money, Jimmy Stewart or no Jimmy Stewart. When you're out of work, of course you might look to get some of your money back from the bank, maybe *all* of your money back. After all, you trusted them with *all* of your money, so you might just want *all* of that money handed back to you, thank you very much. As great as that film may be otherwise, don't let Messrs Stewart and Capra gaslight you. If it's your money, you should get it back. In fact, maybe you should do it today, and set your financing up via alternative solutions. You may, for instance, note the fact that—codified in all that paperwork they make you sign—any money you deposit with a US bank is now, by law, *their* money. You have, by their legal gamesmanship, not deposited property with them for custodial safekeeping; instead, you have forfeited your ownership by converting your simple deposit into an unsecured *loan*. That means, if they go broke, tough; if the Fedgov decides to give you a "haircut" by stealing half the money from your account, tough; if they decide to lock it up because they don't want you to buy from that website they don't like, tough. Unless your banker happens to be Jimmy Stewart and you really do trust him that much, you might want to read all that fine print.

The simple fact is that, while the cause of bank runs may be downturns, the danger from them is caused not by the normal, rational act of people taking their property back, but by the ongoing grift called "fractional reserve" banking. When you deposit your money, did you tell them to "reserve" only a "fraction" of it in the vault, and take the rest out to speculate in real estate on Joe's house? Did you authorize them to use your money to go gambling in the stock market, commercial real estate, or the even wilder derivatives markets? Or did you have, maybe, a good faith expectation that, when you show up next week and want every penny of what it shows on your account statement, that they would happily return every penny of what that statement says they have "reserved" for you? Maybe the "reserve" part of banking should be them reserving your money in the back for you in case you need it, and the "trust" part of their name should mean you can trust it will be there when you come to pick it up.

But the sly practice—commonplace but conniving—of taking in *all* their depositors' money but reserving only 10% (or less!) in cash, means that banks go hog wild speculating the minute the depositor walks out the door. Then, when a slowdown makes it time for them to pay the piper, they have the audacity to blame the victim: how dare you be anxious and worried; how dare you be fearful and desirous to get your money back; how dare you doubt the bank and want to cash out! How dare you "run" to the bank for the money you gave them, the money that their "statement" promises is there! The truth is, they are the fearful, anxious ones, because they know they are skating on thin ice, since they know the day more than 10% of the people show up looking for their money, the bank will fold. They are simply using their depositors' money to hide a fancy Ponzi scheme behind some gleaming furniture and potted plants.

Instead of such grift, let's imagine a *full reserve* bank. The full reserve bank would be an actual repository of depositor wealth. When you put your cash in there, it stays on deposit, secured and insured. This bank understands its fiduciary duty is to safeguard deposits so that—regardless of external events—its customers may rest assured in the knowledge their funds are fully and freely available. There would be no need for bank runs at a full reserve bank. Oh sure, at times things might go bad, and Mary Smith might show up demanding all $250,000 of her funds. So the tellers would dutifully count it all out, and Mary can lug it all home in a suitcase (with help from her eager, young nephew hoping for his cut) and tuck them under her best mattress. But, in all likelihood, a week later, she would begin wondering why she has all her savings sitting under a lumpy mattress, when she could have them behind a foot of steel in a vault...and then sheepishly return them...to a *full* reserve bank.

Now, being libertarian-minded folks, we need not legislate that all banks become full reserve, just transparent about their practices. The different types of banks can compete, some full reserve, some fractional. The fractional reserve banks can say "Look, how often will you really need *all* of your money? With us, I can give you free checking and savings, no fees, and maybe a dividend with the money I make on all my can't-lose speculation." The full reserve bank would have to prioritize customer service and a greater sense of security, and may even have to charge fees to make it profitable. They may provide other concierge services, perhaps a wealth and investment management department, but always with the promise that, "We will be there with your full funds when you most need us." Those banks which simply keep a just, sure accounting and indeed keep your funds safe in their vault, need never fear a "run" on their vaults. The day Mary Smith comes to take all her money out, her withdrawl would be the same as so many other transactions, simply somewhat larger. As long as the banking consumer knows what kind of bank they are working with, we can allow the free market to allow these types of banks to compete, to show which lasts over the long run, which bank the citizens actually prefer. Mary can then decide for herself which type of bank she most needs. But at least a full reserve bank would be available. That way, banks might actually earn the "trust" they so proudly emblazon on their marquees.

FDR's New Steal

"This and no other is the root from which a tyrant springs; when he first appears he is a protector."

— Plato —

FDR was a fellow with exemplary bravado, immense self-regard...and a boundless disregard for the Constitution. Like Wilson, FDR came to the presidency having first practiced the art of authoritarianism by decree while governor and had also forthrightly presaged his approach from the beginning. In his inaugural address, FDR openly vowed to undertake a program of *"bold, persistent experimentation."* Experimentation may be a fine thing in scientific investigation, and even perhaps in testing modes of enacting liberty, but it is surely not needful if, as was FDR's wont, your core pursuit is centralized authoritarianism. And he would, indeed, follow in that Wilsonian tradition of ruling by personal fiat. During his reign, FDR would enact the most Executive Orders (i.e. presidential decrees) of any chief executive by far, 3,728 in total. In other words, over the tenure of his regime, all by himself, FDR and his pen made approximately one new law every day for over a decade.

There are enormous ironies when one examines the immense gulf between such actions and the conventional reputation of FDR (in *Time* magazine's evaluation of the "Person of the Century," for instance, he was barely edged out of first place by Einstein). First, there is the little matter of the Depression and its economic "emergency" which FDR invoked to justify his progressive steamrolling of longstanding pragmatic, effective, and constitutional norms. The initial shock of the stock market Panic of 1929 under Hoover did indeed induce an unemployment rate as high as 9%. However, in the months preceding FDR's election, unemployment was beginning to reverse, reaching its low of 6% just as Hoover, goaded by his critics, began federal intervention. Hoover's "recovery" acts almost immediately slowed the economy and shot unemployment back towards double digits. Thus, FDR did not take over a Fedgov which was following the Coolidge-Harding *laissez faire* approach which had successfully reversed the 1920-21 downturn and thereby created the Roaring Twenties. FDR, rather, took over a Fedgov which was already being steered the wrong way; he simply pushed the socialist pedal to the metal.

His first act was a strongarm closure of all the banks—which he gave the endearing sobriquet of a "holiday"—to stop bank runs. A month later, he followed with an illegal executive order to steal everyone's gold, requiring all citizens to hand their gold to the government (except for keeping your jewellery and a small cache of up to $200 of "monetary" gold); when federal judges properly vacated these illegal acts over the following months, FDR had Congress pass legislation to clean up his handiwork and then sent federal investigators swarming out to seize gold from safety deposit boxes and set up undercover sting operations to entrap citizens still holding gold. At the same time, gold was remonetized from $20 to $35 per troy ounce. By boosting gold's price per ounce, the value of the dollar was being reduced; this revaluation of gold was, in reality, a devaluation of each citizen's dollar by about 40%. It was, in effect, the largest bank robbery of all time, since the citizens had (a) all the gold taken from the safety deposit boxes and (b) the value of their savings slashed by nearly half overnight. And that was just the opening salvo of FDR's great, new "deal" for everyone.

For their part, the banking boys at the Fed immediately cranked up the printing presses to maximum, flooding the economy with phony notes, to balance out FDR's revaluation. All this financialized flim-flam from the Fed and Fedgov produced *numerical* changes in reported "economic activity" and continual, ongoing inflation, as opposed to the previous state of approximately10% annual deflation since the '29 Crash. Indeed, from the moment of FDR's ascendency, the Fed began flooding the economy with cash, boosting the M2 money supply at a scorching average of 12% per year, an inflationary, currency-vaporizing rate rarely matched until the hyperinflationary 2000s. Again, as discussed above, why does the Fed, whose job is ostensibly "stability," single-mindedly pursue inflation, when deflation offers so many correctives? Admittedly, in the short term, deflation entails some credit contraction, which means weak businesses will fail as they cannot pay on their loans, but in the long run pensioners, savers, and profitable businesses prosper. In a free coin economy, metal producers will make up the balance soon enough. And no one gets to manipulate the economy from back rooms through uncontrolled issue of no-value scrip to whomever they wish. But, as the nation was already taking a first step toward renouncing gold, silver and sound money, FDR et al. would continue on a Keyesian/Modern Monetary Theory approach in which they presume the issuance of currency can continue essentially infinitely (although they do generally consider it good form to keep inflationary money growth to "low and slow" single digit rate per annum, lest they rile the peasantry).

FDR's next step was—on the pretense of creating an economy by putting the peasants to work on large-scale Fedgov projects with all that funny money—to create alphabet agencies a-plenty: the Civilian Conservation Corps (CCC), Civil Works Administration (CWA), National Industrial Recovery Act (NIRA), Public Works Administration (PWA), Works Progress Administration (WPA), etc., etc. When the Supreme Court balked at the illegitimacy of such enactments (none of which are granted in Article I, Section 8), FDR, rather than sheepishly apologizing for overstepping the bounds of good sense demonstrated by 150 years of successful governance, played hardball. Overriding any notion of separation of powers, FDR accreted all power to himself by threatening to "pack" the court with four more hand-chosen cronies of his choosing unless the Court rubber-stamped his decrees.

The court caved.

As a result, the free and independent American citizens of Coolidge's "Roaring '20s" were now, to a degree unimaginable even a decade before—let alone to the Founders—working as government serfs for increasingly worthless fiat scrip without the means to acquire real lasting monetary wealth for themselves and their children.

After two terms of such high-handed management, FDR was so proud of his neo-progressive accomplishments that he felt it necessary to further reverse unbroken tradition. He set aside the precedent of a two-term presidency established by Washington and ran for a third term...and, then, not to be outdone, ran for a fourth term in 1944. Apparently, FDR wished to make himself a de facto emperor for life. And, in a sense, he achieved his goal, for only his death at the start of his *fourth* term—which Fate thankfully granted the nation in 1945—finally got him removed from the premiership. FDR was, in actuality, far down the road towards instituting a classic authoritarian government under a lifelong headman with his cult of personality. (It was this fourth run which finally roused the ire of enough American badasses to take up the cry, "No Crown for Franklin," and push through the 22nd Amendment which codified the long-standing tradition of a maximum two terms as president which the emulation of Washington by Jefferson, Madison, and dozens more had long established.)

And what were the results of a dozen years of FDR's socialist largesse? First and foremost, his "New Deal" deepened, lengthened, and worsened the 1929 Panic into a full-blown Depression. When FDR stepped into office in March, 1933, Hoover's interventions had shot unemployment above 20%, and

FDR would manage to keep it between 10% and 20% for almost a decade, right to the verge of the Second World War. Again, while non-intervention by Harding-Coolidge wiped out a market correction in months in 1921, much as did Reagan in 1987, FDR's monolithic governmental overrun of the economy from Washington would ossify a market dip into unrelenting, ongoing despair. Despite FDR's immense debt spending, the unemployment rate and the real GDP remained largely unmoved. Until the advent of Lend Lease military manufacturing for Britain and Russia (closely followed by America's own entry into WWII), there was little boost in real productivity; the only outcome of his "works" plans being a lot of frenetic but unproductive busywork. His much ballyhooed New Deal was, in reality, a lot of spending by Washington on programs it did not need, with money it did not have, on an authority it did not possess. That was how FDR managed to turn Hoover's minor market downturn into a Big Depression. The result of FDR's meddling was not relief, but an ongoing inflationary depression which was only resolved by the great emergency of World War II, which (a) cleared the unemployment rolls, by either drafting, killing or crippling millions of employable men, and (b) gave the Fed a presumptive moral authority to print whatever amount of phony scrip it wanted in order to make weapons and ammo which could in turn be quickly blown up to thence be continually repurchased. Fedgov cannot properly solve the People's problems for them; it can at best prevent problems by resisting the impulse to impose Fedgov tax-and-spend burdens while also maintaining an even playing field where trade, commerce, and growth can flourish. When Washington maintains that kind of self-restraint, the millions of bright, busy people across the nation will figure the way out...and a heck of a lot faster than a handful of closeted bureaucrats will...and without the need for a generation's bloodletting in war.

Somehow, both Wilson and Roosevelt, elected president of an American confederated republic, would feel the need to kill foreign lads to "make the world safe for democracy," while imposing "democratic" socialism at home. But democracy, being the rule of a mob controlled by the propaganda of the oligarchs, is simply a way the people can continually vote themselves into exactly the kind of slavery their overlords want for them, i.e. socialism, which is the granting the state complete power over all persons and property, a form of government which makes authoritarianism possible and slavery inevitable. What FDR's practically unchecked foray in socialism proved most ably is that governments, above all else, are wealth-destroying machines, and it is only a determined, clear-eyed reliance on the wisdom of the American Constitution which forestalls such destruction of the People's money.

Americanism vs Socialism

"Liberty lies in the hearts of men and women. When it dies there, no constitution, no law, no court can save it."
— Justice Learned Hand —

In sum, FDR's administration would use the twin "emergencies" of Depression and War to terrorize the nation into breaking the back of the Constitution. With few exceptions, the Fedgov would forever after churn forward with practically whatever enactment suited its fancy, far too often rubber-stamped by a craven, compliant, and complicit set of black-robed sycophants at the Supreme Court, bending the meaning of the Constitution to the will of the bribed and blackmailed politicos in Congress and the socialist stay-behind networks of the Executive branch.

FDR's regime imposed modernist authoritarianism on a constitutional republic while pretending to foster freedom. The sophistication and dark agency of his approach were perhaps most elegantly revealed in his famous "Four Freedoms" speech of January, 1941. The speech was intended to move a reluctant American people towards interventionism and internationalism, and did so with some crafty linguistic sleight of hand. He proposed that there were four key freedoms which every person in the world should enjoy (note already the speech's internationalist tenor—is he president of the American government, or the world?). The first and second of these freedoms, rightly enough, were simply lifted straight from our Constitution's First Amendment, as these were (1) "Freedom of Speech" and (2) "Freedom of Worship." Oddly, he could have used our own First Amendment, already written up and ready to go in any pocket Constitution; surely, there must be at least one of those someplace in Washington...somewhere. So, it's not clear why he didn't just recite that and encourage more nations to follow suit, maybe fleshing out the story with some inspiring tales of how, back in the day, Sam Adams and Patrick Henry put such rights to good use for the cause of Revolution and, well, Freedom. Even more oddly, our First Amendment freedoms includes the two he noted, plus three more freedoms, including freedom of the press and the right for redress of grievances from government, but he decided not to include any such freedom as those on his little list; maybe a free press and the people talking back to government were not such high priorities for FDR. Even more oddly still, we also have a Second Amendment freedom all written up and ready right next to that first one, and probably many of the Jews living in Germany about that time would have been most keen on looking into having that kind of protection, but somehow FDR seemed to have overlooked that little possibility too.

But that's just the warm up, because the real fun begins *after* he introduces his Freedom of Speech and Freedom of Religion.

Now, bear with a bit of grammar-police technicality for a minute. FDR's first two items were framed as "Freedom-OF-x" or "Freedom-OF-y." His use of the preposition OF is—like the genitive case—creating the possessive sense that the freedom mentioned belongs-to, or comes-from, the agent who owns, uses, or manifests that freedom. That is the kind of freedom that the Constitution contemplates and guarantees, which is called a *negative* grant of freedom; it is "negative" because it gives nothing to, it takes nothing from, the person of agency, for it is the individual citizen who has potential, who acts in the fullness of their power. We are inherently imbued with freedom and agency, and our constitution guarantees only to protect a right to act upon what we already, inherently have, this freedom OF ours—to speak, to worship the Creator, etc. It is a freedom inherent in us, from us, OF us; that freedom receives truth, power, and agency through our personal action. That is why a *negative* freedom is needed, because you best just get out of the way of someone fully manifesting their freedom, because here it comes, baby!

The next two items FDR adds to his shopping list—(3) "Freedom from Want" and (4) "Freedom from Fear"—are framed differently. Why the change from Freedom-OF to Freedom-FROM? In contrast with our first two items, the Freedom-FROM pair indicates an indirect reception—something like a dative case—implying a situation in which the person is indirectly *receiving* the outcome of the action; the freedom herein contemplated comes "sideways," to the person who passively waits on its delivery via government largesse. The freedom-getting here is passive; it's a freedom granted-to the person; it is a gift or privilege given to the peasantry *from* others, *from* the power and agency of others to them. It contemplates, then, technically, a *positive* object, meaning simply a real, actual thing, like a chicken in every pot, or an effective border patrol to keep us safe, Underlying such gifts is also, however, the freedom from working to create it; it is actually a freedom from personal agency, an abdication of responsibility. Thus, grammatically (and hence, psychologically), this freedom-FROM imbues passivity, docility, and helplessness in the instantiation of such freedoms.

That people would like to have lives without any want (i.e. no lack, privation, starvation, etc.) is certainly true and politically admirable. But how does one get there? An American badass knows the rule: you pursue freedom through self-reliant, unconquerable action until you get it. Somehow, that does not seem to align with FDR's approach. Somehow, it seems more like he wanted rows of helpless, hapless foot-shufflers waiting upon his grandiloquent pronunciamentos...and maybe a handout from Big Daddy Frank. For, after all, what had he imposed for America but large-scale, large-state relief programs and a dole? He was simply now looking to take the whole thing international. He would soon be instituting an overseas dole by handing out tanks and bombs to

Russia and Britain in his Lend Lease program in the run-up to the war, and then, after the war, would seek to create giant, international agencies to oversee making the big-state programs he had started in the U.S. an ongoing, international mission everywhere.

So, freedom-FROM is the real play he wanted here. He did not so much want freedom-of, which is bottom-up action from the individual sovereign citizen. He wanted to enact tangible items delivered FROM Fedgov, at the whim of Fedgov, to the slack-jawed proles awaiting his largesse and directives. His administration looked, not to enact "negative" restraints on government intrusion to protect the liberty of sovereign citizens, but to take overt, "positive" action by government to enforce its interventionist programs. So, as he speaks, FDR wants people vaguely dreaming of getting such gifts, e.g. a house, food, clothes, maybe a Universal Basic Income one day; these would be enactments on the national and then international level, much like his earlier real, physical "positive" enactments to seize the gold or create worker armies.

The final "Freedom-from-Fear" would be the final step of teaming up with his internationalist buddies in large organizations, like, say, the United Nations, World Bank, International Monetary Fund, World Economic Forum, Trilateral Commission, etc., etc. to decide what fearful terror-inducing event will next necessitate the further destruction of personal liberties for the peasants in the industrialized world so that they can learn to live in squalid 800 sq. ft. micro-homes, eating bugs, living green on recycled sludge, owning nothing, and being happy.

In actuality, then, FDR's speech is a darkly sophisticated bit of agitprop designed to get the listener nodding in agreement. It creates a mash up of two polar opposite political philosophies, knit together and driven by an NLP "yes-train." He wants his audience entrained throughout all four bullet points, so he starts each phrase with the same American Pavlovian buzz word: Freedom. FDR begins with the "gimme" automatic "yes" granted by the two long-standing, widely-accepted statements of negative freedom under constitutional norms which no sensible person would resist

(Freedom of Speech, Freedom of Religion). Now that everyone is relaxed and agreeing, he deftly slides along to hide socialist principles of government handouts, control, and internationalist intervention under broad anodyne principles, still under a heading starting "Freedom-x" and "Freedom-y" without bothering to paint the concrete picture of how very different such "freedom" is under an international socialist program which promises to give you everything you want only by first taking everything you have. These last two new "freedoms" Roosevelt was proffering were actually Freedom-FROM outward events...by first becoming a helpless ward under government care.

At a deeper level, the final two freedoms, both because of their construction and the program FDR attaches to them, are essentially insane. "Freedom from Want" is a human impossibility. First, on a practical level, the political difficulties of actually delivering material plenty under socialism, is so vanishingly small as to be practically impossible. Besides, human psychology entails that the more you give, the more they want; humans will always *want* something. At every moment, no matter their age and station of life, we want, whether its lunch, wealth beyond measure, or at least please to not die right now. Even the Buddha, who, somewhat hyperbolically, advocated in his Third Noble Truth that we should "end suffering by ending desire," meant not so much that desire is eradicated, but it should no longer be a psychological burden, no longer the driving impulse of our thoughts and actions. Finally, the very notion of wanting to *not* want is itself an inescapable paradox, which the pursuit of this Third Freedom cannot logically overcome. The statement, then, is, at best, no more than a demagogue's trick, a play on the mind, to draw the audience towards his message, to be agreeable to whatever program he attaches to his comforting phrase.

The assertion of FDR's fourth freedom is craftily saved for last, as it is the most irrational and indefensible of all, as no person who isn't already verbally entrained to agree with him would give the notion a second thought. FDR wants to deliver "Freedom from Fear." While, with "Freedom from Want," FDR could at least be pretending he could deliver a sufficiency of dry goods and houses to meet everyone's material needs, with "Freedom from Fear" he is, at the very least, promising something like an internal police force and border defense force so strong that the likelihood of assault is virtually eliminated. While that has some appeal as an abstract goal, it has little real persuasive value when one realizes he is speaking to a people who, at that time, have had within living memory a civil war, three presidents assassinated, and a slew of unarmed, peaceful veterans and their families shot and trampled by their own army in the Capital. Similarly, the explosion of the *Maine*, sinking of the *Lusitania*, and (soon) attack on Pearl Harbor will make assertions of unending border safety ring pretty hollow. Moreover, the straight connotative meaning of "Freedom from Fear" is an implicit promise to render everyone's psyche completely tranquil, without a worry or care in the world. It is, in fact, the very same implicit promise and program utilized as messaging for the post-9/11 "War on Terror." But, how can one rationally expect to make a nation free from fear, or wage a war on the emotional state of terror? This, too, is, at best, a mere verbal trope used by master propagandists to get herds of people nodding in agreement that, "Yes, I would like to not be afraid. Yes, I would like to not to feel terror. Please show me how you will stop me from having these scary feelings, oh kindly and wise leader." These last "freedoms" which FDR promulgates are actually escapism from responsibility, an invitation to voluntary bondage to the state; they are the freedom of penury, an appeal to suckle from the tender sow of big government. This is not the Freedom-OF a free agent undertaking the great adventure of life. That is the "freedom to submit" of slaves. That is FDR's kind of freedom.

In effect, what Wilson and FDR were offering in their Progressivism and New Dealism, was the introduction of a form of socialism-lite into the American body politic. These centralized, authoritarian accretions of power to Washington under an endless array of alphabet agencies is precisely the clawing, envy-motivated type of bureaucrat-operated "freedoms" which Karl Marx promised in his notorious *Communist Manifesto*. Under FDR's "New Deal," the beguiling succubus of socialism had alighted on the sleeping American body politic and was preparing to suck the life blood from its victim. Unlike Americans, who were growing, inventing, and prospering in the 1800s, Europeans had been increasingly drawn to that siren's song of socialism which Marx so beguilingly espoused in his 1848 manifesto. As Marx himself so ironically put it in its opening passage, there was a ghost haunting Europe, and it was indeed communism. Marx and Engels therein outlined the shape of this communist ghost, producing a punch list of the essential elements for manifesting a socialist/communist utopia, the *10 Planks of the Communist Manifesto*, which, in the light of the Wilson-Roosevelt counterrevolution, we might do well to briefly examine:

1. Abolition of property in land (all rents revert to the public fisc)

2. A heavy progressive or graduated income tax

3. Abolition of all rights of inheritance

4. Confiscation of the property of all emigrants and rebels

5. Centralization of credit in a national bank of the state, with an exclusive monopoly

6. Centralization of the means of communication and transport in the hands of the State

7. Extension of factories and instruments of production owned by the State; the bringing into cultivation of waste-lands, and the improvement of the soil generally in accordance with a common plan (a.k.a., "Public-Private Partnerships")

8. Establish obligatory service in industrial armies, especially in agriculture

9. Combine agriculture and manufacturing industries, abolishing the distinction between town and country by redistribution of the populace

10. Free education for all children in public schools. Abolition of children's factory labor in its present form to combine education with industrial production

Note first, how many of these have already been enacted, in varying degrees, both here and abroad: progressive income tax, abolition (or at least heavy taxation) of inheritance, national bank with monopolistic control on credit, control of communication, control of transportation, state partnership with industry, "free" government schooling. Next, note that the general approach of these proposed policies (with the possible exception of schools) are all and only aimed at addressing the disposition of physical resources; they arise from an avowed and unalloyed materialism which is concerned with the control and distribution of material substance (factories, banks, media & transportation facilities) of the nation...of which the citizens themselves are just one more material component. This list is, if you will, a whole wish list of FDR's freedoms-from, i.e. material gifts to be delivered to one's doorstep. For, Marxism is, first and foremost, a form of Historical Materialism; that is, the belief that the totality of reality is the material world, and that its current cultural manifestation indelibly shapes the very nature of individual consciousness. Hence, an avowed Marxist socialist will have an unrelenting insistence on unlimited possession and purview over the nation's material resources, and, to make possible that control, they will seek the centralization of power over banks, schools, credit, communication, transportation, etc. The best means to achieve such control of the material means is via the most centralized and implacable social force possible, i.e. a large, autocratic government. The logic is clear and brutal in its deduction, and clearly brutal in its application.

Recall here the punch line of that old gag: what's the difference between a socialist and communist? A communist is merely a socialist in a hurry. Indeed, one need only read Marx's *Manifesto* (or, if you prefer, Mao's *Little Red Book*) to see that they often use the two terms interchangeably, making little or no distinction between the two ostensibly different systems. Regardless, whichever name one applies to these authoritarian materialist systems, history shows that such centralized governance tends toward economic stagnation and political oppression. Examining the record of avowedly communist or socialist states shows little promise for either personal liberty or communal prosperity under such a system. Not only do we have the obvious and long-standing examples of the failure of nationalized socialist economies in the Soviet Union, Cuba, Venezuela, etc., but—as DiLorenzo has documented in *The Problem with Socialism* (pp 77-86)—even the oft-bruited example of Swedish "democratic socialism" is a chimera. Their actual economic success was built during the period from 1809-1950, when they were the *freest* and thus *most prosperous* economy on the planet. Staying out of the many European wars and cultivating their free markets, the Swedes would amass tremendous wealth and savings. But, beginning in the 1930s, and accelerating by the 1950s, their politicians began adopting the socialist model then becoming fashionable throughout Europe and North America. The result? By the 1990s, their economy had stagnated. In fact, the Swedish economy produced not a single new job from 1950 to 2010, when—in desperation to prosper again—the Swedes finally began peeling back the layers of socialist control in order to allow their people to once again compete dynamically, via lower taxes and greater autonomy. The mid-century "socialist miracle" of Sweden was, in fact, simply the government spending the money their great- and great-great-grandparents had worked so feverishly to amass during the many years *before* the imposition of socialist strictures.

But, one may wonder, is there not something a little backwards here? Why should communist socialism—that system which most especially advertises itself as liberating the proletariat from their poverty and alienation—be the one least likely to do so? Well, since this paradox seems a universal result of instituting socialism, we must surmise it is inherent in its nature, that the very structure of a socialist polity makes that outcome somehow inevitable. That essential element probably lies precisely in socialism's particular political structure, its distribution of power, and its interplay with the weaknesses of human nature. What, then, are the particular, salient features of socialism or communism? First, both of these "-isms" are authoritarian or collectivist social structures, which means they assume that the individual citizen, their person and property, are ultimately subject to the state, which itself has plenary power to undertake any act it deems fit. Socialism or authoritarianism or collectivism—whatever name brute political thuggery goes by—is thus ultimately some form of oligarchy, i.e. a state wherein the few rule the many. Now, under a monarchy, we typically know who the oligarchs are: the king, his kids, and his aristocratic friends and their kids. It's a clear and obvious bloodline dictatorship. Under current technocratic autocracies, the faces change while the structure stays the same. Who, then, would be the persons running the modern oligarchic state? The names and faces you know from the news are hirelings; they are ideologues, i.e. those most blindly and slavishly committed to the state, its power, its programs, regardless of the consequences for the individual citizen. Thus, by its very nature, a socialist state not only accretes full power and wealth to the state, but it hands that power over to bureaucrats most heedless of the citizens, because its power rests in the hands of those who have less regard for practical effect on the masses then for their utopian dreams. It draws to its ranks ideologues driven to enact the vision which overpowers their mind, regardless of outcomes for person, property, or propriety. And, once you give plenary power to human beings, they will use it, with disastrous consequences, for few rulers are either wise or benevolent (let alone both), most especially those ideologically possessed. In fact, research shows that politicos, as a group, are more likely to exhibit sociopathic tendencies than the everyday populace. Thus, a strong central government creates a strong ongoing possibility of abuse, as the opportunities for waste, fraud, graft, embezzlement, oppression, and plain, old sadistic rapine are multiplied as power accretes to the hordes of sociopaths warehoused at the capital. The glowing promises of a "dictatorship of the masses" leading to a "workers' paradise" are therefore most ironically least likely to accrue from those centralized socialist states which typically clothe their depredations under the promise of peace and plenty for the many and needy. Rather, authoritarianism, in whatever form, is the system most likely to produce misery, poverty, despair, and death for everyone save those closest to the central ring of oligarchs.

Taking this analysis a step further, we can mine rich psychological veins which differentiate the mindset instantiated in an American badass versus the socialist ideologue. The socialist, as proper communist materialist, sees the world as a dead thing, an endless scree of dirt and ash over which we apex apes scrape and compete for any marginal advantage. They envision the real and possible as merely what is immediately apparent in the given, surface, "actual" environment—their battleground is the flat, empty landscape of possiblism. They inhabit a loser mindset of emptiness, deprivation, and desperation over what has <u>not</u> been given to them, of their <u>need</u> for what they lack, because of the inherent <u>scarcity</u> of resources, the <u>scarcity</u> of rights, the <u>scarcity</u> of benefits, the <u>scarcity</u> of possibilities. They live in the Land of No Bread. Therefore they must use the power of government kleptocracy (or mobocracy, if necessary), to rob what they unjustly lack from those who have managed to accumulate some bits and scraps.

In contrast, the American badass assumes responsibility for their own circumstances. They inhabit a winner's mindset of envisioning and pursuing what they themselves <u>can</u> generate by producing and providing for others, because their world provides an <u>infinity</u> of opportunities; they exercise their <u>infinity</u> of capacities upon an <u>infinity</u> of possibilities. Therefore, they need nothing from government but the benign neglect to be left alone as they work upwards in a meritocracy of accomplishment, to build for self and family...to eventually evince philanthropy by giving from their surplus in service to those most in want.

Socialism's siren call is a promise of something for nothing; its reality is stealing from everyone while returning nothing. And a large part of why this funnel of greed, graft, and grift characterizes collectivist states is inherent in not only its sociological but psychological effects. Because the promise of something-for-nothing serves to short-circuit the pathways to virtue in the human character, socialism will tend to produce a passive, vicious, inept, and infantilized populace; the result will be a failed state, a "banana republic," unable to manage itself, its people, or its affairs. Americanism, on the other hand, promises us nothing, but thereby gives us everything; it promises only you and your choices, but that essentially forces you to undertake productive self-development, which opens that field of infinite possibilities whose fruits can only be harvested once you have indeed cultivated your personal agency and skills. Because of that prerequisite emphasis on personal responsibility, the fruits of life come only to those who learn to sow, work, endure, and invest—and, since such traits are expected of every person—the republic as a whole begins to exhibits those virtues from the ground up, at every level; the actions which build a flourishing personal life and prosperous household will begin to be reflected in the state itself through the everyday lives and manifold choices of its millions of inhabitants. From this broad contrast, we can articulate a series of paired opposites of virtues and vices, each demonstrative of the differential outcome whereby the American badass emphasis on freedom and self-reliance engenders virtue, while authoritarianism builds vice.

Outcome of Americanism	vs.	Outcome of Authoritarianism	Arena of Activity / Area of Life Challenge
autonomy		*passivity*	*choice of career, lifestyle*

explanation: Given freedom, one either takes on the burden of choice, or fails; under authoritarianism, one learns to meekly succumb and submit, or be destroyed.

industry	*laziness*	*career, business, self-development*

explanation: Given freedom, one either takes on the burden of work, or starves; under authoritarianism, one learns to beg for the scraps offered, and whine for more.

thrift	*profligacy*	*personal and domestic economy*

explanation: Given freedom, one either learns to save for your own future, or suffer during life's exigencies; under authoritarianism, one expects to have given, spend freely from what comes easily, and passively endure when one lacks.

truthfulness	*mendacity*	*verbal and social veracity*

explanation: Given freedom, one either gains reputation and repeat business for one's forthrightness, or soon fails; under authoritarianism, one cultivates the opinion of those in power through whatever words work best, most often using fine embellishment, spin, and dutifully repeating the regime's slogans.

order/cleanliness chaos/slovenliness feng shui—or oi veh!—home

explanation: Given freedom, your place and things are your own to maintain, or wallow in dilapidated squalor; under state-owned authoritarianism, such things are not your problem, but somebody else's responsibility to clean and manage.

altruism   selfishness   philanthropy, public service

explanation: Given freedom, if society is to be made helpful and whole, it is yours to do; under authoritarianism, the state has the job to help those people—it is not my problem.

self-reliance   desperation   internal/external locus of control

explanation: Given freedom, one either takes on the challenges of life, or loses; under authoritarianism, one begs the state for more, and bemoans their lack of generosity on your behalf.

order, peace   disorder, violence   social cohesion or alienation

explanation: Given freedom, one seeks the continuance of an orderly, predictable society to protect the productivity of one's actions; under authoritarianism, one hopes for a means of escape, and may seek to vandalize or destroy one's imprisoning social cage.

morality   depravity   ethical compass

explanation: Given freedom, one learns that such virtues as industry, thrift, honesty, and initiative are rewarding; under authoritarianism, one learns there is no escape but merely scamming the system as often as one can or indulging oneself in mental and sensual escapism.

unconquerability defeatism   learned helplessness...or hopefulness

explanation: Given freedom, one learns there are many pathways and opportunities leading to one's goals; under authoritarianism, one learns that power begets power, and the little person is hopelessly crushed beneath it.

| *impossiblism* | *pessimism* | *basal expectation mindset* |

explanation: Given freedom, one learns that accomplishing little things builds skills to enable you to accomplish larger things, which encourages you to envision accomplishing "impossible" things; under authoritarianism, one finds obedience to narrow rules is rewarded, using one's own initiative is punished, and silent, sullen suffering is safest.

| *optimism, joy* | *despair, gloom* | *basal emotional set point* |

explanation: Given freedom, one learns to envision and manifest one's hopes and dreams, maximizing one's physical and psychological health; under authoritarianism, one learns that one is a mere insignificant piece in a larger machine, and one's lot is simply learning to endure being ground by its gears.

Spirit over Circumstance
"We have to continually be jumping off cliffs and developing our wings on the way down."
— Kurt Vonnegut —

In short, socialism's top-down management style tends to produce passive, sullen, inept citizens waiting on orders, while a republic of freedom engenders initiative-taking activists throwing themselves into their next adventure. That is the difference between socialism's only-possiblism and American Badass' impossiblism (see Part IV). Psychologically, then, socialism produces a stunted imagination, a misunderstanding of the nature of humankind, and the substitution of selfishness and brutality under the color of law for true dignity and hope. Socialism is precisely the triumph of the limits of circumstance over the possibilities of spirit.

Socialism (and its partner, communism) live in the only-possible realm of the merely material. They look around them, and imagine that what they see is all that is; they next imagine that what they imagine is, is all that *can* be. From such stunted phantasmagoria, they project the worst of their dark imaginings into the future and conclude they must wrest whatever they can from their neighbor. Socialism becomes, then, the desperate politics of envy, of purblind pigs fighting for the scraps left in the sty; it is attending to the disposition of the meager leftovers of the day allotted by force to the few who remain to gnaw on the husks and leavings. By failing to recognize (a) that what is possible now is only the springboard to the greater potentialities humanity will soon enough develop, and (b) that the limitations of the physical are merely challenges gifted to your spirit to strengthen itself in patience, resolve, creativity, sacrifice, and love—they rob themselves of the chance to develop true heroism, especially if they give themselves over to the envy, malice, violence, and greed of the failure-oriented socialist mindset. Its outcome is a tendency towards sin, which itself savagely darkens the intellect, for in order to give yourself to sin, to wickedness, you must overlook its dark consequences, so in order to sin abundantly, you must train yourself to avoid thinking clearly of future outcomes, of those you've hurt, or of what you've become. The immoral man is, in sum, an intentionally stupid soul. And continued sinful indulgence simply deepens the self-imposed stupefaction which enables the sin. A free people, however, clearly seeing the heady infinite field of possibility and play arrayed around them, imagine the impossible—dreaming of anything, reaching for everything. Their spirit grows large, their eyes sparkle with incandescent hope, their minds grow bright and eager for tomorrow's next more joyful discovery.

Is it any wonder, then, why authoritarian internationalists love socialism, and hate Americanism? Likewise, is it any surprise that the introduction of centralized authoritarian systems without regard to constitutional strictures in the Wilson-Roosevelt era put this nation on the path of self-destruction? Their regimes were a lead-fisted 1-2 punch to the American constitutional Republic. Not only did their presidencies usher in the third (and most destructive) national bank in the Federal Reserve while also upending constitutional restraints on multiplying new federal agencies (in violation of the minimal powers authorized in Article I, Section 8), but they normalized the *expectation* of large, invasive federalism; that is, they eroded the orientation of the People to self-reliance and unconquerability, instead making the central government the core national agent in molding and controlling finance, industry, agriculture, retirement, philanthropy, and even the arts. Over their tenures—and the several public "emergencies" over which they presided—these administrations shifted America's center of gravity from the citizen to the state. By the end of World War II, then, it was an easy transition for Truman to enact the 1947 National Security Act, instituting the CIA and launching decades of dark projects and covert operations against innocent citizens and free people, both foreign and domestic. The speed with which the money powers began to utilize the powerful levers of central government would so appal lifelong government employee President Dwight Eisenhower that he used his last turn on the national soapbox to deliver a hand-written warning to the People of the burgeoning "military industrial complex." President Washington had used his farewell address to urge us to avoid "foreign entanglements" and remember our duty before God. Eisenhower used his as a monitory cry against the growing danger from within wrought by the power of technological corporations controlling a metastasizing, militarized central government. It was a last gasp by an elected American executive before the black-ops capos capped JFK for having the audacity to actually attempt to run the government by and for the People...a brazen daylight *coup d'état* against the rule of law which thereby openly demarcates a date certain for the quietus of the constitutional Republic,

R.I.P.

American Constitutional Republic

March 4, 1789 - November 22, 1963

With the Republic killed, America entered the Age of Empire. The black budget and military gangs of imperial Fedgov became the operational and enforcement arm of a Pax Americana, orchestrated by offshore, unelected, internationalist technocrats with their "Five Eyes" brethren whose putative goals seemed always to obscure agendas far darker and deadlier than the rainbow-glittered puff pastry agitprop about saving baby seals and "protecting democracy" they fed to the groundlings. Their reign by stealth and deception would lead the nation into an increasingly costly, violent, and interminable international interventionism which would turn the once-vibrant Republic into an indebted, tyrannical Empire.

The Battling Bastards of Bastogne and Beyond
"Better to fight for something than live for nothing."
— General George Patton —

Before the tendrils of the octopus finally strangled the Republic, Roosevelt's regime diverted attention from its economic failures by a second war to "make the world safe for democracy" in Europe, an undertaking which actually laid the groundwork for the institution of internationalist socialism. For, after each world war, as if by magic, a team of technocrats—largely funded by moneyed interests—appeared with a master plan to "end all war" by making all the nations part of a single, worldwide Kumbaya government love party. Surely, it must be just a coincidence that the people behind the League of Nations and later the United Nations were either members of or agents for European plutocratic and aristocratic families with leanings toward world socialist outcomes: H.G. Wells, Aldous and Julian Huxley, Rockefeller Foundation, etc.

Wells predicted in his book *The New World Order* that, in the end, *"the system of nationalist individualism...has to go...We are living in the end of the sovereign states...In the great struggle to evoke a Westernized World Socialism, contemporary governments may vanish...Countless people...will hate the new world order...and will die protesting against it."*

Aldous Huxley gave his own, fictionalized version of this

dystopia in *Brave New World*, replete with babies decanted in incubators, raised in communal barracks, assigned their job and station in life by the overseers, wherein endless drug-and-sex diversions keep the masses from focusing any energies toward political reform or personal rebellion and development.

His brother, Julian, was an avowed eugenicist who helped the Rockefellers et. al. by setting up, under the United Nations umbrella, the UNESCO program whose pamphlet *Toward World Understanding*, Vol. 5 (1949), railed against families which inculcate patriotism in their children: *"As long as the child breathes the poisoned air of nationalism, education in world-mindedness can produce only rather precarious results...For the moment, it is sufficient to note that it is most frequently in the family that the children are infected with nationalism by hearing what is national extolled and what is foreign disparaged...The activity of the school cannot bring about the desired result unless repudiating every form of nationalism."*

The Rockefellers bought the land upon which the UN headquarters was built...and David in his autobiography *Memoirs* (2002) delivered this defiant broadside to his critics: *"Some even believe we are part of a secret cabal working against the interest of the United States...and of conspiring with others around the world to build a more integrated global political and economic structure—one world, if you will...If that's the charge, I stand guilty and am proud of it."*

But, before they could completely enact all their nefarious plans, the Republic would show a bit of what a free, self-disciplined, unconquerable citizenry could do. For, yes, part of American Badass is plain old raw-edged toughness. You want some gumption, guts, and grit? Okay, come and get you some.

The British decided to challenge the American people when we declared our independence, and lost...twice (1776, 1812). So, in straight-up fights between American patriots and the British Empire, that would be America, 2...British Empire, 0.

About a century later, that British Empire decided the

Germans were getting too big for their britches and so, with some helpers on both sides, they started a little do-si-doe called World War I. But those Brits found out they had bitten off more than they could chew, so they came begging for some help from those same Yanks they had been trying to lock down. So—Wilson having talked the doughboys into accommodating the Brits—our boys put on the big boots and steel helmets, sailed over there and, in less than a year, beat down the "Huns."

A couple decades after that, the same group of knuckleheads (plus Japan) got into it again. Guess who everyone called in to clean it up? Yup, the GIs came clattering over in their Sherman tanks to knock out the Nazis...and, while they were at it, send a few dozen aircraft carriers across the Pacific to straighten out Tojo's boys.

By my count, that's America in world wars 2-0.

So, all told, it's looking like a bad idea to start a fight with the American eagle. You wanna go ahead and start a fight? That's fine. We'll damn sure finish it for you.

What made those Yanks so successful? It might could possibly have something to do with those basic Yankee badass attitudes. Let's look at a couple examples of American heroism in those wars to see.

In that first go-round in World War I, the premier model of American military gallantry was probably Sergeant York.

Sergeant York Alvin York was, frankly, reluctant to fight. Due to his Christian faith's call to forbearance and forgiveness, he initially sought conscientious objector status. But, after prayerfully reconsidering and taking a more comprehensive view of the Scripture, his theological understanding deepened, leading him to pursue his military duties with the same zeal with which he had previously resisted them. As part of a group of 17 men sent to attack the German lines in October, 1918, York continued forward even after over a third of his team had been gunned down by enemy fire. Flanked by a couple compatriots, he led the team towards the main objective: a series of entrenched heavy machine gun positions sweeping the front lines. At one point, York found himself cut off and exposed, fighting alone against dozens of Germans with nothing but his rifle—and when he ran out of ammo for that—his pistol. Here his childhood of hunting in the woods served him well, as his single-handed sharp shooting killed over 25 of the enemy. His solo resolve was so extraordinary that the German officer leading the defenders—after vainly emptying his pistol at York but missing—gave up and offered himself and his whole unit in surrender to the gallant lance corporal from Tennessee. York and his team gathered up the remainder of the German battalion, including their 25 machine guns, and marched the whole kit and caboodle back to headquarters. Back at camp, his commanding general called out, "York, I hear you captured the whole German army!" York gave a little shrug and replied simply, "No, sir. Only 132."

He also gathered one more thing for this action: the Medal of Honor.

In World War II, another generation of Americans would demonstrate resolve under trying conditions while maintaining an eye on the bounds of virtue. Here are a couple examples from that second "great" war.

Certainly the costliest, and perhaps most famous, unit action exemplifying American unconquerability in WWII was the Battle of the Bulge. During the depths of one of the coldest winters in memory, in the quiet, thinly-defended woods of the Ardennes forest, when the war was but months from its end, Hitler decided to hit back once more with his elite tank legions. His hope was to slice the Allied armies in half by one last desperate assault towards the strategic port of Antwerp. On December 16, 1944, the Germans attacked with 17 divisions across an 80 mile front, opening a battle which would prove the bloodiest affray fought in the European theatre, with the Americans taking over 100,000 casualties. It was, initially, an unequal and desperate fight since the American forces deployed there were largely untested and unsupported rookies, and they faced the cream of Hitler's army—veteran units sporting their most advanced weaponry—who quickly blew through the thin line. Despite the disparity, again and again, many single GIs, officers and men alike, showed their mettle under the test.

The tenacity shown at the Battle of the Bulge started at the top, with General Anthony McAuliffe of the 101st Airborne Division, whose men were rushed into the defense of Bastogne, the town which was the central road hub through which the German columns needed to pass. The Germans quickly surrounded the town and prepared to assault its outnumbered defenders. With the Americans completely cut off and feeling sure of his victory, the German commander sent a demand for the Americans to surrender. General McAuliffe gave him a crisp, non-nonsense reply, which spoke for everyone protecting the isolated town: *"Nuts!"* That was the kind of dauntless determination imbued within those who would endure that bitter fight in that shocking cold, those "battered bastards of Bastogne." Similarly, when Lieutenant Colonel Creighton "Abe" Abrams—the man the modern tank is named after, the man once called by General Patton the "world champion" of tank commanders—was leading a relief column to those frozen defenders heard that the Germans had the town cut off, he replied, *"The poor bastards, they have us surrounded."*

The 82nd and 101st Airborne divisions which had been rushed into the town as a stopgap against Hitler's churning panzer legions, were technically "mere" light infantry, i.e. armed with only the weapons an individual infantryman can carry, unaccompanied by the heavy weapons of large-barrel, long-range artillery, let alone tanks or air support. In other words, they were a handful of shivering GIs going up against Hitler's elite armor corps, with their state of the art Panther and Tiger tanks. And yet the Germans could not dislodge them.

Why?

Maybe the tale of one lone PFC from the 325th Glider Infantry Regiment, 82nd Airborne Division, and his foxhole will explain it.

Early in the fight, when the elite SS divisions had cracked the thin line of green troops and were pouring through the woods, a gang of those terrified replacement soldiers hitched a ride on a tank destroyer, looking for a ride to the rear, as far from the fight as possible. Behind them, three separate attacking German columns were gaining. The retreating GIs clattered down the snowy road until they found one lone paratrooper, his bazooka and rifle laid aside, digging a foxhole. When they pulled up to ask what he was doing, he glanced up, then went back to his work. *"If you're looking for a safe place,"* he said, *"just pull that vehicle behind me. I'm the 82nd Airborne...and this is as far as the bastards are going."* The formerly terrified replacements couldn't help becoming galvanized by that lone trooper's infectious courage; they jumped down and began digging a trench line beside his. In the hours ahead, other stragglers and squads of retreating men would happen along and join their makeshift roadblock. That one paratrooper, without rank or orders, had built a wall of defiance by the force of his badass will and example.

And he was right: though the siege would go on for many days, neither the veteran SS infantry, nor the finest Panther and Tiger tanks of the 2nd SS Panzer or Panzer Lehr divisions would be able to dislodge the implacable Yankee paratroopers. Mere light infantry—with tireless support from the equally ammunition-starved African-American 969 Artillery Battalion and elements of 10th Armored Division—would gut up, dig in, and hold on until Abrams and his tanks could punch through. It would be some weeks before the Nazis were finally pushed back across the Rhine into Germany, but they never would take Bastogne. That really was as far as the bastards ever got.

Frank Barron and the "77th Marines" One last look at the GIs of WWII involves action in the Pacific with Captain Frank Barron, not so much because of his exploits—which, though courageous, were paralleled by thousands of other officers and men from the era—but because of his ability to also reflect upon and encapsulate their meaning. In this action, Barron was serving as company commander in the 77th Infantry Division—a "ground pounder" unit which the U.S. Marines affectionately nicknamed the "77th Marines" for its demonstrable toughness in battle. While island-hopping towards Okinawa, Captain Barron would be awarded the

Silver Star for exemplary initiative and courage when taking a nest of heavily-fortified Japanese machine gun positions. First, he moved out alone and on foot, under both machine gun and mortar fire, personally leading a self-propelled howitzer forward to the front line so it could bring a withering direct artillery fire onto the dug-in machine gun positions. Then, when his troops still hesitated to advance under the continuing heavy mortar barrage, Barron charged forward, regardless of the danger, personally inspiring and leading his men forward to the objective. His actions were heroic, like many thousands of other soldiers, but he also recognized much of what made such harrowing group combat unique. He later recounted and reflected upon the time one of his comrades—wounded and loaded on a stretcher to be taken back to an aid station—refused to leave until the stretcher-bearers relieved him of his watch and his cigarette lighter, making them promise to hand them out to the other guys in his unit. To Barron, that said more about the greatness of infantrymen than anything else. This is how he expressed the humanitarian side of the badass American infantryman: *"I believe fighting for your country in the infantry in battle is the most purifying experience known to man. These men who trained hard together and fought for extended periods together became so completely unselfish, so absorbed with the welfare of the group, that you could believe their principal concern was for the 'other guy.'"*

Invictus

"For the human soul is virtually indestructible, and its ability to rise from the ashes remains as long as the body draws breath."
— Alice Miller —

Gumption, guts, and grit, that's why paratrooper light infantry was able to beat Hitler's best tankers. It would have been far "easier" to quit, to surrender, to ride out the last few months of the war smoking cigarettes in a POW camp and let someone else do the fighting and dying. It would have been so much "easier," and weaker. But it never crossed that paratrooper's mind; he had a mission, and he dug his foxhole deep, ready to the last. Gumption, guts, and grit was what enabled Captain Barron to walk out alone and lead that artillery piece forward, to personally spearhead that final charge up the hill. But that toughness was counterbalanced by what makes it possible: the will to serve others. As Barron reminds us, true greatness starts with the purpose of service, which is what motivates the toughness to act. What makes badass possible is not so much the dreadful enemy in front of you which you fight, but the beloved family behind you which you protect.

And when you, just one person—just a lone paratrooper or fearless captain—step forward, straight into the whirlwind without flinching, you don't just help your own cause. You become a powerful model for others, even those you may never meet. The resilience, indefatigability, stick-with-it-ness you apply to fulfilling your mission, to making your dreams happen, the unconquerability, perseverance, and determination which enables you to find the pathway to your personal victories, are not just a gift to yourself, but to everyone around you.

Tough and tender, salty and selfless, brave and benign, that was how Barron saw the infantry. That was the story of the American GI. And, yes, frankly it was a toughness sprung from the Christian ethos which renders its follower at once rugged but righteous, *"wise as serpents, but gentle as doves."* It is a fortitude informed by faith. It is superhuman endurance with supernatural self-reliance, because its ground is not earthly, its hope is not worldly, its aim is heavenly. There is nothing necessarily otherworldly about its operations, but a person who fears the loss of soul and spirit more than loss of life and limb is a fierce opponent, a warrior lit afire. Ironically, because the ground of the Christian spirit is beyond this world, it has greater power and effect in this world than most; being grounded in spirit, one is just that much more brave, just that much more bold, just that much more committed to the cause of making right and true the things of this world.

In surrendering one's flesh so that *"Thy will be done, on*

Earth...," one worries less about the body. One seeks to utilize one's flesh—indeed, even surrender that flesh—to reveal the greatness of spirit. And the beauty of God's plan seems to be that the manifestation of His will is to be exacted through human action, human agency, human flesh. God's will of instantiating the good for all becomes most evident—and is usually only concretely realized—through the action of individual humans: Moses, Joshua, David, even Christ. This is the human form being used to manifest the Maker's aim of earthly justice via heavenly love. In God's economy of justice, the human form is the conduit of salvation, human hands the means which deliver His comfort to his suffering children.

But the physical world is a place where action is hard, results take time, and situations are resistant to such change. Thus, the believer must develop the qualities of fortitude, toughness, and resourcefulness necessary to stay in the traces through the challenges to manifest that love. The believer must learn and accept that the work is hard, the timeline long, to begin straightening and softening the world to manifest its full potential to reflect God's greater glory. But it is precisely by the strengthening of one's character, the polishing of one's spirit, that the believer becomes ever more beautiful in their soul while they make ever more bounteous the world.

That explains why those US GIs could come in first with hand grenades, then hand out chocolate bars afterwards, how it was that Americans sent B-17s to pound the Ruhr valley's factories into rubble, and then spent millions in the Marshall Plan to rebuild German industry after the war. Unlike practically all conquering nations throughout history, after WWII, the Americans did not steal the wealth and subjugate the vanquished foe, but rather restored and renewed the fallen peoples of Germany and Japan. This seeming paradox is exactly what is asked of the Christian warrior, of the person evincing the highest capacities of both fortitude and honor: to do the work, no matter how hard; to exact the justice, no matter how difficult; and to render the mercy, no matter how costly. To undertake each of these separate moral tasks with equal application and thoroughness, and, to whatever degree is necessary to most perfectly render it, to demonstrate a full, complete, and heroic humanity—that is truly badass. That is why theirs has been called the "Greatest Generation," for they faced the Depression with stoic endurance, fought the war with unflinching courage, and reaped the postwar bounty with a temperate modesty. It was a bravura display of cultural genius, of a people whose heads and hearts were screwed on straight at an early age, and who kept on that path, doing as they should, without demur and with little fanfare. It was a heroism of heart, manifest in the sacrifice of self, time, and effort in the cause of beautifying the creation. It was a civilizational demonstration that spirit is indeed stronger—that spirit must always stay stronger—than circumstance.

Banana Republics, PetroDollars and Forever Wars

"I believe there are more instances of the abridgment of the freedom of the people by gradual and silent encroachments of those in power than by violent and sudden usurpations."
— James Madison —

That national display of resolve and grit in the Second World War, may, however, have been a final, gleaming reflection of the Republic's setting sun. All the while the boys were fighting overseas, a nascent darkness was overtaking the homeland. For what if all that heroic determination can be turned on its head? What if the American talent for toughness can be used, not as a force for heroism and freedom, but as a tool for oppression and wealth extraction? What if, above Wilson, beyond FDR, there lies a higher level of political control...and levels even beyond that? What if the little fairy tales in your high school civics book do not show you how politics really works in the grown-up world? That is a rabbit hole which is very deep, very dark, and from which you may never return...

Since 1947, while American soldiers continued to display

toughness and fortitude wherever deployed—from the frozen Choisin Reservoir, to the hills of Khe Sanh, to the dust of Fallujah— a dark cloud began to shroud their geopolitical adventures, adventures which produced ever greater destruction with ever dwindling production. The very virtues of American resolve and toughness were allowing it to be used worldwide as that "bad" kind of badass. Yeah, we could roll over them in M-1 Abrams tanks with Punisher logos on the sides and the strains of "Stranglehold" blasting on the speakers, but those one-sided victories were leaving behind dictators and Abu Graib torture chambers.

And the man who saw it all coming a century ago was the youngest two-star general in the Marine Corps, a man who survived over 100 combat actions and had been awarded five different medals for bravery. Smedley Butler was one of America's most battle-tested Marines and never backed down from any fight, on or off a battlefield.

Smedley Butler Smedley Butler, was the most decorated Marine of his time, and is among an elite handful of soldiers to have ever won the Medal of Honor not once, but twice. He also has the distinction of having been the only Marine Corps general to have stopped a coup against the United States. Butler served mostly during the pre-WWI colonial era, seeing action in stations across the planet: Cuba, the Philippines, Honduras, Nicaragua, China, Mexico, Haiti and, finally, France during WWI. At one point, his service was interrupted when President Coolidge dispatched him to Philadelphia, which had requested help cleaning up its crime problem. Butler's efforts were successful there too—though rather unorthodox—as they involved his direct, salty language, cops armed with sawed-off shotguns, and a willingness to root out wrongdoing anywhere, including within the police department and among the posh folks.

During all those overseas deployments, however, Butler had slowly come to realize that his service was less about protecting the integrity of his nation's borders and its People, than the business interests of far-flung commercial conglomerates. As a result, after his retirement from the Corps in 1931, he ran for US senate on a platform of reducing militarism and the excess power of big business over public policy. Butler also penned a short book, *War is a Racket,* to warn America that the practice (and profit) of war itself was the problem, not all the supposed enemies which always seemed to arise every couple years. He had seen his Marines undertake more commercial clean-up operations for the United Fruit Company than any defense of the people. Why must so many American lads go traipsing about Honduras, Mexico, Haiti, China, and Nicaragua killing peasants to protect fruit plantations?

Finally, in 1934, Butler undertook his final service to the nation when he went to Congress with an extraordinary announcement: he had been approached by a cabal of wealthy men who asked him to overthrow the government in a military coup and then install a fascist-style dictatorship under military rule. A congressional investigation was launched. The plot, according to *The New York Times,* was *"alarmingly true"* and, was deemed by the Congress to have indeed been *"actually contemplated."* And the result? As with so many other fancy "blue ribbon" investigations like the Warren Commission, House Select Committee on Assassinations, Church Committee, Rockefeller Commission, 9/11 Commission, NIST Report, etc., etc., the net result was that much was discovered, many fingers wagged...and nothing actually done.

Who do they think they're fooling with their dog-and-pony shows? It is exactly as Arthur Sylvester, Assistant Secretary of Defense for Public Affairs, told the press pool of Vietnam War stringers assembled for his morning briefing: *"Look, if you think any American official is going to tell you the truth, then you're stupid. Did you hear that? Stupid."* (*Southern Illinoisan,* September 9, 1966, p. 11)

As for General Butler, he, at least, refused to back down from his duty, never faltered, nor put self before country. He took to the public airwaves, telling all who would listen that the persons involved were from the highest levels of banking and government, including one politician who sired two descendents that became future presidents: Senator Prescott Bush, a man also later convicted by the Justice Department of trading with the Nazis during WWII. Prescott's son, George would first helm Zapata Oil, running oil and guns in the Caribbean, before going on to become CIA Director, Ambassador to China, and eventually President of the United States, where he promised Americans a *"New World Order"* under *"1,000 points of light"* before initiating the series of ongoing wars which have destabilized the Middle East for 30 years and generated the tidal wave of refugees that overran Europe. Later, Prescott's grandson would be President when two planes hit two Towers on 9/11, 2001, before three towers collapsed at free fall speed each into its own footprint—an event which has never happened before or since to any steel-reinforced skyscraper, no matter if hit by aircraft or lit on fire. Within mere weeks, the Congress had magically produced a 1,000-page piece of immensely unpatriotic legislation called the "Patriot Act," which undermined many provisions of the 1st, 4th, and 5th Amendments to the Constitution—as well as creating a internal police directorate *à la* the Soviet KGB or Nazi Gestapo, comfortingly called the Department of Homeland Security—a bill which Bush II signed, he said, to protect America from those who *"hate us for our freedom."*

You can't make this stuff up.

You see, the way it works is, wrap it in red-white-and-blue bunting, tell them "It's for freedom," and the sheeple will go along with just about anything.

Or...

Maybe, we should stop trusting them so much...because, after all, they are lying liars who lie. It seems like there was once a wise fellow who said, *"By their fruits, you shall know them."* Maybe, instead of their words, we should watch their actions and the fruits of their actions. And if their actions reveal they are traitors, betrayers, and our enemies, we should note their perfidious actions...and defend ourselves accordingly.

In the case of the Deep State—i.e. anyone from that combination of SES apparatchiki ensconced in the bureaucracy for decades, the military-industrial-technological complex of snoops, Pentagonistas, technocrats, and their supervening managerial class of white-paper proffering and WEF-attending traitors...right up to and including the nameless ruling class of the Committee of 300 and Black Nobility/Bloodline Families who know better than to make themselves publicly known—it seems like, after the JFK coup, that the Deep State had at last wrapped its craggy claws around the throat of the American Republic. (And, briefly, if you're having trouble understanding or accepting who these Deep State people are, then you might research the long march of slow-burn socialism: the Fabian Society; H.G. Wells' *non*fiction books *The Open Conspiracy* and *The New World Order*; the Royal Institute for International Affairs, Council on Foreign Relations, and the League of Nations; Lenin, Trotsky and the trainloads of bankster gold that funded their little revolution; FDR's connivance in the thousands of Americans killed at Pearl Harbor to ignite WWII on the *Day of Infamy*; enslaved Jews making trucks for Hitler in factories built by GM; the incestuous relationships between Rockefeller's Standard Oil, I.T.T., G.E., IG Farben, and the Nazi regime, including the amazing coincidence of our B-17s Flying Fortresses bombing factories across Germany, except for these U.S. collaborator subsidiaries; tycoon Armand Hammer running asbestos mines in Soviet Russia; the connection between the ubiquitous Rockefeller plutocrats and such organizations as the United Nations, Trilateral Commission, Bilderberg Group; the rise of eco-fascism in the 1960s at the behest of the Club of Rome whose neo-Malthusian text *Limits to Growth* concludes with the admonition that, *"the real enemy, then, is mankind itself;"* that "green" ideology's dissemination and defense through the work of such luminaries as Gorbachev, Maurice Strong and their "Earth Charter;" the thinking of Bertrand Russell in *The Impact of Science on Society*, or Obama's science czar John Holdren whose book *Ecoscience* advocates reducing human population by compulsory chemical sterilization; the eugenicist roots of family planning advocates Margaret Sanger and Marie Stopes, William Gates, *père* (and little Billy "Vaxx Man" Gates III); the interface between these persons, families, and groups and the rolling series of international wars and crises erupting with increasing frequency throughout the 20th century; how the membership rolls of these groups interface with the upper echelons of political and administrative governance worldwide since 1947; the Federal Accounting Standards Advisory Board, Statement 56 (Oct., 2018) which, in effect, creates a secret, second set of federal accounting books run by unknown bureaucrats given complete accounting control of all federal expenditures but no public oversight—which may explain why Bloomberg can report that in 2019 the Defense Department racked up 35 *trillion* dollars in accounting "adjustments"—otherwise known as, "Oops, we just sorta lost all the money"—in one year; etc., etc., etc.).

Each of the ensuing Deep State-ballyhooed "wars" (largely UN or NATO-led "police actions") took us further from protecting the Republic's borders and farther into protecting the goals and interests of the world plutocrats and pedovores. Some wars, like Korea, served to start or protect communist regimes like N. Korea and Maoist China, while belittling the capacities of NATO nations. Other wars, like Vietnam, served to unify nations under a single communist regime, while undermining American confidence and international stature. And all the while, they were building over 100 overseas bases under red-white-and-blue banners of armed occupation throughout Europe, Asia, Africa, and the Middle East, thereby creating an *imago* of a bullying, militaristic America while draining this Republic of valuable resources, siphoning off its most moral and courageous youth to die needlessly, and undermine its moral stature as a bulwark for peace and liberty.

The last 70 years has evinced a singularly brilliant, dark, and dire design, which is only possible because the American people managed to continue believing we still live under the Founders' constitutional Republic. At one time, we did, and it was beautiful. Its dream was born through a thousand prayers and sacrifices, its reality planted on this earth by patriot's blood...all launched, won, and paid for, centuries ago. But somewhere beginning with the Progressives and ending with the Bushes, that nation was converted, inverted, and perverted, from that constitutional Republic into a Red-White-and-Blue fascist Empire. From *"Live Free or Die,"* we morphed into the economic hit man for the

International Monetary Fund. From *"I have not yet begun to fight"* our navy became, "Have gunboat, will travel," and it did travel, far and wide in furtherance of the petrodollar empire of the internationalist kleptocrats...all paid for by American blood, American money.

Listen:

If no one is attacking our shores, and your sons and daughters are flying off somewhere to die in some land you can neither spell nor find on a map, you can bet it is for their benefit...not for you or your Republic.

If someone in Washington is voting with the "bipartisan majority" to pass another trillion-dollar bar tab (since, how can any serious person call such a spendthrift monstrosity a "budget"?), you can bet it is for their benefit...not for you or your Republic.

If the news is pushing today's latest "crisis" or "terror" or "emergency" that necessitates more taxes or spending or lockdowns or restrictions on your speech, movement, or freedom, you can bet it is for their benefit...not for you or your Republic.

Wake up.

In Part IV, we will talk about victory and solutions. But, for now, remember:

Oceania is at war with Eurasia. Oceania has always been at war with Eurasia, and has never been at war with Eastasia...or is it the other way around?

"If my people, who are called by my name, will humble themselves and pray and seek my face and turn from their wicked ways, then I will hear from heaven, and I will forgive their sin and will heal their land."

— II Chronicles 7:14 —

Chapter 6

"No!" Power:
Citizen & Strength

Mayflower Chronicles, pp. 197:

"March 24. Dies Elizabeth, the wife of Mr. Edward Winslow. N. B. This month thirteen of our number die. And in three months past, dies half our company; the greatest part in the depth of winter, wanting houses and other comforts, being infected with the scurvy and others diseases, which their long voyage and unaccommodate condition brought upon them; so as there die sometimes two or three a day. Of a hundred persons scarce fifty remain; the living scarce able to bury the dead; the well not sufficient to tend the sick, there being, in their time of greatest distress, but six of seven, who spare no pains to help...

"May 12. The first marriage in this place is of Mr. Edward Winslow to Mrs. Susanna White, widow of Mr. William White."

America's unconquerable spirit was first displayed by these Pilgrim homesteaders the widow White and widower Winslow—each having lost their mates mere weeks before—mastered their grief, mustered their strength, and joined together in the work of building this new civilization. Half the colonists were gone within months, yet the rest carried on and built a nation which would revel in such unconquerable determination, as later would Washington and his troops at Valley Forge, the marines fighting their way up Iwo Jima, or the current generation bearing the subjugation of quisling traitors and globalists technocrats.

AS A PEOPLE, 20TH CENTURY Americans inherited unconquerable will and agency; they strode mightily onto the world stage, to showcase their Great White Fleet and boundless commercial enterprise, both for their own good and—as it happened—the malign manipulators behind the scenes. At the same time, the individual citizen was not a hapless urchin, buffeted helplessly by circumstances. Individual Americans continued to flex their capacities, to advocate for their constitutional prerogatives. The application of the Constitution to the internal problems of tyranny and liberty proved to be problematic in instantiation, but powerful in actuation. What could the individual citizen do against the 20th century's rising tide of tyranny? Perhaps they could draw inspiration from a rebel whose cause was always freedom, Patrick Henry.

PATRICK HENRY
"The battle, sir, is not to the strong alone; it is to the vigilant, the active, the brave."
— Patrick Henry —

Homeschooled, self-taught lawyer, politician, and outspoken rabble-rouser, Patrick Henry was Virginia's tireless voice of liberty. Afire with burning eyes and brimstone prose, Henry grew from his youth attending the rolling, orotund sermons of the Great Awakening preachers of his day. In the 1740s, his mother often took young Henry into town from his woodland home in the Virginia hills to hear their revival services. Rapt in admiration by the finely turned scriptural perorations, the lad would mimic the ministers to perfection in his childhood and emulate them as an adult in building his mature success.

After a couple false starts in farming and innkeeping, Henry found his calling as a country lawyer fighting for the cause of the little man, a profession where he could put his loquacity and persuasive fervor to good use in moving juries to his client's side. It was only natural that he turn such oratorical talent to politics, and in 1765 he became the standard bearer for the cause of liberty in the Virginia House of Burgesses. Likewise, although a devout lifelong Anglican, he continually fought for freedom of religious conscience, believing that, regarding one's relationship with the Creator, everyone has *"an equal, natural and unalienable right to the free exercise of religion."*

As uncompromising on liberty as Thomas Paine, Henry also railed against the practice of slavery; despite such protestations, the institution's popularity amongst the many landed gentry in the Virginia House was too great, and neither he nor Jefferson could win enough votes to overturn it. Nonetheless, by the 1770s, Henry had emerged as one of the two voices most undisputedly foremost in rallying the nation to the cause of Colonial independency: Sam Adams in the north and Patrick Henry in the south. As one of the loudest, clearest, and earliest advocates for colonial liberty, Patrick Henry would carry the Virginia House of Burgesses forward to adopting independency on the river of his famous honeyed words and mellifluous oratory.

Yet, like so many of the Founders, Henry was not just a man of words but also of action. He did not just rail against the Stamp Act but led marches against it at the capital. This combination of practical leadership and oratorical skill made him a natural choice to be sent as a staunch advocate for independency to the first Continental Congress in October of 1774. There, he was notable in his eloquence and energy, but unable the shift the many loyalists who were not yet ready to break with the home country.

Once back in Virginia, Henry—true to the character of a badass—continued to pursue the good in both thought and deed. He returned first to earning his daily bread as an attorney to provide for his wife and growing brood of eventually 17 children. At the same time, he continued to lobby tirelessly for the cause of liberty in the House of Burgesses. Despite his indubitable talent and growing fame as an orator throughout the Colonies, we have only one near-verbatim account of any of his eloquence, which happens to be from this fraught pre-revolutionary moment. In

March of 1775, a month before the shots were even fired at Lexington and Concord, he vehemently urged his fellow Virginia delegates to raise a militia against the Crown, and closed with this immortal exhortation: *"The war is inevitable and let it come! I repeat it, sir, let it come...Gentlemen may cry, Peace, Peace but there is no peace. The war is actually begun! The next gale that sweeps from the north will bring to our ears the clash of resounding arms! Our brethren are already in the field! Why stand we here idle? What is it that gentlemen wish? What would they have? Is life so dear, or peace so sweet, as to be purchased at the price of chains and slavery? Forbid it, Almighty God! I know not what course others may take; but as for me, give me liberty or give me death!"*

A month later, he would march on the state capital in Williamsburg at the head of a band of Virginia patriots during the Gunpowder Incident of 1775. After Lexington and Concord, British marines had been sent out to seize the gunpowder stored by the Virginia Commonwealth in Williamsburg, a precaution undertaken by many British colonial administrators as a means of preventing more uprisings by colonial militiamen. Hearing of the confiscation—and unwilling to be outdone by the patriots in Boston—Henry immediately called out the Virginia militia. George Washington and others advised caution. since the British Governor was threatening to respond to any rebellion by reducing the capital "to ashes." Undeterred by such threats, in early May, Henry marched at the head of hundreds of men on Williamsburg, armed and intent on giving the British another taste of American gunpowder. At the last minute, a payment-in-kind of £330 was arranged to settle the matter and forestall bloodshed. But the message had been sent and received: don't tread on the Virginians.

This episode bolstered Henry's rising reputation in the state, and—coupled with his eloquence in debate at the Continental Congress—placed him among the most notable patriots in the *de facto* rebellion. As rebellion turned into insurrection, and insurrection into revolution, it was only natural, then, that once independence was declared in July, 1776, Henry—

that firebrand and electrifying exemplar of leadership—would be elected the first governor of the independent Commonwealth of Virginia, the leader of those who would rather die on their feet than live on their knees. He would run the commonwealth's government during its troublesome infancy over two different tenures, once at the start and once at the end of the Revolutionary War.

When at last the victory was secured, Henry's attentions turned to the proposed new federal government. Since in his estimation even the tenuous ties under the Articles of Confederation had been too tight, the new federal Constitution being proposed in 1787 raised his suspicions. He immediately made common cause with Thomas Paine and the Anti-Federalists in advocating for the addition of a Bill of Rights before any adoption of the proposed charter. Once again, it was primarily Patrick Henry and Sam Adams (this time joined by Paine and George Mason) who spearheaded the cause of liberty, though this time in the cause of defending, not national, but individual independence. Primarily, the Anti-Federalists sought to pare back the centralization and power of the federal government by ensuring the explicit codification of essential personal liberties. This struggle reached a chaotic apogee in Rhode Island on July 4, 1788, where 1,000 armed militiamen marched on the state house to protest ratification of the overweening Constitution. Thankfully, that struggle never degenerated into civil war. Rather, the Anti-Federalist protests moved the states to adopt many of the additions which are now considered the most essential such as the 1st, 2nd, 4th, and 5th Amendments, protections to which the public have recourse and draw succor every day.

Like Thomas Paine, Patrick Henry's rebellion, in a sense, never stopped. He came into the cause fighting the injustice and oppression of slavery, fought the big fight of the Revolution, and finally won the smaller but essential victory for Anti-Federalism which enhanced the Constitution. His love for liberty proved so great that he would even fight against the Constitution he had helped birth in order to keep free the country and countrymen he loved.

With the ascendency of Fedgov over the ensuing decades, much of Henry's work would be tested and, indeed, undermined by illicit legislation and alphabet agency overreach. But while Fedgov (and its arachnid overseers) were pushing their grand plans, with wars engulfing the whole world, the disasters and panics which trammelled the tiny plans of the little people—many of these "little" Americans would push back. They were too busy being free to stop or care who objected. They were proving the worth of those Amendments Henry had fought so hard to enact. They were fighting back with their minds and speech, their community and the law. Like Patrick Henry, they would not be cowed, they would not be silenced, and they would never surrender: liberty or death.

The Power of the Peaceful: the First Amendment

"A man who won't die for something is not fit to live."
— Martin Luther King, Jr. —

To assemble together and speak in search of redress for your grievances, these are essential protected practices in a constitutional Republic, protected for us under the First Amendment. Yet, Wilson's thugs would beat pacifists in the street, and Hoover order the Bonus Army veterans camped out in Washington to be rousted, shot, and burned out. In the aftermath of FDR and WWII, the political center of gravity was moving ever more steadily away from the citizen and towards Washington. Overseas, the Marines and Navy were making the world safe for the devouring maws of the United Fruit and Standard Oil companies. The conglomerates and combines were consolidating control, moving with haste towards their ideal outcome: continual war and infinite corporate profiteering on the backs of a blind and bullied populace. The pieces seemed nicely aligned as fear of the dreaded Soviet boogeyman would cow the quiescent and TV-anaesthetized herd into a fearful obedience willing to march mindlessly into endless proxy wars in far-flung forgotten lands.

Except...for one preacher from the South. This preacher—

who, like Patrick Henry, was from his boyhood a wonder-worker with words—would rise up, speaking his truth with a southern preacher's gift of cadence, an orotund resonance, and a range of articulation and wit born of a doctorate in theology from a northeastern university; this one man from the backwoods of Alabama, would unapologetically bring the trouble. Today, amidst all the revisionism and hagiography, it can be hard to clearly track the real history and person who was Dr. Martin Luther King, Jr. But, in the early 1950s, he seemed just another nameless pulpit-pounder, and America was still a country in the first throes of empire-building, before the CIA had declared hegemony over the American people by publicly slaughtering their president in a motorcade. In studying the real King, you find someone whose courageous yet compassionate approach to political confrontation truly evokes American Badass.

King decided he would take on Caesar, under the light of Christ. He would bring down segregation and Jim Crow through protest, confrontation, and truth-telling, without touching a gun, without lifting his hand against his fellow man; he would do so by turning the other cheek as the blows rained down upon him, his family, and his reputation. He fought the fight just as his Master had, through speaking truth and humbly submitting to the consequences...over and over again, until the victory was won through his sacrifice. And, at each step, he exhibited that rare combination of adding thoughtfulness and prudence to courage and resolve.

In 1955, King began his public outreach to overcome the ongoing Jim Crow laws. Meeting with other preachers in Alabama who were seeking a means of bringing effective attention and resolution to the belittling treatment of black Americans, they sought a cause, an example, to illuminate the moral degeneracy of racial segregation. They examined many individuals and protests, until Rosa Parks' refusal to move her tired feet to the back of the bus made a clear-cut and defensible case, one that had iconic power. But, when the rest of the ministers demurred to speak out—for fear of backlash and losing church membership—King, though the new kid in the group, tremulously accepted the dread task. Still a rookie, he nonetheless took himself to the pulpit and spoke out, and his characteristic eloquence and dynamism moved his listeners, rapidly bringing others to the cause. A year-long boycott of the Montgomery bus line ensued which eventuated in the desegregation of all public transportation. During the dispute, King did indeed pay the price for daring to speak out; he was continually attacked and vilified; his family was threatened, his house firebombed. But he neither allowed himself to resort to personal calumny of his assailants, nor firebomb anyone back. He gutted up, took the abuse, and continued to speak truth boldly and clearly, moving forward without surrender.

From then on, King would lead a coalition of ministers and allied supporters—the Southern Christian Leadership Conference— as a springboard to promote direct, non-violent action toward social change in situations akin to the Rosa Parks case. In 1960, King went to Atlanta to bring sit-in and boycott pressure on the city to desegregate their lunch counters. Within a year, the city would open up those lunch counters and institute other broad-based desegregation measures. In 1961, however, when King joined with others in seeking broad-based civic equality in Albany, Georgia, his efforts failed. Realizing his approach was only successful under the right circumstances and to not seek for too much too soon, King became selective. He looked for cases where his methods could be useful; he avoided rushing into situations where his techniques would prove either unwanted or ineffective. He very consciously sought venues which could produce positive, constructive results, not merely opportunities for grandstanding, let alone powder kegs which would induce chaos or violence. It is a necessary part of the dual nature of badass, to develop the prudence and judgment to discern when to apply peace and patience, and when to apply pluck and pressure.

King's iconic moment came in 1963 when he delivered the "I Have a Dream" speech at the reflecting pool before the Lincoln Memorial. Here was a man whose followers marched straight into assaults by police dogs and fire hoses, who shut down bus lines with boycotts and restaurants with sit-ins. But King would employ no such grand activist gestures that day. This was a man who would be arrested 29 times for—according to the segregationist laws of the time—being in the wrong place, doing the wrong thing, at the wrong time. But the pressure he brought that day would come not from street mobilization, but moral suasion. His speech would ring out across the capital, and eventually the nation. With his straight, bold challenge—that the nation should abide by its own core promise of the rule of law, wherein all persons receive just and equal treatment—he would move more people than any militant march ever could:

"I have a dream that one day this nation will rise up and live out the true meaning of its creed: we hold these truths to be self-evident, that all men are created equal...

"I have a dream, that my four little children will one day live in a nation where they will not be judged by the color of their skin but by the content of their character.

"I have a dream today..."

One way to parse this oration is simply as a request for constitutional justice. At the same time—and more importantly—he was asking only that his children be judged on their character. He sought no handout, no payback. He was, in effect, simply hoping for his children to enter the constitutional arena of freedom which renders every citizen more self-reliant, more unconquerable, more morally sound overall. All he was really seeking was a world which challenged his children to live badass.

Because he was only seeking the justice stamped on his birthright ticket as a U.S. citizen, because he sought nothing more than that his children become their best selves, it gave his speech a clarity and rigor which was well-nigh unassailable; he was enunciating a case with such moral force as to command assent. That—combined with non-violent, though insistent, protest—leant his cause a moral ascendency which could never be achieved by any kind of violent reprisals or verbal ripostes. His very meekness— that quietist respect for orderly discourse in the face of unjust and violent assaults—disarmed his opponents by contrasting so markedly with the ugly brutality of their calumny and assaults.

Beyond that, it allowed onlookers to focus not on his motions and methods, but on his message, so they could hear the clear, unassailable logic of his cause and see the fruits of his patience and moral strength contrasted with the brutality and vitriol of the opposition.

Because of the eloquence of his words and elegance of his approach, the Civil Rights Act passed within a year, followed thereafter by the Voting Rights Act, Fair Housing Act, etc. His efforts over the previous decade had broken the segregationist dam around the issues of racial inequity, without the need for a second civil war like the one that had rent the country asunder in the previous century.

He also, shortly thereafter, took home a well-earned Nobel Peace Prize.

Fighting without any firearms, Dr. King took American freedom to its next level, to a level rarely contemplated on this planet. Freedom in America finally became as simple and powerful as this: are you human? Then here, in this land of liberty, you are free under the law, no matter your looks, your past, your beliefs. Be a burden to none and a friend to all, and all of our bounty is yours to pursue and enjoy.

In fact, King, a trained scholar, was able to make explicit his rationale for using direct, nonviolent citizen action, which epitomizes much of the best of American Badass. In *Strength to Love*,—an apologia King penned during one of his many prison sojourns—the first chapter, "A Tough Mind and a Tender Heart," describes two broad ways of approaching life's challenges, which echo much of what we have seen from other exemplary Americans. He begins by delineating the tough mind:

"Let us consider, first the need for a tough mind, characterized by incisive thinking, realistic appraisal, and decisive judgment. The tough mind is sharp and perpetrating...The tough-minded individual is astute and discerning. He has a strong, austere quality that makes for firmness of purpose and solidness of commitment."

Next, he considers the importance of tenderness: *"But we must not stop with the cultivation of a tough mind. The gospel also demands a tender heart. Toughmindedness without tenderheartedness is cold and detached, leaving one's life in a perpetual winter devoid of the warmth of spring and the gentle heat of summer...*

"Jesus reminds us that the good life combines the toughness of the serpent and tenderness of the dove."

He concludes by commending those who can combine the tough with the tender in a prudent manner: *"A third way is open to our quest for freedom, namely, non-violent resistance, that combines toughmindedness and tenderheartedness and avoids the complacency and do-nothingness of the softminded and the violence and bitterness of the hardhearted...Through non-violent resistance we shall be able to oppose the unjust system and at the same time love the perpetrators of the system. We must work passionately and unrelentingly for full stature as citizens, but may it never be said, my friends, that to gain it we used the inferior methods of falsehood, malice, hate, and violence."*

As he moved to national prominence, King's vision of what evils beset the citizens broadened, moving beyond the difficult and sometimes divisive issue of race alone (which can be leveraged to pit American against American) to the universal burdens and ravages brought by war. Contrary to the mantra of men like Chairman of the Joint Chiefs of Staff Lemnitzer, National Security Advisor John Bolton and other acolytes of the military-industrial complex—who seem to hold that one must never doubt that there has always been a Pax Americana, there will always be a Pax Americana, and that all which is good on this Earth comes from the Pax Americana—King dared to speak out against the Vietnam War. It was perhaps a fatal mistake.

The international plutocracy can allow the minions to struggle in groups against each other—since divide-and-conquer is good for the business of tyranny—but the helots must never touch the political third rail of asserting that maybe peace is better for children and families than war.

JFK made an open and honest speech about peace with Russia on June 19, 1963.

He was shot dead on November 22, 1963.

Bobby Kennedy made an open and honest speech about peace in Vietnam on February 8, 1968.

He was shot dead on June 6, 1968.

MLK made an open and honest speech about peace on April 4, 1967.

He was shot dead exactly one year later: April 4, 1968.

LBJ, George Bush I, Bill Clinton, George Bush II, Donald Rumsfeld, Dick Cheney...none of them ever made an open honest speech about peace (or much of anything, from what I can tell); rather, they led us into war.

Not one of them got shot dead. Ain't that interesting?

Citizen No!

"There's always someone telling you not to do something. The main thing is just to ignore them."

— Tim Robbins —

What lies implicit in King's bold insistence that America should institute racial justice is the essential ascendency of the citizen's sovereignty over the state. That is, the belief that the state is only there as a necessary evil, a kind of public utility agreed to by consent and therefore amendable (or even removable) by public decree. If the state fails in its duties, it should be reformed...or removed. That principle is *the* declaration of the *Declaration*, the constitution of the Constitution.

That essential principle is also the bedrock of the core practice of *citizen nullification*, and is thereby the root of American common sense and common law. At any point where the public utility of government oversteps its bounds or outlives its usefulness, it is the right—nay, duty—of the citizen to stand up and say: "No!" Citizens must continually treat government, and its operatives, like a wayward 3-year-old, which has been given a modicum of resources and responsibility, but which almost always misuses and abuses it, tantrums when remonstrated for its recalcitrance, and finally needs to be given a time out when it responds to restraint by breaking things which do not belong to it.

The gentlest path to citizen nullification is to simply do the right thing. In most cases, that means merely to continue in your particular practice of liberty, no matter what nattering decrees are announced by the nabobs being paid by your tax dollars to sit in air-conditioned offices inventing illicit dictates. Now, they can make whatever fancy declamation they wish in decrying you doing that thing—which is not bothering anyone and none of their dang business anyway—which they want stopped because they happen to not like it so good. But, frankly, that's just kinda tough on them: if they want to use your tax money to tell you not to do what you want with the time and money you have left over—after paying them to tell you what you can and can't do—because you're just going to go on doing whatever harmless thing you want to do anyway. Because, if you are a free and sovereign citizen on the land of your birth harming not one living being just living your life, then there is no call for anyone's interference in anything you do. And what anyone else thinks or says about it—even anyone who draws a Fedgov paycheck—won't change any of that.

This ignore-them-and-hope-they-go-away approach was attempted by Henry David Thoreau in his one-man tax resistance at Walden Pond. This was Thoreau's initial, haphazard one-night experiment at this thing he called *civil disobedience*. It was a first attempt at a more peaceful methodology, but, as a lone practitioner of a method with no historical antecedent, he was just one crazy guy who spent a night in jail and got bailed out by his aunt. Memorializing his ideas in his manifesto *"Resistance to Civil Government,"* however, Thoreau seeded ideas picked up and—under the light of the Gospel—amplified by Tolstoy, whose book was read and applied by Gandhi, whose work was read and applied by King. Thoreau's thinking thus was cultivated by others into an accepted, even commonplace, mode of protest, and, because of its gentle suasion, broad notoriety, and eventual familiarity, it has become one of the most effective means of moving men and nations. It was thus that the Revolutionary War's tools of blockade, blunderbuss, and burning in effigy were augmented by non-violent non-cooperation, and American pioneer patriots gave to patriots worldwide another means to quell government overreach and expand the ground of liberty everywhere, without the necessity of bloodshed.

Still, even today, as with Thoreau, when you try singleton non-cooperation, the Fedgov hirelings will usually not appreciate it, and they may make scenes and break things, and then might go on to get some other bullies with badges and bullets involved, so it becomes a whole thing. Thus, it's often a good idea to plan that sort of protest with friends, all at once, and to be clear and outspoken about why you are doing it, so you can explain it clearly to other people...just so everyone knows you're not crazy; it's just another case of the government being kooky (again). This, second level of *group* citizen nullification is now what's usually contemplated by the term *civil disobedience*, and it's oftentimes needful in order to get the government back on track. It's a more stern but still amicable way of saying: "Look, Mr. Fedgov, there are many of us doing this thing, and even with all of us doing it, there still is no one being hurt, so please go back home, have yourself a nice donut, and leave us alone like you're supposed to."

Such civil, everyday flaunting of stupid and oppressive laws is, of course, the central tenet that underlies the entire Revolution: that the ultimate measure of justice within a nation lies with the judgment of the citizenry...while, at the same time, the center of gravity for government is always a slow, continuous centripetal drift toward the arbitrary imposition of coercive and counterproductive dictates, i.e. tyranny, This eternal polarity between the rulers and the ruled makes it necessary for citizens to continually decide—in each and every generation—on the best course by which to slow, stay, and subvert government overreach.

The *civil* part of civil disobedience is a particularly ambiguous terminology. By the strict denotation, civil disobedience can be any disobedience to a civil (i.e. government) order or authority. This, however, can take many forms, so the more common use of the phrase particularly contemplates the secondary connotation of "civil," meaning something done in a courteous, i.e. "*civilzed*", manner. Thus, in most instances, for most citizens, civil disobedience will be action which is direct and confrontational in advocating for political ends, but still avoids violence and bloodshed. Such efforts at redress of grievances are often relatively mild and polite; that is, they undertake to fix the government via the rather tame modality of words: speeches, editorials, marches, or petitions. That is the reason a broad-based, articulate, insistent, but still non-belligerent approach like King's has such appeal, while violent revolutions like John Brown's often wind up with bodies "a-molding in the grave" without producing any lasting results. It appeals to people's moral compass when citizens politely request a rectification of misguided policy by asking if the thugs wouldn't mind please lifting that boot of dictatorship off my neck, thank you very much.

If, however, such "civil" entreaties fail, people may move to the third step: active resistance, where matters become increasingly frenetic, hectic, and kinetic. The actions in this third stage of civil disobedience are now no longer circumscribed by gentility and politeness, but will tend to be disruptive, intrusive, and catalytic of a need to respond. Herein we find shaming, shunning, slowdowns at work; there is picketing and pamphleteering, placards and graffiti, hunger strikes and perhaps picnics at inconvenient places with inconvenient ideas; there is even, if you're the Yippies, running a pig called *Pigasus the Immortal* for president (sorry, kids, he did not win). Is a sit-in at a lunch counter non-violent? Probably initially, as you quietly order a ham sandwich. But when the ruffians come to throw you out on your ear, matters have become pretty physical and personal. How about a boycott? If your boycott is truly successful, someone is not getting paid somewhere. Is it a harm to the person or company at the receiving end? The fact is, resistance to tyranny is easier with an earlier, lighter touch, but rare is the patriot who will stop short of any means necessary to ensure that their children not bear the shackles of slavery.

Equally important for civil disobedience is the readiness of the protesters to pay the price. The greater the willingness of the protesters to accept the pain and punishment, the greater the effect of their action, whether those actions be shunning the malefactors (which takes little real toll on the practitioner), to boycotts (produces inconvenience, maybe cost), to strikes (loss of livelihood), or marches (arrest, assault, even assassination by security forces). For non-violent protests to work, the protesters must be prepared to make whatever sacrifice is necessary to elicit the brutality and despotism of the other side; it is a peculiar kind of war—a moral war—but it is nonetheless war, and there will be real casualties, and, like in shooting war, the real heroes are those who pay the ultimate price for their cause.

In general, the size of the protest (and its public support) gives some measure of how far afield the tyranny has travelled from the *sensus communis*, and the relative merits of the disobedience itself. That is, a civil disobedience of one person will probably be ineffective and might still be in need of groundwork to either (a) clarify its aims and methods or even overall worth, or (b) put in the time seeding and nurturing the ideas until they achieve enough public support to carry a sufficient community assent in action. These are matters of judgment. Few would say John Brown was wrong in wanting to overthrow the institution of slavery, but it's (a) clear that his choice of method was ineffective, and (b) possible that his precipitate violent action actually slowed the acceptance of abolitionism. In contrast, Dr. King, the primary American exponent of civil disobedience, used a variety of practices and degrees of pressure, from successful bus boycotts in Birmingham, the March and suasion at the Lincoln Memorial, to abandoning such attempts when they later proved a practical impossibility in Chicago. There is simply a degree of pragmatic judgment and political craft needed to make use of such a non-linear, affective tool.

But the information age has somewhat changed the tactical landscape. Where before, a tyrant might expect to hide his graft, grift, and grotesquery, he is much more likely to be discovered and publicly pilloried today. Indeed, one of the remarkable ironies of current political contretemps is to watch the superannuated politicos attempting to gaslight the public with impunity as they were wont to do in the big-media controlled 1980s and 1990s, when three networks and CNN marked the veritable limit of national "news." But an internet, social-media, Wayback Machine-fueled information arena is a vastly different environment. Their long-standing practice of bamboozling the public with every tactic from verbal evasion and equivocation to outright lies have simply created a vast sea of doubters and disbelievers who, having been fooled once, twice, and more, won't be fooled again. The Naked Emperors continue to tell each other how marvelous they look in their latest flim-flam finery, but the peasants have already turned their backs on the revolting spectacle of their naked depravity.

Civil disobedience, then, is exhibited along a scale, across a distribution. While the Revolution had undertaken direct resistance to the Crown in both violent (Lexington and Concord) and non-violent (boycotts, Tea Party) ways, there was nothing like the self-conscious, self-sacrificial street action which came to characterize such actions under King. The British Empire which faced the Colonials with triple-masted man-o-war sporting dozens of cannons was also not the same regime which, 150 years later, voluntarily returned India to the Indian people. Gandhi could work his media magic against the British because their conscience had become sufficiently tender to be moved by the massacre of hundreds and even by this one man's simple act of weeks of self-starvation. In contrast "tank man" standing alone before a column of Chinese armor in 1989 did not stop the CCP from massacring its own citizens *en masse* in a hail of gunfire at Tiananmin Square. Effective resistance always entails, as a starting point, a prudential judgment, knowing who one is playing for, the mood and size of the forces involved on both sides, in order to develop effective strategy and tactics, messaging and methods.

Still, the development and widespread implementation of a set of citizen tools recognized by regime and populace alike as both legitimate and meaningful—as in the case of Gandhi and the British Raj, King and the cities of the South—is an important civilizational watershed. Such implicit understandings as, for instance, that a sufficient number of people in the street checkmates the efficacy of governmental mass slaughter can be reckoned a kind of implicit social contract; it is a political rock-paper-scissors pavane which circumvents the need for actual violence. If the people will not get themselves up to an uprising until they have sufficient numbers to quell any pushback—while, for its part, the regime undertakes to sit on its hands when sufficient numbers do indeed appear on the streets—then the arena of competition moves from physical force to moral persuasion and social perception. Political suasion becomes a competition in information (some might say propaganda). It is, at least, far closer to a civil dispensation of power along more democratic principles, which heralds the potential for the People to speak truth to power without recourse to full revolutionary urban combat. That the mere demonstration of numbers should demand regime reform (even resignation) is an immense accession to democratic principles...and the development and preservation of this implicit social contract having emerged as a multi-generational, internationally-understood paradigm, actually portends a more free, less violent future.

The degree of force employed is, ultimately, however, the choice of the regime—i.e. the goons with the guns—for their response decides which road reform will follow: the easy path of accommodation, or the hard road of struggle. A burdened people may start with the restraint of a Martin Luther King, but the oligarchy that fails to listen will next be dealing with the no-holds-barred relentlessness of a young Malcolm X.

Jury Nullification: You Decide What is Right

"I consider trial by jury as the only anchor yet imagined by man by which a government can be held to the principles of its constitution."

— Thomas Jefferson —

One of the most powerful yet oft-overlooked tools of citizen nullification of unjust laws and out-of-control prosecution is jury nullification. While public protest and the quiet potency of an armed citizenry quells tyranny in the legislative arena, the power of the juror stops it in the judicial arena. Codified as elemental in our courtroom processes is the fact that you, the juror, and no one else, decides who is guilty, who is not, what is justice and what is not. Here, even a protest of one person can prove immensely powerful, as a jury hung by one vote can stave off a gross injustice.

By law, no judge in the United States may command a jury to deliver a particular verdict. Guilt or innocence is decided by the judgment of the jurors, each member freely and in their individual conscience. Likewise, no juror may be threatened or punished for their decision, no matter what their particular reasoning or rationale may be on the matter. Finally, once rendered, no verdict of innocence (not guilty) can ever be overturned. In short, in a courtroom, the judge may be the boss, but the juror is king.

Such jury nullification has commonly been used by the citizens to nullify persecutions for "victimless" crimes which produce no harm nor seem the business of anyone else. Under slavery, American juries were known to ignore the laws and allow violators of the fugitive slave laws to go free as a protest against human enslavement. During Prohibition, it was not unusual for juries to nullify the restrictions against alcohol production and distribution by returning verdicts of not guilty. Similarly, marijuana prohibition has been overturned by juries returning not guilty verdicts for someone arrested for growing a few weeds on his back lot. Likewise, American juries have signaled their displeasure at government overreach by setting free folks arrested for such inconsequential acts as gardening in their own yards, collecting rainwater from their roof, installing alternative energy systems, or protesting against war.

The principle of the supremacy of the jury over both judge and law—as a demonstration and protection of the will of the common citizen—has existed from the beginning of this nation. Even to the extent of voting for an accused person's innocence, not because they did not commit the act, but because you find the law itself repugnant to justice—you, the jury decide what is right. This bulwark against unjust laws was always understood to be precisely one of the main reasons to preserve juries. The Supreme Court, 1794:

"[O]n questions of fact, it is the province of the jury; on questions of law, it is the province of the court to decide. But...you [the jury] have nevertheless a right to take upon yourselves to judge of both, and to determine the law as well as the fact in controversy"

— *Georgia V. Brailsford*, 3 U.S. 1 Dall. 1 (1794) —

The fact of your sovereignty in the courtroom, as a representative of the American People in judgment not just of the defendant but of the justice of the law and its enforcers continued into the modern age. The Court in 1972:

"[There is] an unreviewable and unreversible power in the jury, to acquit in disregard of the instructions on the law given by the trial judge....John Adams; Alexander Hamilton; prominent judges— [held] that jurors had a duty to find a verdict according to their own conscience, though in opposition to the direction of the court; that their power signified a right; that they were judges both of law and of fact in a criminal case, and not bound by the opinion of the court."

— *U.S. v. Dougherty*, 473 F 2nd 1113, 1139 (1972) —

And your duty as a juror—to protect the country from criminals by finding them guilty, the innocent by setting them free, and all of us by stopping any judicial overreach by always choosing the decision which best meets justice—continues to our day. Again, the Supreme Court in *Dougherty* (1972): *"The pages of history shine on instances of the jury's exercise of its prerogative to disregard instructions of the judge."*

The principle of juror supremacy—and jury nullification—goes back deep in the common law, and its greatest hero, who made it all possible, may be an ordinary commoner of unrelenting resolve by the name of Edward Bushel. In 1670, William Penn (yes, that same Pennsylvania-founding Mr. Penn) was once arrested for believing and acting on a Christian worldview at variance with the state religion of Anglicanism. Penn believed in the "Primitive Christianity" propounded in his book *No Cross, No Crown* and felt called to proclaim his faith publicly in pursuit of the salvation of souls. He (along with a companion, William Mead) was arrested on the streets of London by constables for the horrid crime of "preaching seditiously and causing a great tumult of people."

Penn was brought to trial at the Old Bailey at a time when judges routinely harangued and bulled jurors to return exactly the verdict desired by the bench, despite such a practice being repugnant to Magna Carta. One judge, the capricious and despotic Chief Justice Sir John Kelyng, was so notorious in the practice of fining and imprisoning jurors that even Parliament was alarmed and remonstrated against his excessive use of the illegal practice. Yet he, and other justices, continued in flagrant disregard of the law and public censure. Once, when a juror protested that Kelyng could not tell him how to vote since that was against Magna Carta, this supposed exemplar of British justice replied, *"Magna Carta, Magna Farta!"*

It is exactly as a bulwark against this sort of pompous, puerile potentate that your constitutional privileges and the practice of jury nullification were instituted.

In Penn's case, the jury initially found him guilty of the act of public speaking, but refused to find him guilty of speaking to "an unlawful assembly." This raised the ire of so-called Justice Howell, who reared back and gave them the full force of his vengeance: *"Gentlemen, you shall not be dismissed till we have a verdict that the court will accept; and you shall be locked up, without meat, drink, fire, and tobacco; you shall not think thus to abuse the court; we will have a verdict, by the help of God, or you shall starve for it."*

Besides jailing and starving the jury, he also ordered Penn to be bound, gagged, and dragged away. Before the bailiffs could do so, Penn shouted to the jury, *"You are Englishmen. Mind your privilege! Give not away your right!"*

From the jury box, the single valiant voice of juror Edward Bushel cried back, *"Nor shall we ever do!"*

Thus began the test of wills.

Judge Howell kept the jury jailed for two days for having the temerity to not agree with him. By the time he recalled the jury pool back to the courtroom, his abuse had only strengthened their resolve. This time the defiant jurors brought back a verdict of plain not guilty...on *all* counts; they refused to convict Penn (or Mead) of anything. Infuriated, but having a not guilty verdict which could not be voided, the judge lashed back in the only way he could: he declared the jury in contempt of court for returning a verdict contrary to their own earlier finding of fact, fined them, and had them remanded once again to prison, this time until they each paid their fine for contempt. While the others jurors paid the fine and walked away, Edward Bushel refused to pay...on principle.

Bushel would face the time for refusing to pay the fine; he was willing to pay the price for being right when his government was wrong. He would also, however, appeal Howell's fine and imprisonment to the Court of Common Pleas. There are many persons within government of good sense and noble intent, and they occasionally appear in enough numbers and at the right place and time to have a salutary effect. The higher court in this case stood up for justice and found that the practice of instructing verdicts and punishing jurors was itself repugnant to the law and thus they summarily forbade it. That principle of the inviolability of the juror and their vote, i.e. jury nullification, became thenceforth a cornerstone of English common law and was adopted into American jurisprudence.

As John Adams said of jurors and their duty: *"It is not only his right, but his duty... to find the verdict according to his own best understanding, judgment, and conscience, though in direct opposition to the direction of the court."*

Because of the fortitude of Bushel (and temerity of Penn), jurors are free today to protect the accused from injustice in any court of law. Because of Bushel, we have jury nullification as an understood principle of law and cornerstone of American freedom. In this country, the People alone decide who is guilty and who is innocent.

Citizen Nullification: Just say "No!" to Bullies and Thugs
"Freedom lies in being bold."
— Robert Frost —

Nullification is not just for juries. The ability and duty of the public to stop bad governance is the root of American history, the core of its success. The Pilgrims said "No!" to being told to worship God according to another church's opinions, and they had the courage and determination to find a place to make that possible. The Founders and Framers said "No!" to the Crown's tax-and-steal plans, and had the temerity to stand up to the redcoat army to make it stick. Edward Bushnell said "No!" to bad law and lawless prosecution and had the prudence to seek court reform to secure jury nullification. Smedley Butler said "No!" to the fascist plutocrats who wished to turn the United States into a Hitlerian dictatorship, and had the backbone to bruit the fact to the whole world. Martin Luther King said "No!" to generations of Jim Crow laws, and he had the strength of love to triumph through nonviolent resistance.

American history is one long denunciation of efforts by amok bureaucrats to impose their mad despotism on innocent citizens. Only through widespread, public, and unrelenting citizen pushback, do the bullies get put in their place. The primary point of power for the oppressed citizen is the willingness to say "No!" and the wherewithal to back it up.

But the "No!" in citizen nullification is, properly, not just a one-way act. The "No!" must also be directed inward. That is, while it is absolutely necessary to hold government overreach within bounds through the Constitution and citizen watchfulness, the more important principle is for the citizens to say "No!" to their own impulses. In a free republic, for the citizens (and the nation) to prosper, they must be able to exercise moral restraint and self-control; their own personal "No!" is more essential to the long-term success of the land than anything the government may do. If the citizens develop such integrity, then they have not only the self-reliance but the clarity of moral vision to both eschew the temptations of government handouts and maintain the government within its proper bounds. To say "No!" to self indulgence, is also to say "No!" to the need for government intervention, help, and snares disguised as gifts. *No Power* is the initiation point of liberation, the implicit reaffirmation of one's freedom, and the starting point of the long road to true fulfillment and flourishing as a person and nation. True negation of the detrimental is, by extension, positive affirmation of the beneficial. It is not just to call out the negative but to call forth the affirmative, to push away the foul while being pulled toward the fine. Hence, building up one's "No!" muscle is an essential exercise for becoming a well-developed citizen. As Katharine Lee Bates so elegantly expressed it in the second verse of "America, the Beautiful," to make the maintenance of freedom possible, the nation's citizens must build personal integrity, each person must, *"Confirm thy soul in self control/ Thy liberty in law."*

One place where that "No!" muscle remains essential for the health of the Republic is on the long-running, unrelenting fight for gun rights.

Ain't Gettin' the Guns

"Firearms are second only to the Constitution in importance; they are the people's liberty's teeth."

— George Washington —

The 2nd Amendment is the ultimate expression of citizen nullification, the ultimate tool of "No!" power. It is the *last* resort...if we ever fail to stop the bullies in the early stages, if we ever let them slink up behind and take us unaware...and, precisely if we find the need to reach for a last gasp, back-against-the-wall measure, we shall need that rifle above the mantelpiece. Therefore, we shall never surrender it.

You ain't gettin' the guns. As long as there's America, there will be a free people who have the full wherewithal to defend themselves from street toughs and state thugs. Every living being has a self-evident need and right to have the means to defend itself, for how else can it maintain itself as a living being? Likewise we, as that creature who uses the power of the mind to artifice tools to enact our purposes, must have access to the best tools of such defense, i.e. we're gonna keep our guns.

You—who would prefer a disarmed and helpless people grovelling at your feet—can not and shall not have them.

On whatever square yard of ground a true American stands, there will always be a 2nd Amendment.

The Second Amendment is, in fact, the rock upon which the rising wave of technocratic tyranny will crash, break, and eventually recede to insignificance. Without it, the American People, for all their much ballyhooed aspirations and brave bluster about freedom, would become just another subject serfdom clamoring for a less loathsome cage. With it—and the determination to use it—they are an immovable force, a fortress secure.

The right to personal self-defense—both of self and the Republic—is the one sure, concrete, physical means of ensuring that power flows *from* the People to their representatives, not *to*

243

the People from their governing overlords. That is why those hungriest for power itch most ceaselessly to seize the People's weaponry.

But they daren't try it. Think the deep-think AI at the Rand Corp doesn't run the confiscation calculations every hour? And those algos always sum to the same conclusion: some 100,000 Fedgov goons against 100,000,000 armed American militia patriots = about two weeks of ugly street action, and then a Gadsden flag flying above the US Capitol Building...shortly to be followed by the hangings. Precisely because of the Second Amendment which confers overwhelming force in the hands of the People, its use should never be needed. The largest standing army on the planet is the American citizen militia, at least 100,000,000 strong...that's about 50 times larger than even the largest government mercenary army on the planet.

And, to traitors or invaders, the American militia gives no quarter.

So try it.

Fool around, and find out.

Or...

Realize that the People are—always and everywhere—ultimately ascendant, justified in their consensus opinion, and have absolute sovereignty over their person, their home, and their homeland. No enactment of so-called "law" which encroaches upon fundamental human liberties to autonomy over one's own body or the disposition of one's own property—even when dressed up by being declaimed in an ornate chamber by self-proclaimed "stakeholders"—no such encroachments have any standing in justice, but are always and everywhere repugnant to morality and destructive of social order.

"Congress has no power to disarm the militia. Their swords, and every other terrible implement of the soldier, are the birth-right of an American...[T]he unlimited power of the sword is not in the hands of either the federal or state governments, but, where I trust

in God it will ever remain, in the hands of the people."
— Tench Cox, Founding Father —

No creature—neither otter nor ocelot, not the skink nor skunk—is shamed or shunned for taking up the means to defend itself and its kin from prowlers and predators....so too, the human adult—fitted with perhaps the least fearsome claws and fangs of any predator—naturally seeks nothing short of the surest means to provide for and defend itself and its progeny.

If you need it made more formal and explicit, the argument's logic is immensely simple to parse.

First Syllogism:

Premise 1: *All creatures seek* (indeed, require) *a means of defending life* (their life, their "self") *from the exigencies of existence and its myriad dangers.*

Premise 2: *Humans are creatures.*

Ergo, *Humans require a means of defending life* (called "self defense").

Second Syllogism:

Premise 1: *Guns are a most ready, powerful, and cost-effective means of defending life (self defense).*

Premise 2: *Humans require a ready, powerful means of defending life (self defense)*   (per above)

Ergo, *Humans require guns.*

In other words—as the song says—gimme back my bullets.

Of course, all humans are free agents, so they are not literally *required* to always do what is most expeditious and prudent, even in their own self-interest. They could, for instance, sit on their hands and meekly hope the state will protect them. But no competent human, anywhere, can properly be barred the means to self-defense. Not one. And anyone who seeks to deprive you of this basic right to your own self-defense is not doing it for your benefit. Anyone seeking to deprive you of the right to your best means of self defense has their own agenda, and it probably serves their interest, not yours.

Living 2A Large: The Battle of Athens

"The powers of the sword are in the hands of the yeomanry of America from sixteen to sixty...The people are confirmed by the article [2nd Amendment] in their right to keep and bear their private arms."

— Tench Coxe —

On August 2nd, 1946, the ordinary citizens of Athens, Tennessee, having been bullied and brutalized beyond bearing by their local sheriff's department, turned to the 2nd Amendment to rectify the situation. The event is a clear exemplification in recent times of the power of the Constitution and wisdom of the Framers.

Beginning in 1936, the citizens of McMinn County in Tennessee's eastern Ridge-and-Valley territory would labor under the heavy hand of Paul Cantrell, a scion of local gentry who wielded practically unchecked power for nearly a decade with the connivance of the local sheriff's department. Ensconced as state senator, Cantrell—through his gang of badge-wearing thugs under head lackey sheriff Mansfield—ran the county as his private fiefdom, twisting the organs of government into instruments for bribery, false arrest, voter fraud, corruption, and intimidation. For instance, one Tennessee statute gave law enforcements officers a small commission for every arrest they made. This motivated Cantrell and his rapacious deputies to start manufacturing crimes. They devised a lucrative cottage industry of arresting innocent folks on charges of public drunkenness—solely on the testimony of the deputy making the arrest, of course—not only of local citizens but even of travellers merely passing through. Buses traversing the town would be routinely pulled over, and sleepy, bewildered passengers rousted out to pay the $16.50 fine for public drunkenness...all just for riding through Athens. These were the kind of shenanigans that thrilled Cantrell's greedy minions but galled the citizens of McMinn County. The sheriff's department was the core element of Cantrell's money machine, and he used iron-fisted election fraud and intimidation to guarantee the vote went his way so the profits kept flowing in. McMinn county's citizens had petitioned the federal Justice Department for redress of their grievances over election irregularities in 1940, 1942, and again in 1944, but never received a single response. They seemed without recourse.

The beleaguered McMinn citizens fell back on telling each other, "*Just wait till the GIs get back.*" Come 1945, when the war finally did end, thousands of GIs who had just won the Battles of the Bulge and Iwo Jima did indeed come flooding home. The deputies, however, were undeterred by their veteran status and simply continued making faux arrests. It turned out, however, that these veterans—who were simply looking to enjoy a couple hard-earned beers with their comrades—were in no mood to be pushed around, not by anybody.

Unwilling to abide by the false arrests, the veterans—being properly-trained and dutifully-disciplined military men—first went up the chain of command and turned to federal law enforcement for help. They petitioned the FBI for election monitors for the upcoming 1946 election. But, once again, there was no response; there would be no federal help forthcoming. The veterans, however—being properly-trained and eminently capable military men—knew that when you get no orders from headquarters, you use your own initiative. So, they decided to choose and promote GI candidates against Cantrell's corrupt machine in the upcoming elections, running on a ticket for reform and honest government. Having just defeated Hitler and Tojo, they refused to abide any taint of tyranny and injustice in their own home town. They publicly announced their displeasure and intent to rectify matters in the local newspaper (*Daily Post-Athenian*, 17 June 1946, p. 1): "*The principals that we fought for in this past war do not exist in McMinn County. We fought for democracy because we believe in democracy but not the form we live under in this county.*"

The election was held on August 1st, 1946. Both sides sent out poll watchers to monitor the voting and confirm the ballots were properly counted, but the poll watchers sent out by Cantell's sheriff turned out to be approximately 200 "deputies" who were both armed and aggressive. Reports came in throughout the day of intimidation, threats, and beatings of voters and GI poll watchers. Some GI poll watchers were even detained.

Finally, at about 3:00 in the afternoon, Tom Gillespie, a black man, showed up to vote. As he approached the voting station, however, the sheriff's boys started beating him, shouting, *"Nigger, you can't vote here today!"* Undeterred, Mr. Gillespie shrugged them off and kept moving toward the ballot box. An enraged sheriff's goon pulled out his pistol and shot Gillespie in the back. The wound, while fortunately not fatal, drew a crowd of horrified onlookers, and that began the day's battle royale.

The crowd of angry McMinn citizens challenged and harangued the lawless shooter. The nonplussed sheriff's men retreated inside the precinct site, the business office of the Athens Water Company. Finding the two GI poll watchers still inside, the sheriff's men ordered the GIs to sit in the corner and watch while the sheriff's team counted the ballots on the other side of the lobby (which would give their vote-stealing the pretence of having been a "publically witnessed" ballot count). But the two intrepid GIs instead boldly broke out the front plate-glass window of the establishment and dove onto the street. Cut and bleeding, the slightly dazed GIs stood blinking, trying to get their bearings before a crowd of shocked onlookers when one of the deputies clambered out behind them, brandishing his gun and threatening to kill anyone from the crowd who dared cross the street toward the water works building.

With tensions mounting, the deputies called the sheriff, who ordered his men to break the law: he told them to quit counting and instead carry the box of uncounted ballots away from the polling place—in contravention of state law—and instead take them back to his jailhouse, where they could be counted in secret. When the deputies hurriedly grabbed the ballot box and drove off, the GIs called a meeting; they knew that the only way to protect the vote was to get those ballots back, fast! They rushed to the nearby National Guard and Tennessee armories, broke down the doors, and gathered up pistols, rifles, and a couple machine guns. Now armed, they converged on the sheriff's jailhouse. They arrayed themselves along the ridgeline above the brick structure (though leaving the back door unguarded to give the sheriff and his men an easy way out).

"The government, with its institutions, belongs to the people who inhabit it. Whenever they shall grow weary of the existing government, they can exercise their constitutional right of amending it, or their revolutionary right to dismember or overthrow it."

— Abraham Lincoln —

The GIs demanded the ballots; the sheriff and his men refused. An anxious standoff followed as the two sides scouted each other out. By nightfall, Cantrell himself, his sheriff, and a posse of 50 jumpy deputies were hunkered down in the jailhouse with all their ballot boxes, while a growing band of veterans overlooked their position. At last, the besieged sheriff's men opened fire, wounding two GIs who had broken cover to warn off a passerby driving along a nearby road. The GIs returned fire, and a general gunfight broke out, with several more GIs wounded. This uneasy exchange, punctuated, by lulls, continued until about 2 a.m., when the GIs decided to quit playing games. Gathering sticks of dynamite, they hurled the lit explosives against the jail's edifice; the barrage cracked the jail's brickwork and demolished its front porch. That was enough for the sheriff's deputies, who decided they weren't so interested in those ballots after all and surrendered. By that time, Cantrell had long since fled out the back door. The remaining deputies were locked in the jail overnight, for their own protection from vengeful crowds.

The GIs—now the *de facto* government of the town—immediately set about restoring order. First, they cleaned and returned the bulk of the weapons to the armories. Next, with all the sheriff's deputies either in jail or long since fled, the GIs set up *ad hoc* citizen patrols to maintain town safety. Then the votes were counted in an open and orderly manner. Sure enough, the GI candidate for sheriff, Knox Henry, handily beat Cantrell's candidate, as likewise the other GI candidates won their races against Cantrell's machine. In other words, by a single day's no-nonsense confrontation, the rule of law had been restored, and the cleanup of McMinn County government begun.

No less a notable than First Lady Eleanor Roosevelt regarded the event with grudging approbation, remarking a few days later that (*The Daily Post-Athenian*, August 7, 1946 page, 6): *"In this particular case, a group of young veterans organized to oust the local machine and elect their own slate in the primary. We may deplore the use of force but we must also recognize the lesson which this incident points for us all...If we want to continue to be a mature people who, at home and abroad, settle our difficulties peacefully and not through the use of force, then we will take to heart this lesson and we will jealously guard our rights. What goes on before an election, the threats or persuasion by political leaders, may be bad but it cannot prevent the people from really registering their will if they wish to...The decisive action which has just occurred in our midst is a warning, and one which we cannot afford to overlook."*

Within days, GIs in other states were following the lead of the Athens veterans, and calling for immediate voting and government reform in their counties, lest they too resort to rioting which, they said, would make Athens seem *"mild in comparison."* (*The Knoxville Journal*, August 10, 1946, p. 1) Plainly, there was a long-standing demand for reform in many county governments, and it needed a kick start, even if a bullet-fueled one.

As Ms. Roosevelt opined, we would all prefer that recourse to violence would not be needful for government to manifest the People's will. Unfortunately, history shows that freedom is rarely given by tyrants; it must be taken by patriots. Occasionally, you might have tyrannical leadership which cedes to the people's moral ascendency after mere peaceful demonstrations. But the wicked seldom stop themselves; they must be stopped by the just and true, who must come with sufficient will and means to prevail in the contest. First Amendment or Second, it's up to the government to have the good sense to decide which the people will use. Either way, the unconquerable American people will win in the end.

Sword or Slave

"Every citizen should be a soldier. This was the case with the Greeks and Romans, and must be that of every free state."
— Thomas Jefferson —

Since ancient times, citizens carry swords; slaves carry burdens. While debating and voting are the civilized, rational person's course to governmental reform and improvement, the badass knows the tyrant will not see the light until he feels the heat. Therefore, the long-standing truth of politics is that the freeman is armed, the disarmed man a slave.

And, this rule of remaining dangerous enough to be worth leaving alone is as true on the street as with the state. When studied scientifically and objectively, the data consistently shows that more guns make less crime. Because the bulk of citizens are moral, responsible individuals (otherwise civilization would not work at all), the ready access to weaponry means lots of moral, responsible people will have the means of stopping the bad guys before they get too far. Restricting the access to weapons for law-abiding citizens means that only the cops and law-breakers (i.e. criminals) are armed, which leaves a helpless citizenry caught in the middle, at the mercy of marauding gangs of thugs, whether from the state house or the crack house. As the citizens of McMinn County showed and the brains behind the Constitution, George Mason, said, *'I ask, sir, what is the militia? It is the whole people, except for a few public officials."*

Consider the classic case of the town nicknamed "the safest place in America," Kennesaw, Georgia. When the town enacted an ordinance that every homeowner keep at least one firearm in their household, burglaries plummeted by 89%. Likewise, when the Orlando Police Department, concerned over increased sexual assaults, trained 2,500 women in firearm use, the incidence of rape plunged nearly 90%. Finally, not to belabor the point, even the CDC reported that, *"almost every major study of defensive gun use has found that Americans use their firearms defensively between 500,000 and 3 million times each year."* And virtually all of those defensive uses were stopping the criminal simply by displaying the weapon with a willingness to use it...without a shot being fired, without anyone being hurt. The mere presence of an "equalizer" which makes the victim strong enough to resist will most often stop the criminals in their tracks.

More guns, less crime.

More guns, more freedom.

Any questions?

The 2nd Amendment Personified: Lily for Liberty
"To disarm the people is the best and most effectual way to enslave them."
— George Mason —

As one exemplar voice for the millions—or, rather, the tens, even hundreds of millions—of Americans determined to protect themselves and the country with the most effective tools at their disposal is "Lily for Liberty." A first-generation immigrant from communist China, she is a one-woman militia, who says:

"If you believe more gun control by your government is going to save lives, you are being naïve. The champion of all the mass killings in this world is always a tyrannical government.

"Where I came from, China had killed thousands of the students by its own government during the massacre of Tian An Men square in

1989. I surely wish my fellow Chinese citizens back then had guns like this one I am holding in the picture.

"I am a Chinese immigrant and an American citizen by choice. I once was a slave before and I will never be one again.

"I will always stand with my AR, no matter what my President signs with his pen."

Can it be ugly to have to use a weapon? Sure. Does it make a mess when you do so? Absolutely.

So do mouse traps and chainsaws.

Life is messy.

And the worse the difficulty, the bigger the tool and the bigger the cleanup afterwards.

When you have a mess as big as political tyranny, you might have to bring out the big hammer.

And there definitely will be some cleanup afterwards.

"Let your gun therefore be the constant companion of your walks."

— Thomas Jefferson —

But, again, the recourse to guns is not contemplated as a continual, everyday action; it is last resort stuff. When you carry a gun every day, you likely live in a place where you will never need it; when you do not, you likely live in a place where one day you will actually need a gun, but not even have one. The need for the gun arises when you have lost the fight because you have not proactively fought the cultural and political battles which should keep the Republic safe. If you are grabbing cartridge boxes, it is because you failed to stand on the soapbox and failed to protect the ballot box. The voices of the American People need to be louder and prouder to prevent the need for turning to that messy tool of last resort. Fight if you must, but talk while you can.

"Arms discourage and keep the invader and plunderer in awe and

preserve order in the world as well as property. Horrid mischief would ensue [were] the law-abiding deprived the use of them."

— Thomas Paine —

Too many American People have fought too long and too hard to maintain the freedoms bequeathed to us by the Founders and Framers to let anyone come close to that palace of liberty, the American rifle.

"The great object, is that every man be armed. Everyone who is able may have a gun."

— Patrick Henry —

Forget it, traitors.

You ain't getting the guns.

Happy Revolution Day!

"A militia, when properly formed, are in fact the people themselves. They include all men capable of bearing arms. To preserve liberty, it is essential that the whole body of people always possess arms and be taught alike how to use them."

— Thomas Jefferson —

Without the resolve of the founding patriots to retain their weapons, without their undertaking to store up rifles, cannons, and ammunition at Concord, without their temerity to stand in a thin, anxious, yet determined line on the dewy grass of Lexington green, without the ready willingness of 15,000 armed militiamen to rally from every corner of New England upon the British occupiers in Boston...there would have been no Revolution, no 4th of July, no nation of these united American States, and nothing but the unrelenting pall of English imperialism over a brokeback populace.

The rifle is the final line, the ultimate resource of citizen nullification, whose report rings so loud and clear it simply cannot be ignored. Its fearsome shadow looms in the background of every enactment from the traitor class in Washington. And without the inherited fortitude of their cultural descendents in our age—like those in that distant outpost of Athens, Tennessee who likewise stood their ground behind a rifle and chased off the tyrants of their generation—there would be no 2nd Amendment, no spirit of individualism, no red-white-and-blue-blooded backbone of hillbilly heroism.

So, when April 19th rolls around each year, commemorate the anniversary of Lexington and Concord, that day when the "shot heard 'round the world" rang out...ring it in with flags, with signs, with parades, and—who knows—with fireworks and shootouts. Celebrate the day that started it all, the day that first asserted your absolute right to self-defense and continues to remind us of your right to protect yourself, your family, your property, your nation, and your liberty in the most effective way possible: the rifle.

April 19th and a rifle—Happy Revolution Day, America!

Tavistock, TV, and Dope:
Towards Tyranny, Helplessness, and Hopelessness

"The most dangerous man to any government is the man who is able to think things out for himself, without regard to the prevailing superstitions and taboos. Almost inevitably he comes to the conclusion that the government he lives under is dishonest, insane, and intolerable"

— H. L. Mencken —

America entered the 20th century having supped at the breast of Liberty, and had flourished mightily on her fruits: peace, prosperity, and plenty. But the sated, self-satisfied American eagle presented a most appetizing target, a heedless rube, fattened and ripe for the taking. Life was all too easy, what with all that liberty and fecundity...and who would ever suspect or worry that there were malign forces—the devious agents of moneyed plutocrats—

who would want to use that liberty to enrich and empower themselves at the expense of others? But there are always just such pusillanimous souls, and their numbers are legion. For a handful of silver, there will always be any number of hirelings available who will ceaselessly worry at the foundations of freedom with the frenzied urgency of termites.

And so, from its noontime splendor, the seemingly long, slow sunset of the Republic began. At the same time that the United States was outwardly coming into its own as the ascendant world power—delivering the *coup de grace* in World War I, flexing both the military and industrial might to bring victory in World War II—a dark vale was being drawn over its citizens' eyes. The virtues necessary for republican governance—the badass foundations made possible through personal independence, strength, and responsibility—were in the decline.

But how could a cabal of craven minions possibly bring down this American superstate, where there seemed a rifle behind every blade of grass? No, an open, direct assault would never do. The malefactors would have to use stealth and subterfuge; they would have to use pretence in the guise of friendship, treason in the mask of patriotism, and perversion of the nation's tastes in the guise of entertainment...and thus they could slowly titrate a vicious immorality into the culture which would lead the Americans to conquer themselves, to surrender without even knowing it. What the traitors envisioned was a new kind of war, one which did not depend on tanks and planes, but rather a weapon to attack hearts and minds. What if one could control the mind of the enemy population, bend them to one's will, without them even suspecting? Wouldn't that be the most effective, most elegant warfare of all?

What if they did indeed pioneer this weapon in WWI, and have been perfecting it in open warfare against the American people ever since?

When an obscure Austrian Archduke—neither on the throne nor heir to it—was shot by a young Bosnian in the summer of 1914, Americans saw little reason they should involve themselves in "foreign entanglements" over a brouhaha between Europeans concerning European borders. That attitude was so firmly and broadly shared, that Wilson ran his 1916 re-election campaign on the (conniving) slogan "He Kept Us Out of War."

But the British people had also begun 1914 equally recalcitrant about getting involved in a border dispute down in that rabbit warren of tangled fiefdoms in the Balkans, and their doubts had been attacked and overcome by the War Propaganda Bureau of the British War Office. Located in Wellington House—and quickly nicknamed the "lie factory"—the Wellington House propaganda unit swung into action a month after the start of the war by secretly recruiting some of England's most prominent wordsmiths, including Arthur Conan Doyle, H.G. Wells, G.K. Chesterton, and Rudyard Kipling. They were hired to begin beating the drums for militarism, and to write in a manner which gave their words *"the element of news without the element of direct propaganda"* but, at the same time, to produce *"nothing to trace it to any government origin."* In other words, they were to dishonestly bruit government messaging while under the pretense they were only speaking for themselves. And, as the war continued, they were ordered to *"especially"* target the United States because Americans showed *"a very extensive anti-war and pacifist element."* Beyond this use of verbal propaganda, Wellington House also found pictorial representations particularly entrancing, like its grotesque caricatures of German soldiers as brutal apes. Its greatest coup, however, may have been the publication of the much-doubted white paper (*Bryce Report,* see above) which purported to reprint firsthand accounts of German atrocities and also just happened to get released a mere five days after the sinking of the American ship *Lusitania,* a ship which was travelling through waters the Germans had warned were subject to attack by their submarines, a ship also carrying ammunition to the British army, which the Germans had likewise warned would subject ships to submarine intervention. That bellicose 1-2 propaganda punch—coming on top of the revelation months earlier that German minister Zimmermann had telegrammed Mexico in an attempt to coax her into invading the U.S.—would prove sufficient *casus belli.*

Under the incessant propaganda barrage, the American ire was soon stirred, and millions would march off to the bloody trenches in France to "protect democracy" in "the war to end all wars."

More important than its efforts during that war, was how Wellington House morphed afterward into an even more powerful, multifaceted entity called Tavistock Institute. The focus of that entity's efforts moved increasingly to the addition and use of highly-credentialed psychological talent to embark on a "long march" campaign to transform the American ideological landscape from its longstanding heroic badass ideals into an engineered hedonic nihilism. Its long-term goal seems to be a kind of engineered mass psychopathy, a maladaptive social construct of a particularly feckless sort.

One of the first steps in engendering this cultural decline was to move debate and reflection about social mores from being disputes on matters of fact to mere expression of emotion, to continually move the "Overton Window" towards relativism and anomie. One of the prime means of achieving this shift of approach was through the institution of "opinion poll" operations, ostensibly set up to gage the public consensus, as if such polls reveal the pulse of the electorate and so safeguard democratic outcomes. In reality, polls provide many avenues for manipulation and opinion-shaping, by methods including over-sampling those whose opinions you wish to emphasize; stacking, wording, and framing questions in ways which tend to elicit one's desired answers from the respondent; by tendentious analysis of the data results; and by the spin and editorializing used when reporting the results. These "polls" became a means of creating the appearance of a scientifically-generated *sensus communis*, when it was little more than agitprop to foment a herd mentality corresponding to whatever opinion the poll-makers wanted; it was opinion *shaping* in the guise of opinion *sampling*. At the same time, rather than fostering critical analysis, discussion, and discernment related to fact-based data, the inordinate attention to mere "poll" numbers, turned the electorate into passive participants in a political horserace in which sound bites, bumper-sticker sloganeering, and "gotcha" memes became most ascendant, substituting gossip and grandstanding for reasoned deliberation and debate on matters of statecraft. The grand "marketplace of ideas" that was meant to be the crucible of reason which shaped the Republic's response to public events, was reduced to the snap and snark of a junior high school playground, a tawdry kabuki theatre—all flash and fireworks but no real discourse on cultural heritage or civilizational aspiration.

Two of the earlier exponents of crowd control through media manipulation were Walter Lippmann (see his text *Public Opinion*) and Edward Bernays (author of the seminal work, *Propaganda*). Lippmann's efforts sought to control people's thoughts by using tools like the polls to create a sense of an imaginary crowd in everyone's head, a phantasm which he denominated *Public Opinion*. This manufactured sense of the general consensus of the populace, then becomes the *de facto* new social norm...and thereby the mandate for the government to enact legislation in accord with this putative consent of the governed. By creating such a phantasm and getting people to believe we should all obey this *Public Opinion* illusion, Lippmann held he could control public events by merely shaping this *Public Opinion* construct in the public's minds to his specifications, through polls, editorials, demonstrations, and public organizations. By such fake, astroturf "evidence" Lippmann would "prove" that the phantasmagorical *Public Opinion* is in favor of whatever Lippmann's fellow travellers desired, which just happened to be the continued growth of the techno-pharma-military-industrial complex that undergirds and bankrolls the worldwide plutocracy. There was therefore no need for objective, reasoned persuasion, just the manipulation of the *Public Opinion* mind virus.

For his part, Bernays was the person who first coined the term "psychological warfare" for brainwashing the populace and was very explicit in *Propaganda* that he considered the public a mere mob ruled by unseen masters (Chapter 1, "Organizing Chaos"): *"The conscious and intelligent manipulation of the organized habits and opinions of the masses is an important element in democratic society. Those who manipulate this unseen mechanism of society constitute an invisible government which is the true ruling power of our country...We are governed, our minds are molded, our tastes formed, and our ideas suggested, largely by men we have never heard of.... It is they who pull the wires that control the public mind."*

The advent of electronic communication (radio, TV, and eventually internet) would magnify the speed, reach, and power of such mental manipulation. For his part, Bernays would take a permanent position with CBS broadcasting company to employ his methods. Similarly, Roper and Gallup would begin nationwide "polling" operations in the 1930s, placing a spotlight on the issues they wished people to concern themselves with, and directing their responses by the nature and range of answers they allowed them to choose. By the 1936 presidential election, the polls began to become the central issue in the campaign—not the issues, not the nation, nor even the candidate, but the horse race according to mere emotive opinions of managed polls.

The ongoing intellectual nexus, training, and breeding ground of these operations moved from Wellington House, to the Tavistock Institute, and from thence were pushed out into the political and corporate sphere through myriad workshops, consultations, and conferences. Continuing to this day in the US, Tavistock hires and trains the personnel for or out of such organizations as:

Center for Advanced Study in Behavioral Sciences	MIT
Executive Conference Center (Arlington, VA)	National Defense Resources Council
Esalen Institute	National Institute for Mental Health
Georgetown University	National Training Laboratories
Harvard Psychological Clinic	Rand Corporation
Hoover Institute (Stanford)	Stanford Research Institute

Institute for Social Research (Michigan)　　　Wharton School of
Economics

Mental Health Research Institute

How to Herd Citizen Slaves for Fun & Profit

"COVID is critical because this is what convinces people to accept, to legitimize, total biometric surveillance."
— Yuval Noah Harari, WEF —

The next generation of crowd-herding psych warfare specialists moved beyond the earlier work of Lippmann and Bernays to develop a simple, powerful methodology for moving the public to their whims. The seeming chaos of events in public life is—at least in part, and most especially in the most dramatic events on the largest stages—a controlled titration of trauma to break the mind and will of the citizen population. It is an ever more sophisticated, ever more destructive, means of driving and culling the human herd. Especially since WWII, such PhDs-for-hire as John Rawlings Rees—one of the founders and medical director for Tavistock, who helped fold it into the Directorate of Army Psychiatry during WWII—and his protégés like B.F. Skinner and Kurt Lewin consciously undertook to commandeer and control the public's *"hodological space"*—i.e. their internal map of choices, options, and possibilities. These psychiatric technocrats had moved from trying to merely evoke particular behaviors, to downloading mind-maps into the subject population so that every citizen could only think, do, and say what had been programmed into them. From mere "behavior change," this next generation of manipulation agents began to pursue "identity change," a broader, deeper mind transformation, an overwrite of the entire personality. It was, in short, straight up "worldview-war" (*weltanschauungskrieg*), an attack on a target population's model of reality designed to supplant it with one more commodious to authoritarianism. To produce so profound a change, they undertook the dark wizardry of creating an environment with which an initially stable, healthy personality cannot readily interface. In other words, they first create confusion, make your life chaos; they seek to produce such disorder that the structure of your personality will collapse. At the farthest verge of continual distress, even the healthiest personality may be reduced to the feral condition akin to a wild, fearful animal. Under such pressures, herd animals such as humans decompensate into a motile, malleable state, which can then be easily reorganized and transformed to their tormentor's liking. These mind warriors seek, if you will, to "dissolve and coagulate" the mind, producing a new personality; they are thus engendering "order out of chaos." That is why the prison guards at Guantanamo detention camp, familiar with such methods, were so inhuman. That is why your whole nation is increasingly turning into a whirlwind of anarchy, a tumult of controlled chaos, all so that your identity may be displaced, even rent asunder, and you reconstituted into a docile neofeudal serf eager to *"own nothing, and be happy."*

Their base formula for this transformation is an age-old means of mental enslavement now known as trauma-based mind control: first expose the mind to events so horrible that it breaks, then fill the broken, confused subject with new programming. Rinse and repeat. This means you live in a war zone of ongoing, wall-to-wall 4th generation (asymmetric, non-conventional) and 5th generation (information, unrestricted) warfare.

And *you* are the target.

This is the age of contrived warfare, disaster on command to produce a prescribed effect on the "enemy" of the psych war operators, i.e. the citizens. Where once upon a time, Genghis Khan would come riding over the steppes with clear intent to capture the land and ravage the women, which naturally roused the watchmen on the wall to call out the men folk to stand stalwart against the obvious foe...today's warlords lurk in back rooms, their names and faces shrouded, their motives blurred and disguised; their weapons are words which shock and confuse; their shields are images designed to terrorize and break your reason. Here follows just some of how you and your nation have been attacked by the warlords of terror over the last century in order to make your countrymen beg to go kill people they did not know, who did nothing to them, on the justification of hysteria and lies:

Fight with Spain (1898): blow up a battleship, so we can join up to "Remember the *Maine*!"

Fight with Germany (1917): blow up a cruise ship (while sailing in a combat zone carrying war supplies to Britain), because "Remember the *Lusitania*!"

Fight with Japan and Germany (1941): blow up a lot of old, obsolete battleships, plus 2,000 American sailors and airmen: "Remember Pearl Harbor!"

Fight with North Korea and China (1950): divide a helpless people's land in half, and then kill many people over which flag should fly over which part.

Fight with Vietnam (1964): send the *USS Maddox* and other destroyers to shoot at some North Vietnamese patrol boats and then pretend the PT boats shot first with an unprovoked attack: "Remember the single bullet hole in the *USS Maddox*!"

Fight with Grenada (1983): assert potential Soviet influence, as if this tiny, random Caribbean island were actually a geopolitically critical lynchpin island of American security, and launch Operation "Urgent Fury:" "Remember the new airport they're building!"

Fight for Panama (1989): under Operation "Just Cause," capture Panamanian head of state Manuel Noriega using both the 82nd and 101st Airborne Divisions in what was undoubtedly the most expensive drug bust of all time...but had the advantage of making Noriega's erstwhile drug-trafficking partners—viz. President Bush's CIA—the undisputed state-sponsored cocaine kingpins in the Caribbean region: "Remember who owns the coke pipeline, Manny!"

Fight for Iraq I (1991): pretend (through NSA lies) that Iraq's "madman" president—that "Butcher of Baghdad" Saddam

Hussein—intends to invade Saudi oil fields; don't forget to bring out the savages-slaughtering-babies trick again (after all, everyone's forgotten WWI by now). This time, make it babies purportedly slaughtered by brutal Iraqi dragoons who supposedly yanked the babies from incubators and then dashed them on the floor...as narrated on CNN by Nairta Al Sabah, the appropriately tearful teen daughter of the Kuwaiti ambassador, who has actually been attending posh schools in Washington, D.C. for years, and was nowhere near Kuwait, nor any of its baby incubators, in 1991: "Remember the Petrodollar must be protected above all else!"

Follow with *Fight for the entire Mideast, "Axis of Evil" Edition* (2001): with just two planes, take down three towers, which all fall at freefall speed in clouds of pyroclastic dust from which no flight-recording black box or passengers survived but yielded a perfectly intact passport proving to the miracle-workers at the FBI who found it that we have absolute certitude that the malefactors behind the attack were brown men with unpronounceable names which, obviously, necessitates that the American people must immediately give up their civil liberties to a new internal Homeland Security Agency who get to strut around in cool black unis and jackboots: "Remember the Twin Towers, plus Pentagon attack where an airliner's twin titanium engines magically disappeared upon impact!"

Follow with *Son of Fight for Iraq II...new and improved edition— now with "Weapons of Mass Destruction" Upgrade!* (2003): Have Bush II dispatch *eminence gris* VP Cheney on a media blitz of 15 appearances in 30 days hawking the lie that old crazy-man President Hussein is at it again, this time backing the 9/11 brown-men-with-unpronounceable-names (false), along with the Taliban (no Taliban in Iraq)—despite CIA and chief UN weapons inspector Blix publicly debunking these tales by explaining that Hussein hates the Taliban and ran them out of his country years ago. Lump all brown-people-with-unpronounceable-names into an "Axis of Evil," even though the Iraqis warred with the Iranians whose largely Shiite people have a checkered relationship with Sunni Al-Qaeda operatives who actually declared *jihad* against the Saudis. Plow ahead anyway, expanding the military ops from Afghanistan to

Iraq, despite no evidence of any truth to any of Cheney's assertions of *"weapons of mass destruction,"* nor *"yellowcake uranium,"* nor long-range rockets which could leave a *"mushroom cloud over Boston."*

(In passing, the above list comprises nowhere near all overseas U.S. military operations. Moreover, the foregoing litany is in no way meant to disparage in any way the professionalism, selflessness, efficacy, and least of all the sacrifices of the military personnel who undertook the actual operations. Indeed, in most cases, the evidence points to the continued tradition of extreme hardiness and grit exhibited by the average American warrior. Rather, it is to call out precisely the wickedness of deploying and endangering such courageous and dedicated individuals for any but the most dire and necessary circumstances, least of all advancing some hidden monetary or political motives.)

In reflecting on all these wars and their tenuous justifications, why in case after case, does war start with a mind-terror op? Simply put, their method is to make you fearful and afraid, then offer you a pacifying "solution" as a pathway to comfort...which also just happens to be their preplanned objective. As Tavistock director Rees put it, he saw himself as developing and deploying a cadre of "psychiatric shock troops." In *The Shaping of Psychiatry by War,* (1945) he held that the mission of his mind-bending army was to fan out across the world to, *"apply the advanced techniques of psychological warfare as we know them to whole population groups that will grow ever larger, so that whole populations may be more easily controlled. In a world driven completely mad, groups of Tavistock psychologists linked to each other, capable of influencing the political and governmental field must be arbiters, the power cabal."*

For such madmen in psychiatrist guise as these—who seek to engender not sanity but neurosis, not happiness but terrified compliance—sufficient *"social environmental turbulence"* will cause a target population to retreat into a *"synoptic idealism,"* a retreat from the outside world into a kind of infantile fantasyland, the adult equivalent of sucking one's thumb. For such manipulators, inducing *"turbulence"* and *"stress"* in the public sphere are not accidental; these are beta tests or full-blown operations of the psych warfare teams, seeing what works in giant national laboratories of social control and manipulation. In pursuit of their ends, they may, as needed, turn up the gain (the amplitude and frequency) of such stressors to push events towards crescendo, while the continual aerial bombardment of radio and TV fear porn screams of "crises" and "emergency" in the subject population's ears to induce full-blown terrified disorientation. Then these ever-so-kindly technocrats can offer soothing anodyne promises that if the herd will just follow the Plan® of the Science®, all of their problems will go away.

Since, however, the first step is breaking the subject's joy and complacency, Lewin and other original Tavistock researchers on mass brainwashing techniques began using repeated trauma and torture—long used on single helpless patients in the tender care of such depraved researchers—turning these mind control measures on society at large. Lewin claimed that, under widespread terror, society will revert towards an infantile *tabula rasa*, a blank slate upon which they can overwrite whatever Tavistock may wish. In their outlook, such shell-shocked populations become *"fluid,"* like little children needing a parental figure to make sense of it all. When people reach a sufficiently agonized state of disorder and disorientation, they will gladly grab at the readymade solutions offered by their psychiatric overseers. Another Tavistock researcher, Dr. William Sargant, in his text *Battle for the Mind: A Physiology of Conversion and Brain-Washing* (1957) put it this way: *"Various types of beliefs can be implanted after brain function has been sufficiently disturbed by...deliberately induced fear, anger or excitement."*

By 1996, such approaches were being lauded as conveying huge tactical advantages in such military white papers as *Shock and Awe: Achieving Rapid Dominance* prepared for the National Defense University, which held: *"The principal mechanism for achieving...dominance is through imposing sufficient conditions of "Shock and Awe" on the adversary to convince or compel it to accept our strategic aims and military objectives. Clearly, deception, confusion, misinformation, and disinformation, perhaps in massive amounts, must be employed...The key objective of Rapid Dominance is to impose this overwhelming level of Shock and Awe against an adversary on an immediate or sufficiently timely basis to paralyze its will to carry on."*

Over the last century, the political struggle in this country has increasingly become what is termed by many an information war, a mind war. The struggle is for the space between your ears...and of all your neighbors. Sure, the would-be controllers are perfectly willing, if necessary, to engage in physical beatings, assassinations, and other "wet work," not to mention false flags, bombings, and ongoing environmental and toxic assaults on you, your air, water, soil, food, and every living thing. But, as these are cowardly sneak thieves, their preferred method is more by stealth than struggle; they prefer conquest by words and pictures, by hypnosis and suggestion, the mind-magic of image, distraction, falsehood, and constructive fraud (i.e. building a beguiling false narrative, otherwise known as gaslighting). They will resort to clandestine cyanide and bare bodkin only when the cheaper, easier use of lies and tall tales falters.

The control of the masses by the slow, crude efforts of newspaper propaganda of the 20th century would become, as the 21st century unfolded, full air supremacy, exhibiting the capacity and commitment to assault with the increasingly speed, ubiquity, and power which electronic delivery offered. Nearly one hundred years ago, the impact of electronic communication over the airwaves was first demonstrated as radio created an immediate, aural access to the mass mind. That millions could be easily and powerfully manipulated this way was demonstrated with dramatic impact in the 1938 "War of the Worlds" beta test by Orson Welles, wherein people took the sonic presentation at face value, overturned their entire life experience, and believed their country was under assault by space alien blobs from Mars. People allowed their worldview to be imploded and reason eroded because of a 40-minute radio show. What if the radio began to provide wall-to-wall fear porn, day after day? Would that induce the kind of "turbulence" and "stress" which engenders a "fluid" suggestible state in the public which was sought by the madmen technocrats? Despite Welles' initial protestations that he never guessed his production would induce such shock, psychologist Hadley Cantril—who just happened to specialize in propaganda and social influence for the Princeton Radio Research Project—was immediately and endlessly fascinated with the event, compiling his findings on Welles' *"mass persuasion"*—i.e. how to move the herd the way you want—in his 1940 book, *The Invasion from Mars*.

Between the world wars, "talkies" would combine radio's sonic element with the silent "moving pictures" of Buster Keaton's time, to produce the multisensory cinematic experience which proved a heady admixture that engaged much of the cerebral ganglia...without asking anything of the pre-frontal cortex as complex as reading an actual newspaper headline. The message masters could now beam their visions straight into the passive, receptive mind of the viewer, without having to ask the public to generate their own cerebral images via print. The manipulators could seed outcomes and scenarios for their subject audience to envision in a full, immersive experience which—if given a well-crafted narrative package to evoke the desired emotional response to the appropriate visual trigger—would produce a continual, predictable Pavlovian outcome in the target populace, especially if done with consistent, long-term repetition. This would be compelling enough in the initially black-and-white "talkies" and color movies which followed, but perhaps most especially so in the colorful animated works which Disney's studios were hired to churn out during WWII. In some ways, animation can be more direct and powerful than other visual media, since a "cartoonish" image may be rendered in a more directly archetypal form, with all the luring, snarling, loathsome elements wedded to emotionally traumatizing triggers, like a patricide (*Lion King*) or senseless violence against an innocent (*Bambi*). While the conscious mind may dismiss the action as "just a cartoon," the emotional resonance will remain, often sticking deep. In this way, it is easy to characterize a Tojo or Hitler into a complete monster, the valiant GI into a stalwart hero. Or, *mutatis mutandis*, transpose whatever face on the cartoonish head, and make whomever you want the vile

1984-style "Goldstein" of the story for a 5-minute cartoon hate session. In either case, the capture and utilization of emotionally traumatizing and value-distorting messaging by the media is a long-standing, conscious effort by well-funded, amoral technocrats to cow and control you.

Or...

We could continue to sleep, to believe such twisted schemes are impossible. We can pretend all the politicians love us, every banker lives only to serve customer and country, and the technocrats stay awake at night wondering how best to protect our freedom.

Surely these are all just random coincidences, right? Maybe it's better to be a *coincidence theorist*. After all, it's not like wicked people ever conspire together to do wicked things, like those who assassinated Julius Caesar, or gave Benedict Arnold £20,000 to surrender West Point, or blew up the *Reichstag* to bring Hitler to power, or arrayed multiple teams of snipers to shoot Kennedy, or gave 30 pieces of silver to Judas. Does it really matter that much since—in the new, imperial Pax America under the national security state, whether the "winner" comes from one party or the other—either way, the Constitution will be continually ignored, the Bill of Rights shredded, the taxes jacked, the dollar torched while war, poverty, ignorance, and disease multiply? You don't think that's unusual, do you? That's not weird, for all of these disasters to befall simultaneously—all of which reverse America's previous history of marching continuously toward burgeoning prosperity and liberty. Surely, it's just an unlucky accident that, try as they might, somehow our politicians and administrators and technocrats always get it wrong. Somehow, no matter what they try, you always wind up with less money, less freedom, and, by the way, the taxes need to go up again. Gosh darn it all, that surely is some awful bad luck.

But it's all just one big coincidence, right?

How can such a profound, ongoing, and steep decline be explained? Is it really some inexplicable "social contagion" of the later 20th century, some nationwide mental incapacity over which we must simply shrug and learn to cope?

Or maybe...just maybe...

Maybe it is as simple as admitting to ourselves that, with the end of WWII, the immense resources of propaganda, mind control, intimidation, and espionage were brought back to the mainland U.S. and—with the 1947 National Security Act—the Tavistock propagandists, thousands of Nazi scientists and Gestapo chieftains secreted here via "Operation Paperclip," the freshly-minted CIA, and such cold-hearted CIA-subsidized mind control artificers as Ewan Cameron, Jolyen West, et. al., turned their full, malignant, power-hungry psychopathy against the American populace under the cover of "national security?"

What did you think would happen, Mr. Truman, when you signed that Act? Which "Nation" and whose "Security" were you protecting with that Act? A fair-minded assessment of the historical outcome surely makes it hard to believe anyone was worrying too much about the security of the sovereign citizens of this constitutional republic.

Looking around at today's political landscape, do you think there is even one single, straight legislative vote at the national...or even state...maybe even county...level? Or are today's politicos just sock-puppets for the nameless operators from the alphabet agencies driving the black SUVs? Do you think there is a reason the United States has almost completely moved to wifi-connected, easily-hacked electronic voting machines? Is precinct voting by paper ballots—counted openly and publicly witnessed by citizens protected by their smartphone cameras and side arms—really so much slower and harder? What would those folks from Athens, TN say about protecting your vote?

When such a government comes at you shouting you should cower in fear and terror, should you assume they are telling you the truth...or lying? When they tell you what they want you to do, should you assume it's for your own good...or theirs? When the Fedgov speaks...how hard should you listen?

Has mind control put the American people in a permanent state akin to shell shock, a kind of deep post-traumatic confusion which makes them unable to sensibly, purposefully respond to the challenges created by the authoritarian agenda? Trauma-based mind control must start with the trauma part. The terrorized human mind does not think; it reacts. Put the mind control subject (populace) into shock, fear, terror, and tell it whatever fairy tale you want about (a) what boogeyman caused their pain, and (b) what big-daddy government plan will make all that ouchie pain go away. When people allow themselves to be emotionally traumatized by the words and images purveyed by their controllers, they enter a mind-numbed thoughtless state. They have been infantalized. That's when the change agents can pour any narrative into the public's motile, needy souls. The bigger the trauma, the bigger the narrative. The bigger the intended social change, the bigger the trauma, and the more repetitive and wall-to-wall the fear-trigger porn pouring from the telescreen.

And, to follow the thinking of two particularly crafty elitists, viz. Aldous Huxley and Bertrand Russell, what if there were a way to make the slaves even more docile, to make them actually *enjoy* their servitude? In a preface he wrote for the 2nd edition of Orwell's *Brave New World*, Huxley opined:

"A really efficient totalitarian state would be one in which the all-powerful executive of political bosses and their army of managers control a population of slaves who do not have to be coerced, because they love their servitude...The most important Manhattan Projects of the future will be vast government-sponsored enquiries into what the politicians and the participating scientists will call "the problem of happiness"—in other words, the problem of making people love their servitude...Under a scientific dictator education will really work -- with the result that most men and women will grow up to love their servitude and will never dream of revolution."

Similarly, professor Russell in *The Impact of Science on Society* conjectured a techno-pharmaceutical dictatorship could induce a false euphoria to ensure the docility of the masses: *"Diet, injections, and injunctions will combine, from a very early age, to produce the sort of character and the sort of beliefs that the authorities consider desirable, and any serious criticism of the powers that be will become psychologically impossible. Even if all are miserable, all will believe themselves happy, because the government will tell them that they are so."*

But could such a purposeful velvet prison actually be constructed? Rather than beating the masses into submission, could you simply lull them into a quiescent, stupefied infantilism? What would happen, for instance, if you feed them a steady diet of sex and drugs and rock 'n roll?

Bezmenov vs. the Beatles

"Once the communists took over, everything...had to be given to the communists, the government. And if [someone didn't] do it, they make an example of them. Bury them alive. I've seen women and children raped and thrown overboard on a fishing boat. I've seen people die because of starvation...and eating flesh to survive. This country is great because of our Constitution. So we have to fight...If we don't, we will lose it all."
— Amy Phan West, refugee from communist Vietnam —

At the same time such ongoing psychic assaults were unmooring the foundations of people's worldview and surrounding them with terror, the public was being offered increasing means of easy, comfortable escape. Why worry about the big problems of the world, the chaos of politics, the shrinking of your buying power? Look at the endless hedonic tech available to take you out of your misery: TV, movies, cartoons, microwave popcorn, sports, comic books, popsicles, the Pill, air conditioning, refrigerators, porn, chats, socials, lite beer, vaping, crank, fentanyl...even "fully-functional" robotic love mates.

Combine the variety and availability of such distractions

and diversions with an ideology which encourages it: the rock and roll lifestyle, whose core payload message is infinite hedonism, driven deeply into the brain via rhythmic, rhyming repetition. Next, add a touch of good, old-fashioned laziness, with all the conveniences we have been able to construct, the many means of ease, comfort, and pleasure at our fingertips. The kitsch of self-pleasuring, from literal onanistic affordances, to La-Z boy chairs, to riding lawn mowers, to all the "conveniences" and take-it-easy gear and infrastructure of hot tubs, foot massagers, and electric can openers. Life is all about having everything easy and titillating, right? Isn't pleasure your sole purpose on earth?

Of course, there is nothing wrong with pleasure, per se. The body was made to rejoice in the beauty and mildness of a soft, spring morn; to frisson with anticipation at the nearness and caress of our beloved's body; to mingle with our senses and emotions in providing feedback about what is appealing to enact and desirable to pursue. But when that pleasure alone becomes the primary—let alone sole—focus of our being and time, we become at first a cipher, and next a subtraction from the world and those around us. Any moral cipher is a social and material net loss to the community. And a community of such leeches, with each trying to extract the maximum pleasure with minimal effort from each and every person around them, will soon result in corruption, chaos, and collapse, as each tries to suck that last little drop of sustenance from the pittance of productive output extruded by their neighbor.

But what if this were not just your garden variety moral degradation we see rising around us? What if this cultural collapse, this ongoing behavioral sink, were given a fillip by those intending to purposefully undermine the country? In other words, what if moral degradation has been weaponized? In fact, if one's goal is to upend that bastion of freedom which was the United States, you basically have to weaponize the people's own worst impulses against them. For, the American land being so vast, its populace so large, and its constitutional foundations so sure, a moral populace keenly committed to its heroic ideals of freedom and self-determination would create an immovable impediment to anyone seeking to overawe such a place. It would be most especially annoying to any persons seeking to establish a unipolar worldwide hegemony over all nations that such a luminous, flourishing exemplar of liberty and self-reliance could stand with such unconquerable vigor. A nation state of that size and power—an indisputable testament to the power and promise of individual liberty and national sovereignty—would prove most inconvenient indeed.

Whistleblower and former Soviet spy Yuri Bezmenov claimed that the KGB, when seeking to establish their Comintern (worldwide soviet state), recognized exactly this situation decades ago, and instituted a long-range plan to overcome the United States from within. In the 1980s, Bezmenov defected from the Soviet Union and spent the rest of his life trying to warn Americans of the plans he was privy to as a member of the KGB. According to him, this nation has long been subjected to an *"undeclared, total war against [its] basic principles and foundations."* In fact, he claimed the vast bulk of the KGB's resources were devoted to a long term form of psychological warfare against the U.S. which was termed *"ideological subversion."*

Was the KGB acting alone, or did it have fellow travellers in its quest for a centralized, single world governing body? Was it possible that some of them were deeply embedded in various psychiatric, political, and entertainment arenas, ready to add their efforts to the Soviets' covert attack?

According to Bezmenov, such Ideological Subversion is a four-step process. The first and longest period is Demoralization, which takes decades. This process is a demoralization of the subject nation in two senses: (a) it is the literal assault and destruction of the society's moral core, its fundamental values; it seeks to de-moralize, to strip away the mores underlying the culture. This was well begun, according to Bezmenov, by the 1960s, where notions of self-discipline, self-sacrifice, moral restraint, and delayed gratification were replaced with the "hippie" hedonic sensibility that, "Anything you wanna do, it's alright," and "If you can't be with the one you love, love the one you're with," and that one should just generally "Let it all hang out." If so, were the ideologies implicit, the images purveyed, by so many 60s icons, from Timothy Leary's pharmophilic "Turn on; Tune in; Drop out" to Gloria Steinem's Feminism—both of them on the CIA payroll—just so much culture war theatre? What of Jimmy Page, Black Sabbath, and Anton Lavey's little satanic outfit—were they, consciously or unconsciously, part of the club? Likewise, does something darker underlie all the mop-top goofiness of, for instance, the Beatles? Was there mayhap any conscious intent in their lyrics designed to unravel one's moral principles? Perhaps it is hardly accidental that they began their career sweetly wanting to "Hold Your Hand," but soon moved to encouraging the listener to undertake a "Magical Mystery Tour" away from the drear world of responsibility and effortful accomplishment by indulging in psychedelic phantasmagoria with "Lucy in the Sky with Diamonds" in an imaginary land of "Strawberry Fields Forever," seeking not rational understanding but the sensual release which is the royal road to all fulfillment because "Happiness is a Warm Gun," so, baby, "Why Don't We Do It in the Road?" Why is this stepwise degradation into moral degeneration—beginning as sweet *ingenue*, thence to indulgent libertine, perhaps even overt satanic icon—repeated again and again as if forging some new cultural archetype, by keynote entertainers from Miley Cyrus to Justin Beiber to Katy Perry? Is this simply a reflection of a general social slide into amorality, or are particular persons and paradigms consciously advanced and then taken stepwise down the pathway of moral degradation to produce emulation within the wider populace?

Demoralization's sybaritic slide into hedonic self-absorption has a knock-on effect of (b) undermining the national morale, i.e. the general willingness to fight for one's homeland, to defend one's culture. When a society shares no core moral commitment—if its people are amoral and rootless—they have no real incentive to fight for much of anything. At the point where such moral indifference is generalized among the young people, Bezmenov believed the process becomes irreversible, as it becomes a self-reinforcing devolution into self-indulgence and depravity. This intentional voluptuousness, unfortunately, reinforces and aligns rather closely with the natural social supercycles discussed earlier. Thus, the pleasure-seeking ethos cultivated by the KGB is easily interwoven into the characteristic self-indulgence of an n-stage civilization which has lost its mojo, its vision, its self-image and heroic ideals. Such a land has reached the stage where the goal becomes turning life into one long carnival: building social structures and soothing affordances which make pleasure faster, fuller, easier, and more continual; finding ways to take on fewer challenges and goals in order to afford more time for leisure and luxuriating. A populace so slack-jawed and softened soon become not only unable to withstand hardship and pain, but find even the slightest inconvenience and annoyance more than their coddled sensibilities can bear. Hence the rise of the pampered poodles—the "Karens" and "Kevins" of the modern age—who demand to see the manager whenever they have to endure such exasperating affronts as waiting in line, substituting an item, or—God forbid—actually foregoing...anything. Every age everywhere sees people of this sort, but when that attitude is commonplace, a people has lost the fortitude of its forbearers, those rustic titans who felled forests to build a homestead and fended off wolves to survive another season. For a civilization to survive, every generation must find and cultivate that inner strength on its own; no one can do that work for you.

Once the population is thus sufficiently weakened in the first stage, a second period of Destabilization of about 2-5 years ensues which is designed to undermine the structural elements of the society, the fabric of its institutions. In this stage, there are more overt destabilization operations against the functions and organizations of society, seeking to monkey-wrench, undermine, and socially assail them in order to create dysfunction within the government, economy, and defense systems. This would be the Cloward-and-Piven stage where one would see the most obvious application of the "pincer" strategy advocated by the Communist leader Jan Kozak, whose autobiographical account *And Not a Shot is Fired* describes how, in just two years (1946-1948), he took Czechoslovakia from Capitalism to Socialism—by means of Parliament. As he describes it, this political methodology involves creating continual waves of assault against the "bourgeoisie" (middle class) to drive them from the public political sphere. These waves alternate between "pressure from above" as the socialists in the government and legislature advocate communist polices, followed by "pressure from below" as street marchers and advocacy groups demonstrate, protest, and riot in insistent support of those policies. This continual, alternating pressure looks, on the surface, like a growing national consensus in favor of the communist movement, when, in fact, it is simply a coordinated effort by two cadres working for the same team. With the unrelenting drumbeat—from the revolutionary operatives "above" in Parliament and the popular masses led by the revolutionary workers' party "below"—the resistance of the "reactionary bourgeoisie" to communist restructuring is worn down and broken. When you see media-promoted caucuses of legislatures pushing for radical reforms being backed by clamorous street actions against "fascists" led by NGOs, you are looking at a classic Marxist op, the age-old Communist coup. If you have a "Squad" in Congress working for the same ends as those whose "Lives Matter" marching in your streets, you may indeed be deep into the destabilization stage of your civilization.

The third stage, Crisis, is reached via whatever revolutionary event allows for the final seizure of power. It could be internal or external, but most probably is a combination of those in tandem as a result of the chaos induced in the foregoing stage. The social dissolution and moral decay being already far advanced, it becomes impossible for such a society to face any significant stressor, so it will likely dissolve under any challenge whose resolution would involve strength of will, adult discernment, and personal sacrifice.

Normalization, the fourth and final stage, is, for the revolutionaries, the fun part. This is when the commies finally get to fan out across the landscape, grabbing guns, blowing up churches, and slaughtering Kulaks. It is the whole point of the all the foregoing drama. Communism is declared the "new normal," and society will be fully reorganized according to its ideals. When Larry Grathwohl went undercover in the 1960s for the CIA amongst the bomb-slinging members of SDS, he was mortified to hear the discussions by Ivy League trained communists estimating they would need to kill about 30% of the US population to settle matters after their revolution. I'll leave it to you to work out the numbers...but were they to have their way in America today, the bloodletting would give Mao and Pol Pot a run for greatest political democide of all time.

Dark Ideologies and Blind Conspirators

"The idea of stakeholder capitalism and multi-stakeholder partnerships might sound warm and fuzzy, until we dig deeper and realize that this actually means giving corporations more power over society, and democratic institutions less."

— Ivan Wecke —

But, you say, who could possibly be behind all this? How can we know for real and for true who and what and why this is happening to this nation?

You can't know, not with complete certitude.

That there is some dark movement toward control and oppression which is internationally coordinated and operates with immense material resources and has no moral compunctions about its mode of imposing its will upon nations or persons, you have just seen the signposts all laid before you in scores of examples. Can you give a better explanation of all these coincident events, statements, actions, and outcomes...or is it not simpler to simply grab Occam's Razor and cut straight to the chase: there's some dirty work afoot.

First, realize you don't and can't know all of it for one very good reason: it works very, very hard to stay hidden. Because it fears the backlash of its detestable goals being revealed, this dark cult prefers clandestine and camouflaged operations—so much so, that secrecy and disguise may be considered its first aim. Immense thought and many resources are invested in obscuring, confusing, and deflecting attention and knowledge of its actions. The more important and vile the undertaking, the less likely they will announce its planning or mission. As particular organizations are uncovered, they will be bankrupted, disbanded, sold, and reconstituted elsewhere with another name, another CEO. Thus, it is purposefully difficult, if not impossible, for the average person to know the exact name, nature, and dispositions of the enemy. By extension, those who pretend or presume to know are as likely to be misled or confused as to be right.

Remember too, the members of this dark club are lying liars who lie. They lie to you. They lie to themselves. And they lie continually and purposefully to everyone in their own organization, above, below, and beside them. As a result, most of them don't even *really* know. All they know is what they have seen and what they have been told, much of which is almost certainly a lie. And the lie may differ from person to person, day to day. In fact, you can presume that they lie as freely—in fact, probably more carefully and craftily—to each other than to the masses. Furthermore, as one climbs the ranks within such organizations, one is ever more managed, watched, regulated, confined, and coerced. They are hardly any more free or well-informed than us mere proles at the bottom; they just get slightly better housing and a flashier wardrobe.

Do not despair, however, for we can know something of their handiwork and intent by the shadows. Like electricity or X-rays, you may not see it, but you sure can see the effects. The exact composition, size, and daily movements of this Beast gang may be nearly impossible to trace, but, while we may not discern the face, we can surely track the footprints and match its fingerprints. And we must not ignore the clear proofs left by its work: world wars, catastrophic depressions, and fearsome governmental brutality tending toward an authoritarian world government. Though we may not know all the names or games, we can know that our enemy rings us in the organs of force fueled by the privileges of wealth and arrogance of power. These are creatures of control and material longing; they lie with abandon to sow chaos and confusion in order to reap strife and division; they make the world a whirlwind of contention as they milk the addled herd for the last drop of wealth. Like greedy snails, however, they always leave a money trail, for you can make no great event happen on this planet without money. They will sow their plans with money, and they will reap their rewards in money. Follow the money flows in and out as you would harken to the rumbling growl of some dark predator looming in the hedgerow, for money is how the Beast lives and breathes and has its being.

Likewise, while there are certainly organized, ongoing meetings (Davos, Bilderberg, Bohemian Grove, etc.) which can be followed wherein they are often shockingly plain in speaking of their wickedness, at the same time much of their action is now beyond the intent or choice of any one person or group. They have metastasized more into an ideological matrix than a mere network of organizations. More than a single planned scam, these would-be controllers have a shared paradigm, a way of looking at and living in the world. Yes, they will undertake particular destructive assaults—while they profit on the side—against this nation or that patriot, but overriding that will be their antihuman authoritarianism. You will know them by their disdain for humankind—its simple virtues and pleasures—and by their lauding that which is destructive, inimical, repugnant, and discordant with a humane, harmonious life.

In this way, it can become as useful to envisage the enemy as a worldview, as much as looking to find any particular name, company, political schema, or plan to meet and overmatch. The names and faces, after all, will come and go, while the greed and grift remains the same. They are a class of persons who are—as Dostoevsky termed it—*ideologically possessed*, that is, their spirits are overcome by an idea, a vision, a demonic mindset, which darkens their understanding of this world and other people. So, while any number of them may well conspire together with exact plans and schedules to inflict harm on the body politic, many more of them have simply fallen under the spell of their shared world view and beaver away at their own little plot of wickedness, whether or not any two of them ever meet at a conference in Davos or around a satanic fire pit.

You might think of the exercise of tracking this dark ideology and its actions as rather like six blind conspiracists trying to describe the scheming elephant in the room. Yes, each conspiracist may manage to get a firm grip on any particular piece of the elephant, but none of them can see or feel the whole thing. So, the one wrestling with the trunk is sure the schemer is like a serpent, the one hugging its leg is sure it's like a great tree trunk, the one hanging on an ear assures us it has got wings which enable it to fly, etc., etc. While there is assuredly an elephant loose in the fine china shop of the American Republic, the full nature of the thing shattering the fine porcelain of centuries of labor is purposefully hidden, perhaps the most jealously guarded dark secret of all those squirreled away by the Deep State minions. Our job—once we know it's there and recognize the danger—is to grab onto whatever bits of dangerous trunk and tusks we might personally grip and lash it down with enough rope to corral it before it brings the whole house down upon the children and bric-a-brac. We may not know the name or kind of creature, but we can feel the icy scales of its roughhewn sides, smell its fetid breath, and see the malevolent end of its tireless handiwork. We need not know its exact name to recognize its malign design. We need not know its exact measure to fight it. And we need not know its home or heritage to defeat it. We simply need to do a better job of getting a tighter grip while we seek the soft spot on its scaly throat.

Leaving aside analogies, vis-a-vis the real, actual dark ideological network, we have adduced enough direct firsthand testimony from their own words to know that persons well-situated in our circles of power have anti-constitution, anti-liberty—perhaps even anti-human—values and objectives. That should be enough for us to know the storm gathering around us is not going to abet on its own. It is ours today, as in every generation, to stop whatever wrong we see with whatever tools we possess.

Ironically, people learning of this malign force often tend to fight it through the same means it uses for enslaving us: anger, enmity, violence, vituperation. But the most complete and effective victory will ultimately come through what it most disdains and opposes: our humanity. Living the good life, sharing our humanity with everyone, are the means whereby people naturally grow in fellowship, building a mutual strength and unity, a social resilience, bound together by the connection of heart, vision, and love which remains unbroken by mere threats and physical loss. It is the difference between those British tyrants who tried to browbeat Ben Franklin into submission at the Cockpit, but instead turned him into a patriot...and Washington, who won more to his side by his honesty and goodwill, than any military strength or intellectual pyrotechnics.

Whatever this malignant opponent may be, its multi-generational, worldwide effort to bring the entirety of humankind to heel via a single superstructure is the inhumane project of an inhuman intelligence which has no regard for the welfare of humankind. More plainly, perhaps we should just admit we face an immense, malevolent, intergenerational, transdimensional intelligence...that seems to hate all of God's creation, and most particularly the healthy, loving human family. So, how do you defeat all that? Maybe, start where you are. If you really want to win the victory, maybe win the day: love your mate, smile at your neighbor, play with the kids. Tell everyone you see today you love them...with or without words.

Maybe that would be a good start.

Still looks impossible?

That's okay. We're Americans; we live to impossible.

Here's how:

"When a strong man, fully armed, guards his own palace, his goods are in peace."

— Luke 11:21 —

PART IV
IMPOSSIBLIST

Chapter 7

Badass Beautiful and Beyond:
Nation and Impossiblism

Mayflower - Chronicles, (pp. 349- 351) When faced with withering drought the Pilgrims, moved by faith, reach out in fasting and prayer for seemingly impossible salvation:

"These and the like considerations moved not only every good man privately to enter into examination with his own estate between God and his conscience...but to humble ourselves together before the Lord by fasting and prayer. To that end a day was appointed by public authority...hoping that the same God, which had stirred us up hereunto, would be moved hereby in mercy to look down upon us, and grant the request of our dejected souls...But, O the mercy of our God! who was as ready to hear, as we to ask; for though in the morning, when we assembled together, the heavens were as clear, and the drought as like to continue as ever it was, yet, (our exercise continuing some eight or nine hours,) before our departure, the weather was overcast, the clouds gathered together on all sides, and on the next morning distilled such soft, sweet, and moderate showers of rain, continuing some fourteen days, and mixed with such seasonable weather, as it was hard to say whether our withered corn, or drooping affections, were most quickened or revived; such was the bounty and goodness of our God...So that having these many signs of God's favor and acceptation...therefore another solemn day was set apart and appointed...wherein we returned glory, honor, and praise, with all thankfulness, to our good God, which dealt so graciously with us; whose name for these and all other his mercies towards his church and chosen ones, by them be blessed and praised, now and evermore. Amen."

Impossiblist

THE AMERICAN CONSTITUTION IS A remarkable machine: in the front end, you feed people and freedom, and out the back you get airplanes, telegraphs, and telephones; jazz, rock, and rap; baseball, football, and basketball. By creating both the ground and opportunity of liberty, you unleash the infinite creative energy of every individual from which untold marvels will flow. Amazingly, you also elicit the personal best from each person, for, in a free marketplace, we will naturally choose to deal with honest, productive people and businesses; thus, to prosper, the citizen tends to evince their most diligent, industrious, honest, and creative aspects. In an open marketplace, virtuous effort beats vicious sloth, and thus overall, the People gravitate towards their most virtuous potentialities. As a result, the People perforce tend to thrive in their individual self-development, contributing thereby to both their familial and social fellows, justifiably proud in their personal accomplishments, and mutually contributory to the good of the nation. It is thereby a soil which naturally nurtures the best fruits of each person and, perforce, prospers both citizen and nation.

And, as such a nation reaches it full, thrumming potentiality, the People and the Republic realize that, the farther one reaches today, the farther one can dream for tomorrow. They become skilful in applying the initiative and resourcefulness acquired by accomplishing a thousand smaller tasks to sketch plans beyond today's limited confines and towards larger goals. As they apply their freedom to express their capacity for action, build self-reliance through unconquerable determination, and wonder just how much is possible, they realize that maybe yesterday's impossibility can become tomorrow's potentiality. They dare to imagine...anything. They develop *impossiblism*, the belief that there is no such thing as impossible.

JOHN ADAMS: Constitutional Colossus

"I know America capable of anything she undertakes with spirit and vigor."

— Abigail Adams —

Of the Founders, John Adams may have been the most exemplary impossiblist of all. An oft-overlooked champion of the "impossible" mission of American independency, Adams applied ceaseless energy and resolve to overcome innumerable difficult and thankless challenges. If his cousin Sam was the brash, irrepressible voice of the Revolution, John Adams was its broad-shouldered back. He shouldered the burden of shepherding the resolution for "independency" through the Continental Congress and, as we shall document, took on the myriad tasks of making real the promise of the fledgling Republic with well-nigh superhuman energy and fortitude. From Congressman to diplomat, vice president to president, Adams put his shoulder to the wheel—while somehow maintaining a law practice, rearing a family, and producing a voluminous correspondence, at once adoring and erudite, with his wife, Abigail.

The son of comfortably middle-class farmers whose ancestry went back to the very beginnings of the Massachusetts colony, Adams rose to prominence in Boston as perhaps its premier lawyer. From his youth, an incisive, determined, and fiercely moral man (it's not often a townsfolk nickname the local attorney *"Honest John"*), Adams—along with his equally brilliant and principled wife Abigail—were well on their way to a quietly prosperous life in the thriving commercial capital of Massachusetts when first the Sugar Act, then the Boston Massacre, and finally the Tea Party drew Adams' tireless energy and unscrupulous demand for justice into the fray. Before the affray with Britain became open war, he defended both the British soldiers who shot patriot protesters in the Boston Massacre and then turned around and defended patriot John Hancock on charges of smuggling tea; he won both cases and, as a result, the general admiration from all involved for his eloquence, veracity, and even-handed justice.

But, besides a talent for litigation, what did Adams bring to the revolutionary cause? He was neither more scholarly than Madison, nor more literary than Paine, nor better spoken than Henry, nor more charismatic than his cousin Sam. No, he seemingly had no such great innate gifts to set him apart. Rather, his "talent" was something available to anyone: a good old-fashioned Yankee work ethic.

There is no substitute for action. No matter how impossible the goal, no matter how immeasurable the action needed to manifest it, John Adams never ran from any task, never quailed at any challenge. Yes, he—like anyone—had days in which he whined and whinged, cavilled and cursed, but he never stopped nor stepped away. Instead, his life would prove the truth of his wife Abigail's observation, that, *"Great adversities call forth great character."*

While Washington could preside with august majesty, Franklin repose in his accomplished eminence, and Jefferson survey the political tumult with his characteristic enigmatic reserve, Adams brought a restless energy, industry, and ambition. His was a heady admixture of resolve and stubbornness that wove the thousand threads that knit the Republic together.

John Adams was, in short, the supreme *macher*, the man who got things done.

You can't fake results: Beginning in 1766, when he first published articles in opposition to the Stamp Act, Adams would devote increasing time to politics throughout his lifetime. As his reputation and responsibilities grew, he would be drawn for increasingly longer periods away from his beloved family to Philadelphia for the Continental Congress and the revolutionary government, thence overseas for long years as ambassador, and then a final stint in the new Capital at Washington, D.C. Those long years of ceaseless toil included many notable efforts, but the most significant was almost certainly the day he single-handedly saved the American Revolution.

John Adams not only helped Jefferson pen the Declaration,

but he was the man most instrumental in its final passage. On July 1st, 1776—after the Declaration had been delivered to Congress but was still being debated, when the future of the Colonies hung in the balance—he delivered perhaps the single most important speech in American history. As the question of America independency at last came to its final vote, to everyone's surprise, intransigent Tory spokesman for rapprochement with Britain, John Dickinson, stood to speak. Over the course of the next three hours, Dickinson delivered a masterful demur, strongly urging the colonial Congress to vote against this Declaration. His address was carefully crafted, closely argued, and so generally stunning that, by the end, the entire chamber was left in sheepish silence; no one seemed to have an answer. It was in that stupefied stillness that a weary but unbowed John Adams—having spent many a long night over the last fortnight arm-twisting hesitant members to the cause of independency, up that morning since 5 a.m. answering correspondence—stood in answer. He spoke without any notes or preparation, for no one had expected another floor fight at the last minute, since the long debates of the previous day seemed to have settled the matter. Adams started softly, low and slow. His words came not with their usual lawyerly elegance and eloquence, but rather more plain frankness and solemnity. He spoke extemporaneously, yes, but true. He spoke of the injustices suffered, the olive branches offered. He spoke of the brutalities returned and liberties squelched by a Crown showing nothing but disdain and disregard for these Colonies. The slouched shoulders and lowered heads of the legislators were raised; they leaned forward to hear. For 90 full minutes Adams held forth, gathering force and purpose in defense of the great cause of colonial liberty until, as Jefferson later recalled, Adams seemed to transform into a giant, a *"Colossus,"* whose final peroration brought the delegates jumping to their feet in shouts of approbation. That was the day, that was the exact moment, when American independency was decided and your freedom won, and it was John Adams—alone, unaided, and unrehearsed—whose bold, heartfelt truthfulness and passion saved the American Revolution.

And he did not stop there: he would go on to shoulder

many of the endless necessities—both large and small—which make any great project succeed. He would:

...sit on over 90 committees during his tenure with the Continental Congress, his statecraft and insights guiding almost every undertaking of the fledgling nation, most especially as president of Board of War which kept Washington's soldiers in the field long enough to overcome the British

...draw up a "model treaty" which ambassadors could proffer to European nations to secure America's interest abroad while not burdening the nation with "foreign entanglements"

...personally travel to France, Holland, and Britain in furtherance of such treaties, returning often enough with concessions, signatures, gifts, and loans to fund the Revolution and its Republic

...single-handedly pen the Constitution of the Commonwealth of Massachusetts, the oldest extant written constitution on the planet

...serve as Vice President for Washington's two terms, then turn around and

...helm the nation as its second President.

But these are mere line items on a CV—a mere, drear to-do list which can in no way unveil his true character. The episodes which may most clearly evince his badass grit and impossiblist mettle were his sea voyages on ambassadorial missions to France. In two seaborne passages—both crossing the churning Atlantic in winter through the teeth of the British blockade—matters did not go well: in 1778, aboard the frigate *Boston* just days out of port, they were forced to outrun three sail of British ships only to speed headlong into a massive storm. Braving the rolling swells, a lightning strike shivered the main mast, injuring 20 and boring a hole in one poor fellow's head that drove him mad before it killed him. Finally coming into fair seas, they encountered an armed British merchantman, and, clearing for action, the captain found both Adams and his young son John Quincy armed with muskets and ready for the fight; fortunately, the *Boston* far outgunned their opponent and the action was soon over. Soon enough, however, another ship-battering storm kept Adams clinging to a mast for five days until, at last, they reached the Spanish coast. A year later, once more Adams took sail to Europe—again with John Quincy but now also with little Charles in tow. This time, again just days out of port, *Le Sensible* sprung a leak so large the crew had to pump water 24 hours a day to keep from foundering; the captain clawed off and made for the closest friendly port, Ferol, at Spain's northwest corner. Once ashore, the ever-restless Adams refused to wait a month while repairs were made to the ship; he immediately set about hiring donkeys and guides and journeyed with his two young charges overland through Spain, up the icy mountain passes—*"nearly perpendicular"*—over the Pyrenees on paths covering over 1,000 miles to finally reach Paris after nearly two months of weary, bitter travel.

Never flinching, never backing down, never was a man less given to indolence. Truly, Adams demonstrates that—in the article of action—excess is always preferable to deficiency. Do you want to live impossiblist? Then take a page from John Adams: pay the entry fee by tirelessly doing the work to turn your ideal into your real.

The Romance that Made a Revolution

"Is there no Way for two friendly Souls, to converse together, altho the Bodies are 400 Miles off?— Yes by Letter.— But I want a better Communication. I want to hear you think, or see your Thoughts. The Conclusion of your Letter makes my Heart throb, more than a Cannonade would."

— John to Abigail —

For all his accomplishments, John Adams was still just a man, and one given to bouts of irascibility, impatience, and insecurity. Alone, he could be his own worst enemy, but under the mollifying influence of his at once plucky and adoring wife, Abigail, through their lifelong—too often epistolary—conversation, she seems to have been the cement which solidified his emotional citadel. Of the woman he gave the pet name "Portia" (in allusion to the incisive and brave heroine of Shakespeare's *The Merchant of Venice*) and saluted in his letters as *"my dearest friend,"* he wrote that *"nothing has contributed so much to support my mind as the choice blessings of a wife."* For her part, John was likewise Abigail's *"dearest friend,"* ever *"my good man,"* and he *"whom my heart esteems above all earthly things."*

Theirs was a shared mutual respect, candid discourse, and most especially a common commitment not only to each other but to duties beyond themselves, to family and country. As one example, amongst the Founders, John and Abigail were the only ones who not only abhorred slavery but never, as a matter of principle, owned a single slave. Honoring temperance, self-discipline, and industriousness, they envisioned their lives with family and community as a continual pursuit of virtue. Towards that end, Abigail's sacrificed her immense honor, wit, and perspicacity, in daily dedication to her husband, family, and farm. She tirelessly ploughed and managed the farm's furrows (rather more ably than under John's stewardship, by all accounts), minded the poxy youngsters, served as John's most trusted political advisor, and assuaged his moods, so that her husband could, in turn, sacrifice himself in service to his family and nation. Without Adams standing in the breech on July 1st to speak as the Colossus of Liberty, there would have been no Revolution. Without Abigail standing in the breech in Braintree, there would have been no John. Behind every great revolutionary, there is a greater woman. Having such an able partner tending the home, John could fully devote his immense energy, intellect, persuasiveness, and determination back to her, his family, and the nation, in a mutual partnership of duty which gifted their homeland both its founding in freedom plus also two presidencies, as immense a bequest to both family and nation as any couple ever gave.

The closest either of them came to self-indulgence was John's bibliophilia. Though he was never wealthy enough to compete with Jefferson's sprawling collection, Adams kept a standing order with his book seller to ship him any new volume related to the law, and amassed a personal library of over 2,800 books. But, even then, he would eventually relinquish his personal collection for the people's benefit, donating his entire holdings as the seed materials to jump start the Boston Public Library.

John and Abigail Adams' communion in mutual love and admiration, their paired judgment and decisions on matters of state, and their shared commitment to sacrificial service for the betterment of each other, their family, and their nation, produced not only a new nation and two of its presidents, but also over 1,000 tender, literary, and instructive letters exemplifying over 50 years of greatness in marriage.

Altogether, one badass romance.

What neither John nor Abigail could imagine, of course, was how much trouble their newborn nation would face two hundred years later, let alone its source.

The Feast of the Beast: N-Stage Crony Banksterism

"People aren't pissed just to be pissed. They're mad because a tiny group of crooks on Wall Street built themselves beach houses in the Hamptons through a crude fraud scheme that decimated their retirement funds, caused property values in their neighborhoods to collapse, and caused over four million people to be put in foreclosure."
— Matt Taibbi —

In the end, the reality of any situation will become evident; the truth always emerges. Even fiat money—a mere say-so decree—will of necessity eventually revert to its true value, which is nothing. Thus, all fiat money fails, for any say-so money based on things of marginal real use like a cowrie shell, crumbling tobacco leaf, or greenskin Federal Reserve Note is, at base, a fraud. Now, admittedly, government-issued phony money is a very fancy fraud, all dressed up with colorful paper notes and ceremonial pronunciamentos delivered in reverential tones at stolid grey buildings emblazoned with words like Federal and Reserve. But it's still a fraud, a sham, a con of a grift of a swindle of a hustling rip-off in which, ultimately, the banksters who issue these prettified notes produce nothing. Central banks deliver no real product; there is no value added to anyone else's life; their paper notes simply insinuate these shysters into every interaction of the real economy, getting a *de facto* override on everyone else's productive labor. It is a civilization-wide theft by men in suits. None of their fancy scrip (or electronic digits) has any intrinsic value and so, at some point, their worthless product will eventually revert to that same intrinsic value...zero. Here is what George Washington had to say about the matter: *"Paper money has had the effect in your state that it will ever have, to ruin commerce, oppress the honest, and open the door to every species of fraud and injustice. "*

And they needn't try hiding behind the "Federal" part of that Federal Reserve name. As has been said, they are no more doing federal work than a Federal Express driver does when he drops a package on your porch. For proof, here is what the federal courts say (Lewis v. United States, 680 F. 2d 1239 (1982): *"[W]e conclude that the Reserve Banks are not federal instrumentalities...but are independent, privately owned and locally controlled corporations...Reserve Banks, as privately owned entities, receive no appropriated funds from Congress... [W]e hold that the Reserve Banks are not federal agencies."*

Frankly, the window-dressing of the "Federal" in their name has worn thin, and the pretence is gone that they do anything other than administer a slow-drip dose of deadly inflation—just enough to pump the balance sheets for their grifter friends in government and finance, but not enough to kill the patient. The typical lifespan of a fiat currency is a few generations—about long enough for the grandparents to get wise and begin telling the younger folks that they're being rooked by the banksters and the government—then it all falls apart. The American people, being particularly well-off and apparently long-suffering, have put up with this particular Federal Reserve scheme for over a century, more than long enough.

The proof that this particular "Federal Reserve" grift has reached its final n-stage is told by the zeros. The entire federal budget which funded the defeat of Britain in the Revolutionary War was measured in millions. The total to defeat the Nazis in WWII took some billions. Today, Fedgov cannot operate for a year without pumping out trillions, as they fight nothing more dire than their own ineptitude and hare-brained boondoggles. But, when actually totalled, the full amount of multi-layered, "mezzanine" derivative fraud and funny-money the kleptocrats have created in their gambling den on top of the M2 money supply is now measurable in the <u>quad</u>rillions. A quadrillion is a number that looks like this:

$ 1,000,000,000,000,000

There's just not enough stuff to pay all that back...in the whole world.

The smooth-talking sharp-dressed crooks have broken the financial system, but they knew they would, because these are money people, after all, and they know how these fiat-money hoedowns always end. They just plan on not being the guy caught without a chair when the music stops.

That's why the banks have been buying and hoarding gold at rates not seen in generations, because they know fiat money is essentially a continual roller coaster terror ride of economic disasters caused by a money supply which has no basis in real hard assets—as opposed to hard money, especially and particularly monetary metals, which can be readily smelted into a durable, uniform quality suitable for any number of commercial or industrial uses, unlike so many other hard asset classes like land, grains, collectibles, timber, or perishable foodstuffs, which can vary tremendously in quality, degrade over time, and be difficult to equitably utilize in a practical context. There quite simply is no substitute for monetary metals.

In sum, if a transaction is not essentially a form of barter—an exchange of real value for real value—then it is a kind of theft. The theft, under fiat currency, ultimately rests on the central banks which demand people trade their real time, services, goods, and wealth for essentially worthless scraps of scrip. But all of us who use that scrip *as if* it is real money with real value—by our acquiescence to their fraud—have become accomplices after the fact as we allow the financial emperor with no clothes to go on ruling the land in naked insanity.

Now you know where you stand, Mr. and Ms. America: at the tail end on a long night's journey into national debt. Now, when these fiat money schemes fail, the central bank managers have essentially two choices: to allow failure in either (a) their system or (b) your currency. Of course, the currency is their "product", so that's bad when it fails, but the system is, well, their whole system. That's their bread-and-butter, their magic milk cow that churns out the profits. So, they will save their system, which means they will sacrifice the value of your greenbacks, which will just have to go up in smoke. Obviously, they will tinker and temporize to keep the peasants from grabbing the pitchforks, but eventually—when enough market players beyond their control (and ability to coerce and cover up with hyper-monetization) walk away—their pseudo-dollars will vaporize. They will simply hyperinflate your greenbacks into oblivion, and American can join Weimar Germany and Zimbabwe as a watchword for financial mismanagement.

But, never fear, they have a plan.

They will offer everyone their wonderful, new Central Bank Digital Currency (CBDC), which is an even less valuable, more intrusive, and almost inherently inflationary version of the paper-and-digital hybrid currency currently clattering gamely along towards its final self-destruction. The very fact that we have to fight for the continued use of the privacy protection of flimsy paper scrip—in itself essentially worthless but at least a tangible object which cannot be tracked, manipulated, or deleted instantly by a bankster minion at a distant keyboard—is emblematic of how far we have fallen from the understanding and use of real money. How many silver coins do you keep in your pockets? I'll bet your great granddaddy carried some in his.

What are you gonna do on the day the dollar dies, when your income—or savings, or retirement fund (measured in mere thousands)—buys nothing in a market flooded with greenbacks (measured in trillions)? Wouldn't it be nice if the money you made today would still be worth something when you retired, rather than it being "inflated" away to nothing? Wouldn't it be nice if the money you saved and handed on to your children would have the same—or even more—buying power as the day you earned it?

And who is doing all that "inflating" anyway? Who keeps blowing that money balloon bigger and bigger, so that each individual dollar is worth so little? Is it you? Do you have a printing press in your basement? How does all this "inflating" happen? Is there some magical inflation genie somewhere sprinkling dollar dust everywhere? Or are there people—real flesh and blood human beings with names and faces and being paid from the public's coffers—who go out and publicly announce that they will "issue bonds" and "backstop banks" and "quantitatively ease" to the tune of trillions of Federal Reserve greenbacks? It is much as John Adams said: *"All the perplexities, confusion, and distress in America arise, not from defects in their Constitution or Confederation, not from want of honor or virtue, so much as from the downright ignorance of the nature of coin, credit, and circulation. "*

What if, instead of these inflation games, there really were some kind of real, hard assets that these crazed money minions could *not* control, but rather controlled and held directly by the People themselves? What if the Treasury Department were mandated to acquire real money that was dug from the ground, then properly weighed, assayed, minted, and issued to the People? What if your Constitution already said (Art. I, Sec. 10) that *"No State shall... emit Bills of Credit; make any Thing but gold and silver Coin a Tender in Payment of Debts"*? What would your savings be like if that clear, simple sentence were actually followed as our foundational law? How would that affect the value of your house or your children's inheritance?

And even if, for whatever reason, we as a people broached that provision and allowed the federal government to emit bills—like Lincoln did when, rather than pay the London bankers 30% on borrowed millions to fight the Civil War, he printed his own greenbacks—why would we hire foreign bankers to manage and distribute them? Why would we subcontract that primary, sovereign act of emitting our currency to some foreign-owned subcontractor...let alone for a profit? Isn't the issuance of United States currency the business of the American People directly, and not of the hidden, unnamed owners of a private "Federal" Reserve conglomerate?

What if you were in the n-stage unfolding of a collapsing money scam, and nobody had bothered to tell you? What if the big names on the little screen were really fancy criminals with one foot already out the door, ready to bolt as soon as the financial *Titanic* they're steering plows into that looming debt iceberg?

What would you do? What should you do?

When, at last, the hyperinflationary death spiral takes out first the worthless scrap scrip at the edges of the Empire (sorry, Turkey, Japan, Mexico) and at last claws back to the Fed's lynchpin kingpin, the pseudo-dollar, we shall have our inflection point: we will either restore sound, decentralized money or drown under a deluge of bankster-controlled electro-bucks. This is the "crisis" the banksters have long been anticipating, as they have piled up mounds of gold (again, central bank gold reserves are at their highest in generations) and also laid the foundations in many a soporific white paper apologia for the CBDCs which shall turn the serfs into electro-slaves. In their vision, the pseudo-dollar's implosion will be just another engineered crisis which will lead us all a step closer to a tightly-managed worldwide control system. In the next, CBDC, stage, your e-bucks will be sent weekly to your smartphone from your employer (or Fedgov itself, if you have opted for direct enslavement under their oh-so-generous universal (very) basic income), which you may use anywhere (as long as they

approve of what you are buying and from whom you buy it).

You see, when you own the casino, it becomes really easy to rig the games.

This time, obviously, the scam is to roll immediately into the backup: *"Gosh, what a shame that all those ignorant foreigners forgot how great our "dollars" were and its value crashed overnight, but that's okay, because we just accidentally happen to have this handy-dandy tracked and controlled CBDC all shiny and ready to go. But don't worry; we gave it a friendly, perky new name: say hello to "FedBux!" How much can I send you? And, by the way, our buddies in Congress made it a law: ya gotta do it. How much did you say you wanted?"*

American Imperialism: the Weakass Badass of Empire

"I am an anti-imperialist. I am against the eagle putting her claws on any other land."

— Mark Twain —

What if the national badass established by Washington, Adams, and Jefferson had been hijacked by agents of financial criminals? What if, instead of the balanced, virtuous badass practiced by your forbearers, those criminal usurpers finagled guileless Americans into practicing weakass badass? What if they demanded, not the freedom and self-reliance of yore, but an imperialist badass that (a) revels in a scheme of macho brutality and global resource extraction in which the poor boys from rich nations are sent to steal from the rich boys in poor nations...and also (b) converts this once proud Republic into an authoritarian empire, having lost its vision of the—admittedly difficult— balanced nurturance of true republican virtue?

Add the burgeoning currency collapse to the engineered social service collapse which will follow in the Cloward-and-Piven driven overbloat of Fedgov payout systems, and you are sitting on a powder keg. What happens when the Fedgov money scam fails? What happens when the dole payments are cut off? Hungry people get cranky. Hungry people after three days start rioting. Hungry people after seven days go hunting...for anything.

The long-running (purposeful?) mismanagement of the national books—now kept afloat only by the use of the largest national credit card in the history of ever—all while the tax receipts no longer even keep up with the interest "due" on the bonds issued by our ever-so-wise money masters at the "Fed"...all this is, in effect, a reverse revolution: this is a government which has overthrown its constitutional mandate and replaced it with socialist collectivism; this is a government which believes it can fund anything and declare whatever "law" is needful under whichever "emergency" or "crisis" demands its benevolent paternalism, lovingly delivered special delivery to you, the citizen, by many men with large-capacity automatic weapons.

Gosh, ain't that some awfully bad luck...all of that mess happening all at once like that?

Caution: Chaos Ahead!

"The whole aim of practical politics is to keep the populace alarmed—and hence clamorous to be led to safety—by menacing it with an endless series of hobgoblins, all of them imaginary."

— H.L. Mencken —

All tyranny is marked by oppression at home and aggression abroad, but the greater of those two wars is always the war of the government against its own People. The first—and most essential—intuition of any tyranny is that its primary enemy is the citizenry itself, for no People enjoy being bullied and enslaved. And those restive, downtrodden, murmuring citizens are always more numerous, closer, and ubiquitous than any foreign adversary. Thus, a tyrant's primary war is always the war at home, always against you, the vassal serf.

Expect, therefore, that the Great Beastie's minions will suddenly discover an "emergency" of such urgency and magnitude that it absolutely *requires* a global solution, which they will be forced to manage for your own good, completely out of the goodness of their hearts and not expecting anything at all in return...for real and for true! In fact, don't you even worry your pretty little head about it because—just by accident—the UN already has a fabulous plan all drawn up and ready to go, just in case some completely unforeseen and absolutely unexpected scary-big global-style catastrophe might happen...which just happens to be exactly like this "emergency" that actually and by complete accident just happened to happen. And, oh my gosh, we also just happen to have signed a completely legal and absolutely equitable treaty in case of such an accidental completely coincidental catastrophe like this which says we have to lock you up in your home, take away your food, and make you shut up and quit complaining about it on the interwebs. Oh...and one last thing: give us all your guns.

To break the spirit of a People once as strong and determined as those who successfully fought for their revolutionary freedom twice and carried the Allies to victory in both world wars, you either have to overawe them with a great terror, or sneak up on them...or both. We have already talked about the sneaky, stealthy Tavistocky path to tyranny. The other way is the Terror of Terrorism which leads to the Error of Authoritarianism.

Emergency is ever the cloak of tyranny.

Every small "Yes" to the UN—that unelected, unaccountable entity, completely unchecked by the rule of law—is a giant surrender to tyranny. Every acquiescence to that coterie of unelected nabobs—whose New York grounds, buildings, charters, and leadership, were foisted and funded upon the world by the usual suspects in international finance—lays the groundwork for the most massive, least responsive, egregiously dangerous tyranny in the history of the world.

Or do you trust an organization whose Human Rights Council is run by such standout bastions of personal freedom as Communist China and Saudi Arabia?

The very notion of building a single entity and giving it plenary power in any single arena of significance—health, finance, communication, transportation, environment...let alone *all* of these—should give pause to any sensible person with any understanding of history. To *purposely* found and fund such an operation and then hand it plenary power across the full range of core human social, political, financial, and political activities is, frankly, begging for disaster. It is tantamount to summoning the demon...the demon of lawless lust for power which will wreak its will on that hapless humanity which docilely snuggled its collective neck under its clammy, spiny heel.

Remember there is an essentially inverse relationship between the size and distance of government and the justice and freedom it produces. That is, we may formulate the *Inverse Scale Rule of Governmental Democide* this way: the larger and more distant a government is from its constituents, the more tyrannical, violent and even democidal its policies. Hence, genocides—while almost always visited at the local level somewhere—are more commonly formulated and ordered by those miles distant. While there are examples of dictatorships assaulting their own citizens *en masse* virtually under any and all circumstance, the generalized tendency is for the most virulent orders to initiate at the capital and radiate out in their full, sanguine barbarity to the periphery of the regime. Hence, a world-engirdling UN regime, with blue-helmed minions loosed everywhere, should eventually prove a bloodbath indeed.

Authoritarianism usually starts innocently enough, with the usual draconian intrusive and invasive control over what your say, do, and eat, but it typically ends in full-on democide, the savage, wholesale slaughter of innumerable innocents. We need only reflect on history's two most bloody mass murderers. Pol Pot and his Khmer Rouge garnered control of Cambodian and managed, in the "killing fields," to slaughter 1/3 of the entire population in just two years. That's mass murder in a hurry. Or, perhaps you would find more impressive the work of (CIA puppet) Mao Tze-Dung, whose bloodletting was so vast it will forever remain beyond exact enumeration, but whose sanguine exploits—between his civil war, Great Leap Forward, and Cultural Revolution—produced, by some estimates, a final body count anywhere from 50 to 80 million or more Chinese people. That's what you call mass murder in the giant economy-size. Once in place, a true tyrant needs little time or pretext—once all the guns are collected, of course—to initiate a spectacular bloodletting. Usually, this is done by weaponizing the children against their elders through the classic Communist leverage of grievance and envy, and then eradicating the People's historical heroic models which previously held the civilization together via a literal physical assault on everything old, whether persons, books, or statues. Authoritarianism is most often instituted, as Brandon Smith (of alt-market.us) says, using the rather simple formula of launching *"young useful idiots as a weapon to forcibly introduce massive social upheaval, then lock them up in a slave camp and call it Utopia."*

(Yes, we did leave out the UN and WHO and the democidal machinations of Tedros, Fauci et. al. That's because we are still several years from a full, clear, honest "died suddenly" accounting of the decimation visited upon the trusting, unsuspecting masses via the multi-vector, nanoweapon "pandemic" injections. But don't worry, boys. We won't forget you. No way we'll forget you for the second edition.)

Here, then, is the operative question, patriot: if you have determined that a system is rotten—morally corrupt, financially bankrupt—are you safer in or out of it? If it is a system of fictions built on fictions, are you perhaps safer prioritizing real things? Land, food, friends, family, gardens, metals, tools? Where might your time best be spent? What might be the firm basis upon which your future should rest? Upon what moral and physical foundations from whence will you begin the Great Rebuild, once the Beast falls?

Probably those foundations reside in whatever place lies

farthest from the twisted plans of all the alphabet people.

To All the Alphabet People
"If politicians stopped meddling with things they don't understand, there would be a more drastic reduction in the size of government than anyone in either party advocates."
— Thomas Sowell —

Ultimately, we will laugh you to scorn. You, yes, you...you mincing minions, all of you who seek to swarm over us laden with regulatory chains to lock us away for all of our days in obeisance to your fetid fetishes—you, the great, gabbling hordes pouring forth from all your alphabetic lairs like the UN, WHO, MI6, CIA, WEF, CFR, RIIA, IMF, EU, UNICEF, etc., etc. You, you gabbling, nattering flock of imitators, mimics, flatterers...you mental mirrors who cling to baubles and titles, who wrap yourself in the cloak of dark ideology, who suckle the frigid teats of the Beast-of-International-Settlements.

Who died and appointed you experts on running the world? At what point was there a plebiscite of nations to unite under anything except the natural bonds of trade, amity, and hospitality? Why would we need power-mad plutocrats to design and build a formal "United Nations" to issue bombastic charters and declarations making it a law unto itself, by treaty immune from the laws of the land it inhabits (or any other nation), whose acolytes travel about the world wherever they will, without restraint—untaxed, unregulated, unsupervised—whose heavily-armed thugs overrun helpless countries in times of distress, despoiling the people's goods, raping their women, kidnapping their children...and all the while this Kafkaesque monstrosity—along with all its alphabet accomplices—lectures everyone else to obey its ever-more-intrusive directives on what they must eat, drive, build as a house, teach to their children, inject in their bodies, and, of course, think or speak?

Who elected these unworthies? When did the People ever review their resumes, assess the worthiness of their character, assay their perspicacity and moral fiber, and then proceed by free and open election to elevate them to such august positions of terrible responsibility in order to enact plans which are never transparently debated nor fully published? Or, in fact, were these alphabeties selected under cover of darkness in that special midnight club of sanguine festivities, the same club that bequeathed us such genteel humanitarians as Anthony Fauci and Albert Bourla? Are they from the same club that subjected us to the derivative puffery of Yuval "free-will-is-fake-news-you-hackable-uselessly-eating-animals" Hurari and the necrotic medical innovations of Bill "Mosquito-Man" Gates? Are these the same psychopathic know-it-alls who envision us greedily lapping up our meager daily pannikin of 8 grams of bug protein, while shivering in our 200 square foot microcondo with the thermostat kept just above freezing and the 6G radiation turned up to maximum brain melt so we can fully enjoy our neo-feudal serfdom?

Why should anyone know or care what a single one of these self-important, self-apotheosizing buffleheads from the talking-shops thinks or says about anything? Who are these bureaucrats amongst bureaucrats, these walking echo chambers, these least likely people on the planet to have any acquaintance or understanding of the life, thought, work, decisions, aspirations, or absolute majestic glory of the everyday man, woman, or child on the planet? These coddled nabobs, these mental mirrors, these stale puffs of better men's flatulence...

...may they one day—through the grace of God and mercy of mankind—turn and find the humility of heart and depth of soul to bring forth something noble, beautiful, and true which will be for the betterment of society and improvement of souls...

...but—until that blessed, far-off day—yo, Beastie gang...

...go pound sand.

Lying Weapons for Next-Gen War

"It is patently impossible to discuss social engineering or the automation of a society, i.e....(silent weapons) on a national or worldwide scale without implying extensive objectives of social control and destruction of human life, i.e. slavery and genocide."

— *Silent Weapons for Quiet Wars,* opening paragraph —

Of course, the alphabet people's theft via the money system is only the first and most obvious part.

After that, things really get bad.

Only a government engaged in an undeclared war against its own People would undertake the following: eradicate its border so that millions of undocumented, untested, unvetted strangers pour deep into its interior; shut down energy production in oil at the same time it sells off nearly its entire strategic reserve of petroleum to our fiercest geopolitical rival; slaughter innumerable chickens and cows at the same time as aberrant, inexplicable fires have destroyed scores of food storage and processing facilities across the nation; seek to mandate direct injection of woefully undertested, provably deleterious experimental potions into federal workers, military defenders, and the public at large; encourage that same military to abandon the bulk of its equipment in its largest overseas station, then ship off the majority of its remaining fighting vehicles and ammunition stockpiles to foment an unwinnable proxy war at the doorstop of a geopolitical rival with the world's largest nuclear arsenal in an attempt to have the two largest Christian nations bleed each other dry; and all the while, ignore the ongoing bombardment from high overhead by jet planes spewing immense plumes of nanoparticulate heavy metals (aluminum, barium, strontium), in a never-ending omnicidal deluge.

Such a list of assaults on the average citizen (not to mention the Republic itself) can amount to only one thing: war. This goes beyond mere bumbling incompetency or even quisling treachery; this is out-and-out warfare, a "soft kill" assault on the very fabric of the nation and the People themselves. The "leaders" whose words enable, belittle, or ignore such atrocities are mere smokescreen, "air cover" for their ongoing assaults; the truth is in the deed, and their deeds are deadly, their end goal obvious: that the plebs of their omnipotent socialist superstate shall be accosted, beset, tracked, controlled, vilified, mocked, starved, and, eventually, slaughtered by the trainload.

Or...Prove me wrong.

Show us there is some deep humanitarian purpose, Deep State minions; reveal your hidden patriotic resolve, SES apparatchiks. Reverse course. Beginning tomorrow, institute sound and sensible government which upholds and exemplifies the constitutional provisions which once enabled this nation to grow with an easy dignity and exemplary prosperity: free speech, free commerce, strong borders, low taxes, unobtrusive police, sound money, able military, and amicable foreign policy.

Any time you're ready, sweetheart.

The Little Island of Lost Souls
"There you have the gist of it all: somebody expects something fine and noble and unselfish of us; someone expects us to be faithful."
— Walter MacPeek —

Listen, dark minions, we know of one way you are just like the rest us: you are each and every one of you different; each of you has a unique story about how you got there. Some of you were born into the club; you had no choice as you were beaten, raped, and terrorized into submission from childhood. Some of you were seduced into it, by friends, mentors, lovers, piles of cash and prizes. Many of you simply sleepwalked into it through your work, maybe feeling something was not quite right, but studiously ignored the signs, just trying to follow orders and make a living.

And some of you were always psychopaths in your own right and eagerly sought membership so you could indulge your darkest fancies.

To those of you who are true believers and desire it, don't worry: you will have your chance to fight and die ignominiously in service of your indifferent, heartless Master.

Soon, however, the rest of you will want out. You will see the walls closing in. You will see the scorn in people's faces; you will see your bosses disappear, one by one; you will look over your shoulder and the fancy jobs will be gone, the graft and grease will be gone, the vaults full of cash empty. You will hunt around desperately for an exit. Fortunately, there is one: the path of truth.

Take the 500 pound monkey off your back. Find a place to confess—confess it all—so you can, for once, rest in the peace of a clear conscience and whole mind...maybe even find some godliness and try to live in the joy of a clean, whole soul.

But, in either case, becoming a whistleblower and truthteller—that's your escape hatch. Going down with the ship is a long, dire descent into nothingness, and you know what awaits you at the end. Those who foolishly cling with ever more desperation to the Beastie's clammy scales will get the full treatment.

So, you wanna live? Here's the deal. One time offer: surrender.

Come clean with all the facts, and you may live. No deals on the cash and prizes, however. All that swag and booty you piled up? Those are the fruits of theft and fraud which make them illicitly acquired; you have no moral right to those: they will be *droits* of the state, to be remunerated to the People for the general welfare.

Fortunately for you—if you are part of that vast middle-management pool between the People and the administrators at the very top the Dark Network—it is possible that you may prove sufficiently ignorant and insignificant and innocent to be released on your own cognizance. Maybe there's some jail time; maybe there's banishment to the Island of Lost Souls; maybe you actually get to walk among us. Recognize, however, that your disservice to your fellow humans will make it impossible for us to ever again allow you into any office of public trust, or to operate in management of any entity formed or organized under the laws of any state. Basically, you can stay home minding your own business hanging out with your family...maybe run a lemonade stand. Do that. Be quiet. Try to stay out of trouble. Learn to be a nice person, a friendly neighbor...and get up every morning ready to practice being thankful you're even alive.

If, however, you were direct party—or suborned others—to treason, murder, or democide, all bets are off. For your soul's sake, I would suggest you come forward, confess, and fall on the mercy of the court and God. Frankly, however, I expect you lot to continue fighting with all the humanity and politesse of cornered rats, so we'll just hunt you down and deal with you. It's up to you. My advice: come to the party with a contrite heart...and remember to bring the receipts.

Walk Away

"Always choose silence with liars, cheaters, cowards or spineless people...Ignore, avoid, stay away."
— Jyoti Patel —

The worst, traitorous elements of the federal government are—consciously or unconsciously—at war with the best, freest element of the general public. There are vast swaths of go-along, get-along non-entities in between, so the final ideological showdown will be at the extremes, between the patriots and the Beastie gang.

The best elements of the American patriot class will have to lead the People out of Babylon, out of Egypt, to the next Promised Land of milk and honey prepared for the people of God. There will always be another Pharaoh, Nebuchadnezzar, Nimrod, George III, always another brat given power when what they really needed was a good spanking; this is just another such test of our hearts and wills. As the Hebrews did so many times before with the Egyptians and Babylonians, the People will ultimately have to simply walk away. We are, once again, in one of those times. It is time for those of you who hear the call to prepare to stand up, blow the *shofar*, and lead the People on the trek out of the wreck.

While their all-knowing Great Telescreen will continue to screech and scream, delivering an endless array of mis-, dis-, and faux information, the People shall turn their thoughts elsewhere. As the zombied enforcers will continue to cavil, coerce, and cajole the masses, the patriots who dare to speak in truth and live in freedom shall be building parallel economies and municipalities. The Beastie gang will shriek and threaten, and we will grow vegetables and raise children; they will reprimand, and we will dance and pass around the carafe.

They cannot eradicate freedom: freedom is inborn.

They cannot kill an idea: ideas are bulletproof.

Sooner or later, enough of the People shall fully awaken, remember their true, free, compassionate self, and simply live a human life. They will love their families and tend their plots and invent microprocessor-controlled electromag-driven gensets, laughing and dancing, singing and praying with their neighbors. And, one day, they will look over and wonder at the strange, irrelevant man screeching vicious nothings from that rusty, far off megaphone...and then have a good laugh at his expense before they go back to picking a handful of chard for the night's salad.

A government whose debt-to-GDP ratio is reaching historic proportions, whose bonds are increasingly rejected in the open market, whose base essential industries were long since either shipped abroad decades ago or overregulated out of existence, whose armed forces have become an increasing playground for the exhibition of unprecedented social engineering, adoption of morbidly overpriced yet underperforming ordinance, and promotion of sycophantic careerists with all the military perspicacity of a kumquat...such a government is a dead thing walking, and it is best to be standing to one side when it topples.

Walk away from the whole, corrupt, collapsing system, whose ideological roots are the illogical, impractical, and nonsensical...and whose finances are founded on the quicksand of fake money and phony speculation.

Actually, maybe you should run, boys and girls, just run!

In whatever way you can with whatever means available, look to move aside from the wheezing, pustulant corpse of Uncle Sam. Don't worry, we patriots have the tools to revivify the corpse, but we will do so in our own time, on our own terms.

So, maybe you should just move away and find a tall mountain promontory from which to watch it all collapse in a spectacular conflagration—some place high above the fray, holding hands with your local tribe of sages and visionaries, eye to eye, heart to heart, ready to Build Back Human.

Doing Impossible

"It is human nature to try hardest to accomplish the very thing we are told is impossible...Because innately we know that nothing's impossible."
— Richelle Goodrich —

We are, as a civilization, standing at the edge of the precipice, the very edge of the abyss from whence we either plummet to our death...or rise to the skies and fly.

Listen, patriot, you have been given the greatest gift ever: to live at the time of greatest challenge in the history of humankind. Humanity has burgeoned across the planet, in numbers and with productive capacities which make it possible for us to turn this garden of possibilities into a wasteland...or a paradise of potential for every glorious human child. This is a time which no longer calls for the back-breaking gumption and grit of our ancestors, who had to dig and delve in the dirt for every calorie, every mere sip of water. We have made the earth yield its plenty, have tamed the lakes, routed the rivers, so that we may harvest bountifully and drink and bathe freely. Now is the time to leverage that material advantage into a psychological abundance of every-unfolding wonder and discovery.

But there seem to be that handful who hunger to enslave and dehumanize, who seek to transition the human form and individual person into a subspecies under their febrile control. Psychopaths run loose amongst us, whose arrest, prosecution, and eventual legal restriction may prove the great political challenge of the next generation.

That means you—yes, you—are the inflection generation. You have the glorious privilege to fight the greatest death match of all time. You are the people whose every decision can shape this world for years...generations...perhaps centuries to come.

Take a deep breath: you are guaranteed to live in interesting times, times that will make heroes or fools of us all.

All of the challenges, inconveniences, impediments, which will come your way are nothing more than bountiful opportunities to become your heroic self. What would you have, to be perambulated about in a baby buggy and fed ice cream sandwiches by hand the rest of your life? Is that the kind of legacy you wish to leave behind?

Or will you be the person that the grandchildren look upon in wonder—awed at how anyone could have made it through, how anyone could have found such guts, grace, and passion to boldly, joyously face all that was thrown at them?

First, we must reject their anti-human, self-loathing narrative. We must recognize the falsity of their neo-Malthusian, Peak-Oil, Global Meltdown fearmongering storyline—if, for no other reason, than because their narrative has an abominable prognosticatory track record whose P value has a diminishingly small differential from flat zero. In normal people talk, that's called *lying*. Today, we have the means of abundance for all. The reality of humanity's overall prosperity will be expiated upon later, but, for the present, just understand that ours is no longer a time merely to survive, but to thrive. Now, having solved the physical problems of sustenance and shelter, humanity faces a more demanding challenge, that of character: we must demand of ourselves the practical prudence to broadly deliver abundance to everyone.

This is the time to face the seemingly impossible challenge of feeding, housing, and caring for all in a healthy, nurturing manner. Children no more, we must take on the grown-up task of stewardship for our fellows and our home world. Rather than wrestling over the toys in the sandbox, maybe we can start learning how to distribute and share amongst everyone. We must recognize we no longer need only to engineer the physical world, but also to ameliorate our own character, to perform a firmware update on the dark recesses of our own mind, heart, and will. Our wills must become integral with our purpose, our acts aligned with our ethos, our spirits fulfilled more by generosity than greed.

If we are to survive this "Great Filter" moment, this civilizational funnel which weeds out axiologically weak cultures, we will need to enter an age of wisdom, a time of internal housecleaning; we must undertake a mental hygiene wherein we recognize we must step aside from the mind viruses of conceptual malware offered by those who would cow and control us for their benefit; we must instead walk into the open vistas of new understandings and contextualizations where we stand back in reflection, unafraid to coolly reconsider even our most cherished and longstanding beliefs. We must think critically, debate honestly, listen humbly so that we can write a new, more humane, more synoptic story of who are we; where we have come from; what our true history is; and, thence, what we shall make of ourselves in this vast land of potential, without naysayers and overseers to hold us back.

In short, we must get wise or die.

Difficult? Yes.

Impossible? Who cares?

Impossible...is nothing—the proof of which comes next.

But, first, know that any seeming social collapse will be an engineered peak crazy, a maximum madness wrought by those who hope to employ the chaos to their advantage. Every crisis devised by mind-bending manipulator-magicians will be thrown at you—thick and fast, as they scream from their telescreens that you are weak and useless and so must become completely terrified because soon you will surely die and be dead and face a deadly dying death...unless, of course, you come running home to the tender mercies of their velvet slavery.

Be stalwart. Be prepared and resolute.

Better: laugh, as you realize their desperation, bathed in lies and drowning in insignificance.

Then, return to the foundations: family, faith, freedom. Great truths are simple, though, admittedly, living in full accord with great truths often requires equally great deeds. You will need the strength of character to do the difficult. You will need to badass up.

Ultimately, you must become as badass as you are wise.

To keep on through the storm, let your spirit therefore be guided by impossiblism. As Adams took on every task placed before him, the spirit of impossiblism takes on every project and asks not *whether* it can be done, but rather *how* will I do this thing. Any obstacle becomes simply a challenge, and one simply goes over, under, around, or through it to reach the goal. To any one goal, there are many paths forward, and you only need to find and follow one of those paths. This assumption—that any goal is achievable, any problem solvable, any outcome possible—is the sinewy resilience of mature American Badass.

As a mature badass, you act with a far-ranging freedom of thought, your agency—your ability to choose, adapt, innovate, and discover—is fully engaged; you bring to the situation a potentially limitless set of possibilities for action. You are likewise self-reliant, fully engaging your capacity for free action by awaiting neither help nor direction, nor halting at the recognition of occasional obstacles or looming limitations, but instead you utilize your personal resourcefulness to do what you can, with what you've got, right where you are. With those two modes of action engaged, one naturally becomes an agent of unconquerability, who will continue on the task, toward the goal, to achieve the mission, through continual, iterative efforts, without surcease, until its completion.

And when you do all that, you can achieve what, to others, seems the impossible, but to you is just doing your daily duty. Look at the history of how many seemingly impossible things have already been achieved by those wild-eyed Yankee badasses.

Listen:

When the Colonials took to this continent, there were many disparate, disjoint, and disconnected rivers, lakes, and tributaries which could—if connected—provide the fastest, easiest transportation of persons and commerce. Oh, how the Colonials wished this land were connected by a series of canals linking all those waterways for easy integration and navigation. So, with the opening of the Frontier after the Louisiana Purchase, they went out and dug over 3,000 miles of canals which did indeed connect all those waterways in a network which stretched from the eastern seaboard to the Great Lakes and into the further reaches of the western and southern states. It was a lock-building frenzy that would culminate with an expedition far to the south in order to connect the very Atlantic and Pacific oceans through the Panama Canal in 1914.

In 1867, Andrew Carnegie wanted to build a bridge connecting St. Louis directly to Illinois, but was told it was impossible to build iron spans that could bridge over a mile of rushing water across the mighty Mississippi. His reply: *"Nothing is impossible."* By choosing first to build the bridge with steel, then hiring engineering wizard James Eads—who produced 40 unique, patented techniques for that single construction job...and whose perfectionism actually drove Carnegie from the project—that "impossible" bridge was built and opened in less than 10 years.

Through the resulting Eads Bridge, Carnegie and Eads would revivify St. Louis' economy, launch the structural steel industry which made skyscrapers possible, and render a bridge whose over-engineered steel spans made it at one time the longest in the world and which is still in daily use 150 years later.

Want your impossible problem solved? Maybe tell an impossiblist American engineer about it.

Can't see at midnight without a candle? How about get someone like Mr. Edison to whip up an electric light bulb that will burn for hours with the flip of a switch?

Can't communicate important news to far-off relatives? How about a telegraph line, and have your message there in seconds, thanks to Mr. Morse and his fancy code? Or, better, get a telephone and tell them yourself in plain English, thanks to Mr. Bell. Or, heck, send them a picture, thanks to Mr. Eastman with his Kodak camera, or even better, that handy little Brownie. Or, why not just grab an iPhone and instantaneously send them a complete motion picture with sound and moving pictures, thanks to Apple?

Talking and pictures not good enough 'cuz you'd rather give grandma a good, old-fashioned hug in person? Then how about you just fly in the sky, free as a bird in an airplane thanks to those whiz-bang bicycle-building Wright boys from Ohio?

Can't get high enough in that airplane? How about shoot to the edge of space, like William "Captain Kirk" Shatner did, thanks to SpaceX?

Can't get enough firepower downrange? How about try one of those rapid-fire "machine gun" things, thanks to Mr. Thompson?

What can't you do? Line it up. Some American will put it on their To-Do list of "impossible" things to solve. That's what we've been doing for hundreds of years.

Everything is impossible...until it isn't.

Everything is impossible...until someone does it.

Everything is impossible...until you engineer it.

Translation: Nothing is impossible.

So, when you say today's Beastie gang political problem is too big for them American folks in the hills to solve, well...

AmRev 2.0

"I must study politics and war, that our sons may have liberty to study mathematics and philosophy. Our sons ought to study mathematics and philosophy, geography, natural history and naval architecture, navigation, commerce and agriculture in order to give their children a right to study painting, poetry, music, architecture, statuary, tapestry and porcelain."
— John Adams —

Be girded. Be ready.

American Revolution 2.0 is coming, and things are gonna get pretty random.

We are entering a time of inflection, of peril, promise, and potential. Never has humanity unleashed such terror upon itself...and never had access to greater promise. The greatest natural power on earth is human creativity, and the sheer weight of numbers—racing towards 10 billion of us—means there are more engineers, scientists, poets, visionaries...more Einsteins, Teslas, Gandhis, and, yes, even George Washingtons and Thomas Jeffersons...alive today than ever.

If we must study politics and war, then so be it....

This planet surges with human power and potential; we have but to restore the People's badass hope, their big-smile dream of the glorious future which will repay their efforts. Doomsayers are always backward-casting; they take the past as predictive and the present as indicative. They believe there is no way out. They are in-the-box, small-minded, believing that what they see now is the only possibility.

But what has the American adventure proven over and over again? We can be unconquerable...and thereby achieve the impossible...that we have but to open our mind and set our hearts upon that which we would have, and we can build it out for ourselves and our posterity.

What do we wish? Do we not wish for a world where the citizen is sovereign, where the People are free and flourish in their freedom? Then that is what we must set as our goal, determine as our outcome.

So let it be decided. So let it be done.

Understand this, however: the bad guys will not stop. The British did not stop; they had to *be* stopped. We tried talking; we tried pleading; but the British ultimately had to be stopped with guns, cannons, blood, and years of heartache and destruction. Twice.

So that our children may live in a world of prosperity and power...

Our opponents today are at least as tenacious as those Brits, albeit we fight on a different battlefield. Today, the battlefield is often electronic and psychic: a flickering screen, a wavering mind. Today, the tactical challenge is different: they want to play mind games and convince you to surrender, to voluntarily give your consent to slavery, for their good, for your supposed good, for what they claim is the good of the polar bears and baby seals...and most certainly not because they want to control you or own all the land...no, not at all for such selfish reasons at all.

Of course, if they want it kinetic, we can do kinetic. Americans can do kinetic all day long. Just pack a lunch, buddy, because you're gonna be here a minute.

Either way, if they wanted a fight, they better believe they got one.

This time, however, the roles are sort of reversed. It's the ones riding above and controlling our traitorous government who seek a revolution. You see, we, the People, already have a Constitution on the books that British Prime Minister Gladstone called, *"the most wonderful work ever struck off at a given time by the brain and purpose of man."* This time, the tyrants in Fedgov are the revolutionaries; they are the ones looking to overturn the legal government—our constitutional Republic—to replace it with another "new boss, same as the old boss," another unfettered authoritarian regime, just like most countries in most places in most ages, just like they had set up around the world under their British Empire years ago and now want to bring online as a worldwide global money IMF/BIS/UN alphabet hegemony where millions of children dig in mines for pennies, or are swallowed into the filthy maw of their unspeakable sex-slave-and-slaughter machine.

Will you stand by and abide that? Will you pretend that is not happening so you can coolly sip a tall drink at poolside...and pretend you don't hear millions of children screaming?

And then their children may live in a world of poetry and wonder...

This time the patriots are not the ones overthrowing and rebelling. This time the patriots are restoring our unique, irreplaceable system, our invaluable Constitution which controls government and liberates citizens. Never let the enemy's rhetoric confuse the issue: they are the insurrectionists, the anarchists, the iconoclasts, the Jacobins-in-waiting, who would as gladly run a guillotine as a rigged voting machine to get their hands on the levers of power. Chaos, confusion, lies, and division are their tools; your tools are order, clarity, truth, and unity; that is why any one of you is worth any ten of them.

That is why this nation is always in their crosshairs. The greatest threat to their worldwide neo-feudal hegemony is the American Republic, and the greatest force multiplier in the Republic is a well-informed, motivated American patriot.

Welcome to AmRev 2.0, gang, it's going to be bigger, hotter, and wilder than the first one. Unlike others, ours will be a restorative revolution, a reclamation with renovation, the Great Restart will be the restoration of the American Constitution.

And this time nullification will be your weapon and information your ammunition. Aren't you excited? I can hardly wait to see what the history books write about you.

The Great Restart

"A faithful friend is a strong defense; And he that hath found him hath found a treasure."

— Louisa May Alcott —

This Great Restart will be fought more with hearts than swords, minds than guns. Yes, some of it will get brutal and in the street. But you ultimately will win it in the grocery store and neighborhood. Yes, some will fight with fists and fury, but you will win most with words and love.

Show your neighbor how much you care for them. Then remind them that this nation—any great nation—is only as great as its People are good; that only person to person, heart to heart, can we be one people, one nation; that we can only grow and prosper as one unified nation when we bend our wills to duty, sacrifice, and self-discipline; that we need each other, each and every one of you, more than all the tanks and bombs and politicians; that each person is essential to the unity and power of the People to reclaim the government, to restore the Republic, and to shape a future of peace, prosperity, and freedom.

Peer-to-Peer

"United we stand, divided we fall. Let us not split into factions which must destroy that union upon which our existence hangs. Let us preserve our strength...and not exhaust it in civil commotions and intestine wars."

— Patrick Henry —

The battlefield they have chosen is 4th/5th generational warfare. Such actions are less about hardware than software, more about control of the mental and emotional space between your ears than physical ground. Such a contest is primarily informational, asymmetric, nonviolent; it is about winning hearts and minds.

The winner in this war will be the side that can best fight with peace, can most conquer with love. We play now within an information arena, a planetary stage with the eyes of the world upon us through a million smartphone images. Every motion is judged by the hearts and minds of the billions. That is why they fight so hard to control the blogosphere, the social, search, broadcast, and edutainment media: those are the primary means to achieve air supremacy over a population's wetware. The first question of 5G war is what can speak best to those millions of intentions, those billions of hearts, to move them to accept and adopt our ideology?

Fortunately, as the People, we already hold the high ground. Our hearts and minds are the ground they want to conquer, and our natural humane intentions are the ideology they wish to subvert. When you refuse to surrender your citadel to their blandishments, you become unconquerable. Then, as you sally forth from your keep and speak peer-to-peer—one real human heart to another—embracing in fellowship your neighbor, you take that ground from the enemy. As the People move toward consensus—without the interference of ginned-up narratives which divide-and-conquer Americans along prescribed racial, religious, ethnic, social, political, doctrinal, identity, wokeist, long march through the institutions, critical racist theory divisions—that consensus of the People towards humane ends wins. No longer the hierarchical, top-down, pyramidal structure of domination and decree by the "ruler" enforcing "rules" upon the "ruled," the People move toward those few, clear, family-, faith-, and freedom-friendly needs we all share. The People, in their human commonality of purpose, find their modest needs are most simply met by keeping the law small and the possibilities great. Once we've gone peer-to-peer, why do we need government? What are we fighting about? Who got us fighting against each other in the first place?

The Great Restart of liberty will start local, but end worldwide. It may stumble and falter and lose its way, be hesitantly begun, sloppily rebuilt, slowly reoriented...but it will eventually stretch across nations, and ring with shouts and songs and hymns, and move the millions to raise their lands to greatness once again.

Populist, nationalist, patriotic, the People will win because a nation is ultimately nothing more than the People, and the People love their freedom. We will fight lawfare with lawfare, wordfare with wordfare, we will win this battle at the local level, peer-to-peer, person-to-person, one backyard conversation at a time. The technocrats will shout of gloom and doom; they will threaten and cajole and declare, *"The end is nigh!"* And we will calmly speak of the infinite love of the human heart and the beautiful future when all the little guys simply agree to agree. And then, one day, our smiling hordes of impossiblists will lead that tiny gang of traitors out of the People's offices, and we will take our country back.

If they insist on fighting, we can fight, for we are strong and we are many.

If they insist on shouting, we will answer with the quiet assurance of eternal truths.

If they insist on killing, we will pray, for we know the Lord is mightier than any sword.

For we are legion and we will never stop, for we know that our cause is just, and, in the end, our lives our best when we serve not ourselves but our ancestors who gave us this gift of freedom, and our children who justly deserve to receive that jewel of liberty—whole and unbroken—from us.

Patriots of the world, arise! You have all of your rights to reclaim!

Patriots Beat Bad Guys 10:1

"You cannot be disciplined in great things and undisciplined in small things."

— General George Patton —

I (sorta) hate to break it to the bad guys, but patriots win. See, there is a fundamental and ineluctable truth about the difference between patriots and traitors: patriots are moral, traitors immoral. The end result of that moral math is that patriots will outthink, outwork, outfight, and therefore outdo the traitors 10-to-1.

The basic fact is, patriotism is a core moral virtue. Someone who is a patriot of necessity has a generosity of spirit and consideration for others which, of itself, provides useful service to a cause. A person with sound emotional and moral spirit is naturally affectionate for those people and things around them. They find joy in the comforts of their family and local community; they wish the best for both. This communal affection for one's familial home is called loyalty or love; for one's homeland, it is called patriotism. Patriotism is thus a subset of love and loyalty, akin to one's love of family.

Hence, a patriot is, most likely, a person with a keenly developed moral sensibility. By extension, that means a patriot will tend to exhibit other moral traits like self-discipline, honesty, prudence, industry, conscientiousness, selflessness, frugality, determination, gumption, guts, and grit. In short, they are built for badass. They may at times be too trusting, too kind, too slow to react, but beware the man who reacts with a slow burn. His ire may kindle long and low, but he will likewise have thought very clearly and thoroughly about the injustice done to him and will not be stopped until he has moved with implacable determination to fully settle matters. Cross not the honest man, lest he nails your broken bones on the cross of your own sins.

In contrast, let's think about the sad sack poltroons arrayed on the other side, the satanic sycophants scuttling about the Beastie's suppurating nether regions. This side—the side arrayed against the team of loving, loyal, self-sacrificing patriots—are weak-willed self-servers who evince few, if any, moral aspirations. An unpatriotic person, a person who is capable of betraying their nation, perforce necessarily lacks other core moral strengths or virtues. They may thereby, and most likely do, exhibit all manner of other vicious immoral qualities like self-indulgence, mendacity, foolishness, laziness, irresponsibility, prodigality, fecklessness, timidity, cowardliness, and fragility. In short, they are built for weakass; they build for failure. They will tend not only to treat their own managers and colleagues with indifference, forgetfulness, and disdain, but also exhibit the full range of their amoral, immoral ineptitude, malfeasance, and querulousness upon each other.

Thus, when the two organizations meet in the full-contact, 24/7 grind of open conflict, the patriots have the advantage. While the People will exhibit unwavering resolve and resourcefulness, the craptastic narcissists of the traitorous opposition will most likely underperform, underdeliver, and just plain underwhelm at all the wrong moments. When orders are sent to their team of rascally rapscallions and lying losers, it's at least a 50/50 bet they'll be misplaced, half-followed, or plain old ignored. How do they really expect to conquer the world with such a confederacy of dunces? Or, perhaps you think American badasses can't roll such pimping poseurs as Klaus "garters-on-the-strand" Schwab in his pleather faux-Klingon bathrobe seconded by his pencil-necked sidekick Yuval "Toffler-and-Ehrlich 2.0" Harari.

I know which team I'd bet on.

At base, the malefactor's motivation resolves down to just two things: me and my stuff. It's all about selfishness and material goods; the wicked person lusts for the things of the world in order to titillate their little self. Thus, even when working in teams or

324

partnerships, each of them is always ultimately only seeking a personal material advantage. Hence, they will always and everywhere be seeking some edge, even amongst their comrades, large or small. To whatever degree they succeed, they will seek to gain supremacy over more of their fellows. If they grow immense, they will look to attack anyone and everyone who might take even the slightest thing from them in the slightest way. The empire of evil, then, is always a barely controlled Hobbesian war of all against all, a constantly-simmering every-man-for-himself game of king of the hill. It is the most inefficient, dangerous, and destructive form of organization built on a cultural foundation of narcissism, greed, and savage competition which invariably leads to its own destruction, for the more material resources and people which are fed into it, the more every greedy creature indulges their all-consuming lust for material control, pleasure, dominance, and acquisition. Therefore, the more it succeeds, the more spectacularly it fails. If you doubt any of this, simply read any history of the struggles and foibles of the inner party members of Stalin's Soviet Union, Hitler's Reich, or the billions shovelled into the kleptocratic swamp of Ukraine's Potemkin Village of a war against Putin.

A kingdom of goodness, however, built on the ideology of devotion to the "abstract" (i.e. spiritual) ends of selflessness, amity, and compassion, will tend the other way. Mere material wealth is not its sole end, but merely a subsidiary effect of the industry, orderliness, and conscientiousness demanded of a virtuous spirit. Because such people are not fighting in a zero-sum game over a diminishing handful of material goods, but are seeking to instantiate intangible ideals of heart and soul, their organization can actually scale infinitely. In fact, the more people of such caliber that can be brought into their ideological scheme, the larger and faster the organization can grow...and with greater efficiency, as more and more hardworking and dutiful shoulders selflessly lean against the wheel. An organization of the good for the cause of good, therefore, tends to overawe an organization of the bad seeking to do bad, on the order of at least 10-to-1.

Republic of Dreams, Land of Visions

"Some men see things as they are, and ask why. I dream of things that never were, and ask why not."

— Bobby Kennedy, Sr. —

And why are citizens of a republic more likely to be good guys?

Because a republic is the most badass form of government possible: it demands badass at every level, from every citizen, and the more the citizens badass themselves, the more they and their republic thrive. A republic—because it is solely a set of abstract agreements to act right, to live in accordance with rational, lawful behavior—demands of its participants that they run their outward lives in a rational, lawful way. It puts the burden on the People to be virtuous enough to live within the law, so that they do not need the dictatorship and bands of thugs requisite within failed authoritarian states to enforce dictatorial mandates on lawless mobs. A healthy republic, rather, depends on citizens strong enough to defend their lawful rights from the inevitable crew of crafty thieves and traitors who attempt to use the color of law to usurp the equitable distribution of power.

Healthy republics—wherein the People have internalized the need for moral self-regulation and expect the same from their fellows and the government—thereby tend to produce less bribery, corruption, waste, fraud, and abuse at both the public and private level. In contrast, wherever the law is the imposition of restraint upon a restive and ill-disciplined people, chaos lurks around every bend in the road. The slightest hitch can unleash the selfish impulses of the masses: failure to deliver the dole produces riots; ineffective policy during disasters erupts in looting and pillage; any unpopular enactment becomes a pretext for vandalism, arson, assault on public officials or even random strangers.

There is, therefore, a positive (in both sense of the word)

feedback mechanism built into a properly-ordered republic, wherein engendering and cultivating personal moral order supports and maintains the health and vitality of the nation; so likewise, does the republic's establishment and maintenance of the laws (those *res publica*, those "public things," i.e. those legal standards we must mutually share and uphold) provide the order and stability needful for the individual to indeed live a rational, orderly life. In a republic, therefore, there is an essential moral reciprocity between the state and citizen, each mutually interested in the maintenance of public lawful order and personal moral discipline.

In short, healthy republics tend to produce healthy citizens, and vice versa. As the state keeps to its place, the citizen must keep to their peace, and the whole prospers. If not, then comes the need for corrective adjustment and renewal.

If, then, today's citizens recognize the power and worth of a republican form of government, we citizens will likewise recognize the need to act so as to undergird and nurture such government. How do we citizens thereby support our Republic? Quite simply by living in the most virtuous manner possible, and then demanding the same from the government itself. The reciprocity of the rule of law is lawfulness of the government and the self-mastery of the citizen to behave in a virtuously lawful manner. Likewise, if one or the other party imbalances that equation, then both the written, juridical laws and the unwritten, natural laws provide mechanisms of correction.

That's how republics are built, that's how republics are kept, and that's how republics reclaim their glory.

Too Much Americanism in America to Lose

Fiat justitia ruat cælum. "Let justice be done though the heavens fall."

— Motto, Tennessee Supreme Court —

So, all things considered, it looks like there is still too much America left in those Americans for their Republic to be conquered. As it was 250 years ago, the European overlords just don't know who they're messing with. Like anybody, they think that we think like them, but American patriots are not like them, scurrying little sycophants awaiting table scraps from the great money Beastie. Those little servitors of the moneyed class obviously have no acquaintance with the backbone and grit of the everyday peasant class in America. So, now, the irresistible force of the great globalist monopoly will once again meet the immovable object of American impossiblism.

Americanism wins.

For, the immovable object needs to do nothing but be: be itself, be unmoved by the screeching vaporings of the onrushing force. That force, however, must continually expend energy in its pursuit...and so must ultimately fail, for, while it is surely convinced of its own invincibility, its force—though indeed mighty and great—is ultimately finite.

So, after many years of mincing around, the struggle has finally reached its climax, wherein the forces of tyranny have dropped the mask, manifested openly their plans for complete enslavement and democide, exposing the immeasurable depths of their depravity.

They have shown that they are in open warfare against the common folk.

And for that, they will pay.

For there are a lot of common folk, a whole lot more common folk than sociopathic globalists. So, now that it's open war, let's do the math: the People have the numbers; the People have the moral high ground; the People have the gumption, grit, and guts. We've done it and won it before, so we'll just have to get in it and win it again.

It's just a matter to time now.

And here's the beauty part: this time the stakes of the

game are all-in, winner take all for the whole world.

They will come hard for America: it will be called the bad boy of the whole world for hanging on to all those old-fashioned ideas like God and guns and grit, while all the cool kids in the UN club delight in running their fingers through the motley plumage adorning the Beastie's back, and party all day guzzling the sweetest high-fructose corn syrup energy libation, nuzzling the fastest microwave-blasting phones close to their heads, and disporting in weaving lines of unclad erotic randomness, as they prance about the ritual circle, piling up the logs in anticipation of the sacrificial fire to the Ancient Ones.

And the American cowboy will squint, spit one last time in the dirt, kicking up just a touch of dust beside his boots, rack the bolt on his select-fire long gun, and—knowing that he must win, so that the world can witness the majesty of one more impossible victory—stride boldly toward that setting sun. For the reinstitution of the American Constitution means the world's liberation.

"For nothing will be impossible with God"

— Luke 1:37 —

Chapter 8

Your Infinite "Yes!":
Citizen & Impossiblist

Mayflower Chronicles, pp. 250 -251

"At our arrival at New Plymouth, in New England, we found all our friends and planters in good health, though they were left sick and weak, with very small means ; the Indians round about us peaceable and friendly ; the country very pleasant and temperate, yielding naturally, of itself, great store of fruits, as vines of divers sorts, in great abundance. There is likewise walnuts, chestnuts, small nuts and plums, with much variety of flowers, roots and herbs, no less pleasant than wholesome and profitable. No place hath more gooseberries and strawberries, nor better. Timber of all sorts...cover the land...The sea affords us great plenty of all excellent sorts of sea-fish, as the rivers and isles doth variety of wild fowl of most useful sorts...Better grain cannot be than the Indian corn, if we will plant it upon as good ground as a man need desire. We are all freeholders ; the rent-day doth not trouble us; and all those good blessings we have, of which and what we list in their seasons for taking. Our company are, for the most part, very religious, honest people; the word of God sincerely taught us every Sabbath; so that I know not any thing a contented mind can here want."

American Impossiblism

"Like all Americans, he had no talent for bowing to the inevitable. The word 'impossible' is not in his vocabulary."
— Romain Gary, Frenchman —

THE AMERICAN "IMPOSSIBLIST" IS THE achiever of visions, the maker of dreams. The best of what American Badass evokes is a kind of maximization of the human spirit wherein one dares to "dream the impossible dream." Yet, as we saw in Chapter VII, the Beastie gang has built a challenge indeed, a challenge to political and economic freedom which seems truly insurmountable, truly impossible, and, truly, can only be defeated by American impossibilism.

Fortunately, being American is precisely the art of turning the "impossible" into reality, to be both enough of a dreamer to see the ideal, and enough of a doer to make it real. Practically everything great America has ever been or become was "impossible"...until it wasn't:

The freedom of religion was impossible in Europe, until the Pilgrims came here.

The freedom from the world's strongest empire was impossible, until the patriots won AmRev 1.0...and then the Son of AmRev 1.0 in the War of 1812.

The ability of citizens to be sovereign and preserve their rights under a lawful republic was impossible, until the Constitution was instituted.

The chance to start over and build your life anew was impossible, until Lewis and Clarke, Daniel Boone, and the settlers opened the Frontier and the West.

And that is just the start of that unending quest, for impossiblism means always challenging yourself and your nation to see farther, to do better. Impossiblism means anything possiblism: to reach out with hopeful optimism and see the possible beyond the horizon. Of the Founders, probably the most soulful and visionary impossiblist of them all—the one who seemed to most freely dream and fully embody all that he dreamed—was Jefferson.

THOMAS JEFFERSON

"Timid men...prefer the calm of despotism to the boisterous sea of liberty."
— Thomas Jefferson —

Thomas Jefferson was, perhaps, at once the most visionary dreamer yet most pragmatic idealist of the revolutionaries, an embodiment of the Renaissance man, a veritable artist of imposibilism. He believed in and worked toward living a life and building a nation where badass action in pursuit of excellence lifts humankind to its greatest potentialities. Notoriously the least voluble of the Founders, Jefferson was a man more inclined to think and then do, than to merely talk and then wish.

As a young man, rather than live in the family estate, he personally envisioned, designed, and oversaw the (never-ending) construction of his Monticello mansion and gardens, an architectural masterpiece celebrated and studied for generations. At the same time—in those stretches where he was not called away on the nation's business—he improved his time around the estate as a handyman and inventor, producing numerous practical conveniences, the most important of which was a radically redesigned plow through the use of differential calculus, while the others ameliorated any number of domestic endeavors, from a macaroni-making machine to revolving boot stand, from an automatic gate closure to a mechanical letter copier which generated a repository of his voluminous correspondence.

A bibliophile on a magnitude even greater than John Adams, Jefferson amassed a personal collection of thousands of volumes by age 27, which were all destroyed when his first house burned down. Undeterred, he immediately set about rebuilding that collection of texts ranging across virtually every scholarly and scientific pursuit from philosophy and theology to paleontology and mechanics, and most especially his most beloved avocation, architecture. On the strength of such broad learning, Jefferson developed a luminescent ability to organize and formulate his own reflections precisely and powerfully in written expression. When at last, his surveys of the political thinkers concluded, he moved straight to unending action, for, as he said, *"What country can preserve its liberties if their rulers are not warned from time to time that their people preserve the spirit of resistance?"* All his researches and skills came into powerful focus and application in his long-running, exemplary political career.

A man who, at 6'2", literally stood taller than almost all his revolutionary fellows, who seemed always to be scanning the horizon for the sail of some far off ship, Jefferson was also a man who sought to see his visions made manifest, to actually realize some envisioned utopia of sovereign citizens, wherein each was a freeholder of a miniature kingdom like his own, each peacefully perched atop their own little mountain of peaceful liberty. As he saw it, power must continually be devolved towards that local level, for "[t]he People...are the only sure reliance for the preservation of our liberty."

His political efforts towards realizing such a nation of freeholders began in the Virginia House of Burgesses where—as he had from his earliest days as a lawyer—Jefferson spearheaded quixotic efforts to abolish slavery. He would propose legislation to allow slaves to be freed both while in the Virginia House of Burgesses, and later, in initial drafts for the Northwest Ordinance. Both attempts were quickly quashed by recalcitrant legislatures. Yet, over the course of time, Jefferson's utopian abolitionist vision would win the day.

From state representative, he went on to serve the fledgling Republic in ever more consequential roles as first congressman, then ambassador plenipotentiary, secretary of state, vice president, and, eventually, president. His greatest repute, however, came from the clarity and verve of his written expression. By the time of the Second Continental Congress, Jefferson had entered the national stage with a defense of the colonial perspective in his 1774 pamphlet, *A Summary View of the Rights of British America*. On the strength of that pellucid effort, his choice as the man to helm the crafting of the Revolution's Declaration was undisputed. And though he shaped and served in government for decades, his writing never lost its revolutionary zeal: *"The tree of liberty must be refreshed from time to time with the blood of patriots and tyrants."*

Of course, the culmination of his public service was his presidency. Chapter II has already covered his practical skill, fiscal discipline, and expansive forethought during his tenure in the office: dispatching the Marine Corps across the Atlantic to put an end to the continual rapine and sex-trafficking of the Barbary Pirates in North Africa; balancing the budget, reducing taxes, and alleviating much of the national debt from the Revolutionary War; doubling the size of the United States with the stroke of a pen in the Louisiana Purchase; laying the groundwork to double the size of the nation yet a second time by funding the Lewis and Clark expedition to open up the West and knit the continent from the Atlantic to the Pacific; solidifying Washington's precedent by following his example and retiring from office after serving only two terms. Jefferson, by winning the presidency for the Democratic-Republican ticket and then helming the government with such skill, also thereby set the nation on a course of libertarian individualism—and away from the nascent authoritarianism of the Federalists—which obtained for the better part of a century. His tenure thereby set the tone and tenor for the nation, and, as a consequence, the American People experienced perhaps their most peaceful, free, abundant, and prosperous era. By his political efforts, his utopian dream for everyman—a land of individual freedom and personal autonomy—was perhaps brought closer to reality than at any other place or time in history.

After Jefferson at last retired from public service, he spent his final years largely as he had spent the earlier ones: corresponding to his friends and colleagues, living with the largeness of spirit and freedom of mind in the countryside he loved yet had sought little material advantage from, in a house built to his visionary image, in a nation he had founded to his ideal of a republic wherein land-holding freemen were sovereign in their fields and grottoes. He was ever free in his spirit—in reflection and written correspondence, and amongst his beloved books—ever free on his land, and finally free in his nation...all by the work of his hands and power of his words. He lived in the reality of having adhered to and triumphed through his pledge: *"On the altar of God, I swear eternal hostility against all forms of tyranny over the mind of man."*

In his final decades, his immense intellectual curiosity and commitment to public service would impel him to continual, pragmatic efforts at improving American minds. He sought a People who were free and who also possessed the clarity of intellect to defend and improve their Republic. As he said: *"If a nation expects to be ignorant and free, it expects what never was and never will be...The people cannot be safe without information. Where the press is free and every man is able to read, all is safe."*

Thus, when he discovered the British had burned the Library of Congress to the ground in the War of 1812, Jefferson resolved to sell his entire, rebuilt library—then numbering over 6,700 volumes—as the seed collection to begin reconstructing the institution...and, at whatever price the Library choose. Not wishing to unduly take advantage of the generous offer, the Library engaged a bookseller as a disinterested third party to come up with a final valuation; yet, when the books were actually priced, they were adjudicated not on their true literary merit or collectability, but by mere physical measurement, as if they were so many potatoes being weighed. In addition, the bookseller's manifest recorded merely 6,500 books, thereby overlooking over two hundred texts. Thus, the sale—already more than fair—considerably short-changing the former president both in the value of each volume and in the numeric final total. Jefferson, however, did not feel it fitting to make an issue of the matter and never corrected the bill of sale nor ever asked that he be paid the difference. One need not worry, however, that the lifelong bibliophile was left in his final days bereft and bookless in his Monticello mansion. Confessing himself a man who, *"cannot live without books,"* Jefferson immediately began restocking his beloved library and would amass yet a third collection of several thousand over the next decade.

The greatest focus of Jefferson's final energies, however, were devoted to manifesting a long-cherished dream: building a university *"broad & liberal & modern"* for his state, with professors ranking in *"the first order in their respective lines which can be procured on either side of the Atlantic."* So it was that, soon after replenishing the Library of Congress, Jefferson would found the University of Virginia. In a vast undertaking for the "retired" president, Jefferson ushered the legislation through the House of Burgesses, and would wrangle tirelessly with deans, professors, and students in bringing to fruition the institution he modestly called "the hobby of my old age." In October of 1817 the first cornerstone was laid for "Central College" a fledgling institution which, via Jefferson's watchful shepherding, was soon elevated into the University of Virginia, where Jefferson served as its first rector until his death in 1826. Even more monumental than doing the legislative heavy lifting, Jefferson himself served as master architect for the entire project, devising a detailed plan for an *"academical village"* whose sprawling elegance took maximal advantage of the school's pastoral setting. Contrary to the traditional monolithic big brick boxes of that era's other universities, Jefferson devised a lyceum which opened on large pavilions in a neo-Classical style, with a central Rotunda modelled on the Roman Pantheon. Jefferson was, in effect, seeking to resurrect an Athenian bastion of intellectual debate and free inquiry, a center of learning whose porticos would resound with young philosophers deep in Socratic debate, a la Raphael's immortal fresco *The School of Athens*. In that sense, Jefferson's valedictory project may be seen as simultaneously the culmination of his life and of that Attic dream of a democratic polis under the sway of reasoned debate—the university becoming a capstone for both Jefferson's life and the vast arc of western civilization, set so many generations ago and finally realized in the backwoods of Virginia. So ambitious was his project that its final construction took nearly a decade. So long, in fact, that Jefferson was only able to personally visit the completed university once, in June of 1826, near the very end of his life. The vision Jefferson had nurtured for so many decades had at long last been gifted to his state—a school of first repute which would be, *"based on the illimitable freedom of the human mind, for here we are not afraid to follow truth wherever it may lead, nor to tolerate any error so long as reason is left free to combat it."*

Within a month of completing his long journey to build that long-sought university, Jefferson would perish. But—as was true of his life—even his death was marked by one last impossibilism: he passed away on July 4th, 1826, the 50th anniversary of the day he helped found this nation...which was also the dying day as his long time compatriot, competitor, co-author of the *Declaration,* co-founder of the nation, predecessor in the presidency, and closest friend, John Adams.

Thomas Jefferson: you just can't make up that kind of impossiblism.

An Infinity of Impossibilities

"The word 'impossible' ain't in my dictionary."
— Jessica Maria Tuccelli, *Glow*—

Jefferson wasn't the only American to pursue impossiblist outcomes which lie beyond the boundaries of the present moment. This innate belief in impossiblism is deeply baked into the American psyche, for the truly determined, self-reliant, competent badass will reach out ever farther, ever more eagerly, to manifest ever more greatness beyond the verge of today's possibilities.

Get ready, world, because the human family has not yet begun to impossible. Here is a selection of many Americans—from numerous fields—reminding us just how near, how reachable, how actionable, is impossible:

Politics, Policy, Pugnacity

"Most of the things worth doing in the world had been declared impossible before they were done."

— Louis D. Brandeis —

"Impossible is just a small word that is thrown around by small men who find it easier to live in a world they've been given to explore the power they have, to change it. Impossible is not a fact; it is an opinion. Impossible is not a declaration; it is a dare. Impossible is potential. Impossible is temporary. Impossible is nothing!"

— John C. Maxwell *The Difference Maker* —

"In planning any operation, it is vital to remember, and constantly repeat to oneself, two things: in war nothing is impossible, provided you use audacity, and do not take counsel of your fears."

— General George Patton —

Business & Finance

"When you exhaust all possibilities, remember this: you haven't."

— Thomas A Edison —

"Thinking always ahead, thinking always of trying to do more, brings a state of mind in which nothing is impossible. The moment one gets into the 'expert' state of mind a great number of things become impossible."

— Henry Ford —

"Believe and act as if it were impossible to fail."

— Charles F. Kettering —

Sports & Aviation

"Women, like men, should try to do the impossible. And when they fail, their failure should be a challenge to others."

— Amelia Earhart —

"It is difficult to say what is impossible, for the dream of yesterday is the hope of today and the reality of tomorrow."

— Robert H. Goddard —

"The difference between the impossible and the possible lies in a man's determination."

— Tommy Lasorda —

"I won't predict anything historic. But nothing is impossible."

— Michael Phelps —

"Aviation is proof that, given the will, we have the capacity to achieve the impossible."

— Eddie Rickenbacker —

Arts & Writing

"All things are possible until they are proved impossible, and even the impossible may only be so, as of now."

— Pearl S Buck —

"Ordinary people believe only in the possible. Extraordinary people visualize not what is possible or probable, but rather what is impossible. And by visualizing the impossible, they begin to see it as possible."

— Cherie Carter-Scott —

"The limits of the possible can only be defined by going beyond them into the impossible."

— Arthur C. Clarke —

"It is impossible to win the race unless you venture to run, impossible to win the victory unless you dare to battle."

— Richard M. DeVos —

"Many of the things that seem impossible now will become realities of tomorrow."

— Walt Disney —

"The man of the future may, and even must, do things impossible in the past and acquire new motor variations not given by heredity."

— G. Stanley Hall —

"Man is the only creature that strives to surpass himself and yearns for the impossible."

— Eric Hoffer —

"Dreams taught me never to doubt myself, by letting me do the impossible."
— Michael Bassey Johnson, *Song of a Nature Lover* —

"Hope sees the invisible, feels the intangible, and achieves the impossible."

— Helen Keller —

"Faith is the first factor in a life devoted to service. Without it, nothing is possible. With it, nothing is impossible."

— Mary McLeod Bethune —

"Success is determined by those who prove the impossible, possible."

— James W. Pence —

"Once you chose the power of love, nothing is impossible."
— Debasish Mridha —

"In life, nothing is impossible to achieve when you have enthusiasm, optimism, confidence, and commitment."

— Debasish Mridha —

"Her failure didn't matter, because at least she'd been true to her impossible dream until the very end."

— Ruth Ozeki, *A Tale for the Time Being* —

"Darkness comes. In the middle of it, the future looks blank. The temptation to quit is huge. Don't. You are in good company. You will argue with yourself that there is no way forward. But with God, nothing is impossible. He has more ropes and ladders and tunnels out of pits than you can conceive. Wait. Pray without ceasing. Hope."

— John Piper —

"What we can or cannot do, what we consider possible or impossible, is rarely a function of our true capability. It is more likely a function of our beliefs about who we are."

— Anthony Robbins —

"Impossible just means that you didn't do it yet."

— Frank Sonnenberg, *The Path to a Meaningful Life* —

"Nothing is impossible. Some things are just less likely than others."

— Jonathan Winters —

So integral is this impossiblist attitude to American engagement with life's challenges, that we have writers and scholars adducing methodologies of "impossiblizing." Best-selling author Steven Kotler in *The Art of Impossible* asserts the proven path to "impossible" achievements lies through the individual's motivation and learning which develops ongoing "flow" states of maximal creative output. Similarly, Dr. Alan Bernard has taken his impossiblist approach to corporate seminars worldwide. He even encourages one to *make* any task "impossible" by incrementally increasing one's expected outcome and/or shortening the projected time line for completion to the point where it seems impossible to everyone. Only then is one ready to brainstorm to breakthrough solutions, and one does that by asking, "Okay, it's impossible...*unless* what?" This allows the mind to envision the next-level breakthrough pathway to impossible. In both approaches—as in the many quotes above—you are a change machine. You are, at root, freedom itself, made in the image of divine reason and creativity for continual self-improvement and never-ending renewal. *You* are how impossible happens.

How Do You Feast on a Beast? One Bite at a Time

"Any fool can make a rule, and any fool will mind it."

— Henry David Thoreau —

You know who hates it when you impossible? The Beastie. The Beastie cult wants you sad, sorry, sickly, simping, slack-jawed, and self-defeating. Of course, it is a bit of a misnomer to say the big, bad Beastie gang wants you dead. Eventually, yes...eventually, they want their little herd of compliant cattle culled down to what they call a "sustainable" population size—which really means a manageable herd, a herd of slaves just big enough to *sustain* their tidy enclave of kleptocrats in the luxury to which they'd like to become accustomed. But, until then, they don't so much want you completely dead as just half-dead. To them, you are most useful when you are sufficiently tired, dulled, and stupefied to continually grind out your little cubicle quota, but not sufficiently well-rested, well-informed, and physically well to ask pesky, probing questions about the whole exercise.

In short, the Beastie has a fine little plan for you: *"Go along to get along, comrade citizen worker! Be a dutiful member of the herd: stay up till 2am hugging your bestie phonie, take your totally safe and completely effective shots, and imbibe much TV "programming." Stay safely in automaton mode, and all will go well for you. Once you have waddled your way to the end of our 65-year maze, we will have a pension, gold watch and once-in-a-lifetime, very special, very tasty donut for you! Yummy, tasty...just one bite and you will have a long, restful sleep!"*

By putting your head down this way and shuffling along in robopath mode, you become not only the complicit, willing, even eager participant in your own destruction, you become another brick in what is intended to be a 1,000-year, world-engirdling prison block. In a society being slowly reshaped into an open-air abattoir—a giant mechanical combine for the harvesting of souls—it is hard to tell who is friend, who is foe, what is organic, everyday foolishness, and what weaponized mind control chaos and confusion. To stop shuffling in lockstep to the eternal brutalization of the human spirit under the leering, drooling mercies of lizard-hearted psychopaths, one might want to start looking for the exit doors out of one's little rat-racing maze.

Instead of mindlessly complying, one might want to dig down to the foundations of what it means to be human, to construct a life of meaning and purpose, to unearth those half-buried truths of the ages which bring peoples to fulfillment and nations to peace. Fortunately, these foundations are still there, as sure and strong as ever, for true foundations can be neither broken, nor shifted, nor eradicated. Now, look around: what have been the truths of the joyful life and peaceful village for the long history of humankind, those ways which long practice and ancestral memory—handed down over generations—have proven most harmonious for man, woman, and child? What are the ways of humankind's well-being which arise ineluctably from our biological and psychological foundations? Turn from the clamoring voices of confusion on the stage show of clowns and jesters built by today's artificers and overlords. What has been most true in most times and climes for the lives of the people—the average people, the ones who do all the working and yearning and dreaming and striving? What did people portray as life's ideal on murals in Rome, papyrus from Egypt, the teaching tales of East Africa and Old Europe, in Colonial America or cookouts by your grandparents? Slow down; dig down; reach down into the ground of your clan's past, into your own heart and experience, those ancestral memories inherited from innumerable forbearers, knit into your very sinews, and you will find these sure foundations:

Family is the most fundamental of ineluctable biological realities, for the quintessential polarity of man and woman draws them to join in producing the young. Man and woman with child makes family, the most elemental social unit. The essential physical, dynamic duality inevitably renders the most essential psychological framework: family...and thence the custom and comfort of marriage which socially upholds it. The biological compulsion to bring forth in family makes the familial structure the most necessary, fruitful, and thereby precious sociological unit. A civilization can only be as strong as its families, for each relation of that essential father-mother-child triangle must be knit solid, healthy, and whole for those persons not only to thrive in and amongst themselves, but to succeed outside of their familial dwelling. Father and mother must act in mutual respect and furtherance of the family's comity, safety, and plenty. Each of the parents must likewise give of their time and love to the child so that it may know its own worth and gain from their guidance and wisdom. Homes which fail to manage well these basal relations will tend to undermine, rather than contribute to, a healthy, dynamic, forward thinking and creatively flowering civilization.

As no person succeeds alone, so no family flourishes alone. Each person comes arrayed with a range of capacities and limitations, strengths and inadequacies. Hence, few people thrive by only encountering a few people. Every human must, first and foremost, see to their own survival, but, once they have built a family, they then seek outside protection for the furtherance of the loved ones of that family, those family members who are—by dint of love and kinship—the extensions of one's personal identity, who *are* that larger "self" which the family becomes. Thus, from the primal impulses to live, and live more abundantly, the atom of self grows outward and forms the molecule of family, which eventually weaves the polymer of society with its far-flung interlocking chains of community; it is an implicit pact of mutual protection and cultivation which moves us to reach ever outward from self to lover, from couple to family, from home to hamlet, and thence from clan to civilization. Through that mechanism of continual, ever-expanding circles of reciprocal interaction, generosity, and justice, humankind joins person to person, family to family. Paradoxically, the more people learn to work amicably and fruitfully in larger and larger arrangements, the more each person is able to specialize, to more and more exhibit and maximize their peculiar individual strengths, to acquire ever finer skills and tools, knowledge and experience in their unique talent and craft, which then in turn makes their skills and knowledge of greater value when utilized and delivered back to the ever-widening human community. Thus, a society which elicits the maximum potentiality from each individual will perforce reap the maximum potency from its populace overall, in an ever-strengthening circle of interconnectivity, an unbounded positive feedback loop of development, discovery, and victory.

Thence, from that smallest social unit of family—once settled and secure—community grows; around family comes other families, neighbors, and a larger, stable society which enables all those families to mutually nurture and cultivate their individual members. Family, extended family, and the network of local relationships connected with it, is, then, the essential integument of every society, and, at the same time, it is within family that the social duties attendant upon living amongst others are first hard coded into each person in order to form the interpersonal politesse underlying civilization. In other words, society is built on that tiny foundation of inculcating into each child those basal "daughter" virtues that virtually every 10-year-old is expected to exhibit: politeness, respect, courtesy, reciprocity, timeliness, kindness, etc. Hence, a well-formed family culture is the foundation of any civilization, and any civilization failing its families is soon to fail itself.

Faith is the recognition of the larger-than-thou, that great Beyond in whose acknowledgement the larger world's order and beauty is best studied, honored, and emulated. On a basal level, then, for most people, such faith informs not only the metaphysical but the ethical foundation of their worldview. They live best when they live in accord with the order of a world rendered by the transcendent moral Orderer of this lawful realm. This understanding of the *mysterium tremendum et fascinans* may range from the dogmatic monotheism of Jehovah God to the mysterious unity of the Taoist's ineffable Way to the faceless watchmaker or deist Demiurge of *philosophes* and gnostics, but all of these notions point to the recognition of our world's ineluctably complex yet precise wheelwork which evinces itself in beauty, majesty, and fine-grained interconnection. Until we can do better, we do well to simply adore, rejoice, and order our lives in service of such splendor. Within the larger context of society, shared faith in a larger Order typically grounds and encapsulates an entire moral schema, for it will both foreground those ethical attributes it most values as well as stacking or prioritizing their relative import. Such shared value stacks further knit together the members of the community in mutually accepted perception of the nature and purpose of a well-lived life, easing and strengthening their personal interactions and societal undertakings.

Freedom in individual action is the practical engine which enables the realization of the forgoing two foundations. In other words, freedom is that single essential which greases the skids of life's journey. As freedom has been a continual through line of this text, a brief summary should suffice to demonstrate the goods which individual freedom confers: the free trade between craftsmen enables each person and family to develop their craft, while likewise discovering the value of their produce through real world feedback on its desirability and acceptance, and the opportunity to grow and develop in that trade; freedom in marriage enables the man and woman to find the partner with whom they are best suited; freedom of movement allows a family to find a place and path for their child's development; freedom of worship allows everyone to carve out their understanding of the Orderer of this world and how to so comport themselves to live in accord with both that grand Order and their neighbors.

Freedom, then, is truly the universal utility and thereby in a class all its own. It is the substrate for all other human action, underlying any virtue, and may therefore be deemed the *superutility*, the one essential to manifest any human good. Freedom is thus the one good which makes all other human goods possible, for a person bound down in chains can manifest neither industry nor thrift, a man muzzled can neither speak truth nor evoke beauty. Freedom—though no solid, substantial thing of itself—is yet the single thing which makes possible all choices to do good, to live well, to produce beauty, for only in the freedom of choice can we choose the good. Without it, there is no other human virtue. Thus, only through freedom can we unleash the wonders wrought by human heroes.

Besides these three essentials, everything else—*everything* else—in life is a mere utility. All the housing and furniture and jobs and investments and entertainments and repairs and gardening and shopping and appointments and visits and travelling...all of these other things are *used* as means to safeguard and cultivate these three essentials. In short, everything else we encounter in our lives is a tool for protecting, providing, and prospering in furtherance of family, faith, and freedom.

Whenever in doubt, revert back to the essentials: is this thing of use to the big three? That is the surest measure of its true worth. This also proves the need to protect that proven shield of freedom, the American constitutional Republic. If there is any better mode or place—a better Constitution or instantiation of freedom—name and show it, and we shall adopt it...yet history does not reveal any such. Since, then, freedom best protects the faith and family which are most worth protecting, and the American Constitution best protects that freedom, it becomes our duty in turn to protect that Constitution from all enemies, foreign and domestic. Fortunately, freedom and self-reliance, unconquerability and impossibilism, when applied to any problem, tend to quickly yield positive results. The best solution to constitutional protection, then, may be as simple as a daily dose of American Badass.

But note: today the Constitution is too often simply a dead letter, ignored by an unruly and manipulated legislature. It will take a watchful People with the will to *demand* correction to actualize its true promise. The manifestation of freedom is—like marital love—an act of the will. It is not a one-time decision; it must be continually renewed, reinforced, and redeveloped by people of beneficent intent whose recognition of both mission and the need to face and overcome difficulties allows them to transcend the passing troubles of the moment to realize the greater payoff in the offing. Thus, the marital partner may face the greater challenge of the alluring neighbor offering a la carte romance, or the lesser challenge of forgiving the heedless mate mindlessly picking a scab whilst watching *Game of Thrones*. In either case, the continuance in *loving* one's previous choice is a decision made again...and again...and again. We are agents within a Sartrean existential plenum, who must face the continual infinitude of possibilities with a good faith understanding that it is our lot always to *choose;* with varying degrees of rational grounding through a dusky epistemic veil, we *must* choose, which makes every decision some combination of hope, hypothesis, and heroism. Now is the time to make the choice to love your freedom, to love your Constitution, no matter how battle-scarred and beset you both are.

Without true constitutional restoration, the Tavistocked, mind-numbed society of Imperial Amerika will continue towards its catastrophic nemesis. We will raise generations of young people ever more atomized, narcissistic, alienated, and ultimately enslaved to the immediacy of gratification of passing sensual urges. We will see a continual diminution and minimization of human potential down to its most bestial, twitching imbecility. With freedom on the line and our families in the balance, it is past time to renew our love affair with the Constitution. For constitutional freedom to arise again—for there to be a renewal of this nation—it must come by the hand of the patriots, and by their hands, our eyes shall one day feast on the spectacle of the fall of the Beast.

Remember: this is not about any single criminal or despot, any particular arrest or crime. The individual forthcoming arrests are just stepping stones to uncover the organization, and even uncovering the organization is just laying out the puzzle pieces to reveal the ideology beneath, that dark worldview which motivates their multi-generational, worldwide network of inhumanity. That foul worldview must be dragged, screeching and cringing, into the light of truth. The depth of their malignancy, the breadth of the criminality, must be made inescapably evident for all to see. Its revolting reality must be revealed in its full malevolence, so that it may become anathema in every human heart throughout every land for 1,000 years.

At the end, the Beast shall stand alone—having sacrificed every last minion as a pawn in its desperate final stand. Its jewel-encrusted crown shall dangle athwart its crenellated ears, its feeble arms pin-wheel in impotent rage, until at last—beneath the gales of laughter from the gathering crowd—its corpse will shrivel, toppling in flaccid insensibility as its querulous soul is catapulted to its final reward: an eternity of its tiny self turning ever tighter into a self-imposed circle of misery—a tiny ego knotting into itself, by and for itself, a miniscule roiling ball of abject hate forever trapped within a solipsistic annulus of malice, spite, and rage.

Which truly is Hell.

Freedom is the solution

Reclaim the Constitution

Rules for Restorationists

"Calling representatives every single day, arranging local community meetings, and marching in the streets every Sunday: it's not the path to glory, but it's absolutely essential to maintaining a democracy under threat."

— Laura Moser —

Contrary to the surprisingly erudite yet ultimately morally corrupt *Rules for Radicals* by infamous Beastie boy Saul Alinsky, social rectification is <u>not</u> best served by *"ethical elasticity."* A republic—and the patriots who undergird it—depend primarily on a national moral fiber. It is, ultimately, personal responsibility and the preservation of duty to others which both founds, grounds, and rebounds a republic. Victory arises by living in badass, and the practical foundation of badass is self-discipline. *Self-discipline* is the means whereby one ultimately accrues resources within the world, achieves self-reliance, and enables the success and generosity which reciprocally flow back to you as love and honor.

The issue, then, is not a matter of hiring the right politicos to do the work *for* you, but you becoming wise enough to see the dangers, determined enough to act, and strong enough to stand up for the law. That is the challenge for today's patriot. As Thomas Paine said: *"Those who expect to reap the blessings of freedom, must, like men, undergo the fatigues of supporting it."*

This land will again be a republic, only if you can reclaim it.

Do you want the Beastie gang to decide how this nation is run, or you?

A republic, only if you understand its value.

A republic, only if you can live its promise.

A republic, only if you will fight for it.

You, the citizen sovereign, are the point of power.

A Revolution of 1

"What do we mean by the Revolution? The war? That was no part of the revolution; it was only an effect and consequence of it. The revolution was in the minds of the people, and this was effected from 1760-1775, in the course of fifteen years, before a drop of blood was shed at Lexington."
— John Adams —

You are a revolution of 1.

Here is how our nation's Revolution is realized in political union under a lawful Republic: a small handful of just and explicit laws that proscribe the ambitions of government which open the paths for action wherein you—the individual sovereign citizen—can choose to live out your own personal continual revolution in a glorious open field of opportunity, allowing you to express the infinite possibilities of self given by your Creator. In that way, the surrounding world sheds its stolid, drear disguise and reveals itself in its true nature, as a Cosmos—which simply means a *harmony*—wherein, unfettered by capricious despots, your choices abound, surrounded by an infinitude of variegated and differentiated adventures which offer themselves to you in their joyous Harmony, spinning out to the limits of freedom's iridescent, ever-unfolding dance.

And when your field of possibility is thus made infinite, the impossible becomes possible. You are thereby stepping into the fully-realized, vibrant American Republic wherein impossiblism becomes expectant realism, making every dream possible, every tomorrow hopeful.

Thus do you become—as the Framers intended—a never-ending revolution of 1.

You need seek neither a red *county*, nor a blue *city*, but rather an American *country*, a red-and-white-and-blue country. The Great Restart of our Revolution is a populist movement of the People, an inclusive action of the whole of the populace, a reclamation of the promises made 250 years ago *by* the People, *to* the People, and kept *through* the People. The People will drain that fetid swamp in Washington, D.C and bulldoze its Masonic road maze deep underground. That 6,660-inch (555-foot) affront, the Washington Phallument shall be toppled, its long Reflecting Pool no longer continually impaled by the watery image of the Phallument thrusting through its circular uterine apex to fill the Pool's quivering receptive canal. Their perverse masonry shall be flattened, salt sown in the ground, and their fertility cult's iconographic proclamation of conquest over this Christian nation forever eradicated. The new capital—built in the middle of the nation—shall refocus on the republican ideals of truth, honor, and duty before self, wherein sexual impulses find satisfaction *under* the guidance of godliness and reason, rather than the other way around—and that new capital proudly built in the renewed heartland of the country will kickstart another 250 years of liberty lit aflame in the hearts of its citizenry reflecting the badass republican ideals of its founding.

We are already in AmRev 2.0, the second, bigger and better Revolution. This is the ideological phase, where everybody chooses a side. Whose side shall you be on? Here's an easy analytic: recognize the dark goals imagined by the Beastie cult on the other side; remember the dire ends implicit in their ascendency. Look at the encroaching decrepitude of American society as amoral relativism has been inculcated into our youth for generations by the malign agents of the immoral Beastie cult. Contrast that with the universal admonitions by the Founders and Framers that there is no such thing as a successful republic with an amoral public. The American People will either find and renew their generational heroic heritage, or fade to blood-spattered irrelevancy, as another proof of the self-destructive arc of hedonic self-indulgence.

Your mission—and you must choose to accept it—is clear: today, the most morally reprehensible people have unlimited access to the most destructive weapons and technology in the history of history; it is your job to remove these dangerous toys from the hands of these ethical infants and deliver them to the adults on the planet. Pronto.

As with any large undertaking, begin by understanding first principles:

* It is time to make them pay: they must pay a cost, or they will not stop.

*They will not stop on their own, never; they play by no rules; you cannot stop them until they are *physically unable to respond*. It is ugly, but necessary, to impeach, arrest, remove, jail, shame, banish or otherwise cut off all their access to positions of power and leadership.

* No mercy for those who willfully destroy God's handiwork; no quarter. All mercy for those who repent. Give the underlings a way out, a way back into the human family.

* De-comply yourself. As much as possible, be separate from and unattached to any of their systems.

* Work systematically outward, by scale and time, starting small then growing big: begin with where you are and who you know; tell 2 to tell 2 (see below); secure your home; secure your locality; scale up in numbers and terrain; plant the seeds of success with your neighbors and next generations; win what battles you can today, survive to fight tomorrow, and build for the future through unshakeable truths which will found the renewal of our civilization for generations.

Since you win the big victory by first triumphing in your small corner, begin by winning your world. We will only turn our country red-white-and-blue after we have assuredly wrested back control of the key offices by putting true patriots in office at the county level. You must see that true patriots occupy the offices of:

sheriff	school board
attorney general	mayor
county commissioners	judges / magistrates

Does that mean you must run for office? I dunno; only you can answer that. But I suspect that—if you aren't the one to move into the government and run it properly yourself—you know and can provide support, networking, funding, advertising, and rally planning for some trustworthy, sensible person who would protect the interests of the People. If the local government roles aren't filled by the People, those offices will continue to be filled by the enemies of the People. It matters not so much *what* you do as *that* you do. As George Washington said: *"Every post is honourable in which a man can serve his country."*

Not sure where to stare? Maybe try some of these:

* Build Committees of Communication, bottom up; speak and create local networks with people you personally know and implicitly trust. From this network, select a ready spokesperson. These people can network more broadly in planning and communicating action plans for local events, and then the victories will spread, from family to family, neighborhood to neighborhood, county to county.

* Once you have restored constitutionality to your municipality or county, go stepwise up the ladder: reach up and out to build action plans with other Committees, to begin working on restoration of the states. Once the states are restored, the work of scraping the filth from the fetid halls of the nation's Capital can begin. Any attempt to do that too soon will only result in the same footdragging, obfuscation, doublespeak, and tyrannical retribution that has been visited upon patriotic Americans for the past 50 years and more.

* Don't lift the load alone: most people work best—and enjoy working best—in teams, especially in teams with like-minded folks. In this task, you will find comfort in discovering your many patriotic colleagues willing to put their shoulders to the wheel of saving the country. Turn to them; seek their aid and council; combine your energies, wisdom, and numbers to overawe the tiny handful of ne'er-do-wells who would rob your descendents of their heritage. Use the Founders as a treasure trove of models on how to revolt, large and small, soft and hard, quiet and loud; mine that rich legacy of practical demonstrations of how to win. Groups of ten to one hundred people can work wonders in any county, and your power is exponentially expanded by the synergy of many minds and talents in one glorious cause.

You need seek no grand new designs: the Revolution has already been won. You need seek no massive new organization: the Beast loves to capture organizations at the leadership level, seeding them with two-faced liars who will pervert the mission, turning them into controlled opposition which take your money and waste your time by pursuing frustraneous, irrelevant, and useless insignifica.

They hate it most when you know and love your neighbors, your county officials, your laws and customs. That's why they like mandates and directives at the national level to lock you down and keep you away from your neighbors, while they tear up the history books and tear down the statues to eradicate your culture and heritage.

You are a revolution of 1. Reclaim your freedom right where you are, with what you have, alongside those whom you know.

A revolution of 1, by everyone...cannot be undone.

When we come at them from every vector, in every form, in every moment, from across the political spectrum in such a deluge of fructifying constitutional renewal, the Beastie gang will neither be able to track, anticipate, nor respond. Victory will come in a thousand forms, from a million directions, from anti-terrorist cells of patriots springing up everywhere to root out the restrictions and lunacy of the quislings undermining our fundamental institutions. The restorationists of the Great Restart will quell the black op terrorists who have overturned the natural order of our Republic, taking our nation from being a land of fear and loathing and returning it to a republic of joyful liberty.

A revolution of 1, by everyone...is how victory is done.

Choose Your Own Badass

"Freedom is not for the weak."

— Tony Calderone —

Does it look hard? Are you thinking, maybe you don't want to do all that? Well, do you think Washington wanted to freeze at Valley Forge? Did Adams want to drag his two sons to nearly drown in the Atlantic then freeze crossing the Pyrenees Mountains? I'm guessing Mary Corbin didn't like getting her arm and face shot up loading a cannon over her husband's corpse at the battle of Fort Washington.

Patriotism is a full-contact sport. You don't win by quitting. When it's gut-check time, it's gut-check time. As Jefferson said: *"We are not to expect to be translated from despotism to liberty in a featherbed."*

You *don't* want to run the government? Good! Precisely the people who don't want to be in government are the ones that *should* be. Government, especially legislative government, should be filled with people who are fulfilling their short term duty to self-government, showing up to check the books and pare back the overreach, and then will gladly go back to a well deserved retirement in a restored constitutional republic.

From now on, we must accept that *we* are the cavalry. We can't wait on some political savior. If we want representative government, then the People need to represent themselves. The People will need to be the leadership. Step in, take over, do your duty, and go home. Be like Washington; be another Cincinnatus: set down the plow, go fix the government, and then return to plowing your row when you're done. It's the only way. Otherwise the clowns and criminals camp out in the capital, partying on your nickel. Or do you want another 20 years of anti-constitutionalist party functionaries like Lindsay Graham and AOC running your government for you?

Expect it all, patriot, to come at you...and soon.

Expect trouble...and triumph.

Expect difficulty...and deliverance.

Expect vexation...and victory.

What, then, will be your patriotic path? What kind of American badass will you be? Only you can answer that. But you have models; you have history to choose from, to learn from. Maybe you can reflect on which of the revolutionary dreamers and doers speaks to you. Look at how varied, divergent, how wildly particular and peculiar their talents were. Regard the varied characteristics of these powerhouse models of patriotic success:

The selflessness and devotion to duty of George Washington...

...the rabble-rousing brashness and street oratory of Sam Adams...

...the assiduous scholarship and exacting intellect of James Madison...

...the practical inventiveness and public-minded philanthropy of Benjamin Franklin...

...the literary verve and uncompromising idealism Thomas Paine...

...the courage and persuasiveness of Patrick Henry...

...the boundless determination and indefatigable zeal of John Adams...

...the visionary imagination and literary panache of Thomas Jefferson.

Their personalities and abilities varied tremendously, yet each found a way to be of value to the Revolution, showing the way of American Patriots:

We don't cry.

We don't comply.

We multiply.

If we can find half as many true patriots who are half the men the Founders were, we shall surely win the day.

Here is how George Washington put it on the eve of his Revolution, speaking words that ring as true now as they did then: *"The time is now near at hand which must probably determine whether Americans are to be freemen or slaves; whether they are to have any property they can call their own; whether their houses and farms are to be pillaged and destroyed, and themselves consigned to a state of wretchedness from which no human efforts will deliver them. The fate of unborn millions will now depend, under God, on the courage and conduct of this army. Our cruel and unrelenting enemy leaves us only the choice of brave resistance, or the most abject submission. We have, therefore, to resolve to conquer or die."*

Apologize to no one for being American, for being and demanding freedom. Live your life, without compromise, without apology, American and free. You have been given the greatest gift offered any patriot in history: to preserve the beauty of human life from the madmen bent on eradicating it from the earth. (You can thank God later for this opportunity disguised as pain and terror.) Right now—recognizing that your life will be an illustration of either hedonism or heroism—the only question is: what will your impossible be? What will we inscribe on your plaque, in the Great Hall of American Badass?

Non-compliance is Victory

"America was born of revolt, flourished on dissent, became great through experimentation."

— Henry Steele Commager —

Historically, America is entering the age of full maturation. We can no longer hide under the cloak of innocence, for we have seen both good and evil; the Revolution showed us images of the good, but the last century has clearly shown us the evil that lives not only in the enemy but latent in us. Indeed, even if we try to take the craven way out—cower in the pretence of innocent ignorance—we will only be led more quickly and easily into the Beastie's killing fields. We therefore must take up the torch of wisdom, no longer naive but in full understanding of our situation. It is time to grow up: recognize the good and the bad and accept the responsibility of sifting the two in order to follow that path which advances the former and forestalls the latter. It is past time to wrest this nation from the sneak thieves who harvest everyone's labor under the pretense of "managing" the financial system while also manipulating the government in furtherance of their dark cult's dystopian neo-feudalist agenda.

Since we know the government—all three branches—are largely and viciously captured, most of us will just have to do it the old fashioned way: we're just gonna have to do our own thing. That's how Americans do it. We don't need no stinking permission. We'll just fix your little problem for you.

Remember when Britain imposed the Sugar Tax in 1764, shortly followed by the Currency Act? The Colonials made it quite clear that was simply not going to happen. They showed up for marches, boycotts, riots, and, when those didn't fix it, they marched en masse to Governor Hutchison's mansion and pelted it with stones until he got the message.

Parliament backed down.

Message sent. Message received.

And no one was hurt.

But, within months, government repeated its mistake.

In 1767, Parliament came right back with the Stamp Act, requiring a tax on just about anything made of paper. Well, here came the Colonists again, ranting, rampaging, this time putting an embargo an anything made in Britain. The Americans simply refused to pay.

Parliament backed down

Message sent. Message received.

No one was hurt...except a few Parliamentarians in their pride.

But, within months, government repeated its mistake.

Over the course of 1767 and 1768, Parliament first passed the Declaratory Act—basically declaring that it can declare a tax on any dang thing it wanted—then went on to prove it by passing a series of increasingly broad taxes and restrictions called the Townshend Acts. Naturally, outrage, resistance, and non-compliance resumed, broadening across the Colonies. By 1770, confrontational Colonists got themselves shot in the Boston Massacre, which only intensified the street actions and boycotts. Parliament reversed course and rescinded most of the Townshend Acts.

Parliament (partially) backed down

Message sent. Message received.

Colonists were hurt, and Parliament is now on a short leash.

But, within months, government repeated its mistake.

1773 - Parliament's "compromise" to the ongoing power struggle was the Tea Act, yet another tax of a commonplace activity (drinking tea) which ensured the Act's rejection. The Colonists' reply was a "Tea Party," telling Britain what they can do with their tea.

Parliament refused to back down.

Message sent. Message ignored.

Government doubled down on its mistake.

1774 - Parliament punished Boston for abusing its tea leaves with the Intolerable Acts: they closed down the city, the harbor, and the People, beginning wide-ranging, house-to-house, search-and-seizure missions. The other Colonies rallied 'round; a first Continental Congress was convened which sent one final plea to Britain for amity and moderation.

Parliament double-dog refused to back down.

Message sent. Message flouted.

Government tripled down on its mistakes.

1775 - Parliament declared Boston in rebellion. Proving they agree, the patriots of Boston shot up a few hundred redcoats at Lexington and Concord.

1776 - On January 10th, Thomas Paine published *Common Sense*, and six months later the People formally divorced themselves from the idiots in Parliament.

There is a scale of tension between ruler and citizen, from a light touch which is solicitous of the People's liberty to the iron fist which indulges in unrestrained authoritarianism. Those rulers do best who keep the touch light, who listen closely and early to the plight of the populace, as people will not long abide injustice. They may grumble and knuckle under for a while, but, at some point, unjust enactments will bring sharp, sure resistance and retribution. That means the moral calculus of citizen non-cooperation works above the level of mere legal compliance. A tyrannical government may call their unjust enactment a "law," but when repugnant to moral order and duty, it will eventually be treated as what it is: a moral evil and impediment to the good. It will first be circumvented, then ignored, then opposed, and finally overthrown.

Thus, the question is, ultimately, not a matter of steering between legalism and extralegalism. Both sides accept the truth of *extralegalism*, i.e. that beyond the "law" is justice; that an unjust "law" is no law; that, because the purpose of law is provision of justice, that any purported law repugnant to justice is actually an enactment of tyranny and is thereby properly and justifiably opposed by the populace because any unjust "law" is void on its face and thus, *ab initio,* without force. Properly ordered extralegalism is, of course, deployed in pursuit of the good and true, as the Founders enjoined the People to be. An improperly oriented extralegalism however, would partake in, for instance, the Jacobin excesses of the French or exsanguinous anti-clerical excesses of the Russian Revolutions—all too many of whose adherents were, it seems, possessed of the most immoral and unseemly of appetites and despotic of dispositions. Hence, before one aligns with an extralegal undertaking, it is best to be clear in head and heart—and perhaps confer with sage others—that what you are doing is indeed ultimately in pursuit of, not selfish ends, but what is right. But, following, Congressman Crockett, once you've checked that you are right, go ahead.

At the local level, then, if some thug with a badge and gun comes and tells you to stop doing something which is morally sound (i.e. ethically lawful, even if juridically extralegal), a citizen can justly ignore her. If she claims she is "just following orders" from some unknown authority for no legitimate purpose, the citizen can justly reject such groundless non-authority. Such persons and enactments have no local power. They have no local jurisdiction in contravention to the public good and the will of the People. If the citizen—and the hundreds of neighbors who have met and agreed this is a cause worth the cost—have already reached a consensus, then that particular so-called "legal" enactment is no law in their province. If the badge-bearing thug calls for backup, escalates, becomes a physical bully, she is still a local person. Her face is known, her shopping and visiting and seeking friends all happen within the community. Shunning and shaming and social ostracization will be amongst her cost for playing the petty boss. Together, the community can help clarify the moral situation for both the thug and any "lawmakers" involved.

The best victory is won without fighting; the sweetest triumph by capturing hearts, not bodies. A community knit toward one end will harm no persons, yet permit no injustices. A community clear in its purpose and committed to its triumph cannot be defeated. As Thomas Paine said: *"It is impossible to conquer a nation determined to be free!"*

Non-violence is Victory
"Tyranny cannot defeat the power of ideas."
— Helen Keller —

1 person staging a non-violent demonstration is an arrest.

100 people staging a non-violent demonstration is a riot.

1,000 people staging a non-violent demonstration is a rebellion.

1,000,000 people staging a non-violent demonstration is a revolution.

100,000,000 people staging a non-violent demonstration is...

a whole new world.

All Aboard the Freedom Train
"For what avail the plough or sail, or land or life, if freedom fail?"
— Ralph Waldo Emerson —

In the cause of liberty, everyone is invited, even the fallen ones who may have gotten somewhat confused. Once it becomes clear how much more powerful the People are without pursuing the tribalism and fear and handcuffs and submachine guns used by the Beastie gang, the People will go back to living their normal, cordial, hospitable lives because we will be having too much fun getting smarter and stronger and healthier and holier. We will wonder why those silly poltroons want to run around putting walls around everything, when everyone lives so much more abundantly by just moving towards the endless vista of pure possibility. Our job is fructifying the world and nurturing each other. That's enough to keep everyone too busy in loving service to have time to lock each other up.

And come with a smile, because there are all kinds of good times on the freedom train.

Radical Localization

"The proper direction of man's thought is not toward the creation of new laws for government, but toward the acceptance of every person's moral dignity."

— Edmund Yates —

What will it look like, on the other side of AmRev 2.0?

The future is no unipolar tyranny under a single hegemonic state, neither is it that open-air electronic gulag dreamed of by technocratic overlords...it is a congeries of villages-within-villages....of decentralized power and authority under principles of subsidiarity, wherein power is kept in its proper place: the most local level possible.

Radical localization of power, production, and authority most closely mimics our basal social structure, the village, in which those who are given authority are known directly, and directly know, those they direct. This scaling down of scope maintains the human element, an extra level of reciprocity and empathy which is otherwise unattainable. It further allows for greater justice (as opposed to mere legalism), for knowledge of the person and their circumstances is essential to make sound judgment and dispositions. (This is why the 6th Amendment requires a jury of *peers*, i.e. presumably people from the area who know the person and can understand not just the law, but the individual and the totality of their plight, circumstance, and character.)

Read the Constitution carefully: it contemplates a collection of states, that is, a collection of sovereign nations. Every one of those states is itself a sovereign republic in its own right, and—as long as that state abides by the handful of strictures in the general agreement and harms no other state—it is free to act in its own interest and discretion. That is the point of the 10th Amendment: that what few powers were not ceded to the federal authority are retained by the sovereign states...and the People.

This understanding of the ongoing devolution of authority to the most local level was central to Jefferson and Madison when they opposed the 1798 Alien and Sedition Acts. Both of these Founders published declarations to reassert the ineluctable right of the states and citizens to nullify such overweening federal enactments. For instance, Jefferson, in his Kentucky Resolution, opined that the federal government, *"was not made the exclusive or final judge of the extent of the powers delegated to itself; since that would have made its discretion, and not the Constitution, the measure of its powers."*

The government-limiting "Principles of '98" outlined by those two Founders were likewise upheld in the Supreme Court's recognition of "anti-commandeering" as a legitimate exercise of a state's sovereign right of self-determination. No state can be compelled to have its agents or properties commandeered by any federal enactment purporting to order any particular action by any particular state. The state, in its sole sovereign choice, may simply refuse to comply with any Fedgov attempt to legislatively steal a state's time, land, agents, or property.

In *The Federalist Papers* Number 46, Madison similarly upholds the parallel right of citizen nullification, viz. that the *"refusal to cooperate with officers of the Union,"* is a perfectly legal practice. The Principles of '98 and anti-commandeering undergird the necessity from time to time of the states to nullify the Fedgov when necessary, much as the People must likewise restrain Fedgov overreach through direct citizen nullification.

As a counterpoise to the heavy hand of central government, radical localization prioritizes devolution of forms of economic exchange to the most basic, individual level. In terms of medium of exchange, that may mean hard, incorruptible materials like gold and silver, or decentralized blockchain digital assets like Bitcoin, Etherium, and Monero, or any other form of direct, peer-to-peer barter, trade, and commerce.

Radical localization also means recognition of the sheriff as the highest law enforcement officer in the land—who is for that reason directly elected by the citizens of that area—to be answerable to them, because the sheriff thereby knows best the individual citizens and how best to maintain lawful peace and justice for them.

Radical localization likewise means restitution of the militia as the standing defense of each state by armed, trained adult citizens of that state...not standing mercenary armies beholden to Federal paymasters, nor local constabulary whose mission and funding is likewise bent by mandates, messaging, and funding from Fedgov alphabet agencies.

Radical localization further means dismantling most of the Federal superstructure which sucks the life blood from the nation. It means health, welfare, education, art, industry, communication, transportation, and all other matters of daily intercourse are the business of the People and not the province of directives by central committees in bureaucratic ivory towers from agencies captured by corporatist interests. It means restoration of the limitations of Federal powers to that handful enumerated in Article I, Section 8, which gives more than enough grant to provide for uniformity and ease of interaction between the various states and jurisdictions, but not for undue interference from far off agencies, eager to feather their own nest which are all-too-easily captured by corporations and kleptocrats who then profit from and subjugate the citizens. It means, in short, returning true power to the states and the sovereign People as required by the 9th and 10th Amendments.

When Fedgov has become radically cavalier and corrupt, getting radically local is the most simple, effective, and genteel way to rectify their overreach.

Peer-to-Peer Revolution: Localization Across the Nation
"The cure for evil and disorder is more liberty, not suppression."
— Alexander Berkman —

Gumption, guts, and grit are great, but they are only a part, a presage, a mere adumbration, of the full glorious manifestation of fully-realized impossibilism. When Americans say "anything is possible," it's not just words; we really, actually mean that, ultimately, nothing is impossible. Maybe not today. And possibly not even tomorrow. But, at some point, we can solve any dang thing that's worrying you.

When you're badass, you do hard for breakfast. With impossible, it might take a minute, but we'll get there.

How? Simple:

Impossibilism rests on the presupposition that all challenges are, at base, engineering problems. That is, with the right understanding of the factors and elements involved, they can, in principle be resolved. Iterate through the particulars until you find probable practical resolutions and test and rework the most effective pathways until you find the most successful. Rinse and repeat. And this applies in any field: from obvious arenas like electronics and architecture, to the more recondite and emotive arenas of psychology and sociology...and even overturning tyranny. These latter, soft science challenges—though difficult—are as amenable to intelligent, systematic, unrelenting "humangineering" as any other.

Which means, again, AmRev 2.0 is just a matter of time.

Once the revolutionary Great Restart triumphs, the second part of localization begins: de-federalization. The local counties and states will begin to uncouple their actions from the federal "incentives" of tax money taken from the People and then returned to state and local government as federal "mandates" to twist the country around their finger by boomeranging the People's own tax money back against them as perverse incentives to undermine their Republic. That will be when the real fun starts, when all that cash is now kept in the People's hands, and they realize how really wealthy they have really been all along and—finally unburdened by wasteful tax pilfering—they begin to save and build and invest in each other.

The future of radically local is radically prosperous.

Tell 2 to Tell 2

"Let us therefore animate and encourage each other, and show the whole world that a freeman, contending for liberty on his own ground, is superior to any slavish mercenary on earth. "

— George Washington —

How does one move to radical localization?

Start where you are.

Get with your friends and start Committees of Real Solutions.

Await no orders from headquarters.

You are enough: you are a revolution of 1.

The only way through it is to do it, for it is always better to ask for forgiveness than permission. After you have built your palace of freedom, everyone will forgive you.

As you move out looking for engagement and allies, you may find it helpful to apply *Ideological Triage*. Under this schema, you classify another's political understanding into one of three types: (a) *patriots* who are already properly aligned and well-informed, whom you can readily befriend and incorporate into your plans and alliances; (b) *sleepwalkers* who are unconscious to the current realities or, worse, so ideologically possessed by Beastie-think that they are unreachable; and (c) the *dazed and confused* folks in the middle, who are the ones that may profit from your attention, who are willing to listen and may actually be awakened by sensible statements. Learning to recognize the ideological mindset of the people you are dealing with and react accordingly is an essential toolset to winning the ongoing mindwar. Use triage to manage your time and emotional energies: joining with patriots to make things happen, leaving behind the sleepwalkers who are presently beyond saving, and helping those dazed and confused in the middle when you are able.

Wherever you go, whatever you do, be prepared to tell your revolutionary story, to explain why it is time to begin the Great Restart of the Constitution. You do not always need to stand on a soapbox; you do not always need to wave colorful banners; but you do need to make sure, in your own way, in your own circles, that you find ways to bring people along. You can start this way:

Tell 2 to Tell 2. Make it a mission to convince at least two people, and encourage them to each convince at least two more. With that simple commitment, the numbers will grow exponentially and the victorious tipping point reached much more quickly. The power of people is precisely realized in other people, in how we affect and move others. You cannot know how far your lightest touch, smallest word, may stretch into eternity by turning another's heart and mind. Stay the course; live fully in your truth; you will be providing a model and inspiration for someone, whether you know it or not. If you only inspire just one more, you have already doubled your power. If you tell 2 who tell 2, you have septupled your power ($1 + 2 + 4 = 7$)! And it you're that 100th monkey who sets off the "a-ha moment"—like the lone rifleman who fired the first shot on Lexington Green—and you happen to bring on the victory of AmRev 2.0, then you—whether they record your name in the history books or not—will be the person who saved the world.

In *On Tyranny*, Timothy Snyder propounds other core prudent principles for surviving and succeeding in times of oppression, several of which are useful in face-to-face politics. Amongst the most pertinent on street level:

Principle 12: <u>Make eye contact and small talk</u> *"This is not just polite. It is part of being a citizen and a responsible member of society."* It is essential to build and maintain human networks, to recognize that new friends are the first step to victory and old friends the citadel of last resort.

Principle 13: <u>Practice corporeal politics</u> *"Put your body in unfamiliar places with unfamiliar people. Make new friends and march with them."* Get out of the house and into the world; despots want isolated, atomized basement dwellers with nothing to guard. Get out and let the world hear those truths which have been so carefully hidden from them.

Principles 15: <u>Contribute to good causes</u> *"Be active in organizations, political or not, that express your own view of life."* Put your money where your mouth is. Make it real by helping them with a deal. Free association is not only an essential right; it is the building block wherein the people recognize their mutual self-interest and grow into associations of action organized around those common goods. Be around those of similar belief and do something—anything—toward making it real; action-takers are the victors, no matter how seemingly small and isolated. This is fruitful not only at the political but personal level, bringing together persons of like mind for compelling activities spreads the joy all around.

As you move forward seeking to understand, embody, and disseminate truth, remember that the first, continual, and unending tool of the enemy is lies. That is how evil works. Every evil act either directly employs a lie, will be covered and protected by lies, or will later be obscured by lies. Assume, if the enemy's mouth is moving, they are lying. You, instead, stand on truth; truth can be obscured but not destroyed and it will be there for all to see long after the storm has passed.

Besides covering their crimes, lying is often used by the Beasties to serve their secondary purpose of inducing fear and terror. Of all your emotions, fear and terror are those which will (a) cut off your reason (as you tremble in emotional distress), (b) leave you inert (as you feel either uncertain or unable to act), and therefore (c) make you seek outside help (weakening your resolve to resist authoritarian dictates). Thus, to arm yourself against their lying you are wisest to (a) avoid their noxious propaganda as much as possible (b) doubt most especially those statements which evoke the most fear and terror in you, and (c) focus your attentions and actions on the things which most engender the opposite of fear and terror in your life, i.e. those things which evoke love, friendship, trust, companionship, and wholesome fun.

Yes, as simple and stupid as it sounds, much of the way to beat them, is to simply turn your back on them and live a beautiful, joyful life in the company, companionship, and fruitful fellowship of your mate, children, friends, neighbors, pets, garden, and soft, spring zephyrs.

They hate that.

You win by winning. So go home and win today. Make your home a victory castle, where your family is always winning, with that most amazing soulmate of yours, and the smartest and kindest kids of all time.

AmRev 2.0 will take courage. It will take time. You will have good days and bad days, good weeks and bad months. But you will stay the course, prayerfully, faithfully, indefatigably—like the Pilgrims, like the Founders, like Daniel Boone, like Andrew Jackson, like Stagecoach Mary, like the paratroopers at Bastogne, like every other American Badass who, for your sake, beat back every traitor and tyrant, trial and terror, placed before them. You will not quit; you will not falter; you will neither whine nor wail nor apologize for doing what is right when called in your time to do what's right. You will pick up the torch and carry it as far down the road as your body can bear, and then pass it on to the next patriot, until the battle is won.

Then you will have run your race well, good and faithful servant of the beautiful, good, and true.

And, along the way—when there's a moment—may you be able to stop by the roadside with that wisp of grateful smile and easy grace which brings peace and joy, love and happiness, to whomever what you meet.

A Union of Individualism

"When we lose the right to be different, we lose the privilege to be free."
— Charles Evans Hughes —

Thoreau at Walden was a commune of one, suited to his personal vision of a private utopia. The framework of this nation is to be a continual social laboratory like Thoreau's one-man citadel of freedom. America was to be a quilted landscape of many variegated experiments in liberty, much as each of the states are—as was intended—many unique and differentiated republican experiments in freedom. This intentional multiplicity of approaches likewise manifests itself in many individual lifestyles as well in any number of communities organized to instantiate particular ideologies and models of human flourishing.

For instance, the Owenites once even attempted to institute socialist communities within the Republic, most notably at New Harmony, Indiana. There, in 1825, Robert Owen invested a considerable personal fortune in hopes of constituting a "New Moral World." It failed, for all the core difficulties inherent in socialist frameworks discussed earlier—from the freeloader problem to its perverse disincentivization of the morally strong and professionally skilled, on down—but that adventure of nearly five years was actually one of the longest-run of all the socialist communal experiments. Nonetheless, this nation gave Owen the chance to prove the truth of his ideas, and in the end he can be said to have sacrificed his fortune in an expensive but invaluable bench test of socialist ideology for anyone willing to study it.

In contrast, the countercultural Amish have, since 1693, successfully followed in the footsteps of Jakob Ammann, shaping their lives around their understanding of the moral and Christian principles which undergird a flourishing community. Though they have produced nary a skyscraper nor billionaire, they continue to thrive in thousands of households, spending their days in much the same way as their ancestors did 300 years ago. As radically localized and pursuant of subsidiarity as anyone, they seem to have succeeded by pursuing that simple formula of adherence, respect, and cultivation of family and community founded on a clear faith shared by all. Managing to prosper with a quiet continuity—with nary an enemy and any number of admirers—it seems like they must be doing something right if that many people are happy to continue in the tradition.

Farther west, Arcosanti in central Arizona is the brain child of Paolo Soleri, an architect who sought to build a proof-of-concept community for his notion of "arcology," i.e. architecture informed by ecology. Since 1970 the project has moved by fits and starts to proselytize, increase the number of completed buildings on its campus, and increase the range of its public outreach. Never a mammoth organization, it has produced an outsized interest and reputation for its modest budget and staff. Despite Soleri himself passing on, the Soleri Foundation continues to pursue the physical manifestation of the vision he delineated in *Arcology: the City in the Image of Man*, viz. a fully-realized 5,000-member ecological city, a forward-thinking aspiration which the practical dreamers of the Revolution would have understood.

Similarly, since 1971, the Farm intentional community in central Tennessee has taken an approach which may be seen as an admixture of the foregoing efforts. Begun with earth-friendly and communitarian ideals, they have focused on finding ways to exemplify and promote practical methodologies by which to embody them. Thus, they pursue alternatives to society's more conventional interventionist, materialist, and consumerist ethos by fostering natural childbirth via midwifery, vegetarianism, and alternative energy—all with special emphasis on partnerships with native cultures. While sharing much of the uniformity and centralization of the Owenites in its beginnings, a continual ethos of service and outward engagement via publishing, stage performance, midwifery, and charitable work via its Plenty International arm, has given the Farm its own stamp. No longer a strictly communitarian collective in the economic sense, it nonetheless maintains its essential roots in the cultivation of a supportive, integrated social space committed to a simple, sustainable, ecofriendly lifestyle emphasizing family and the instantiation of good works and moral worth.

These are just snapshots of a few of the more public or long-lived efforts by groups of Americans who have used the freedoms afforded by a large and unfettered landscape to renew and improve the social fabric of society from the bottom up. As the Owenites tried to mesh socialism with American libertarianism, Arcosanti to meld the urban with the ecological, so is the Farm attempting to finely balance the pastoralism of the Amish with modern tech, to meld the traditional communal, familial village with today's individualist sensibilities. The members of each of these pioneering communities have, in a sense, volunteered to donate their own lives as real world alpha tests of theories of social development. In many ways, such communes or intentional communities are exactly the kind of disparate, far-ranging exercises in personal and social innovation envisioned by the Framers. For the continuation of such great American experiments in doing your own thing in your own way, for the synergistic payoff of multiple microcommunities testing multitudes of microcultures, for the continual self-improvement of the human community via relentless, reckless just-do-it-ism, we need as many courageous pioneers as we can get.

Simply do your own thing, homesteaders; long live Yankee localism!

The Pragmatics of Praxis
"The essential psychological requirement of a free society is the willingness on the part of the individual to accept responsibility for his life."
— Edith Parker —

In a world where the Beastie gang really dreams of a neo-feudal "hunger game" which leaves you weak, poor, and eventually dead, finding your path to peace and plenty is victory—life is victory.

Survival is victory.

Remember their plan is for a slow, subtle, stealthy attack wherein the victim is lulled into what amounts to a twitching, asphyxiation by slow degrees, easing quietly, oh-so-quietly, into a susurrating, soundless quietus. But your resistance and revelations force them to act, to engage; it brings the reality of their plans into the light; they can no longer work in the dark, invisibly weaving their malign magic towards their dire designs. Sure, they will act under the pretense of philanthropy with a show of invulnerability, but the more they enforce their draconian and tyrannical schemas, the more they reveal precisely how inhumane their plans, the more they will be despised, reviled, and rejected by humankind.

Because their intent is evil, they must lie.

Because even a whisper of truth proves their wickedness, they must shout.

And, because every moral person will oppose them, they must fight.

Eventually—as their "externalization of the hierarchy" increasingly unveils the murderous repercussions of their agendas, causing revulsion and resistance from the mass of ordinary, benign people—they will fully reveal their fangs with the wild ferocity of any rabid miscreant. At the end, they must act openly to manifest fully, and the very nature of their grotesque plans will evoke the resistance which destroys it. At its final verge, their climactic efforts to force slavery and impoverishment, endless beatings and wild chaos, on a species built to win will result in next-level universal rejection. Their final paroxystic leap towards "victory" will prove their culminating defeat.

But the final ride to the finish line where their colossus of destruction collapses of its own wickedness will be increasingly chaotic, kinetic, and demonic. You, with the soulfulness and purpose to remake the world anew in human-heartedness, must come through the forthcoming muddy slog. Real survivability will necessitate first and foremost a solidly-formed mental frame: do you have the gumption, guts, and grit to reach the survival side?

The future needs you to build survivability.

Survival is victory

Whatever you do, look to come out the other side. We will need patriots, lots of patriots, for the Great Rebuild after the celebration party. When they come at you with lies, speak back with the truth. When they lash out at you with lockdowns, lockouts, shutdowns, and scarcities, put your head down and find your way through.

Action is victory; compliance is death

Find a place to ride it out in maximum subsidiarity, where you can most control what is your own for your home with the least dependency on any authority. Own your space; master your immediate domain. Don't fight the dragon until you can face down the lion and the bear.

Defend your own. Stand your ground. Work your land. Love your mate and your life. That is real everyday heroism in the real world. This means a kind of self-reliance based on practical, economically-viable skill sets. They can't move you if they can't uproot you.

First things first: stand in truth. As Timothy Snyder says in Principle 10:

<u>Believe in Truth</u>: *"To abandon facts is to abandon freedom. If nothing is true, then no one can criticize power, because there is no basis upon which to do so."* The Beastie cult will come at you with gaslighting and lying. You will defeat them with logic and facts. Do not allow them to use manufactured narratives to twist measureable, historic, consistent truths into agenda-driven falsehoods. You may have to work a little harder, dig a little deeper, think a little longer, but the truth has an ultimately unmistakable resonance built of solidity, correspondence with manifold well-founded facts, and self-consistency.

Some of us will have to fail, that others may succeed

Doing what's right and doing what's prudent does not always mean you win. Sometimes the numbers and luck and circumstances will be more than anyone could be expected to overcome. Your job is to leave a record of a life lived in the light and the right; ultimately, the outcome is not your business.

Some of us will have to die, that others may survive

Sometimes, your sacrifice will mean more than your survival. Nathan Hale, Jack Kennedy, Bobby Kennedy, Sr., Medgar Evans, Ashli Babbitt—some will go on before to the Other Side, unafraid and unforgotten, honored more for their sacrifice to their cause than for themselves...and often that short, exemplary life will move more people than anything anyone could have accomplished in one hundred more years of living. What is most fearful is not a heroic death, but a cowardly clinging to life.

Resistance everywhere means victory somewhere

Just stand—no knee for thee. As long as one patriot stands undaunted, the battle has not been lost. When a million patriots stand together, victory will surely follow.

Big Freedom on a Small Farm

The function of freedom is to free someone else.

— Toni Morrison —

Man needs woman, woman needs man, and when their needs meet in family their days together complete the circle of life. To support the maintenance of that circle, really, the family only needs three practical fundamentals: water, food, and energy. Any freedom-loving person who understands that fundamental truth is halfway to building the self-reliant footprint needful for a full and fulfilled life. The rest is just putting in the time: time to practice overcoming which builds unconquerability; the years of unconquerability which renders impossibilism; the time as a couple to manifest one's mature vision of life's mission; time as a family to learn the joy in each person's difference as part of that togetherness; and time to look back at the end of the road on a vineyard laid straight and tended well.

Those three essentials added to the foundation of family are most readily and surely met via homesteading, farming, standing on your own land. A handful of acres, well chosen and tended, can bring all the work one can handle with all the room one needs to meet the essentials of life. As of yet, we have not fully mastered reliable independence of local energy generation for the masses, so that remains our epoch's most urgent engineering challenge, the single implement which will produce the greatest humanitarian payoff. Until then, meeting that primal requirement must remain an ad hoc resolution suited to immediate circumstance. Locally provisioning food and water, however, can be done with all manner of current off-the-shelf tools and materials. With the three essentials met, a family can readily leverage its way into building whatever mode of life is most commodious to its shared values and ideal outcomes.

While living directly off the land's abundance through one's own labor is the most direct means to the most well-founded self-reliance, one may—for the sake of occupational, artistic, familial, social, or other obligatory or professional pursuits—undertake more urban adventures, with the proviso that independence and self-reliance will always be more tenuous and subject to third-party interference around the assorted random multitude of the city. Indeed, in the long run, the post-revolutionary city will become a humming hive of blazing innovation and development which produces understanding and products beyond anything imagined today. But that restored urban order must await the post-revolutionary Great Rebuild.

Whichever path suits one's circumstance, some basics will likely prove most helpful. One may, for instance, want to "be a good Mormon," in the matter of backup supplies; that is, in accordance with LDS practice, it might be prudent to aim toward a year's store of dry goods and consumable supplies for the inevitable "black swan" social disruptions which seemingly occur in every generation. In that vein, many folks have found some of the following to be thankful to have on hand in the event of public alarms and disruptions which interrupt normal commerce:

Water Filter/Purifier	First Aid Kit	Toiletries
Firewood	Bleach	Sewing Repair Kits
Fire Starters/Candles	Powdered Milk	Rain Gear
Fuel	MRE/condensed meals	Baby Supplies
Gasoline Containers	Heirloom Seeds	Medications
Garbage Bags	Canning Supplies	Self-Defense Tools

To these may be added some first principles thinking codified by Charles Hugh Smith in *Self-Reliance in the 21st Century*, which lays out a series of core approaches for remaining anti-fragile through the coming years of challenge via personal preparation and *"cooperating with trustworthy others in productive networks."* You might begin by adding these pragmatic frameworks to your badass attitude and hard assets:

- Build cooperative, reciprocal networks for producing and procuring essentials

- Prioritize first producing and sharing, before taking and talking

- Start with projects which can be completed with on-hand, available resources

- Remain flexible and resourceful to build antifragility against supply interruptions

- Develop a variety of practical, hands-on skills for self-reliance and barter

One might suppose that the folks who will come out on the other side of any survivability challenge will most often be those blessed with physical strength, practical skills, and a well-stocked larder. And such brute physical attributes will indeed help...at first. In the immediate onrush of events, those who have built a defensive bastion and stockpiled dry goods will seem to be best off. But soon, the gangs of bandits will come. Eventually, even the best-supplied singleton Rambo in his dugout cinderblock bunker will be overcome by numbers and lack of sleep. An individual's skills and strengths are invaluable, as part of a team...but as one person against the world, even Bruce Lee would be brought down. Any single person's physical strength can be drained in a matter of minutes of life-or-death struggle against a mob. Rather, one might look to have a bigger plan, a bigger team, a longer checklist of options than the next guy. The bigger your network, the bigger will be your victory. Ultimately, any political resolution and reconstitution will be a matter of which side wins the narrative war anyway—i.e. that side wins which gains the moral ascendancy in the minds of the most people. Politics is ultimately retail, personal, and best transmitted by special delivery, face-to-face. While you will indeed need unconquerable personal resolve as a revolution of 1, you will only be able to overcome the beastly swarm with the help of many, many kind-hearted allies, in your neighborhood and beyond.

Thriving is triumph Thrive where you are, building partnerships and networks with trusted peers who understand the worth of liberty and self-reliance. Each peer-to-peer microsuccess is one building block, one individualized paving stone, on the pathway to a restored constitutional Republic. Starting small is starting wise, since the Beastie gang love to infiltrate large organizations by sowing discord, creating chaos, and misdirecting their actions. Build slow, from below, with those you know. As the old saw goes, "The quicker up, the quicker down." Protect and defend the trusted locals of your community. Build Back Human, around the family, faith, and freedom that have undergirded every successful civilization of the past.

Try electrogardening, hydroponics, permaculture, food forest, 1 acre, raised bed, greenhouse, regenerative, and biodynamic farming...try well or catchment or filtered or humidity captured water...try wind, sun, EM genset, LENR, geothermal, or combustibles...solve the three practical essentials of food, water, and energy for you and yours, so others can see how to do it for them and theirs.

When you solve the three *essential* things—food, water, energy—you unleash the potential to pursue the three *magnificent* things: truth, beauty, goodness. And when you're winning like that, who really cares what the dang government is saying or doing, anyway?

Sometimes victory is no more complicated than a happy family and a cozy garden.

Unlock the Land

"The United States is a nation of laws, badly written and randomly enforced."

— Frank Zappa —

While crying overpopulation, overcrowding, and overuse, the Fedgov has locked up vast swathes of land in the western United States at its own behest and judgment. For example, over 80% of the land in Nevada is under federal stewardship, and, overall, nearly 50% of the land in the West is federally held.

Really?

For the love of God, why?

Over 600 million acres of land are sitting fallow, ignored, unused, while people live on the streets and housing costs balloon year over year.

To what real benefit is it to have the central government the largest landowner? Why should we socialize the vast majority of the land in any part of this nation? Why should the people suffer when we have fully half the land in the western continental US locked up? What would happen if we were simply to institute a good old-fashioned land drive? How about a dollar an acre for everything you put under the plow, and a 4-acre grant for anything you put a house on?

Of all the places we put such valuable and precious resources, we leave it in the hands of the timeservers and nincompoops of the Fedgov kleptocracy?

If you want a flourishing, successful People, give them access to the land that is their rightful bequest. If forty acres and a mule—land and transport—were supposed to be the great promise of those once enslaved, maybe it's time for the 130 million neo-serf American households to at least have access to the 600 million acres of land held by Fedgov.

Let's see, that's more than 4 acres per household...

And, at the same time, we sent, for instance, well over $100 billion in US military aid to the grifting confederacy of whining dunces in Ukraine who either sold it, stole it, or got it blown up by Russia's endless supply of missiles, drones, cannon shells, and bullets. So, just funding the proxy war in Ukraine ran over $300 per person, or about $1,200 per family of four...which won't exactly get you a Lexus, but it could possibly get you the down payment an old Toyota beater that rolls.

So, here's a question: if Fedgov had all that land and cash lying around which they either kept for themselves or gave to their kickback buddies in Ukraine, how come they never offered any of it to you for land and transport?

It seems like...maybe...the next time you see a Fedgov rep on the street, you might could ask 'em: *"Hey, where's my dang 4 acres and a car?"*

The Death of Taxes: Voluntary Contributory Government
"One short sleep past, we wake eternally
And death shall be no more; Death, thou shalt die."
— John Donne —

They say the two eternal inescapables are death and taxes.

But, is that how you want it?

Death, sure, that's kinda baked in the cake—kind of a big ask to end death right now. But mandatory taxes? We do that to ourselves. Who says we really need taxes?

A truly voluntarist nation, after all, would never institute any type of coercive payments from its citizens. The government might beg; it might plead; it might even cajole to the limits of the People's ability to stand its simpering importuning...but it would never send armed thugs to drag its sovereign masters—the citizenry—to jail.

Any government so constituted—demanding money at the end of a gun—is a straight up thief. You can paint that pig in whatever lipstick you want, but a government is either engaged in a free exchange as a social contract with each individual citizen—making it voluntary—or it is a criminal mob where guys with guns come grab what the boss says is his stuff, at his discretion.

There is no in-between. There is no cute negotiation.

And the way to really keep the government beast in its cage is to maintain absolute clarity and boundaries on that one issue: you have no right to my money. The limits of its capacity to "tax" should reside in its ability to persuade. Put more sharply: the limits of government's capacity to spend must reside in its ability to persuade. In other words, government must pony up the proof which would encourage us to donate, not rely on its smug willingness to extort. Ultimately, the rule must become: government receives from the citizens only what is voluntarily given. That would mean that it would first need to provide persuasive, demonstrable, sure-nuff proof it is doing what is right, before it could ever wheedle a single cent from the strapped electorate.

Put another way: all forms of coercion over both the mind and money of humanity must cease.

And that includes any notion of obligatory taxation.

After all, if, indeed, the federal government is providing services of such inestimable value to the American nation, they should have no problem making that case. Therefore, let's just make it obligatory that they actually make that case. It should be especially obligatory to explain how they always seem to spend every penny and never seem to save any money left over, when—not only do many prudent families typically look to save a certain portion of their income for emergencies and exigencies—but our most incisive and successful presidents, like Jefferson, Jackson, and Coolidge, made it a point to routinely return more money to the Treasury than they spent.

Is there some shortfall in the number of calculators and adding machines issued to our agencies? Is there a need for remedial arithmetic instruction within the federal accounting corps? Or are they just spending to spend, knowing that the boys in body armor with submachine guns can always be dispatched, fanning out across the nation to swarm over the hapless citizenry and swipe all the cash from you all, you greedy peasants!

Maybe—instead of continuing with this inveterate extortion—we could create positive incentives for those agencies, divisions, and departments which produce demonstrable savings and reduction of their expenditures. It would seem more sensible to create some bonus, merit, comp time, or other concrete expression of the People's appreciation for such efforts than our current system whose perverse incentives encourage continual waste, fraud, float, bloat, and abuse.

Back in the 60s, many a dorm room had a poster which read, "It'll be a great day when the schools have all the money they need and the Navy has to hold a bake sale to buy a battleship." Maybe we could have the annual naval Telethon-for-the-Fleet. Even better, the CIA could have a bake sale and the IRS try opening a lemonade stand—provided, of course, the local code enforcers would allow that kind of unrestricted economic exchange without proper documentation and licensure. It might be quite a useful exercise for them to stand before the People and detail exactly all the wonderful services they are rendering for the public weal.

Of course, so sudden a change to just and fair taxation may prove a rather abrupt transformation for the masses (and especially the apparatchiki) to wrap their heads around. We may need a transitional stage whereby we at least revert to pure constitutional governance, viz. no internal taxation, but only excise duties at the borders for import and export. Maybe we should start with pure constitutional simplicity: the People have all the guns and money, and the Fedgov gang gets to walk around disarmed and begging.

In either case, I'm betting everyone will be glued to the tube the night of the first FBI telethon.

Or, to put it another way:

One short fight past, we wake in liberty
And the IRS shall be no more; Taxes, thou shalt die.

Bucky Fuller: Operating Manual for Human Freedom

"Dare to be naive."

— Bucky Fuller —

What, really, does embodied impossibilism look like, to live in the creative freedom of a liberated soul? What actually happens when you set your life on the pursuit of improving the world by concentrating your focus on producing good for everyone? R. Buckminster Fuller was a man who set himself exactly that task and thereby became one of the most singular and original minds of the 20th century. He may be, therefore, a prototype of the next stage of American Badass. Designer and visionary, twice expelled from Harvard, Fuller went on to become one of the most prolific and creative innovators of the 20th century, producing 28 patents, popularizing the geodesic dome, inventing "dymaxion" engineering, and earning a Presidential Medal of Freedom for a lifetime at the forefront of speculative design.

Yet, Fuller spent the first thirty years of his life largely confused and directionless. It was not until 1927, at 32, that his personal awakening occurred. Desperate, head of a growing family yet facing extreme financial pressures, he stumbled along the icy shoreline of Lake Michigan, edging towards the choppy swells, contemplating suicide as the only way out. But—at that moment of darkest despair—somehow, a small voice from deep inside pulled him back from the edge of self-destruction. He suddenly saw that, rather than throwing his life away, he could offer his remaining days to the service of humankind. He dared to ask himself: what if I quit waiting on permission and approval, and instead simply went out and pursued projects I think will make things better? In an instant, his moment of despair and self-doubt became a resolution for positive action: *"From now on you need never await temporal attestation to your thought. You think the truth. You do not have the right to eliminate yourself. You do not belong to you. You belong to the Universe. Your significance will remain forever obscure to you, but you may assume that you are fulfilling your role if you apply yourself to converting your experiences to the highest advantage of others."*

That resolution allowed Fuller to release his full energies towards helping all of humanity; he was free to dare, to think, and to express all the unique, unconventional notions which had made him such a poor candidate to follow the conventional, prefab dogmas offered by Harvard. Endlessly fascinated with number and geometry, his talents tended toward discovery and innovation in the engineering arts, most often involving design and improvement in the construction and building trades. But he also engaged in continual metacognitive reflection on the act of creation, on modes of design, on the process and optimization of engineering for function, outcome, and humanity's success. For instance, Fuller postulated that one of the core outcomes of effective design solutions is *ephemeralization*, which he defined as practical modalities to *"do more with less,"* whose ultimate outcome would look something like humanity producing practically anything from basically nothing. He would systematize this principle into *synergetics*, a catch-all term for understanding both the physical and metaphysical universe via an original framework of geometric concepts, with most especial emphasis on empirical study of systems in transformation. At their apex, Fuller's visions projected the ability of humankind to manifest in practical application what he called the *Dymaxion*, a blending of the words **dy**namic, **max**imum, and ten**sion** to sum up the goal of his work: *"maximum gain of advantage from minimal energy input."*

The efforts of this "friendly genius," then, tended toward producing an elegance and simplicity which was simultaneously productive of power. In effect, he looked for geometric efficiencies which could yield disproportionate, synergistic results. Hence, his fame often revolves around his fascination and championing of the geodesic dome, a structure confining the most space for the least material cost, yet with immense tensile strength and resilience. Such structures, like his schematics and models, evoke a clean, direct, efficacy of design which is the hallmark of a kind of beauty in engineering. As he said, *"When I am working on a problem, I never think about beauty...but when I have finished, if the solution is not beautiful, I know it is wrong."*

In sum, his work may be said to evince a kind of engineering impossiblism: the use of imagination in design to evoke more from matter than material science currently says that structure or substrate can yield. How? Through the use of thought, through the imagination's access to geometric and arithmetic reconfiguration which enables as-yet-unseen structural, chemical, metallurgical, or process redevelopment. There were, for Fuller, no impossibilities, only questions still to be asked, and an alluring infinity of engineering possibilities yet to be tested.

You Have to Fail to Succeed

"If you are not free to choose wrongly and irresponsibly, you are not free at all."

— Jacob Hornberger —

Since the mistakes of his early life brought him to the point of failure—even suicide—yet also proved the springboard to his eventual success, Fuller never feared failure. In fact, he emphasized the importance of actively seeking to fail—hanging out beyond the edge of your competency to see what's happens and how far you can get—and knowing that failure is the royal road to success. As he put it: *"Mistakes are great, the more I make the smarter I get."*

Giving people the permission to fail, gives them the courage and resolve to win. Without finding those limits and edges, they will not discover the full range of their capabilities. Without having the courage to test, fail, recoup, and try again, they will never discover how to enlarge those capacities and outcomes. To do more with less, you first have to do the trying...and failing.

To fail like Bucky, you have to fail fast and often, in dymaxion directions. One of the greatest beauties of a republic of freedom is precisely that ability to fail. For that reason, Fuller believed the current political landscape—with its competitive, zero-sum model—was ultimately counterproductive. Instead, he envisioned a world which made such competitive approaches increasingly irrelevant as the capacities of humankind were released through engineering innovations which made possible such limitless abundance that political wrangling over the distribution of power and resources became irrelevant. He was, for instance, one of the first to recognize that—by the middle of the last century—humankind was already producing enough food to feed everyone. We did not really have a food *production* problem or even, properly understood, a *hunger* problem: we had a food *distribution* problem. We simply were not yet wise enough—not properly socially constituted—to reliably get the food to everyone.

Fuller's solution was not to shake his fist and demand the politicians solve that mess. His idea was to get in the fast lane and engineer so beautifully and well, that we could feed everyone, without hardly trying. To Fuller, we live in a synergistic creative field of infinite possibilities and outcomes, a place wherein humankind is designed to be a success. The practical realization of that success was his dymaxion vision for everyone.

And, by failing more grandly than most of us, he got closer to that vision that most of us.

If you're not failing, you're not really trying. Fail fast; fail oft; fail hard. You'll get there sooner.

How have you failed today?

Dymaxion Man: I Seem to Be Freedom

"You never change things by fighting the existing reality. To change something, build a new model that makes the existing model obsolete."
— Bucky Fuller —

In his creatively quad-formatted manifesto *I Seem to be a Verb*, Fuller laid out his dymaxion vision for the unfolding possibilities of human potential, a potential virtually without limit. He declared: *"Real wealth is indestructible and without practical limit. It can be neither created nor lost—and it leaves one system only to join another—the Law of Conservation of Energy. Real wealth is not gold. Real wealth is knowing what to do with energy."*

That: *"Man's intellect has the ability to tap the cosmic resources of energy and make them work for him."*

And: *"The new life needs to be inspired with the realization that the new advantages were gained through great gropes in the dark by unknown, unsung intellectual explorers"*

He sought to realize these potentials by one simple but powerful practice: *"I always say to myself, what is the most important thing that we can think about at this extraordinary moment."*

Fuller's ability to rise above the explanations and projections of prevailing, conventional analysis allowed him to see beyond the drear, pessimistic narratives of the only-possibilists, the stinking thinking of those whose dreams and optimism have been driven out of them. He believed instead that every person had been born a genius and had been *"de-geniused"* by miseducation. And yet the solution was as simple as turning back to your true, endlessly-possible, always-inquisitive, fully-engaged self. He offers us the understanding that the human mind—once released from the shackles of boxed-in, narrow-view thinking—unleashes our capacity to envision better strategies to thrive. We are, at base, not static, fixed personalities, but rather a self-aware, unfolding process of self-discovery: *"I live on earth at present, and I don't know what I am. I know that I am not a category. I am not a thing—a noun. I seem to be a verb, an evolutionary process— an integral function of the universe."*

Reflecting on his life, Fuller believed he was proof of everyone's ability to thrive in their own journey, and to bring everyone else along with them: *"I am now close to 88 and I am confident that the only thing important about me is that I am an average healthy human. I am also a living case history of a thoroughly documented, half-century, search-and-research project designed to discover what, if anything, an unknown, moneyless individual, with a dependent wife and newborn child, might be able to do effectively on behalf of all humanity that could not be accomplished by great nations, great religions or private enterprise, no matter how rich or powerfully armed."*

Bucky is living proof that the most valuable resource on the planet is human creativity. The more people—the more minds—the better off we will be. Get out of the People's way, let them blossom, and watch the world thrive.

This belief in the inherent power and potential in humankind arises from his recognition of the self-evident integrity of the universe itself, that the very integument of reality reveals a unity, harmony, and *"interaccomodation,"* in which love is the *"metaphysical gravity"* which binds everything together, a force you may not see, but can feel. The universe is far more than mere random rocks in Brownian, scattershot disarray, but a glorious, ongoing display of limpid, interwoven order. The more one understands the universe, the more one realizes its inherent integrity, its hidden but palpable design which militates for a Designer, its set of eternal laws implying a limitless, regenerative, universal "force."

Such metaphysical realizations are essential in understanding ourselves, for *"Ninety-nine percent of who you are is invisible and untouchable."* As part of that hidden, primordial *urstoff,* you are an outgrowth of the greater cosmos, one harmonizing element of the greater Harmony.

More simply, it's one great act of love in a million forms. Life's journey always goes back to love. It's never been anything but love. Or, as Fuller put it: *"I'm not trying to counsel any of you to do anything really special except dare to think. And to dare to go with the truth. And to dare to really love completely."*

In such a cosmos, where order is evident and love the underlying foundation, your ability to recognize, reflect, act, and embellish that order makes you a being of magnificent majesty and beauty. He tells us to remember who we can be: *"Never forget that you are one of a kind. Never forget that if there weren't any need for you in all your uniqueness to be on this earth, you wouldn't be here in the first place. And never forget, no matter how overwhelming life's challenges and problems seem to be, that one person can make a difference in the world. In fact, it is always because of one person that all the changes that matter in the world come about. So be that one person."*

Over nearly ninety years of exploring how close to impossibly well one can live on Spaceship Earth, Fuller's life always challenges us to harken back to *I Seem to Be a Verb* and its final, powerhouse passage: *"MAN CAN DO ANYTHING HE WANTS"*

Superabudance: More People, More Plenty
"Political freedom includes in it every other blessing. All the pleasures of riches, science, virtue, and even religion itself derive their value from liberty alone."
— Benjamin Rush —

Contrary to neo-Malthusian declarations, the People are not the enemy. Human imagination is, in fact, a truly limitless natural resource, and it is therefore the resource we should most assiduously collect and cultivate. Rather than limiting or reducing population, the immense, ongoing proof of humanity's capacity to realize Fuller's dymaxion principle of "doing more with less," mandates that we create, nurture, and release "into the wild" as many primed and empowered human spirits as possible, for that is the quickest way to reap the harvest of all that potential mind power.

Did you know that a wisp of cotton dipped in tar can make light? Neither did Thomas Edison, until he imagined it and tested it by putting an electrical current across it: the first electric light—and, soon after, the first light bulb—all from the most common and cheapest of materials. Only the infinite, limitless capacities of the mind to test and investigate the resources afforded it, and then to engage and rearrange them under the power of reason and imagination—disciplined by the laboratory and workbench—can take humankind from the back of a cave to the empyrean verge of space.

Contrary to the simplistic projections of Malthus—which treat human beings as if they are mere consuming automatons, eating without inventing, each a mere black hole of material waste—the social, economic, and technological outcomes of the last 100 years shows that the neo-Malthusian, Club of Rome, Extinction Rebellion hysteria is more the outcome of cultish indoctrination and multimedia propaganda than any well-formed empirical analysis. In counterpoise to the screeching Chicken Littles of the political realm, three tightly-argued scholarly works, amongst others, make a clear and compelling case for the fallacy of such apocalyptic doomcasting.

In *The Ultimate Resource*, professor Julian Simon propounds the contrarian position that not only are we not headed for destruction, but the burgeoning human population is itself the best indication that we shall prosper long into the future. His research shows that, over time, there is an *inverse* relationship between wages and the cost of metals, across the board. That is, as the population has increased, things have gotten cheaper. He furthermore demonstrates this phenomenon of humankind producing more with less across a wide range of agricultural products as well as mining and metal manufacturing. Looking at corn, lumber, aluminum, iron, lead, arable land, televisions, air conditioners, and per unit productivity vs. scale of the business, he shows that bigger, more complex societies continually win by continual dymaxion microimprovements, an ongoing process of doing more-with-less that improves per-unit production and thereby drives down prices while it drives up personal wealth. At the same time, objective data collected by the EPA shows levels of pollutants declining. In other words, population growth over time—rather than producing scarcity and high prices due to competition for a diminishing supply of goods—correlates with the prices of basic commodities actually dropping—all while public demand for clean manufacturing has improved environmental quality.

So sure was Simon of this price trend that he made a famed public wager with celebrated population pessimist Paul Ehrlich, author of the neo-Malthusian rant *The Population Bomb* and an always-wrong alarmist who claimed in 1980 that *"England will not exist in the year 2000."* The two decided to track five commodities of Ehrlich's choice over the ensuing decade (until 1990), to see if the prices would go down—as Simon's data suggested—or up—as Ehrlich's scarcity alarmism predicted. Sure enough, while population actually increased over that period at the fastest pace ever recorded, the per-unit commodity costs—measured in either nominal or inflation-adjusted terms—fell. To his credit, Ehrlich paid up. More importantly, Simon—unlike many professors—had proven his thesis in a public, practical, real-world test. Furthermore, economist Mark Perry has widened the chronological analysis and, by examining the data from 1934 to 2013, demonstrated that Simon's thesis is no one-off fluke, but, rather, underscored by contemporary data.

But, the pessimist may ask, how is that possible? How can prices drop when there are more people chasing the same goods? Short answer: because human capital reduces costs. Why? Because human beings are clever and inventive, they find ways to do more with less, to produce more cheaply and effectively, and hence they will continually create ways to make goods more readily available at lower production costs. Simon therefore makes the bold proposal that it might be most accurate to assert that, *"Natural resources are not finite."* For, the amount that can be extracted, and thus the amount of use and output per unit extracted increased, on a scale with no known limit. Basically, the more time and human minds you put to work on production, the more output you are going to get while your costs continually diminish. He concludes, in examining the per-unit costs of everything from metals to grains over the long march of history is that, *"There is no physical evidence or economic reason why human resourcefulness and enterprise cannot forever continue to respond to impending shortages and existing problem with new expedients."*

Simon likewise shows the truth that more people mean more wealth by examining how the population size and rate of population growth affects innovation. His data shows that when both ancient Greece and Rome experienced times of population reduction through famine and war, their rate of innovation and development dropped; with fewer human minds entering the workforce, their civilizations stalled. Thus, it appears that the faster you bring human brainpower on board, the better your civilization develops.

Through such statistical, empirical studies, Simon concludes that humankind is the *"ultimate resource"* exhorting us to understand that, *"The ultimate resource is people—skilled, spirited, and hopeful people who will exert their wills and imaginations for their own benefit, and so, inevitably, for the benefit of us all."*

Similarly, J. Peter Vajk in *Doomsday Has Been Cancelled* provides compelling evidence that, almost without exception, despite the ballooning population, the prices of all the commodities of extractive industries (agriculture, mining, fishing, and forestry) were driven down tremendously in the period from 1870 to1957. Considered broadly, this suggests that inventive innovation makes it possible that, *"economic wealth has no intrinsic limit, since we can certainly see no intrinsic limits to knowledge."*

Likewise, in parallel with Simon's recognition that pollution was being *reduced* while industrialization increased, Vajk asserts that humanity recognizing our potentiality to problem-solve will actually make environmental destruction less likely. The longer an industry works, the more it utilizes every element of the material it extracts, much as the oil industry now generates numerous products from every barrel extracted from the ground, leaving nothing behind after the distillation process except a smattering of tar. Because people seek ways to "do more with less," this tends to reduce the waste and by-products of production, as they seek to squeeze the most value from every ounce of the raw materials. Moreover, as people recognize that we are not saddled with a no-win scarcity window closing on a dwindling resource base, they will lose any frenetic urgency to gorge on every available resource before the shrinking pile disappears. We can instead build a world of advanced technological abundance which yet lives with the balance and equanimity of the pastoral era: *"If we know that the world is open-ended, with more than enough for everyone, then we can afford a leisurely pace, take only what is needed, when it is needed. If we can exorcise the mentality of the zero-sum game, we can be as kind to the environment as the Indians were, and recognize the boundlessness surrounding us."*

One of the core concepts which drives ecologically-framed fear porn is the notion that there is a fixed *carrying capacity* for the planet, i.e. that there is some determinate physical limit to the number of people that the planet can maintain, beyond which all will collapse in a Mad Max scramble for the last table scrap and ounce of oil. Vajk responds to such fears of shortage by first asking us to consider: how big is the biosphere? The biosphere—which is all living things, plus their leavings and decomposing leaves, animal carcasses, manure, mud in the oceans, etc.—is about 1 million million kilograms. But, while that is surely a big number, it actually amounts to only about 1 *sixth* of 1 *millionth* of 1 *millionth* of the *total* mass of the earth. In other words, all the living plants and animal parts of the planet that so consume our attention, are but the merest scrape along the surface of the vast planet. In fact, the bulk of the world's mass—about 99% of the total—are, reasonably enough, those essential elements of oxygen, carbon, hydrogen, and nitrogen. Chemically considered, the only difference between us, as living beings, and the dead are the arrangement of those elements. In other words, we haven't even scratched the surface of earth's "carrying capacity" for life. There are, for our purposes, atoms without limit for humankind to grow practically without end.

He then examines particular classes of materials to show how abundant the actual supply is. Looking first at the most commonly used nonmetallic materials (sand, gravel, salt, limestone), at our current levels of use, we have a large enough supply to last for literally millions of years. Maybe we don't need to worry about those right now. Of the other non-metallic elements, the one in shortest supply may be phosphate, which could run out under current modes of use after 1,000 years. Again, this seems like not a matter of immediate concern.

How about metals? There is enough iron (in the form of taconite ore) for centuries. Of course, from iron, we produce steel by creating alloys with the addition of carbon and usually other trace elements. The particular elements added vary in availability and utility, but even if we encounter a shortage of any single element, there are all manner of substitutes, plus there are always more rare but useful metals like titanium or tungsten waiting in the wings. Again, seems like no emergency here.

What about hydrocarbons? Under current modes of operation, we may soon reach a point where the energy cost of extraction for fuel-grade oil may surpass the energy return of pumping it up. This looks like one of those engineering issues still underdeveloped. At the same time, for all the other uses of hydrocarbons—from plastics to lubricants to pharmaceuticals—the oil shale supplies are sufficient for about 3 million more years.

Furthermore, careful analysis of past data indicate we can better project future outcomes not by measuring the current piles of inert substances and drawing straight lines into the future, but by recognizing that the creative engineering limitations will be continually overcome which changes the projections and, according to the historical trends, always in an upward manner as human beings continually do more with less. This ephemeralization of output which makes humanity increasingly powerful in enacting our designs with greater ease and facility, may perhaps indicate we are entering the "Age of Substitutability." That is, humanity seems to be getting ever better at devising workarounds for near-term problems. The intellectual disciplines and routines of the sciences allow us to transmute almost any physical challenge into a kind of engineering problem...all at a time when there are more engineers walking around the earth than ever! If anything, that would seem to imply that the future will see us only get better at getting better.

Sorta like, human beings for the win!

Perhaps—rather than cowering in fear or shrieking in rage under the sway of the Beastie gang's pronuniciamentos of "global boiling" and imminent planetary doom for all—we should break their spell, that magician's trance which is a combination of distraction, dissimulation, and reorientation designed to induce helplessness and despair. Maybe their messaging is more about engendering fear to encourage compliance with centralized control by globalist directives rather than any real, objective peril. Maybe a life lived in cultivation of civilization and nurturance of neighbor would be far more fruitful than one devoted to morbid self-loathing arising from horrid imaginings which pale in comparison to humanity's history of bounteous fructification of the planet.

But wait! Won't we stink ourselves to death with pollution doing all this design, development, and deployment? Sometimes, yes, we will be very careless. We will doubtless continue to rush forward and make mistakes. But pollution is itself an engineering problem. It is amenable to rectification by the same principles which enabled us to produce it, as the U.S. has conclusively proven since 1970 when it created the EPA and began driving down particulate pollution ever since. If past is any predictor, ultimately, most of what is presently lost as waste will eventually be cleverly repurposed as resource to be fed back into some kind of productive use. Again, in the late 1800s, the main craze in the oil industry was for the kerosene fuel which lit peoples' homes without recourse to candles (or even dung fires!), and is only pulled from petroleum crude as a fractional distillate in the in the 300-525° F temperature range; the rest of the petroleum which had been pumped out of the ground was then cavalierly discarded as mere "waste"...until the chemists got to work and reimagined employing the other distillates as resources. Soon enough—while the kerosene continued to get the primary attention—gasoline, heating oil, lubricants, wax, and other uses were found for what before had been sloughed off as mere industrial "by-products" and waste Population growth means our brainpower will continually magnify, meaning our ability to ephemeralize and conquer challenges in transportation, information, medicine, construction, distribution, and environment. There will indeed continue to be a myriad of engineering challenges, but—boy, howdy!—ain't we gonna have a lot of engineers to throw at them.

As one obvious but dramatic example of ephemeralization, just look at your smartphone. In 1945, ENIAC, the first electronic programmable computer, took up 2 rooms and needed one hour of repair time for every one hour of run time...all to operate at a processing speed of about 5,000 Hz. Compared with that—only about eighty years later—your typical smartphone is processing almost one million *times* as much data...all day and all night, for years on end...in a device small enough to hold in your hand...and take anywhere. That is some badass engineering ephemeralization. That is not a "flawed species;" that is not some basically maladaptive animal; that is a collection of winners, a species built for victory.

Perhaps, it is time for the social and political understanding to catch up with our engineering capabilities and demand we design ourselves into a successful civilization. Perhaps, we should adopt one, simple, single focus, without demur or compromise, because we have the proof and the truth of the power of the human mind to make real the ideal through the transmutation of matter into the resplendent imaginings of our minds. In that way, we may more readily move beyond fear and confrontation to amity and cooperation, in the abundant garden we have wrought, living out our long lives of...100 years? 200 years? Who knows? Maybe we'll engineer ourselves Methuselah-style and live out 969 years rich in truth, beauty, and goodness. Vajk challenges us to not, *"shirk responsibility to ourselves for creating that future; to do so leaves the future to be chosen for us by default. Now is the time for each of us to take up the task of creating the present positive, the dawn of the humane and positive futures toward which our values urge us."*

Lest you think today's circumstances have undermined the conclusions of Simon and Vajk, the latest research is, if anything, even more encouraging. Tupy and Pooley in their recent work *Superabundance,* apply the metric of "time price" to measure how much people must pay to acquire any good. This single measure allows them to generate a cross-cultural, pan-historical analysis of the cost (i.e. time invested via human labor) to acquire an item. Looking back as far as 1850, primarily focused on 50 of the most fundamental commodities (e.g. cotton, wheat, iron, crude oil, lumber, etc.), the indications are that the time cost in hours worked to acquire all of these has dropped remarkably. In fact, on average, the typical price decrease for each commodity has been about 98%. Similarly, one may measure the acquisition cost of a particularly useful human affordance, viz. getting an hour of light at night. Being able to work or enjoy oneself with family and friends after sundown obviously provides a tremendous boon to individual productivity and felicity. In 1800, the price of an hour of light—primarily using pre-industrial candle power—was three hours of human labor. Today, for you to flip a switch for an hour of light runs about one-sixth of a penny...by comparison, practically free.

That such a tremendous abundance in so fundamental an advantage is rarely considered, demonstrates how much today's superabundance—quantum leaps beyond anything conceivable to our ancestors of just a couple centuries ago—is woefully ignored and insufficiently appreciated. Our current level of wealth and abundance makes the lives of the Founders—who worked by candlelight and travelled by horse—look like cavemen by comparison, yet it is taken for granted today. Moreover, humankind is far from done. The research in *Superabundance* indicates that the rate of abundance growth means your real wealth (in terms of actual time cost to acquire worthwhile products) doubles approximately every twenty years. Overall, over the last two centuries, worldwide, the time cost of goods has dropped so fast that people are now about 50 *times* more wealthy—live life 50 *times* more abundantly—than just a couple centuries back...and it's growing fast.

But, once again, the naysayer may wonder, how can that be possible? How—in a finite world with ostensibly finite resources—can having more and more people make it *easier* to acquire resources? The simple answer, again, is human brain power. Knowledge is power; knowledge is wealth, for knowledge is the means by which humans produce the artifacts and process which produce the goods which maximize human success on the planet. And how do we acquire such innovative knowledge and power? Through the human mind:

thought, deduction, classification, calculation, imagination, innovation, and creation. Thus, if you want to prosper, you need to maximize human mind power. Tupy and Pooley do offer the caveat that to truly utilize that mind power, there must be sufficiently free expression of ideas, i.e. free speech and publication. In order for competing notions to be presented, tested, and developed in the marketplace of ideas, people must be able to communicate, debate, and mutually assess theories and data. With that proviso accommodated, the formula for human flourishing becomes simple:

(People + Freedom) x Time = Prosperity

In sum, people are not the problem; people are the solution. That means that free people in a free market are victory, family is victory, and big families in big, free countries are big victory.

So, bring on the people, and let the fun and games begin.

Limitless
"America's abundance was not created by public sacrifices to the common good, but by the productive genius of free men who pursued their own personal interests and the making of their own private fortunes."
— Ayn Rand —

Once free, self-reliant, and unconquerable, you become limitless, the vista of possibilities endless; you become the center node of a life of infinite adventure. No longer the victim in a tragedy, encumbered by the heavy hand of Fate in an ever-more-burdensome round of toil and trouble, you become the hero whose wit and substance can ken the path to triumph over every obstacle.

In the land of the free, every man is a conqueror, every woman an adventuress.

You write your own story. You star in your own movie time adventure, more real, raw, and powerful than anything the glitz of a cinema camera might distract you with for a couple hours.

The end, then, is a limitlessness even beyond the dreams of the

Founders. Today's patriot badasses have every reason to believe the future of humankind will raise itself to unimaginable capacities which make today's "impossible" difficulties look like the mere risible bugbears of childhood.

Patriot Badass Worldwide

"Nobody's free until everybody's free."

— Fannie Lou Hamer —

By its appeal to the most optimistic qualities in humankind, our Republic has become a magnet of magnificence; over the last 200 years, America has had the good fortune to attract to itself some of the most brilliant souls from every land. The promise of freedom has drawn immigrants who come bearing the optimism which dreams of a better world, the courage to sacrifice the comfort of their familiar lives in pursuit of those dreams, and the determination to begin building those dreams with nothing but their own hope and grit.

I have met them, by the dozens, first generation Americans from Asia, Africa, Europe, the Mideast...from Iran and Armenia, Senegal and Syria, Russia and Jamaica...who fled from oppression, who ran to opportunity, who came with nothing but the hope in their hearts. They had only what they could carry with them. They expected nothing but a chance to labor unfettered towards their dreams, and, thereby, they indeed discovered their greatness. They built businesses and families; they went back to school and became leaders in their professions; they came here searching for the American dream and found it in themselves.

They came with nothing, and, in a sense, America gave them nothing in return, nothing but the emptiness of pure freedom...because that's all the human spirit needs: given an open field of opportunity, the human heart will step out, imagine a better tomorrow, and remake the world in its own brilliant design; give the human imagination the negative space, and it will paint a dreamscape of incalculable beauty.

Such are the spirits that have continually recharged American Badass; surging to these shores from all around the planet have come many of humanity's most hopeful, courageous, determined, and energetic souls. Now, at last, comes the time for America to pay that back. All of today's American dreamers—whether American by birth or by choice—have one looming, magnificent challenge offered to them. You, patriots, have only to stave off the Beastie assault on this Republic, give one final proof of the worth of republican liberty, and you will create a victory and example which will free patriots everywhere.

Yes, patriots, you will win this coming victory for yourself, your family, and your country. But beyond that, you owe this victory to the world...for all the free spirits languishing in all those other nations, those nations which have over the years, if you will, donated their best and brightest souls to America, those glimmering seedlings which have constantly renewed our ethos of opportunity. Now, from a joint victory of American patriots and worldwide dreamers, an even greater future can blossom than anyone has yet wishcast towards an impossiblist paradise. Benjamin Franklin reported that the Founders foresaw the greater import of triumphant American Badass centuries ago: *"Tis a common observation here that our cause is the cause of all mankind; and that we are fighting for their liberty in defending our own."*

This realization of the enormity of America's challenge and opportunity was echoed by Sam Adams, who said: *"Our contest is not only whether we ourselves shall be free, but whether there shall be left to mankind an asylum on earth for civil and religious liberty."*

Now, as the Beastie imagines itself lord of all, comes the time. Now comes the chance to enter the next amazing stage of the wondrous human saga. Now can the American badass—those of us who have inherited the dreams and aspirations of the Old World Pilgrims and immigrants who fled here from so many lands in search of nothing more than freedom, who sought any chance to realize their full capacities without hindrance—now must we triumph here and then venture back to those ancestral lands, bestowing on them pragmatic proofs of how to fully manifest triumphal victory and practical liberty. Thus will those long-held dreams—sent as seeds of hope across the sea and at last grown to their full magnificence—be returned to their homeland and joyfully shared as the fruits of freedom. Then may Badass patriotism—love of family, polity, and liberty—blossom worldwide, so that every region may revel in its own unique mode of lively, lawful liberty.

Sure, the American Republic was the first to venture forth, the place that started it all by taking those initial uncertain, stumbling steps in humanity's journey to establish a polity of sovereign citizens. That doesn't mean it has to be the last. In fact, first rarely equals best. Humankind is always just getting started.

As this Republic was a call to instantiate the democratic principles of self-governance in the Americas, so shall the liberation of the American People from the handcuffs of the globalist controllers be the starting gun for the liberation of the planet into an age of exploration, development, and unification under those ideals of personal growth, individual autonomy, and universal compassion...an age of the humane treatment *of* humans *by* humans in their human realm.

Let's bring the whole world into the full efflorescence of these principles. Let's see who can best answer the challenge—by experimenting in a thousand places in a million ways, in a joyous race to the infinite horizon— and find out who in the world can badass best.

Surely, that will be the baddest badass of all.

Prayer Almighty
"Of all the dispositions and habits which lead to political prosperity, religion and morality are indispensable."
— George Washington —

Of course, when taking on impossiblist goals, it might be nice if one were to have some greater leverage, some transcendent source of illimitable power. What if there were, in fact, some access to unimaginable power which required little or no physical effort on your part? Wouldn't that be a useful adjunct in your endeavors?

Such, of course, is the promise of the power of prayer. The notion of tapping a direct through line to the intent and action of the Great Orderer and thereby accessing immeasurable energies towards one's intentions is heady stuff. To undertake the metaphysical and epistemological heavy lifting necessary to underwrite full warrant of prayer's miraculous efficacy, however, would necessitate immense demonstration far beyond the scope of this work.

Without going down the fraught conceptual pathways to deductive proofs or close analysis of testimonial claims, let us merely mention a few suggestive points in passing.

Probably the most common use of prayer is the petitionary request for miraculous intervention, i.e. that something wondrous happen. The current *locus classicus* for examination of such claims may be Keener's scholarly and compendious *Miracles* (2011) which provides enormous evidentiary testimony supported by his carefully parsed critique of the arguments and claims of those dubious of such reports. A more popular approach using contemporary testimony is Strobel's *The Case of Miracles* (2018), which documents both personal accounts and the investigations and conclusions of scholars in the field. Finally, we will take one of the most dramatic and widely-documented uses of prayer to which is attributed immense effect as an exemplary, if obviously controverted, case: the Battle of Lepanto.

In the 16th century, the long-running fight over control of the Mediterranean Sea between the rising Ottoman (Muslim) and European (Christian) forces was approaching its climax. Tapped to command the Christian fleet, Don Juan of Austria—sometimes called "the last true knight of Europe"—commanded his armada to undertake a series of devotional acts. He forbade any blasphemous talk or inducements to fornication (i.e. prostitutes) aboard ship, that the sailors fast for three days, that they make acts of contrition and confession, and, on the eve of battle, distributed rosaries to the entire fleet, which the men dutifully prayed. When the fleet arose on October 7, 1571, they attended a prayerful mass and—when they happened upon the Ottoman fleet by the town of Lepanto off the Greek coastline—raised a cross at the bow of every ship and headed into battle. Both sides came into the fight with over 200 galleys and nearly 70,000 men, but the Ottoman complement was better equipped, trained, and bore the experience and confidence of a navy that had not lost a sea battle in a century. The Europeans had Don Juan, their faith, and a mass of ill-trained and inexperienced crewmen. Worse, as the two fleets closed, headwinds blew in, stalling the advance of the European fleet and bringing in a dense fog that obscured their vision and confused their ranks. Yet, just as Ali Pasha—grand admiral of the Ottoman forces—careened headlong forward in the belief that victory was at hand, the wind suddenly shifted, giving the Europeans easy sailing and, better, shepherding the clouds alongside their ships, which hid their movements. The two forces smashed together in a tumult of shot, sword, and flame. Over five long hours they clawed and hacked and bombarded one another. But, at last, Ali Pasha fell, his ship was taken, his fleet's line broken, and his armada scattered. At the end, Don Juan's untested crews sunk or captured 187 Ottoman ships while losing only 13, a rate of over 10 to 1. It is said that Pope Pius V—who had ordered fasting, masses, and rosaries in support of the contest—received a stunning vision of the victory that day, two weeks before couriers would arrive with written reports of the victory. In any case, the pious attributed the victory in large measure to the power of faith and prayer to Jesus through Mary, and the pope made October 7th thenceforward the feast of Our Lady of Victory. Did all that prayer and fasting really make the difference at Lepanto? I dunno, but it obviously sure didn't hurt.

We must acknowledge, however, Zuckermann's commentary ("Does Prayer Work?", 2019) which notes that the two most comprehensive longitudinal studies of medical outcomes do *not* seem to support the claim of any measurable positive effects attributable to prayer. Since that hard data runs counter to immense anecdotal observations from numerous qualified witnesses, we may reasonably draw two tentative conclusions: (a) the interactions of human thought and intent, faith and doubt, with outside events through these modalities like prayer and intentional conscious intervention are rather more complex and variegated than our current methodologies allow us to fully capture; and (b) such limitations of our understanding militates against making any extravagant claims either for *or* against its efficacy. Nonetheless, what does seem universally-acknowledged as both palpable and proven are the psychological benefits arising from the practice, which—alongside both its anecdotal beneficence and physical safety if not benefits—suggest we should be rather more permissive than dismissive of so richly storied a practice which produces no hint of harm while offering every hope of help.

Pray on, brothers, pray on, and let the doubters worry over their doubts. As for me and my house, we shall serve the Lord.

At one time, prayer opened every session of Congress, the Supreme Court, and every day of classes for the schoolchildren of America, for the faithful of this nation revelled and rejoiced in the battle which strengthens you, glorifies God, and prepares your reward in Heaven. It's been written that (Job 7:1), *"The life of man upon earth is a warfare,"* and so we may do best to recognize that the war is ultimately not physical but spiritual and thus our greatest weapons are not swords and guns but prayerful intentions and mindful supplications. Maybe we just need to step out from the great lie that there is no other world than what our senses behold. Maybe, just maybe, the world is more wild, wide, and wonderful than what we behold with our eyes.

In any case—historically considered—the faithful mind in its many forms has proven itself as the foundation of most great civilizations. Whether the ancestors of Heaven in China, the devas of India, the Sky Father of the Plains Indians, the innumerable deities populating the pantheons of Greece, Rome, Egypt, Scandinavia...let alone the finely-wrought dogmas of the Levantine monotheist creeds, the source of much of a people's moral sense and moral urgency flows from their faith. And the summative practice of that faith is almost always rooted in—or accompanied by—the most fervent, frank, and heartfelt prayer.

A people will live spiritual truths only when they know Spirit truly lives.

Can we have political peace and accord without faith? Will there be worldly goodness without spiritual acquiescence? Perhaps. But it appears as if that unspiritual approach is precisely what the American people have tried for the greater part of the last century, and it is a miserable failure and galloping demonstration of what the human spirit, completely released from all moral bounds, devolves into.

Thus, through prayer, one obtains both the potential for immense—perhaps even miraculous—benefits, plus the guarantee of the cultivation of some of our most refined and admirable qualities, with the added bonus of a grounded, centered imperturbability rendered by this most beneficent, blessed, and beautiful practice. Maybe we should try God for a change. Maybe that service and sacrifice and acknowledgement of the greater-than-self, the greater than anything of this world, is the greatest victory of all.

Maybe the ultimate badass is the goodness of godliness.

Maybe, what lies beyond impossibilism is the truly infinite.

Maybe God waits for you.

Pray today.

Pray like your life depends on it, like your soul depends on it.

It just might.

Tomorrowland

"I am well aware of the toil and blood and treasure that it will cost us to maintain this Declaration, and support and defend these states. Yet, through all the gloom, I can see the rays of ravishing light and glory. I can see that the end is worth more than the means."

— John Adams —

(What, then, might that look like...when the Republic rises reborn...when the Constitution is fully restored...when an infinity of possibility opens before the People?)

The sun was hot, and little Santiago squinted up at the skyscrubbers flying low across the sky, cutting through the white haze and leaving behind a swath of the sharpest blue of the week. His sis Amelia had worked in the seascrubbers last summer scooping up the oceans, and she said soon the sky would always be blue, but he was not so sure. She said he should join the skyscrubbers when he got big and make the sky always clear, but he thought he would wait and see.

Little Santiago was tired of skipping along the sidewalk, and he did not need any more frogs for his collection from the pond. So he decided to go down to the school and see what his sis Anna was doing.

But when he found her classroom, they were all standing with their hands on their chests and saying the "Pledge of Protection" to the flag, and when Anna spotted him she shook her head and gave him a stern look. So he crouched low outside the door and tried to whisper all the words along with the class, but could not remember the 5th Great Freedom...but he could usually get the end: *this Pledge of Protection of the Free States of North America...and to our Republic of Laws, one people, free by birth, upholding liberty and justice for all.*

But then the class sat down to do math, which always made little Santiago sleepy, so he decided to go to the marketplace where there were many booths, and see if there were any new model rocket ships worth buying with his allowance. Mr. Nguyen was at his fruit stall, and he gave little Santiago some grapes and told him to grow big very fast so he could make Santiago very rich as a delivery boy and then laughed and laughed with his big loud cackle. Then Mr. Nguyen told him the Model Mart next store was closed because the owner had been picked up by two agents from the Federal Liberty Agency; it seems the G-Men came by asking if anyone needed any more rifles or ammo, and the Model Mart's owner said he could probably use a little more ammo for his Revolution Day shootout, so they were giving him a ride downtown right quick to grab a couple extra cans of .50 cal for the big fun. Then Mr. Nguyen started teasing Santiago again about becoming his new delivery boy, saying he would give him many silver coins so he could buy all the fanciest model rocket ships when the Model Mart's owner got back from his ammo run. But little Santiago knew he didn't want to become Mr. Nguyen's new delivery boy because you will not get very rich being a delivery boy working for Mr. Nguyen with his craggy cackle and crooked teeth, so little Santiago thanked him for the grapes, and decided to go down to the church.

At the church he saw Father Gomez, who smiled and offered him lemonade and cookies. So little Santiago sat a while, taking little sips of the lemonade, but not too much, because father always put too much sugar in his lemonade. But he did eat both cookies, which little Santiago could tell were baked by Mrs. Morris, who always put extra chocolate chips, so they were always kind of juicy, even after a couple days. And father said he was very busy that day, with two weddings, but said there was always time for a rosary and started to take one out of his desk drawer, but little Santiago said no. The rosary always made him sleepy, but maybe one day he would not be so sleepy saying it.

Instead, little Santiago wandered down to the skydocks, where they were rolling the battered lift containers up to the Mrstik Elevator, a giant steel scaffold stretching miles and miles overhead, a floating, linked ladder of rails and tubes allowing low-air, low-grav factories to work high above, brewing up super-superconductors and growing megaveggies and other things little Santiago didn't understand, but big sis Allie did, riding up there on one of the people pods every morning. She used to bring home a bushel of mega-'matoes every couple weeks and make amazing spaghetti sauce. He sighed. He missed her making mega-'mato sauce since she had transferred over to the superceuticals department. Then another huge shipping container—the paint on its ribbed sides flaking where the clasping bars grabbed it for its ride up—was rolled onto the great elevator platform, was snapped hard into place by the clasping bars, and then, with a loud hydraulic hiss, shot skyward on its long maglev assent toward the floating factory outpost way overhead. He blinked into the sun and sky, wondering what things looked like from way up so high and far away. But then another loader skid was coming behind him, and the foreman was shouting, and somebody spilled a 55-gallon drum of something that smelled like bad pond water, so little Santiago decided now was a good time to go to the Park.

He loved the Park, where the lawn was soft enough and the hill short enough he could climb up the gentle slope to the monument, lay down, and roll downhill until the grass tickled his arms and his head would gently spin and spin. But today Santiago did not feel like spinning.

Today, he was thinking about his grandpa Jose and wanted to read the plaque again. It said:

"The Battle of Three Rivers, where Jose Almanza's Militia surprised the Invaders"—that was the part Santiago liked best, the part about his grandpa Jose and the militia. He knew militia was many brave men with guns. And he thought about the way his grandpa would tell the story, putting little Santiago on his knee and—between the coughing fits he used to have before they brought him a regen bed—tell him of the battle. That the war seemed all but lost. That the bad men were so very sure of themselves. That everyone was saying it was impossible to win, that the bad men were too many. Grandpa Jose would explain that the bad Invaders never expected them, because bad men never expect God. They never see God coming because they never look to Him. And while the bad men were all so busy thinking they would attack the last of our army and kill them all, they never saw the militia.

"Tell me about the surprise!" little Santiago would say then.

Then grandpa Jose would look both proud and embarrassed all at once. "Yes, then, when we had them surrounded, I gave them the surprise," he would say. "I walked out from my headquarters."

"And then," little Santiago would shout, "you took off your helmet!"

"Yes, and I took off my helmet, and tucked it here, under my arm, right here," he would say, crooking his left arm.

"And then your shirt, you tore your shirt!"

"Yes, little Santiago, and then I reached with my other hand and ripped open the front of my jacket and shirt...and I stood there,"—here his voice often got quavery and quiet—"my bare chest to their guns, but their guns grew still, as I wondered if they would shoot me down like a dog. And then I shouted: '*Will we all just fight and fight and fight like madmen drowning each other in mud until the end of time? Then shoot me down now! Shoot me here, where I stand! Or will you have the courage to try peace? If you are men who love your families, then have the courage to stand with me here...have the courage to try peace!*"

Then grandpa Jose would look at little Santiago with a wistful glimmer in his eyes. "That was the longest ten seconds of my life," he would say, "waiting for them to shoot me."

"But they didn't shoot you, grandpa!"

"No, little Santiago, they did not shoot me. They came out. One...and then two...and then many more."

"And then they made your president of the whole *Esados Unidos*!"

Grandpa Jose would chuckle. "No, that was many, many years later, little Santiago."

"But, grandpa?"

"Yes?"

"Why did the men not shoot you?"

And Grandpa Jose would lean back in his chair, looking very far away. "I think God made them kind of blind." Then grandpa Jose would look at him with sparkling eyes and say, "And because God wants everyone to see: impossible, is nothing." And then he would talk about how many men had died—good men and bad men—and all the terrible fighting, until that day when many saw a way out, the day the Invaders began to lose heart and ran and ran, and that battle was the "high water mark" of their attack on the country and that because of that, the war was soon over and now today the country could live at peace with itself and the world.

And little Santiago sighed because that was the same thing it said on the plaque: "high water mark." But water can't be high. Water sits low, in a puddle, or a pond. Water can't be high, like a mountain or a Mrstik Elevator.

So he shrugged and went to look at the flags. There were three mighty flag poles, with three glorious flags, and they furled and unfurled, waving in the breeze in slow majestic rolls under the wide, endless sky. He was proud of his grandpa Jose, and proud that grandpa had won this place and won the peace so that these beautiful flags could wave so proudly and so that grandpa could become the president because he was so brave.

And so, that day—standing there under those beautiful flags, thinking of that far off battle—little Santiago decided what he would do. He decided he would be a man as brave as his grandpa Jose, but not in war, because there was no war. Little Santiago knew big sis Allie wanted him to study at the Vollmer Institute of Vibratory medicine like her, but he decided he would use the peace grandpa Jose had won and bravely fly. He decided he would fly beyond those flags, higher and higher—beyond even the skyscrubbers sis Amelia wanted him to join—even beyond the sky. That day little Santiago decided he would reach for the highest heaven at the very verge of space itself...because impossible, is nothing.

Then our mouth will be filled with laughter, and our tongue with joyful shouts. Then shall the nations say: 'The Lord has done great things for them.'

The Lord hath done great things for us: we are become joyful.

May those who sow in tears, reap in joy,

May he that goes out weeping and casting seeds,

Return home shouting with joy, bearing sheaves of wheat.

— Psalm 126 —

APPENDIX 1

Quotes on Constitutionalism

"[T]he American Constitution is, so far as I can see, the most wonderful work ever struck off at a given time by the brain and purpose of man."
— William Gladstone, British Prime Minister —

THE COURTS, IN APPLYING AND interpreting constitutional jurisprudence, utilize what may be thought of as a "least harm" or "least intrusive", principle, viz. that the document contemplates the least intrusive allowance for government action and the least restrictive range for citizen liberty. This basic approach is captured in a pair of Latin tags: positively, as *Potestas stricte interpretatur* (A power is strictly interpreted), or negatively as *In dubiis, non praesumitur pro potentia* (In cases of doubt, the presumption is not in favor of a power). In either case, the message is clear: the grant of power to government in your founding charter was intended to be—and rightly should remain—minimal, so that you may fully flourish in the maximal exercise of your freedom.

Does the Constitution really give you that much freedom? Is the government really as legally constrained as you are reading? If there were ever any doubts about how great the citizen's sovereignty is in our Republic, take a look at what those who wrote it, studied it, and adjudicated it have to say.

The following citations come, almost universally, directly from the Founders, Framers, and federal court decisions, demonstrating the original intent of that document with robust and uncompromising clarity: by right and by law, you are a freeborn citizen, and thereby afforded every liberty due the full, sovereign use of your faculties.

***   ***   ***   ***   ***

"[A]ll men are born equally free and independent, and have certain inherent natural Rights...among which are the Enjoyment of Life and Liberty, with the Means of acquiring and possessing Property, and pursuing and obtaining Happiness and Safety."

— George Mason. *Virginia Declaration of Rights*, Article I (1776) —

"The state governments represent the wishes, and feelings, and local interests, of the people. They are the safeguard and ornament of the Constitution; they will protract the period of our liberties; they will afford a shelter against the abuse of power, and will be the natural avengers of our violated rights."

— Fisher Ames to the Massachusetts ratifying convention (1788) —

"The powers delegated by the proposed Constitution to the federal government, are few and defined. Those which are to remain in the State governments are numerous and indefinite. The former will be exercised principally on external objects, as war, peace, negotiation, and foreign commerce; with which last the power of taxation will, for the most part, be connected. The powers reserved to the several States will extend to all the objects which, in the ordinary course of affairs, concern the lives, liberties, and properties of the people, and the internal order, improvement, and prosperity of the State.

"The operations of the federal government will be most extensive and important in times of war and danger; those of the State governments, in times of peace and security. "

— James Madison, *Federalist Papers*, No. 45 (1788) —

"The accumulation of all powers, legislative, executive, and judiciary, in the same hands, whether of one, a few, or many, and whether hereditary, self-appointed, or elective, may justly be pronounced the very definition of tyranny."

— James Madison, *Federalist Papers*, No. 47 (1788) —

"If men were angels, no government would be necessary. If angels were to govern men, neither external nor internal controls on government would be necessary. In framing a government which is to be administered by men over men, the great difficulty lies in this: you must first enable the government to control the governed; and in the next place oblige it to control itself."

— James Madison, *Federalist Papers*, No. 51 (1788) —

[On creating a national bank, and congressional powers generally:] "I consider the foundation of the Constitution as laid on this ground: That "all powers not delegated to the United States, by the Constitution, nor prohibited by it to the States, are reserved to the States or to the people." (Xth amendment.) To take a single step beyond the boundaries thus specially drawn around the powers of Congress, is to take possession of a boundless field of power, no longer susceptible of any definition...Nor are they within either of the general phrases..."to lay taxes for *the purpose of* providing for the general welfare." For the laying of taxes is the *power,* and the general welfare the *purpose* for which the power is to be exercised. They are not to lay taxes *ad libitum for any purpose they please;* but only *to pay the debts or provide for the welfare of the Union.* In like manner, they are not *to do anything they please* to provide for the general welfare, but only to *lay taxes* for that purpose. To consider the latter phrase, not as describing the purpose of the first, but as giving a distinct and independent power to do any act they please, which might be for the good of the Union, would render all the preceding and subsequent enumerations of power completely useless...

"It would reduce the whole instrument to a single phrase, that of instituting a Congress with power to do whatever would be for the good of the United States; and, as they would be the sole judges of the good or evil, it would be also a power to do whatever evil they please. "

— Thomas Jefferson, letter to President Washington (1791) —

"[T]he habits of thinking in a free Country should inspire caution in those entrusted with its Administration, to confine themselves within their respective Constitutional Spheres; avoiding in the exercise of the Powers of one department to encroach upon another. The spirit of encroachment tends to consolidate the powers of all the departments in one, and thus to create, whatever the form of government, a real despotism."

— George Washington, farewell address (1796) —

"When an instrument admits two constructions, the one safe, the other dangerous, the one precise, the other indefinite, I prefer that which is safe and precise...Our peculiar security is in the possession of a written Constitution. Let us not make it a blank paper by construction...Let us go on then perfecting it, by adding, by way of amendment to the Constitution, those powers which time and trial show are still wanting."

— Thomas Jefferson, letter to William Nicholas (1803) —

"Certainly all those who have framed written constitutions contemplate them as forming the fundamental and paramount law of the nation, and consequently...an act of the legislature, repugnant to the constitution, is void...Thus, the particular phraseology of the Constitution of the United States confirms and strengthens the principle, supposed to be essential to all written constitutions, that a law repugnant to the Constitution is void..."

— *Marbury v. Madison*, 5 U.S. 137 (1803) —

"On every question of construction [of the Constitution] let us carry ourselves back to the time when the Constitution was adopted, recollect the spirit manifested in the debates, and instead of trying what meaning may be squeezed out of the text, or intended against it, conform to the probable one in which it was passed."

— Thomas Jefferson, letter to Judge William Johnson (1823) —

"[T]he object of a Constitution, is to restrain the government, as that of laws is to restrain individuals...[I reject] the novel, the hazardous, and, I must add, fatal project of giving to the General Government the sole and final right of interpreting the Constitution;—thereby reversing the whole system, making that instrument the creature of its will."

— John C. Calhoun, *The Fort Hill Address* (1831) —

"It is this negative power—the power of preventing or arresting the action of the government—be it called by what term it may—veto, interposition, nullification, check, or balance of power—which, in fact, forms the constitution."

— John C. Calhoun, *A Disquisition on Government* (1850) —

"The Constitution of the United States is a law for rulers and people, equally in war and in peace, and covers with the shield of its protection all classes of men, at all times, and under all circumstances. No doctrine, involving more pernicious consequences, was ever invented by the wit of man than that any of its provisions can be suspended during any of the great exigencies of government. Such a doctrine leads directly to anarchy or despotism."

— *Ex parte Milligan*, 71 U.S. (14 Wall.) at 120-121 (1868) —

"The Federal Government has no general police power and that of the states is beyond the reach of Congress, except in rare cases where the people in whom it inheres have released it by the terms of the Federal Constitution."

— *U.S. v. Fox*, 94 U.S. 315, 320-21 (1877) —

"The court is to protect against any encroachment of Constitutionally secured liberties."

— *Boyd v. U.S.*, 116 U.S. 616 (1886) —

"An unconstitutional act is not law; it confers no rights; it imposes no duties; affords no protection; it creates no office; it is in legal contemplation, as inoperative as though it had never been passed."

— *Norton v. Shelby County, 118 U.S. 425* (1886) —

"We are bound to interpret the Constitution in the light of the law as it existed at the time it was adopted."

— *Mattox v. U.S.*, 156 US 237, 243 (1895) —

"The Constitution is a written instrument. As such, its meaning does not alter. That which it meant when it was adopted, it means now."

— *S. Carolina v. U.S.*, 199 U.S. 437, 448 (1905) —

"The police power under the American constitutional system has been left to the states. It has always belonged to them and was not surrendered by them to the general government, nor directly restrained by the constitution of the United States...Congress has no general power to enact police regulations operative within the territorial limits of a state."

— *Shealey v. Southern Ry. Co.*, 127 S.C. 15, 120 S.E. 561, 562 (1924) —

"Your rights must be interpreted in favor of the citizen."

— *Byers v. U.S.*, 273 U.S. 28 (1927) —

"Those who won our independence believed that the final end of the state was to make men free to develop their faculties, and that in its government the deliberative forces should prevail over the arbitrary. They valued liberty both as an end and as a means. They believed liberty to the secret of happiness and courage to be the secret of liberty."

— *Whitney v. California*, 274 U.S. 357, 375 (1927) —

"Experience should teach us to be most on our guard to protect liberty when the government's purposes are beneficent. Men born to freedom are naturally alert to repel invasion of their liberty by evil-minded rulers. The greatest dangers to liberty lurk in insidious encroachment by men of zeal, well-meaning but without understanding."

— *Olmstead v. United States*, 277 U.S. 438 (1928) —

"No state shall convert a liberty into a privilege, license it, and attach a fee to it."

— *Murdock v. Penn.*, 319 US 105 (1943) —

"The claim and exercise of a Constitutional right cannot be converted into a crime."

— Miller v. U.S., 230 F.2d. 486, 489 (1956) —

"No state legislator or executive or judicial officer can war against the Constitution without violating his undertaking to support it."

— Cooper v. Aaron, 358 U.S. 1, 78 S.Ct. 1401 (1958) —

"Where rights secured by the Constitution are involved, there can be no rule making or legislation, which would abrogate them."

— Miranda v. Arizona, 384 U.S. 436 (1966) —

"If the state converts a liberty into a privilege, the citizen can engage in the right with impunity."

— Shuttlesworth v. Birmingham, 394 US 147 (1969) —

"Waivers of Constitutional Rights, not only must they be voluntary, they must be knowingly intelligent acts done with sufficient awareness."

— Brady v. U.S., 397 U.S. 742, 748 (1970) —

"If you have relied on prior decisions of the supreme Court, you have the perfect defense for willfulness."

— U.S. v. Bishop, 412 US 346 (1973) —

"Government may not prohibit or control the conduct of a person for reasons that infringe upon constitutionally guaranteed freedoms."

— Smith v. U.S., 502 F2d 512 CA Tex (1974) —

"When a judge acts where he or she does not have jurisdiction to act, the judge is engaged in an act or acts of treason."

— *U.S. v Will*, 449 US 200 (1980) —

"Officers of the court have no immunity, when violating a Constitutional right, from liability. For they are deemed to know the law."

— *Owen v. Independence*, 100 S.C.T. 1398, 445 US 622 (1980) —

"The Constitution is not neutral. It was designed to take the government off the backs of people."

— William O. Douglas, *The Court Years 1939-75* (1980) —

***   ***   ***   ***   ***

"Go forward, in one hand bearing the book of Christian truth and in the other the Constitution of the United States. Christian truth and American liberty will make you free, happy, and prosperous."

— Vatican representative to the World Columbian Exposition
(Chicago, 1893) —

APPENDIX 2

Quotes on Liberty and Morality

"Righteousness exalteth a nation."

— Proverbs 14:34 —

"The only foundation of a free Constitution, is pure Virtue, and if this cannot be inspired into our People, in a greater Measure, than they have it now, they may change their Rulers, and the forms of Government, but they will not obtain a lasting Liberty—They will only exchange Tyrants and Tyrannies."

— John Adams —

"We have no government armed with power capable of contending with human passions unbridled by morality and religion. Avarice, ambition, revenge, or gallantry would break the strongest cords of our constitution as a whale goes through a net."

— John Adams —

"Our Constitution was made only for a moral and religious people. It is wholly inadequate to the government of any other."

— John Adams —

"Liberty can no more exist without virtue and independence than the body can live and move without a soul."

— John Adams —

"Public virtue cannot exist in a nation without private, and public virtue is the only foundation of republics."

— John Adams —

"The laws of man may bind him in chains or may put him to death, but they never can make him wise, virtuous, or happy."

— John Adams —

"Honor is truly sacred, but holds a lower rank in the scale of moral excellence than virtue. Indeed the former is part of the latter, and consequently has not equal pretensions to support a frame of government productive of human happiness."

— John Adams —

"Human nature itself is evermore an advocate for liberty. There is also in human nature a resentment of injury, and indignation against wrong, a love of truth and a veneration of virtue. These amiable passions, are the "latent spark"...If the people are capable of understanding, seeing and feeling the differences between true and false, right and wrong, virtue and vice, to what better principle can the friends of mankind apply than to the sense of this difference?"

— John Adams —

"[N]either the wisest constitution nor the wisest laws will secure the liberty and happiness of a people whose manners are universally corrupt. He therefore is the truest friend of the liberty of his country who tries most to promote its virtue, and who, so far as his power and influence extend, will not suffer a man to be chosen onto any office of power and trust who is not a wise and virtuous man."

— Samuel Adams —

"The diminution of public virtue is usually attended with that of public happiness, and the public liberty will not long survive the total extinction of morals."

— Samuel Adams —

"[M]en will be free no longer then while they remain virtuous."

— Samuel Adams —

"No people will tamely surrender their Liberties, nor can any be easily subdued, when knowledge is diffused and Virtue is preserved. On the Contrary, when People are universally ignorant, and debauched in their Manners, they will sink under their own weight without the Aid of foreign Invaders."

— Samuel Adams —

"A general dissolution of the principles and manners will more surely overthrow the liberties of America than the whole force of the common enemy...While the people are virtuous they cannot be subdued; but once they lose their virtue, they will be ready to surrender their liberties to the first external or internal invader...If virtue and knowledge are diffused among the people, they will never be enslaved. This will be their great security."

— Samuel Adams —

"Our liberty depends on our education, our laws, and habits...[I]t is founded on morals and religion, whose authority reigns in the heart, and on the influence all these produce on public opinion before that opinion governs rulers."

— Fisher Ames —

"[T]he very best forms of government are vain without public virtue."

— William A. Cocke —

"When was public virtue to be found when private was not?"

— William Cowper —

"The life of the nation is secure only while the nation is honest, truthful and virtuous."

— Frederick Douglass —

"We have never stopped sin by passing laws; and in the same way, we are not going to take a great moral ideal and achieve it merely by law."

— Dwight D. Eisenhower —

Leges sine Moribus vanae ("Laws without morals are useless," Motto of the University of Pennsylvania)

— Benjamin Franklin —

"Sell not virtue to purchase wealth, nor Liberty to purchase power."

— Benjamin Franklin —

"Liberty cannot be established without morality, nor morality without faith."

— Horace Greeley —

"I consider the domestic virtue of the Americans as the principle source of all their other qualities. It acts as a promoter of industry, as a stimulus to enterprise and as the most powerful restraint of public vice...No government could be established on the same principle as that of the United States with a different code of morals."

— Francis Grund —

"The American Constitution is remarkable for its simplicity; but it can only suffice a people habitually correct in their actions, and would be utterly inadequate to the wants of a different nation. Change the domestic habits of the Americans, their religious devotion, and their high respect for morality, and it will not be necessary to change a single letter in the Constitution in order to vary the whole form of their government."

— Francis Grund —

"Virtue, morality, and religion—this is the armor, my friend, and this alone that renders us invincible. These are the tactics we should study. If we lose these, we are conquered, fallen indeed...[S]o long as our manners and principles remain sound, there is no danger."

— Patrick Henry —

"No free government can stand without virtue in the people, and a lofty spirit of patriotism."

— Andrew Jackson —

"A nation as a society forms a moral person, and every member of it is personally responsible for his society."

— Thomas Jefferson —

"No government can continue good but under the control of the people; and...their minds are to be informed by education what is right and what wrong; to be encouraged in habits of virtue and to be deterred from those of vice...These are the inculcations necessary to render the people a sure basis for the structure and order of government."

— Thomas Jefferson —

"It is in the manners and spirit of a people which preserve a republic in vigour...[D]egeneracy in these is a canker which soon eats into the heart of its laws and constitution."

— Thomas Jefferson —

"Dependence begets subservience and venality, suffocates the germ of virtue, and prepares fit tools for the designs of ambition."

— Thomas Jefferson —

"Liberty...is the great parent of science and of virtue; and...a nation will be great in both always in proportion as it is free."

— Thomas Jefferson —

"The order of nature [is] that individual happiness shall be inseparable from the practice of virtue."

— Thomas Jefferson —

"No people can be great who have ceased to be virtuous."

— Samuel Johnson —

"History fails to record a single precedent in which nations subject to moral decay have not passed into political and economic decline. There has been either a spiritual awakening to overcome the moral lapse, or a progressive deterioration leading to ultimate national disaster."

— Douglas MacArthur —

"To suppose that any form of government will secure liberty or happiness without any virtue in the people, is a chimerical idea."

— James Madison —

"[R]eligion, morality and knowledge, being necessary to good government and the happiness of mankind, schools and the means of education shall be forever encouraged."

— Northwest Ordinance of 1787 —

"Unless virtue guide us, our choice must be wrong."

— William Penn —

"A state is nothing more than a reflection of its citizens; the more decent the citizens, the more decent the state."

— Ronald Reagan —

"The laws by which the Divine Ruler of the universe has decreed an indissoluble connection between public happiness and private virtue, whatever apparent exceptions may delude our short-sighted judgments, never fail to vindicate their supremacy and immutability."

— William Cabell Rives —

"To educate a man in mind and not in morals is to educate a menace to society."

— Theodore Roosevelt —

"[L]iberty without virtue would be no blessing to us."

— Benjamin Rush —

"The only foundation for...a republic is to be laid in Religion. Without this there can be no virtue, and without virtue there can be no liberty, and liberty is the object and life of all republican governments."

— Benjamin Rush —

"Republics are created by the virtue, public spirit, and intelligence of the citizens. They fall, when the wise are banished from the public councils, because they dare to be honest, and the profligate are rewarded, because they flatter the people, in order to betray them."

— Joseph Story —

"Somehow strangely the vice of men gets well represented and protected but their virtue has none to plead its cause—nor any charter of immunities and rights."

— Henry David Thoreau —

"No polity can be devised which shall perpetuate freedom among a people that are dead to honor and integrity. Liberty and virtue are twin sisters, and the best fabric in the world."

— James H. Thornwell —

"[Liberty] considers religion as the safeguard of morality, and morality as the best security of law and the surest pledge of the duration of freedom."

— Alexis de Tocqueville —

"Of all the dispositions and habits which lead to political prosperity, religion and morality are indispensable supports. In vain would that man claim tribute to patriotism who should labor to subvert these great pillars of human happiness—these firmest props of the duties of men and citizens...[R]eason and experience both forbid us to expect that national morality can prevail in exclusion of religious principles."

— George Washington —

"The aggregate happiness of the society, which is best promoted by the practice of a virtuous policy, is, or ought to be, the end of all government."

— George Washington —

"Human rights can only be assured among a virtuous people. The general government...can never be in danger of degenerating into a monarchy, an oligarchy, an aristocracy, or any despotic or oppressive form so long as there is any virtue in the body of the people."

— George Washington —

"Lastly, our ancestors established their system of government on morality and religious sentiment. Moral habits, they believed, cannot safely be on any other foundation than religious principle, nor any government be secure which is not supported by moral habits."

— Daniel Webster —

"[I]f we and our posterity reject religious instruction and authority, violate the rules of eternal justice, trifle with the injunctions of morality, and recklessly destroy the political constitution which holds us together, no man can tell how sudden a catastrophe may overwhelm us, that shall bury all our glory in profound obscurity."

— Daniel Webster —

"In selecting men for office, let principle be your guide. Regard not the particular sect or denomination of the candidate—look at his character. It is alleged by men of loose principles, or defective views of the subject, that religion and morality are not necessary or important qualifications for political stations. But the scriptures teach a different doctrine. They direct that rulers should be men who rule in the fear of God, men of truth, hating covetousness. It is to the neglect of this rule that we must ascribe the multiplied frauds, breaches of trust, speculations and embezzlements of public property which astonish even ourselves; which tarnish the character of our country and which disgrace our government. When a citizen gives his vote to a man of known immorality, he abuses his civic responsibility; he not only sacrifices his own responsibility; he sacrifices not only his own interest, but that of his neighbor; he betrays the interest of his country."

— Noah Webster —

"[I]f the citizens neglect their Duty and place unprincipled men in office, the government will soon be corrupted; laws will be made, not for the public good so much as for selfish or local purposes; corrupt or incompetent men will be appointed to execute the Laws; the public revenues will be squandered on unworthy men; and the rights of the citizen will be violated or disregarded."

— Noah Webster —

"[P]erfect freedom consists in obeying the dictates of right reason, and submitting to natural law. When a man goes beyond or contrary to the law of nature and reason, he...introduces confusion and disorder into society...[W]here licentiousness begins, liberty ends."

— Rev. Samuel West —

"[A] free government...cannot be supported without Virtue."

— Samuel Williams —

"Let a man's zeal, profession, or even principles as to political measures be what they will, if he is without personal integrity and private virtue, as a man he is not to be trusted."

— John Witherspoon —

"So true is this, that civil liberty cannot be long preserved without virtue."

— John Witherspoon —

"[A] republic [in disarray] must either preserve its virtue or lose its liberty, and by some tumultuous revolution, either return to its first principles, or assume a more unhappy form."

— John Witherspoon —

APPENDIX 3

Quotes on Bankers, Bonds, and Bolsheviks

"[B]anking establishments are more dangerous than standing armies and...the principles of spending money to be paid by posterity, under the name of funding, is but swindling futurity on a large scale."

— Thomas Jefferson (1816) —

"The few who understand the system, will either be so interested from its profits or so dependent on its favors, that there will be no opposition from that class."

— Rothschild Brothers of London (1863) —

"This [Federal Reserve Act] establishes the most gigantic trust on earth. When the President [Wilson} signs this bill, the invisible government of the monetary power will be legalized....the worst legislative crime of the ages is perpetrated by this banking and currency bill."

— Congressman Charles A. Lindbergh Sr. (1913) —

"From now on, depressions will be scientifically created."

— Congressman Charles A. Lindbergh Sr. (1913) —

"The [Federal Reserve Act] as it stands seems to me to open the way to a vast inflation of the currency...I do not like to think that any law can be passed that will make it possible to submerge the gold standard in a flood of irredeemable paper currency."

— Henry Cabot Lodge, Sr. (1913) —

"These 12 corporations together cover the whole country and monopolize and use for private gain every dollar of the public currency."

"A great industrial nation is controlled by its system of credit. Our system of credit is concentrated in the hands of a few men. We have come to be one of the worst ruled, one of the most completely controlled and dominated governments in the world—no longer a government of free opinion, no longer a government by conviction and vote of the majority, but a government by the opinion and duress of small groups of dominant men."

— President Woodrow Wilson (1919) —

"Should government refrain from regulation [taxation], the worthlessness of the money becomes apparent and the fraud can no longer be concealed... By this means government may secretly and unobserved, confiscate the wealth of the people, and not one man in a million will detect the theft."

— John Maynard Keynes,
The Economic Consequences of the Peace (1920) —

"From the days of Spartacus-Weishaupt to those of Karl Marx, and down to Trotsky (Russia), Bela Kun (Hungary), Rosa Luxembourg (Germany), and Emma Goldman (United States), this world-wide conspiracy for the overthrow of civilisation and for the reconstitution of society on the basis of arrested development, of envious malevolence, and impossible equality, has been steadily growing. It played, as a modern writer, Mrs. Webster, has so ably shown, a definitely recognisable part in the tragedy of the French Revolution. It has been the mainspring of every subversive movement during the Nineteenth Century; and now at last this band of extraordinary personalities from the underworld of the great cities of Europe and America have gripped the Russian people by the hair of their heads and have become practically the undisputed masters of that enormous empire."

— Winston Churchill, "Zionism versus Bolshevism",
Illustrated Sunday Herald (London), February 8, 1920, pg. 5 —

"The people are naturally conservative. They are more conservative than the financiers. Those who believe that the people are so easily led that they would permit the printing presses to run off money like milk tickets do not understand them. It is the innate conservation of the people that has kept our money good in spite of the fantastic tricks which financiers play-and which they cover up with high technical terms. The people are on the side of sound money. They are so unalterably on the side of sound money that it is a serious question how they would regard the system under which they live, if they once knew what the initiate can do with it."

— Henry Ford, *My Life and Work* (1922) —

"The people must be helped to think naturally about money. They must be told what it is, and what makes it money, and what are the possible tricks of the present system which put nations and peoples under control of the few."

— Henry Ford, *My Life and Work* (1922) —

"The financial system has been turned over to the Federal Reserve Board. That Board administers the finance system by authority of a purely profiteering group. The system is private, conducted for the sole purpose of obtaining the greatest possible profits from the use of other people's money"

— Congressman Charles A. Lindbergh Sr. (19123) —

"I am afraid that the ordinary citizen will not like to be told that the banks can, and do, create and destroy money. The amount of money in existence varies only with the action of the banks in increasing or decreasing deposits and bank purchases. Every loan, overdraft or bank purchase creates a deposit, and every repayment or bank sale destroys a deposit. .... And they who control the credit of a nation, direct the policy of Governments and hold in the hollow of their hands the destiny of the people."

— Reginald McKenna, emeritus Chancellor of the Exchequer,
addressing shareholders as of the Midland Bank (1924) —

"We have, in this country, one of the most corrupt institutions the world has ever known. I refer to the Federal Reserve Board. This evil institution has impoverished the people of the United States and has practically bankrupted our government. It has done this through the corrupt practices of the moneyed vultures who control it."

— Congressman Louis T. McFadden,
Chairman of the Committee on Banking and Currency (1932) —

"Some people think the Federal Reserve Banks are the United States government's institutions. They are not government institutions. They are private credit monopolies which prey upon the people of the United States for the benefit of themselves and their foreign swindlers"

— Louis T. McFadden, (1932) —

"The Great Depression was not accidental; it was a carefully contrived occurrence. The international Bankers sought to bring about a condition of despair here so that they might emerge as rulers of us all."

— Louis T. McFadden (1932) —

"Capital must protect itself in every way...Debts must be collected and loans and mortgages foreclosed as soon as possible. When through a process of law the common people have lost their homes, they will be more tractable and more easily governed by the strong arm of the law applied by the central power of leading financiers. People without homes will not quarrel with their leaders. This is well known among our principal men now engaged in forming an imperialism of capitalism to govern the world. By dividing the people we can get them to expend their energies in fighting over questions of no importance to us except as teachers of the common herd."

— *The Civil Servants' Year Book*, "The Organizer" (1934) —

"The present Federal Reserve System is a flagrant case of the Governments conferring a special privilege upon bankers. The Government hands to the banks its credit, at virtually no cost to the banks, to be loaned out by the bankers for their own private profit. Still worse, however, is the fact that it gives the bankers practically complete control of the amount of money that shall be in circulation. Not one dollar of these Federal Reserve notes gets into circulation without being borrowed into circulation and without someone paying interest to some bank to keep it circulating. Our present money system is a debt money system. Before a dollar can circulate, a debt must be created. Such a system assumes that you can borrow yourself out of debt."

— Willis A. Overholser, *A Short Review and Analysis of the History of Money in the United States* (1936), p. 56 —

"We are completely dependent on the commercial banks. Someone has to borrow every dollar we have in circulation, cash or credit. If the banks create ample synthetic money, we are prosperous; if not, we starve. We are absolutely without a permanent money system...It is the most important subject intelligent persons can investigate and reflect upon. It is so important that our present civilization may collapse unless it becomes widely understood and the defects remedied very soon."

— Robert H. Hemphill, Atlanta Federal Reserve Bank (1939) —

"The Federal Reserve bank buys government bonds without one penny."

— Congressman Wright Patman (1941) —

"The entire taxing and monetary systems are hereby placed under the U.C.C. (Uniform Commercial Code)"

— The Federal Tax Lien Act of 1966 —

"Neither paper currency nor deposits have value as commodities. Intrinsically, a 'dollar' bill is just a piece of paper. Deposits are merely book entries."

— *Modern Money Mechanics Workbook,*
Federal Reserve Bank of Chicago, (1975) —

APPENDIX 4

O, Canada: Invitation to a Super-Nation

(Flag of the United States of North America)

AND, BY THE WAY, ISN'T it time we finally annex Canada? Canadians would make great Americans, and, together, these two peoples would agglomerate into a region of freedom so dauntingly vast and full of half-drunk, well-armed rednecks as to last for centuries and serve as a touchstone of liberty for the ages.

Indeed, if Benedict Arnold had not been such a greedy, unprincipled scoundrel, we might all have been a union of free, united North American states long ago—an unbroken sea of liberty stretching from the Arctic Circle to the Florida Keys.

O, Canada, glorious and free, bring me your tired, your hungry, your shivering masses yearning to be Yankee!

Let's, peacefully and voluntarily, annex Canada and show the world how a real united States of North America—a really free peoples freely joined together to live in amity in the celebration of humanity's infinite capacity—can thrive in one, united, free, prosperous, and joyous accord across a stupidly vast land mass...about 7½ million square miles, but who's counting?

I invite the Canadians to draw up petitions of grievance against their overweening technomasters in Ottawa, collect signatures towards a national referendum whereby the Northlands applies for formal admittance of all your free and frosty provinces as states of this union, and load up the world's longest truck convoy—swinging by Parliament Hill to drop off some copies for the jokers up there—and then hand-delivering the originals to our boys in the Border Patrol (along with, maybe a couple dozen of those cinnamon-sugar beaver tails and a couple pots of hot joe, just to soften up those BP boys...what with it being first thing in the a.m. and them about to have a very long day and everything). Heck, even our Congress may be smart enough to accept a deal that good when they see it.

One vast continent of anglophone, self-reliant citizens with the same liberty-loving ideals would become such a shining bastion of freedom and bacon-larded breakfasts of gargantuan proportions as to be well-nigh indomitable.

To be fair, we would be glad to have you annex us under your Constitution, except for that still having all those trappings of the British Crown and Commonwealth part. No kings or queens—we're still kinda touchy about that, thank you very much. I'm sure you will soon learn to enjoy life without worrying about any of those inbred mouth-breathing royals showing up anyway.

So come on over to the free side, Canada. We can play some baseball—and might even let you win a game or two...and then you can hit us in the head with hockey sticks, until the Molson runs out. And then we'll discuss exactly how to team up and hook up those Mexicans with a little gringo liberty love...for an eventual trifecta of north American forever freedoming, a jazz trio of free-form liberty in the *Esados unidos de Norteamérica.*

Anyway, for starters, I'm thinking a flag with 50 stars, then maybe 9 dashing maple leaves (or is it 12? I don't really get how y'all do that territories thing) would look pretty sweet as the upgraded banner for the United States of North America.

As wild-eyed revolutionary Ethan Allen wrote to Congress back in 1775 when he was dreaming of wresting Montreal and thence the whole continent from the Crown...Canada *"might rise on eagle's wings, and mount up to glory...unconquerable freedom, immense wealth, inexpressible felicity, and immortal fame."*

Now, wouldn't that be badass, eh?

Free Canada! Annex the Canucks!

P.S. ...and later, like this, guys...

(Flag of the *Esados Unidos de Norteamérica*)

APPENDIX 5

Happy FreedomFest, America!

"It having pleased the Almighty Ruler of the universe to defend the cause of the united American States...to establish our liberty and independence upon a lasing foundation, it becomes us to set apart a day for gratefully acknowledge the divine goodness, and celebrating the important event, which we owe to His divine interposition."

— George Washington —

ONE OF THE MOST GLORIOUS traditions of the Chinese people is New Years, basically a whole week of a whole country having a party. Why should we let the Chinese folks have all the fun? Over here, we have all these federal holidays, but they are all spread out, and they don't always really correspond to exact historical dating, so...

What if, instead at worrying about all the particular scars and scabs of past wounds, we looked to a future we could build together with our shared freedoms and capacities? Might there be a better way to holiday, a way we could help America celebrate its best qualities, including its ability to self-correct and strive for the best?

What if, instead of dividing American Federal holidays into so many blocks for particular persons and events, we perhaps build a more meaningful and celebratory event, a kind of nationwide block party...for a whole week...and just blow it all out in *FreedomFest?*

Like, what if we made it the week running up to July 4th...something like...if we moved Memorial Day back a little, Veterans Day up a bunch (because the end of WWI was, really, over 100 years ago already), Juneteenth and MLK back a bit, and the same with the George Washington and Lincoln birthdays...stacking those 6 national holidays right before the final 4th of July extravaganza? Same number of holidays, but we just make it one big, ole festival of Americanism, doing it in grand style. It would be like Christmas season, only in July, and for freedom.

What if we just double-down on loving our freedom—like the Chinese love their New Year—and just take all those federal days off at once as a national celebration...of Freedom...plus plain old Family, Food, and Fun? Wouldn't you love to live in that country? Wouldn't that put a lot of smiles on a lot of faces every year, planning for it, driving to see grandma for it, just laying on the beach pretending not to snooze in the sun for it?

How might we do it?

Well, we might designate each day, maybe sorta like this:

June 28th - Memorial Day I for overseas Freedom Fighters: parades, ceremonies, and memorials for those who fought for freedom and the principles of this country, *abroad*, - e.g., especially veterans and active duty military. Also commemorates the day the freshly-written Declaration of Independence was delivered by Thomas Jefferson, John Adams, and the rest of the committee to the Continental Congress for its final debate and vote.

June 29th: Memorial Day II for domestic Freedom Fighters: parades, ceremonies, and memorials for those who fought for freedom and the principles of this country, *at home* - i.e. activists, speakers, politicians, writers, and dreamers. MLK, Malcolm X, RFK, Dorothy Day, John Brown.

June 30th - Day of Personal Penance, Prayer, and Reconciliation: reflection on the question what have I *individually* done for freedom? What have I *individually* failed to do for freedom? What part of our national heritage and conscience can stand reconsideration and recalibration, from the history which caused Juneteenth, to the Trail of Tears, the Japanese internment camps, or the protests of Martin Luther King, Jr.? Is there anyone I have *personally* wronged, denied or abridged in the article of freedom? What can I do better next year to bring more freedom to myself and those around me?

July 1st - Constitution Day - Day of reflection on the Constitution, its adoption, its continued significance, and the qualities which it defenders and inheritors must embody to maintain it. Celebrations of the history of its formulation and the biographies, words, and deeds of the Founders and Framers, including the commemoration of John Adams' "Colossus" speech winning the vote for independency in the Continental Congress.

July 2nd - Bill of Rights Day - Day of reflection on the Bills of Rights, each of these Amendment's significance, the historical precursors for its consideration, and the history of law and public use and defense of these. Encouragement of citizens to "Flex your favorite Right," most especially with lots of speeches, marches, and worship services in demonstration of First Amendment Frenzy, and shootouts, gun shows, and marksmanship demos by the militia for Second Amendment Swagger.

July 3rd - Day of national Prayer, Penance, Thanksgiving and Reflection - Day of reflection and prayer for the rectification of the *nation* in matters of freedom for all peoples, both nationally and those we interact with abroad. Petition and fasting before our sovereign Lord that the American people may better manifest liberty and justice for all. What might the *nation* do better to live out its promise of freedom? How can I contribute to that *national* effort?

July 4th - Freedom Forever Day This remains *the* national day in recognition of Independency and all the gifts of liberty guaranteed to us by the Constitution through the Revolution and the sacrifices of the heroes who came before us. Readings of the great documents on our freedom, reenactments and recitations about the Founders and Framers, and of course, lots and lots of food, beverages, joyous people...and fireworks forever.

Now, what could be more freeing and fun than that!

Select Bibliography

Alinsky, Saul. (1989) *Rules for Radicals*. New York: Vintage Books.

Astor, Gerald. (1995) *Operation Iceberg*. New York: Donald I. Fine, Inc.

Barnard, Alan. (2019) *It's Impossible...Unless?* Cambrige, MA: Global Research, LLC.

Bennett, William. (Ed.) (1993) *The Book of Virtues*. New York: Touchstone.

Bethune, James J. "Davy Crockett's Electioneering Tour," *Harper's Magazine* April, 1867.

Brookhiser, Richard. (2011) *James Madison*. New York: Basic Books.

Butler, Smedley. (1935) *War is a Racket*. New York: Round Table Books.

Calloway, Donald. (2016) *Champions of the Rosary*. Stockbridge: Marian Press.

Capaccio, Anthony. "Pentagon Racks Up $35 Trillion in Accounting Changes in One Year" *Bloomberg*. January 22, 2020. Retrieved at: https://www.bloomberg.com/news/articles/2020-01-22/pentagon-racks-up-35-trillion-in-accounting-changes-in-one-year#xj4y7vzkg

Chernow, Ron. (2010) *Washington: A Life*. London: Penguin Books.

Cockburn, Alexander; Jeffrey St. Clair (1998). *Whiteout: The CIA, Drugs and the Press*. New York: Verso.

Coleman, John. (1969) *The Tavistock Institute of Human Relations*. N.P.

Connell, Janice. (2013) *The Spiritual Journey of George Washington*. N.P.

Cuddy, Dennis. (1999) *Secret Records Revealed*. Oklahoma City: Hearthstone Publishing, Ltd.

DiLorenzo, Thomas J. (2016) *The Problem with Socialism*. Washington, D.C.: Regnery.

Estulin, Daniel. (2015) *Tavistock Institute: Engineering the Masses*. Walterville, OR: Trine Day, LLC.

"Federal Land Ownership: Overview and Data" (2020) Washington, D.C.: Congressional Research Service.

Felkerson, James. (2011) "$29,000,000,000,000: A Detailed Look as the Fed's Bailout by Funding Facility and Recipient" *Working Paper No. 698* Red Hook, NY: Levy Economics Institute, Bard College.

Franklin, Benjamin. (1961) *The Autobiography and Other Writings*. London: Penguin Books.

Fuller, R. Buckminster. (1970) *I Seem to be a Verb*. New York: Bantam Books.

Green, Thomas Andrew. (1985) *Verdict According to Conscience: Perspectives on the English Criminal Trial Jury, 1200-1800*. Chicago: University of Chicago Press.

Hsieh, Paul. "That Time the CDC Asked about Defensive Gun Uses" *Forbes*. April 30, 2018. Retrieved at: https://www.forbes.com/sites/paulhsieh/2018/04/30/that-time-the-cdc-asked-about-defensive-gun-uses/?sh=46c606aa299a

King, Martin Luther. (1963) *Strength to Love*. Glasgow: William Collins Sons, Ltd.

Kotler, Steven. (2021) *The Art of Impossible*. New York: HarperCollins Publishers.

Kozak, Jan. (1999) *And Not a Shot is Fired*. Appleton, WI : Robert Welch University Press.

Lane, Rose Wilder. (2012) *The Discovery of Freedom*. Baltimore, MD: Laissez Faire Books.

Liang, Qiao and Wang Xiangsui. (1999) *Unrestricted Warfare*. Brattleboro, VT: Echo Point Books.

Lind, William and Gregory Thiele. (2015) *4th Generation Warfare Handbook*. Kouvola, Finland: Castalia House.

Madison, James. (1999) *Writings*. New York: Penguin Putnam, Inc.

McCullough, David. (2002) *John Adams*. New York: Simon & Schuster.

O'Neill, Tom. (2019) *Chaos: Charles Manson, the CIA, and the Secret History of the Sixties*. New York: Little, Brown, and Company.

Paine, Thomas. (2021) *Common Sense*. Asturias: King Solomon.

Register of Debates, House of Representatives (20th Congress, 1st Session) "A Century of Lawmaking for a New Nation: U.S. Congressional Documents and Debates, 1774 - 1875", pp. 2085-2090. Retrieved at: https://memory.loc.gov/cgi-bin/ampage?collId=llrd&fileName=006/llrd006.db&recNum=310

Ross, Tara and Joseph C. Smith. (2008) *Under God: George Washington and the Question of Church and State*. Dallas: Spence Publishing Company

Royall, William Lawrence. (1880) *Andrew Jackson and the Bank of the United States*. New York: G.P. Putnam's Sons.

Rummel, R.J. (1994) *Death By Government*. New Brunswick: Transaction Publishers.

Shlaes, Amity. (2013) *Coolidge*. New York: Harper Collins Publishers.

Sieden, Lloyd Steven (1989) *Buckminster Fuller's Universe: His Life and Work*. Basic Books. pp. 87–88.

Silent Weapons for Quiet Wars. n.p. n.d. (samizdat, controverted)

Smith, Charles Hugh. (2022) *Self-reliance in the 21st Century*. Hilo, HI: Of Two Minds.

Snyder, Timothy. (2017) *On Tyranny: Twenty Lessons from the Twentieth Century*. New York: Tim Duggan Books.

Sutton, Anthony. (1976) *Wall Street and the Rise of Hitler*. Seal Beach, CA: '76 Press.

Third Report on the work conducted for the Government at Wellington House. (Sep. 1916) Catalogue Re. CAB 37/156/6. The National Archives.

Tupy, Marian and Gale Pooley. (2023) *Superabundance: The Story of Population Growth, Innovation, and Human Flourishing on an Infinitely Bountiful Planet*. Washington, D.C.: Cato Institute.

Ullman, Harlan and James Wade. (1996) *Shock and Awe: Achieving Rapid Dominance*. Washington, D.C.: National Defense University.

Walter, Paul and Lorraine. (1899) *The Coming Battle*. Chicago: W.B. Conkey Company.

Wren, Christopher S. (2018) *Those Turbulent Sons of Freedom*. New York: Simon & Schuster Paperbacks.

Young, Alexander. (1841) *Chronicles of the Pilgrim Fathers of the Colony of Plymouth from 1602 to 1625*. Boston: Charles C. Little and James Brown.

Zuckerman, Phil. (2019) "Does Prayer Work?" Retrieved at: https://www.psychologytoday.com/us/blog/the-secular-life/201909/does-prayer-work

Website

To get yourself even more American Badass—news, videos, and even hats and shirts—including the printable .pdf version of the *One-Page Constitution*, check out:

americanbadass.store

Made in the USA
Columbia, SC
25 January 2024

30195493R00246